EMEN'S ALLIANCE ✝ CROSS

Story & Art by
Arina Tanemura

Vol. 10

GRAPH
TANEMURA
V. 10

CONTENTS

CHAPTER 40: ONE SECOND AHEAD

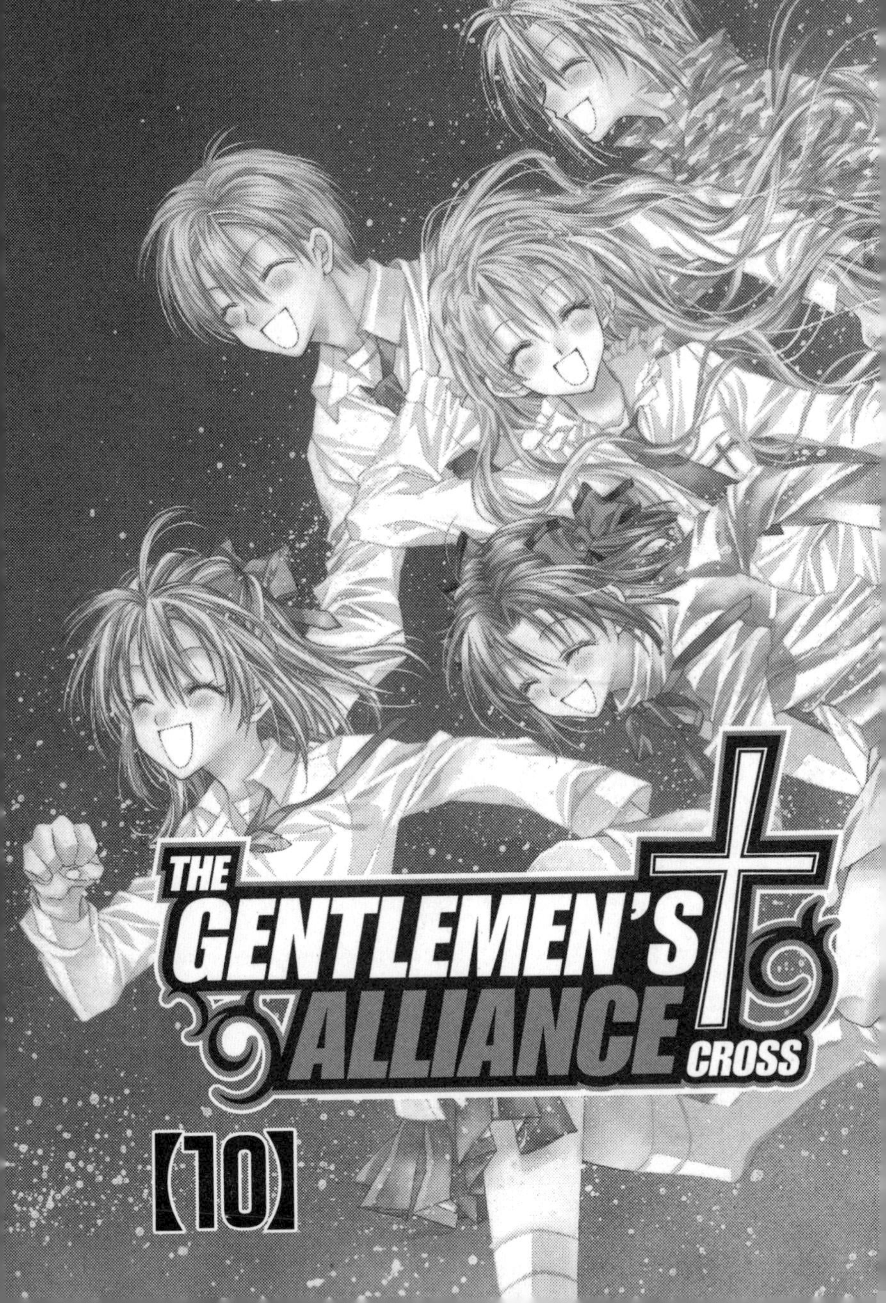
THE GENTLEMEN'S ALLIANCE CROSS
[10]

CHARACTER INTRODUCTIONS

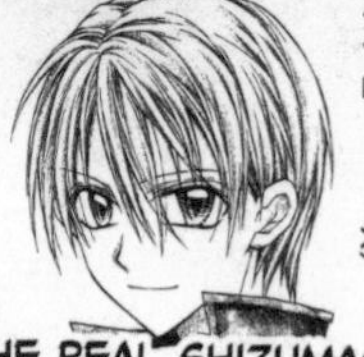

(Younger Twin)

THE REAL SHIZUMASA

An illness prevents him from attending school. He helped Haine mend her yanki ways.

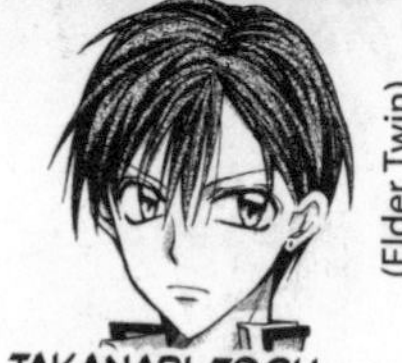

(Elder Twin)

TAKANARI TOGU

Student Council President

The double. Referred to as "the Emperor" and is the highest authority in school. Wrote Haine's favorite picture book.

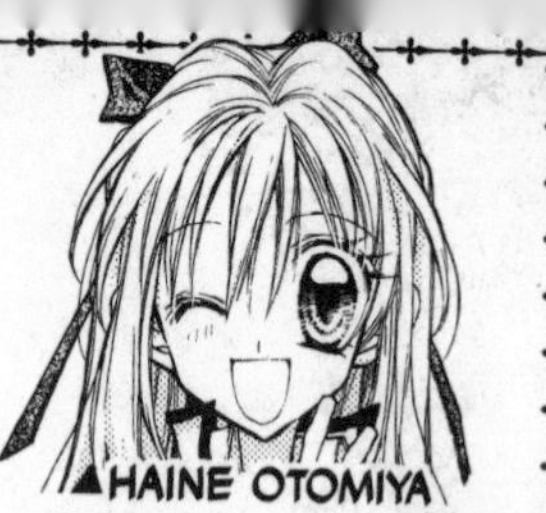

HAINE OTOMIYA

Bodyguard & General Affairs

A cheerful girl who is in love with Shizumasa-sama. Former juvenile delinquent. Adopted into the Otomiya family in fourth grade.

MAGURI TSUJIMIYA

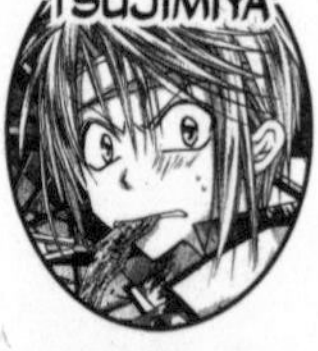

Vice President

Childhood friends with Maora, and now they've become lovers.♥

MAORA

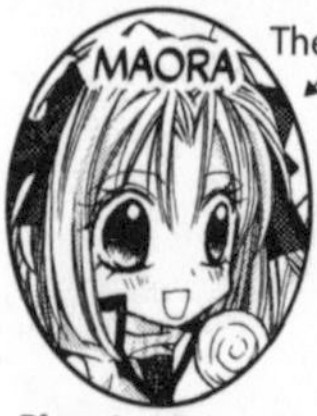

The Same Person!!

POSTMAN

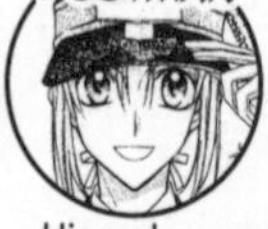

Planning Events & Accounting

Childhood friend of Maguri.

His real name is Ichinomiya Yoshitaka. A very cute boy!!

USHIO AMAMIYA

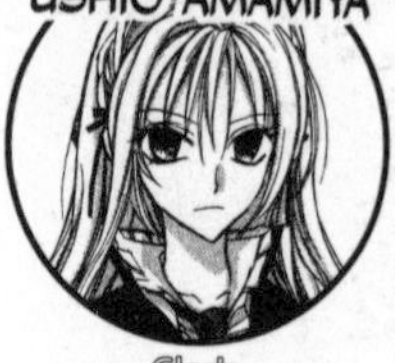

Clerk

Haine's friend. Haine is dearer to her than anyone.

THE GENTLEMEN'S ALLIANCE CROSS

Haine Otomiya is a former juvenile delinquent who attends Imperial Academy. One day, she is appointed the rank of "Platinum" as Emperor Shizumasa Togu's fake girifriend.

Haine has discovered her real father is not Kazuhito, but Itsuki, her foster father. Also, after learning Kazuhito had forcefully taken her mother Maika away from Itsuki to marry her, she decides to break into the Kamiya mansion with her old yanki friends.

On the day of the attack, Takanari and Shizumasa give Haine a letter written by Kazuhito. After learning about Kazuhito's feelings for her, Haine stops the attack. But then a fire breaks out at the Kamiya mansion! Haine rushes in to save Kazuhito and Maika, but she faints from exhaustion. All three are rescued.

After the fire, Kazuhito decides to return Maika to Itsuki. But Maika loves Kazuhito and chooses to stay by his side. Haine is happy to finally be able to connect with Kazuhito.

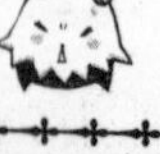

STORY THUS FAR

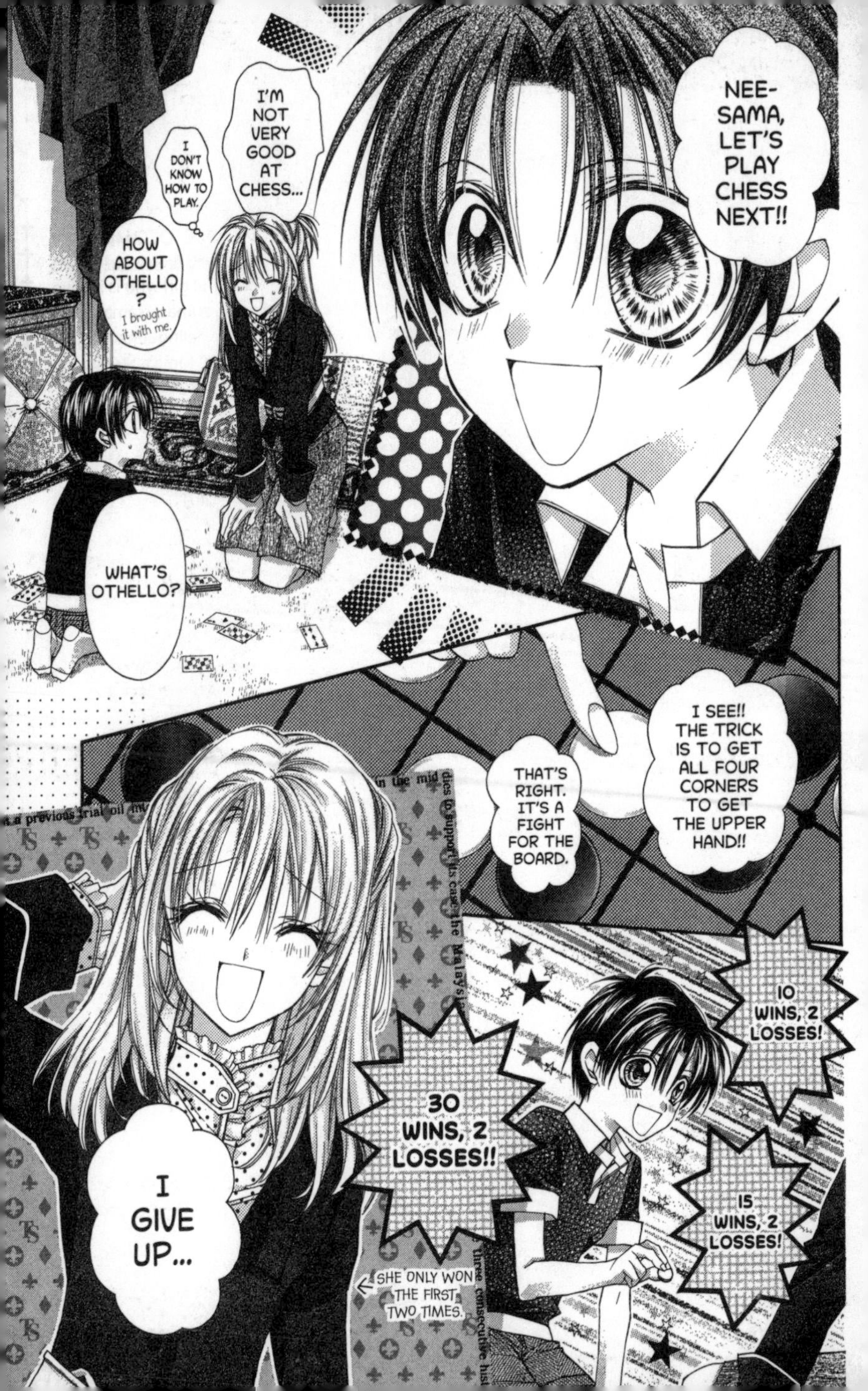
NEE-SAMA, LET'S PLAY CHESS NEXT!!
I'M NOT VERY GOOD AT CHESS...
I DON'T KNOW HOW TO PLAY.
HOW ABOUT OTHELLO?
I brought it with me.
WHAT'S OTHELLO?
I SEE!! THE TRICK IS TO GET ALL FOUR CORNERS TO GET THE UPPER HAND!!
THAT'S RIGHT. IT'S A FIGHT FOR THE BOARD.
10 WINS, 2 LOSSES!
15 WINS, 2 LOSSES!
30 WINS, 2 LOSSES!!
I GIVE UP...
SHE ONLY WON THE FIRST TWO TIMES.

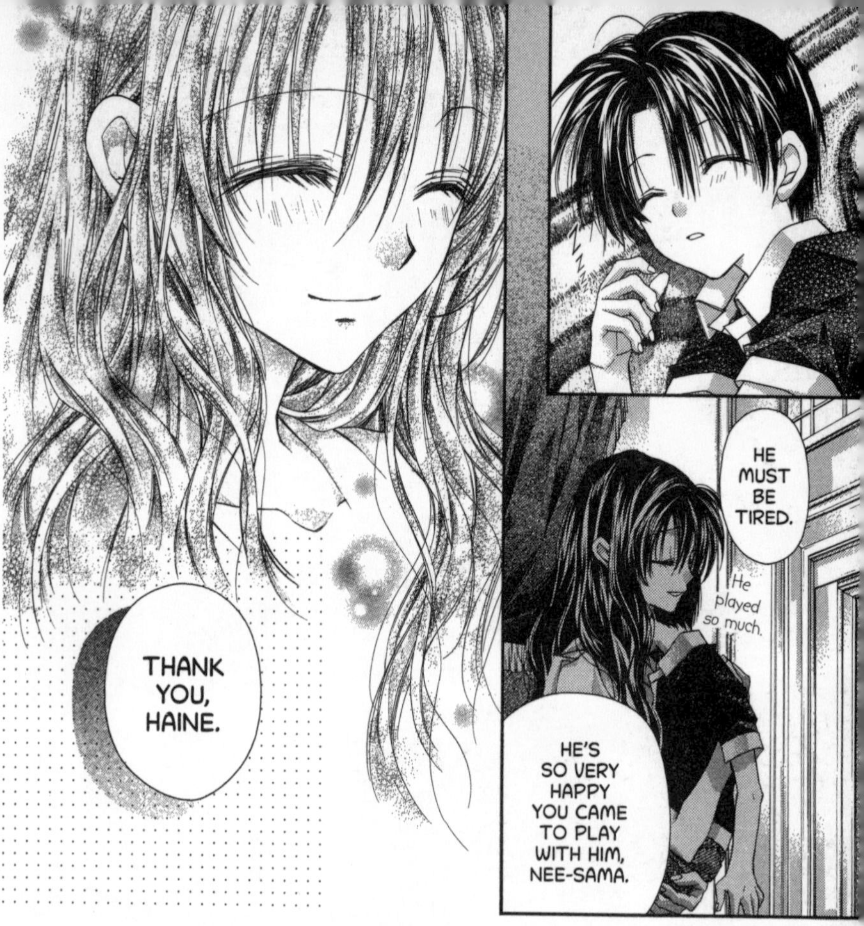
HE MUST BE TIRED.
He played so much.
HE'S SO VERY HAPPY YOU CAME TO PLAY WITH HIM, NEE-SAMA.
THANK YOU, HAINE.

Chapter 40: One Second Ahead

Lead-in Run to the sky!!

※ I'm giving away the story.

Aaah, I'm sorry... (laugh) For the first and second page, I just wanted to draw Tachibana and Komaki, that's all!

And, believe it or not, this is the beginning of the final chapters. Whoa... (People above had been pressuring me not to say it, but I've decided to tell you.)

The Takanari and Shizumasa arc. I've also included Ushio and Senri because they have a role to play.

Eh... The scene in which Haine-chan and Takanari are kissing... Toya-kun is there too.
But that's okay, he can be there. He's like air to Takanari-sama... But I bet Haine-chan felt very uneasy...

Some fans may have realized this is the beginning of the final chapters, I guess? I've already decided on the ending... Well, I had decided on it from the very start (though there have been many twists and turns). Now, just because I like Takanari, it doesn't meant that Haine and Takanari will get togeth—mumble, mumble, mumble...

Waaah! Takuto, you idiot...!
Give Mitsuki back to me...!

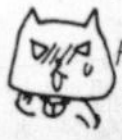
Huh ?!

In *Full Moon*, I liked Eichi-kun more.

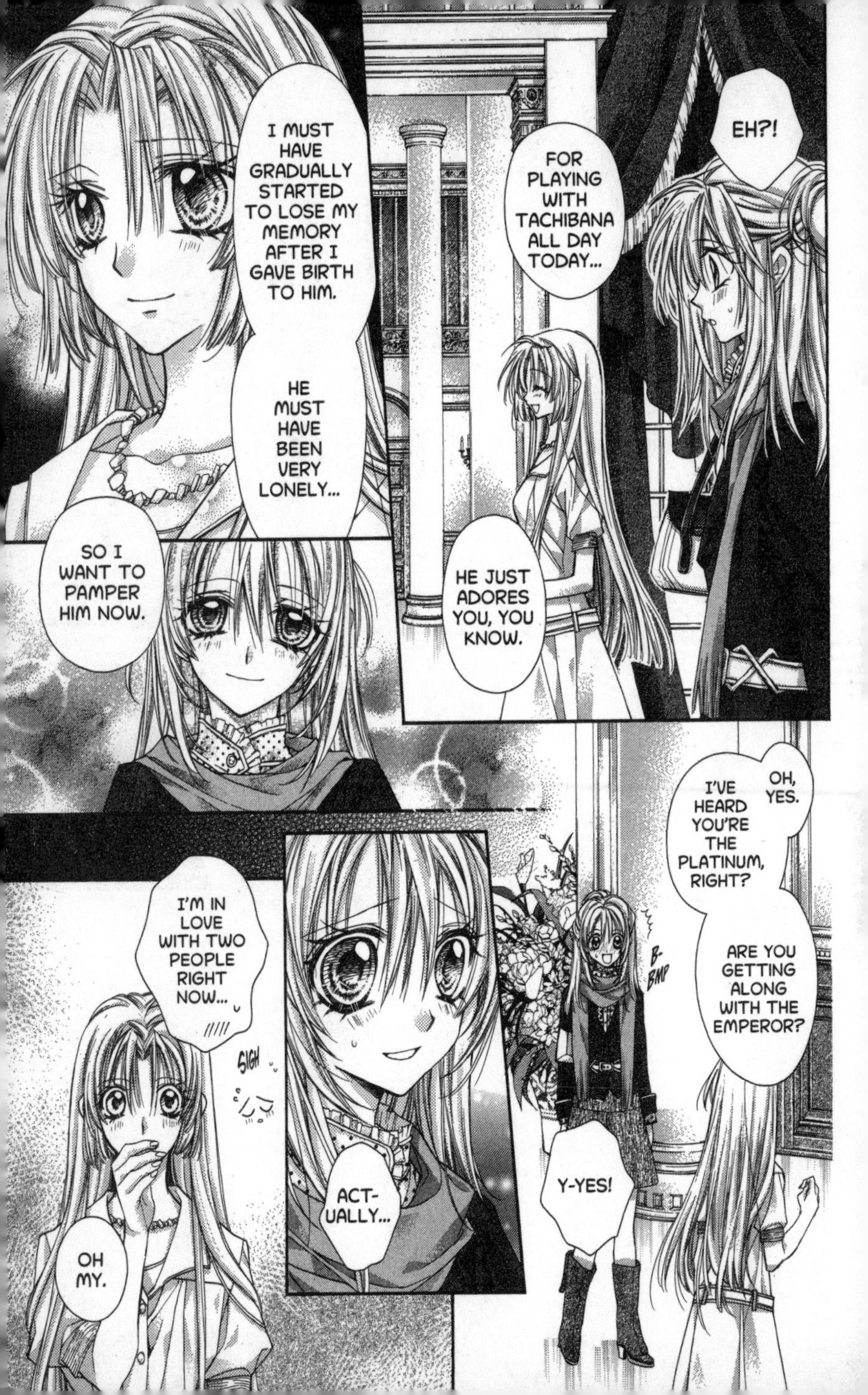
FOR PLAYING WITH TACHIBANA ALL DAY TODAY...
EH?!
HE JUST ADORES YOU, YOU KNOW.
I MUST HAVE GRADUALLY STARTED TO LOSE MY MEMORY AFTER I GAVE BIRTH TO HIM.
HE MUST HAVE BEEN VERY LONELY...
SO I WANT TO PAMPER HIM NOW.
OH, YES.
I'VE HEARD YOU'RE THE PLATINUM, RIGHT?
B-BMP
ARE YOU GETTING ALONG WITH THE EMPEROR?
Y-YES!
ACT-UALLY...
I'M IN LOVE WITH TWO PEOPLE RIGHT NOW...
SIGH
OH MY.

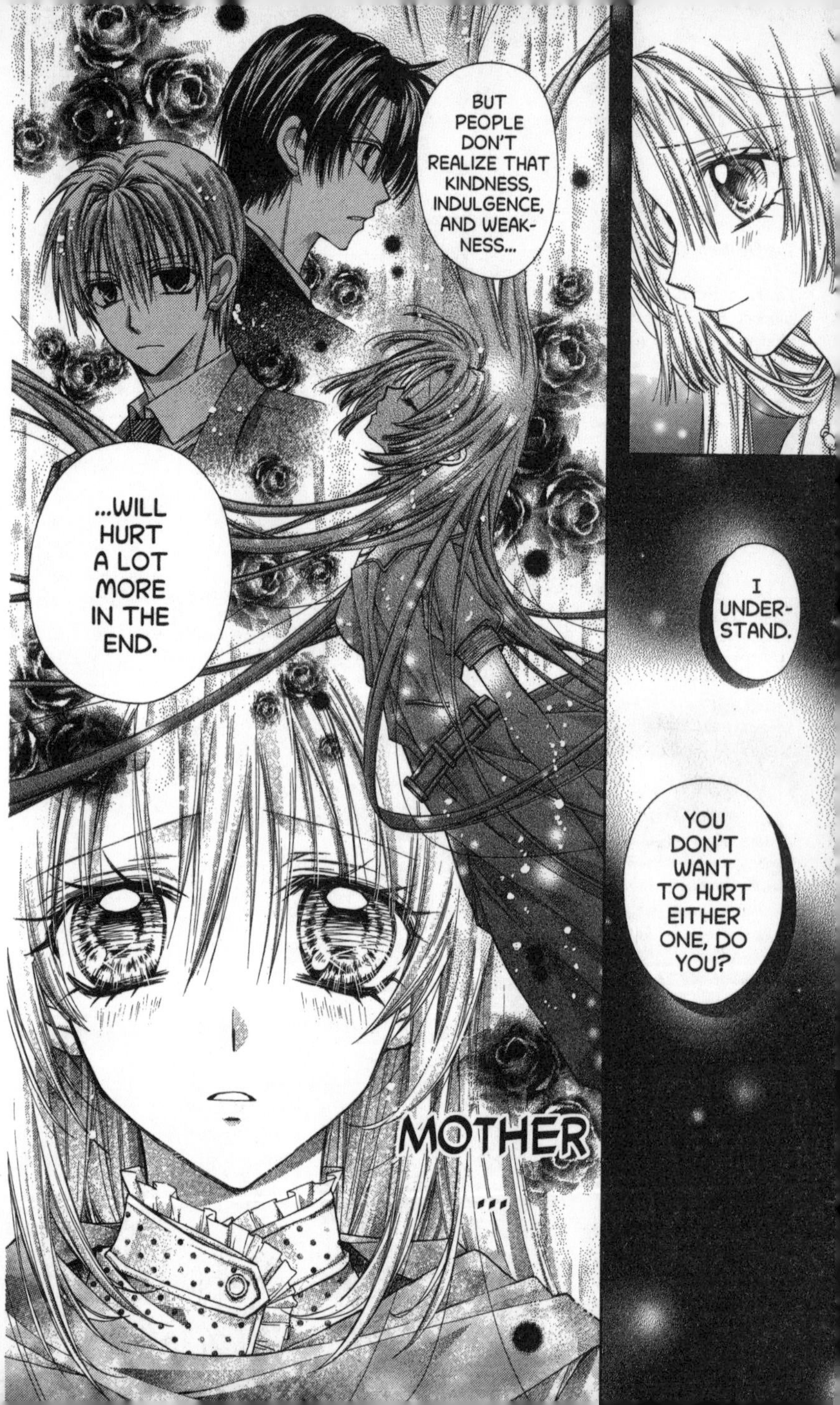
I UNDER-STAND.
YOU DON'T WANT TO HURT EITHER ONE, DO YOU?
BUT PEOPLE DON'T REALIZE THAT KINDNESS, INDULGENCE, AND WEAK-NESS...
...WILL HURT A LOT MORE IN THE END.
MOTHER
...

Hello

Hi, hi, hello. Tanemura here. We've finally arrived at volume 10 of *The Gentlemen's Alliance* †.

I'd like to thank you all for the support. And for those who are reading this manga in Japan, I would like you to read the last chapter in the July edition of *Ribon* magazine.

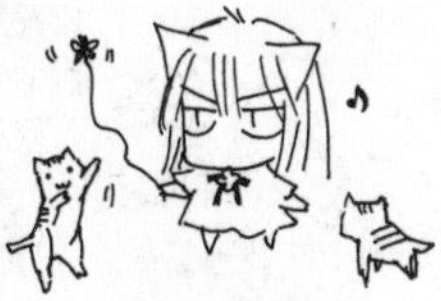

A lot of things will be announced in the July edition! (I'll talk about the details at the end of this volume). ↑ Actually, the announcements will start in the June edition, but for those of you who like to read my manga in tankobon form, the news will also be announced in the July edition.

This volume is filled with rather serious chapters, so I haven't written any sidebars. I'll talk about everything at the end.

Thanks.

It looks like I'm even going to have more work to do this year.

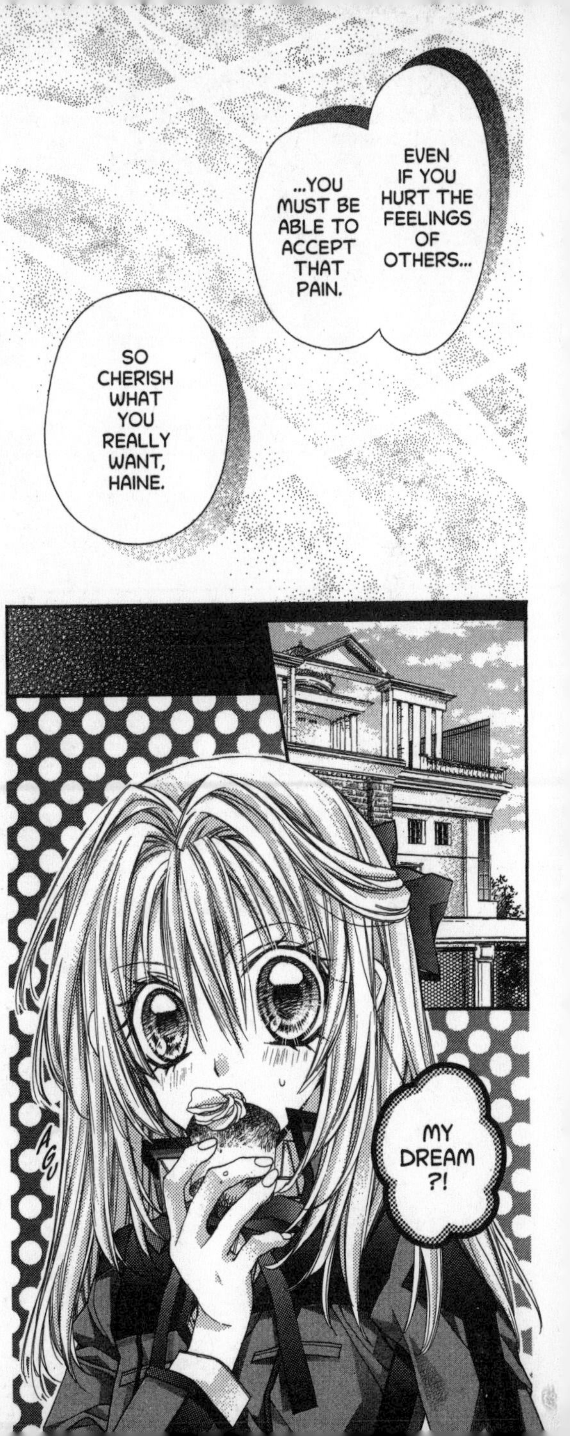
EVEN IF YOU HURT THE FEELINGS OF OTHERS...
...YOU MUST BE ABLE TO ACCEPT THAT PAIN.
SO CHERISH WHAT YOU REALLY WANT, HAINE.
MY DREAM?!
AGU

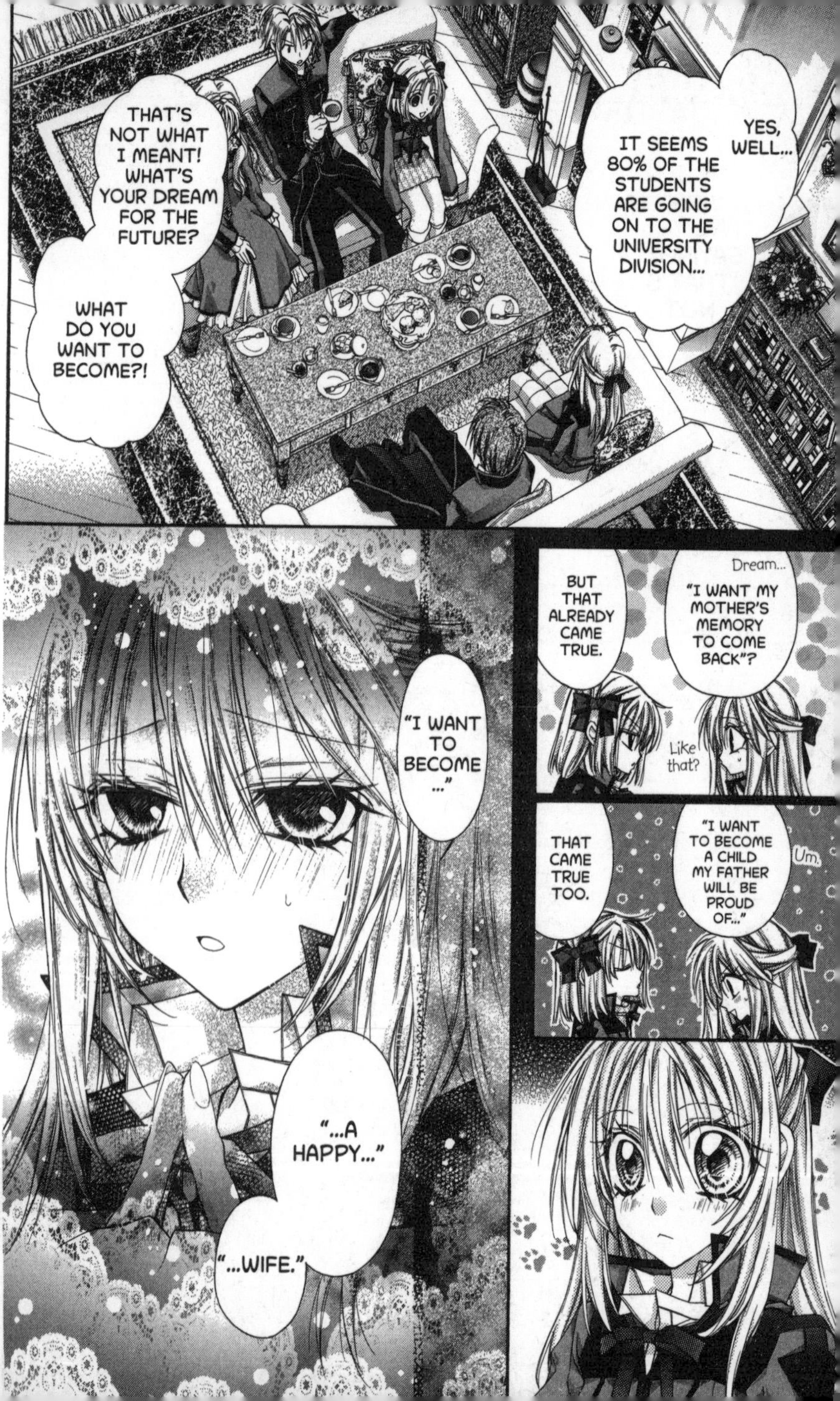
YES, WELL...
IT SEEMS 80% OF THE STUDENTS ARE GOING ON TO THE UNIVERSITY DIVISION...
THAT'S NOT WHAT I MEANT! WHAT'S YOUR DREAM FOR THE FUTURE?
WHAT DO YOU WANT TO BECOME?!
Dream...
"I WANT MY MOTHER'S MEMORY TO COME BACK"?
Like that?
BUT THAT ALREADY CAME TRUE.
Um.
"I WANT TO BECOME A CHILD MY FATHER WILL BE PROUD OF..."
THAT CAME TRUE TOO.
"I WANT TO BECOME ..."
"...A HAPPY..."
"...WIFE."

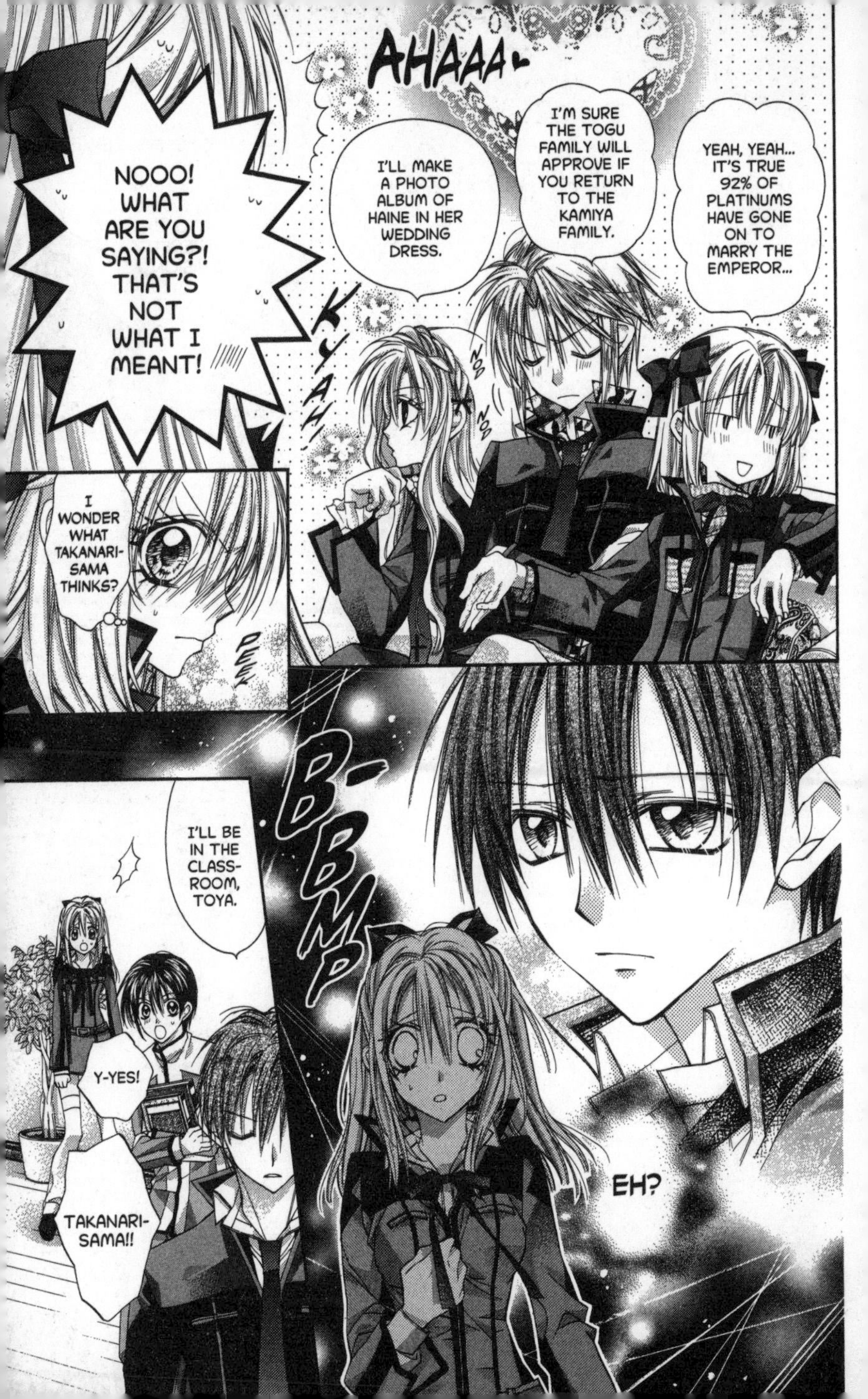
AHAAA
YEAH, YEAH... IT'S TRUE 92% OF PLATINUMS HAVE GONE ON TO MARRY THE EMPEROR...
I'M SURE THE TOGU FAMILY WILL APPROVE IF YOU RETURN TO THE KAMIYA FAMILY.
I'LL MAKE A PHOTO ALBUM OF HAINE IN HER WEDDING DRESS.
KYAAH!
NOD NOD
NOOO! WHAT ARE YOU SAYING?! THAT'S NOT WHAT I MEANT!
I WONDER WHAT TAKANARI-SAMA THINKS?
PEEK
B-BBMP
EH?
I'LL BE IN THE CLASSROOM, TOYA.
Y-YES!
TAKANARI-SAMA!!

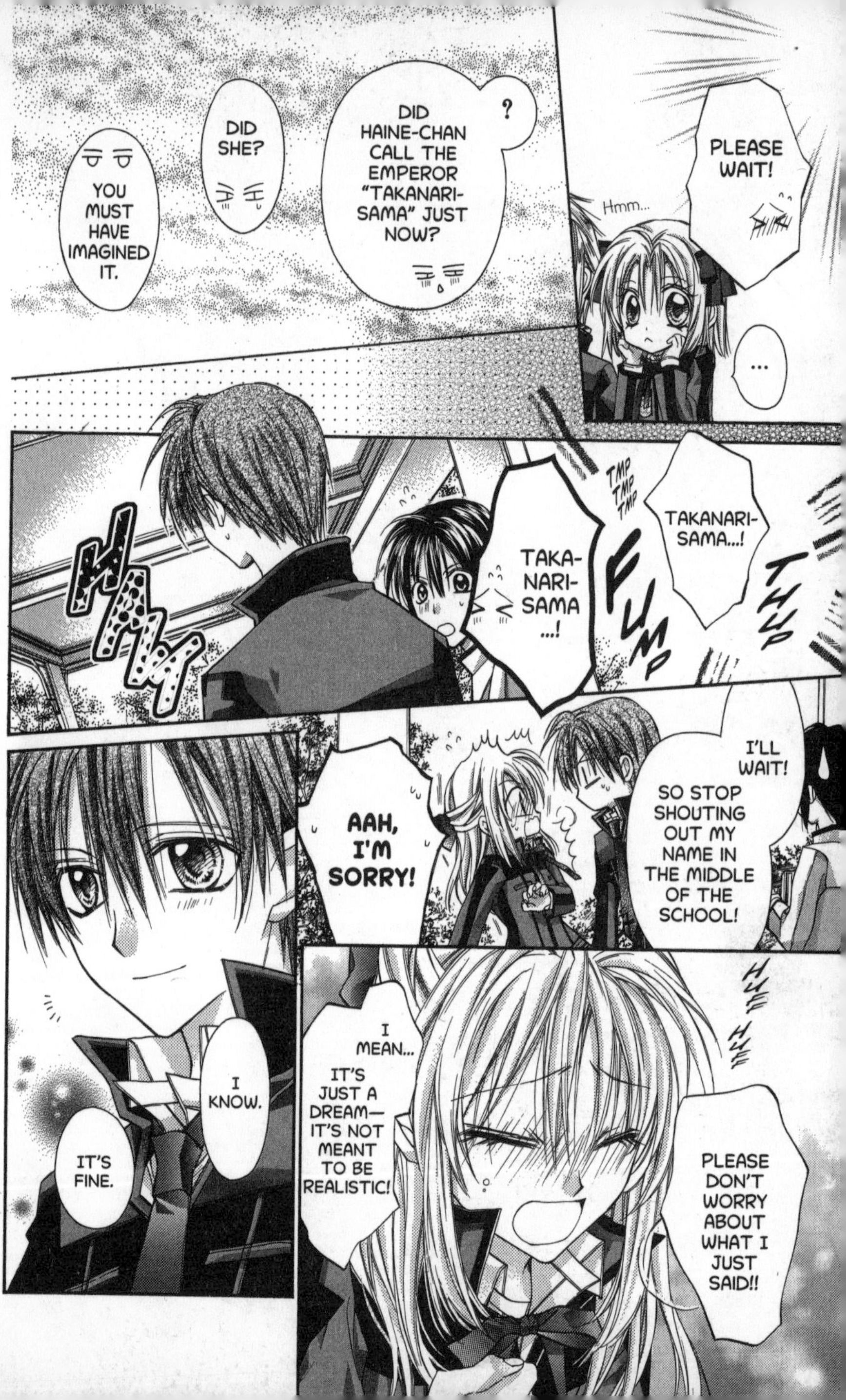
PLEASE WAIT!
Hmm...
...
DID HAINE-CHAN CALL THE EMPEROR "TAKANARI-SAMA" JUST NOW?
DID SHE?
YOU MUST HAVE IMAGINED IT.
TAKANARI-SAMA...!
TMP TMP TMP
FUMP
TAKA-NARI-SAMA...!
I'LL WAIT! SO STOP SHOUTING OUT MY NAME IN THE MIDDLE OF THE SCHOOL!
AAH, I'M SORRY!
PLEASE DON'T WORRY ABOUT WHAT I JUST SAID!!
I MEAN... IT'S JUST A DREAM—IT'S NOT MEANT TO BE REALISTIC!
I KNOW.
IT'S FINE.

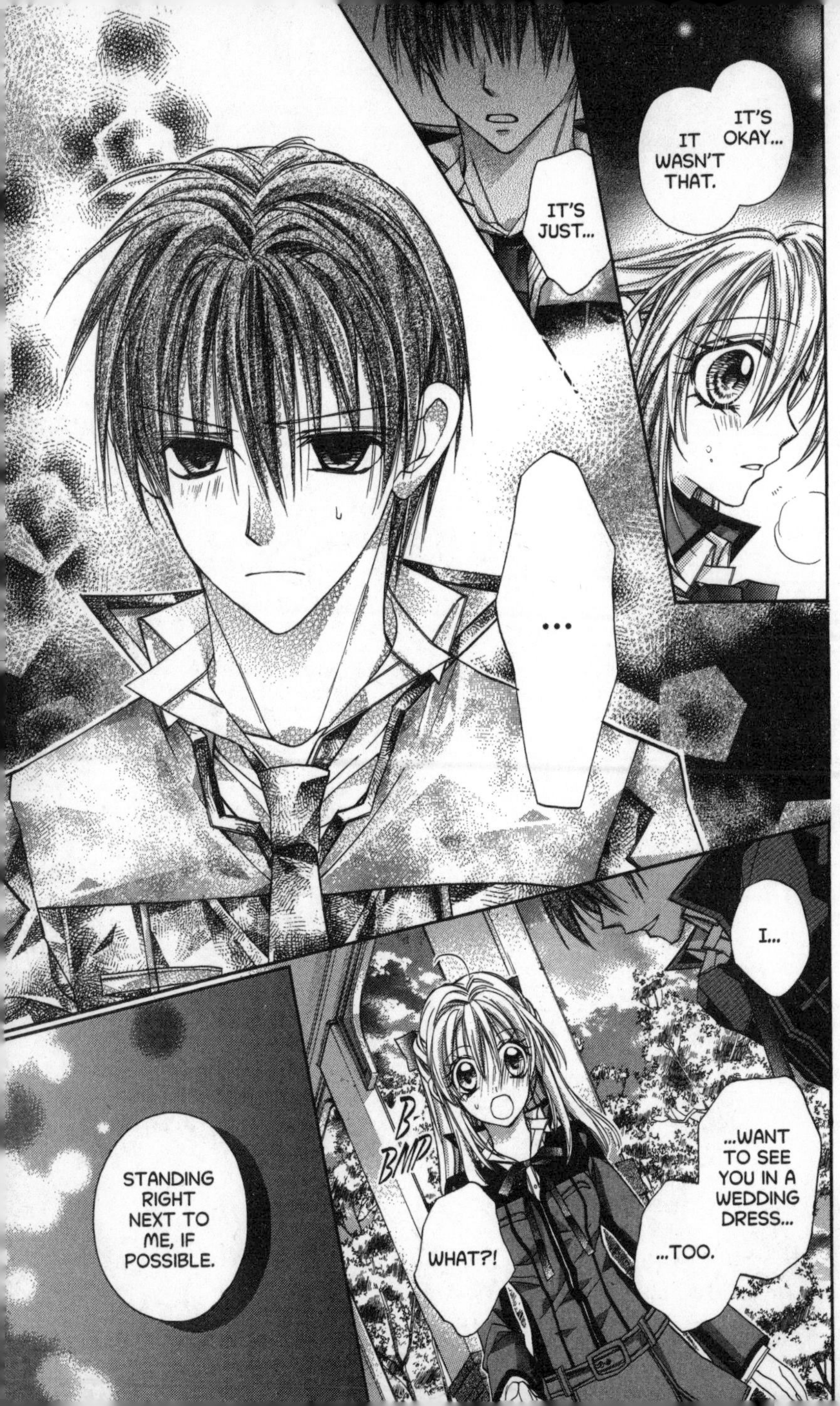
IT'S OKAY... IT WASN'T THAT.
IT'S JUST...
...
I...
...WANT TO SEE YOU IN A WEDDING DRESS...
...TOO.
B-BMP
WHAT?!
STANDING RIGHT NEXT TO ME, IF POSSIBLE.

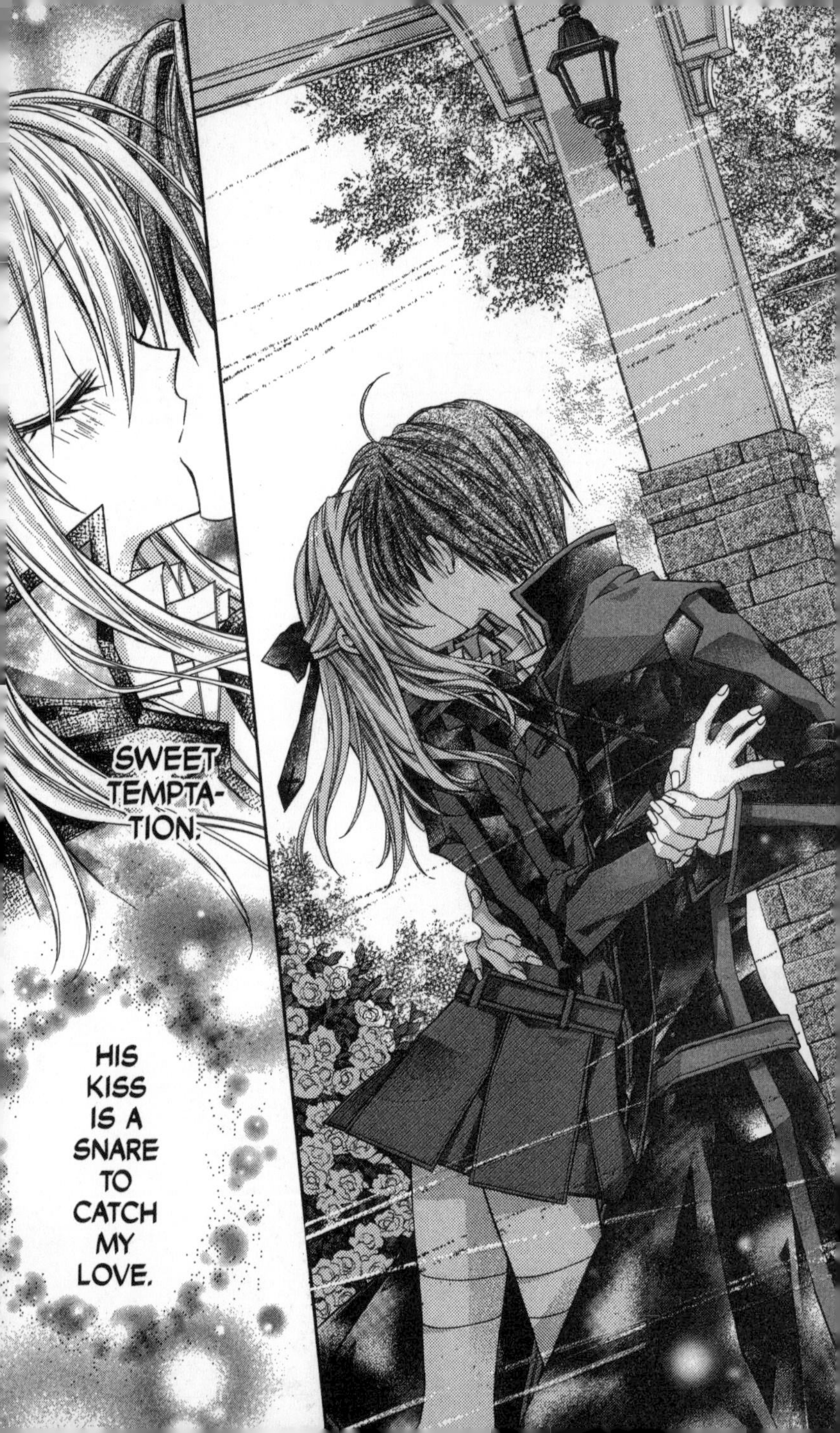
SWEET TEMPTATION.
HIS KISS IS A SNARE TO CATCH MY LOVE.

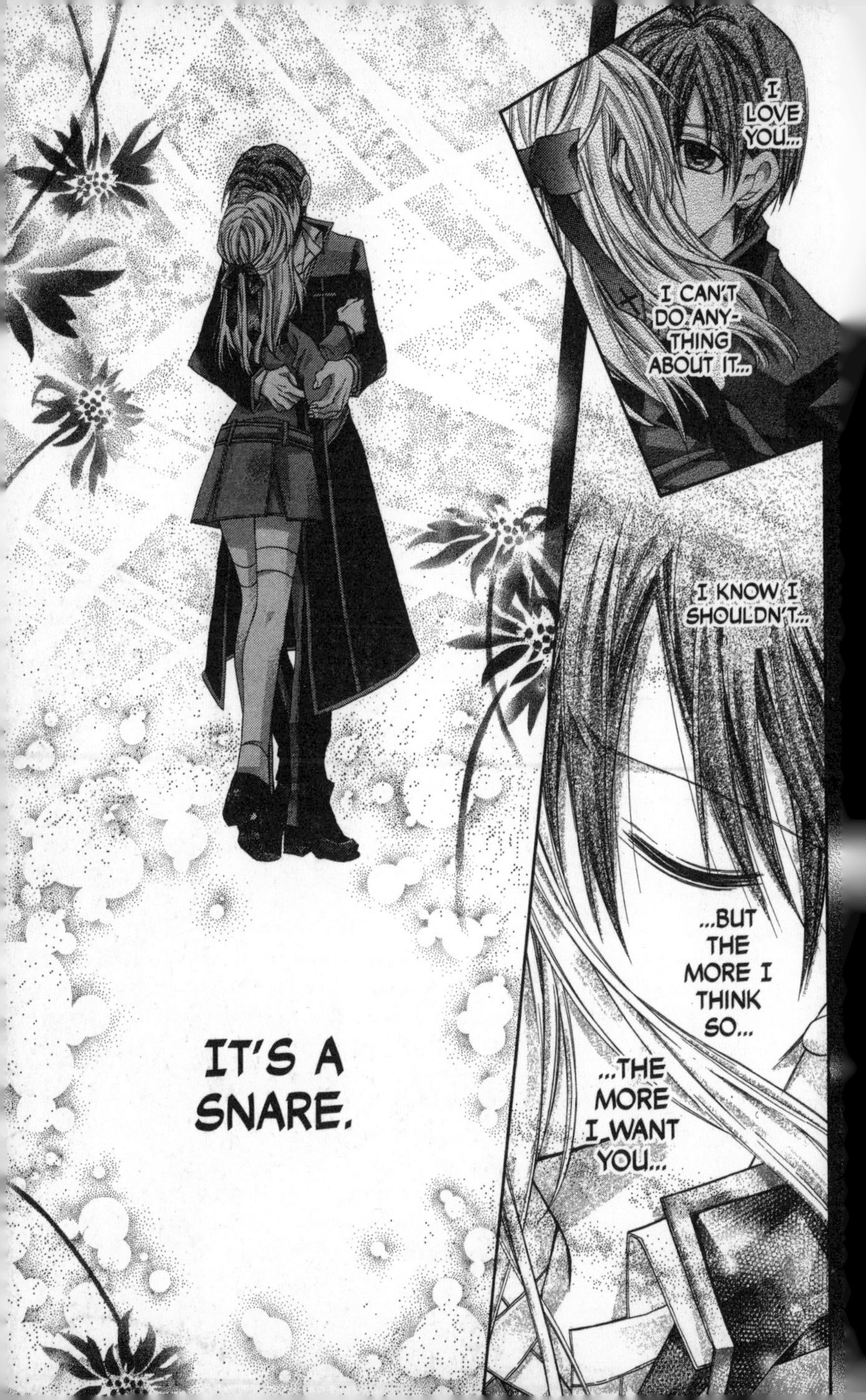
I LOVE YOU...
I CAN'T DO ANY-THING ABOUT IT...
I KNOW I SHOULDN'T...
...BUT THE MORE I THINK SO...
...THE MORE I WANT YOU...
IT'S A SNARE.

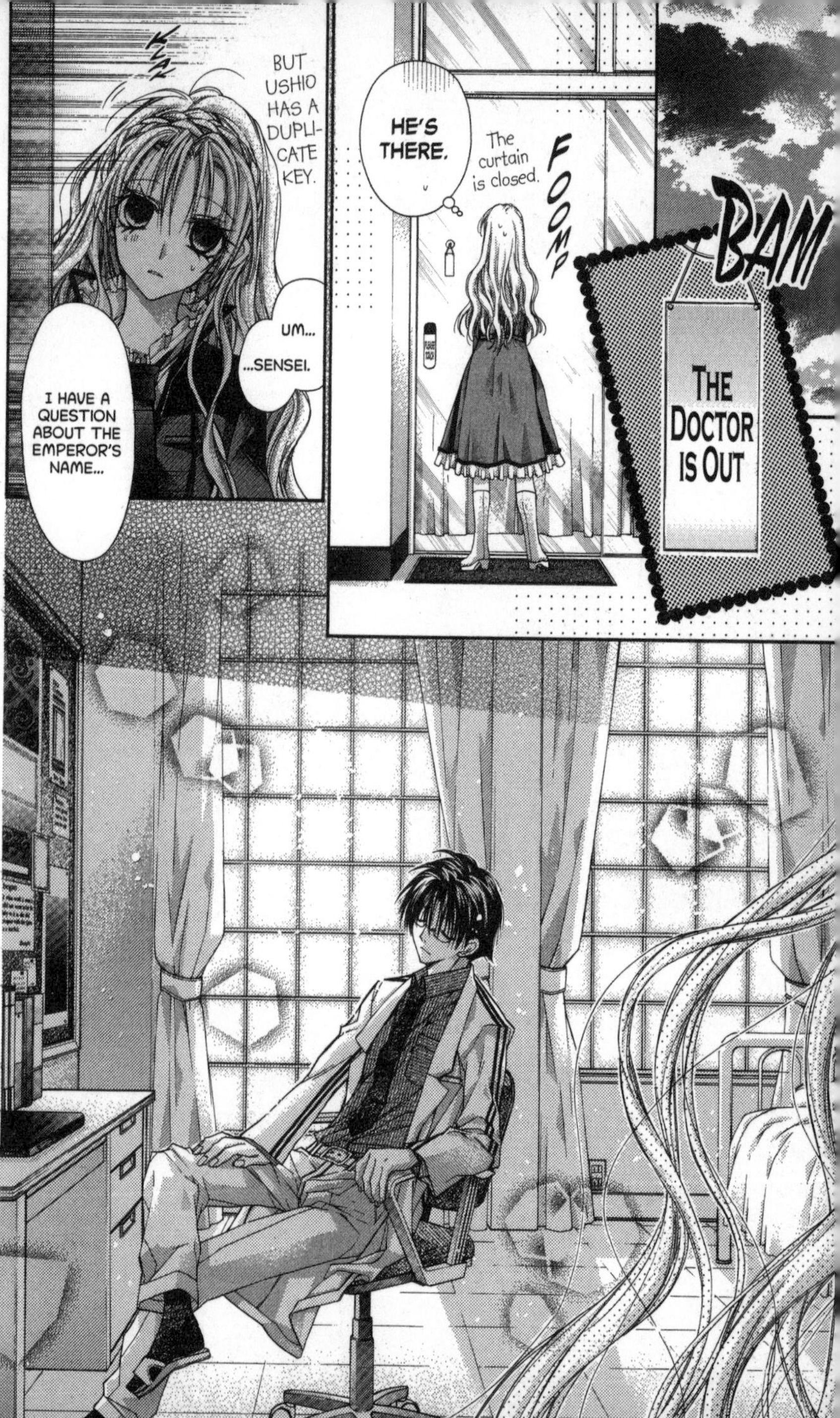
BAM
THE DOCTOR IS OUT
FOOMP
The curtain is closed.
HE'S THERE.
BUT USHIO HAS A DUPLICATE KEY.
KLAK
UM...
...SENSEI.
I HAVE A QUESTION ABOUT THE EMPEROR'S NAME...

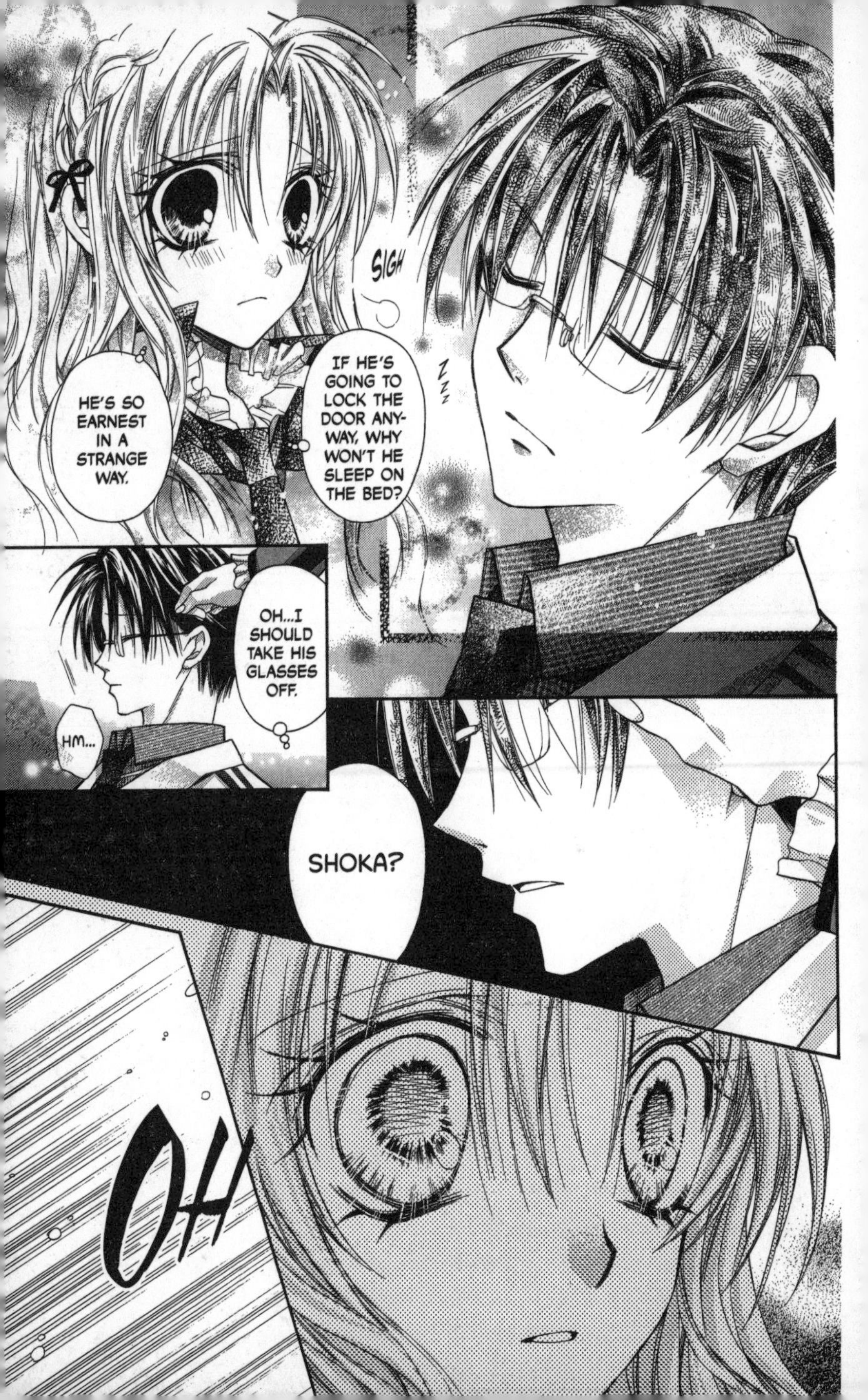
SIGH
ZZZ
IF HE'S GOING TO LOCK THE DOOR ANY-WAY, WHY WON'T HE SLEEP ON THE BED?
HE'S SO EARNEST IN A STRANGE WAY.
OH...I SHOULD TAKE HIS GLASSES OFF.
HM...
SHOKA?
OH

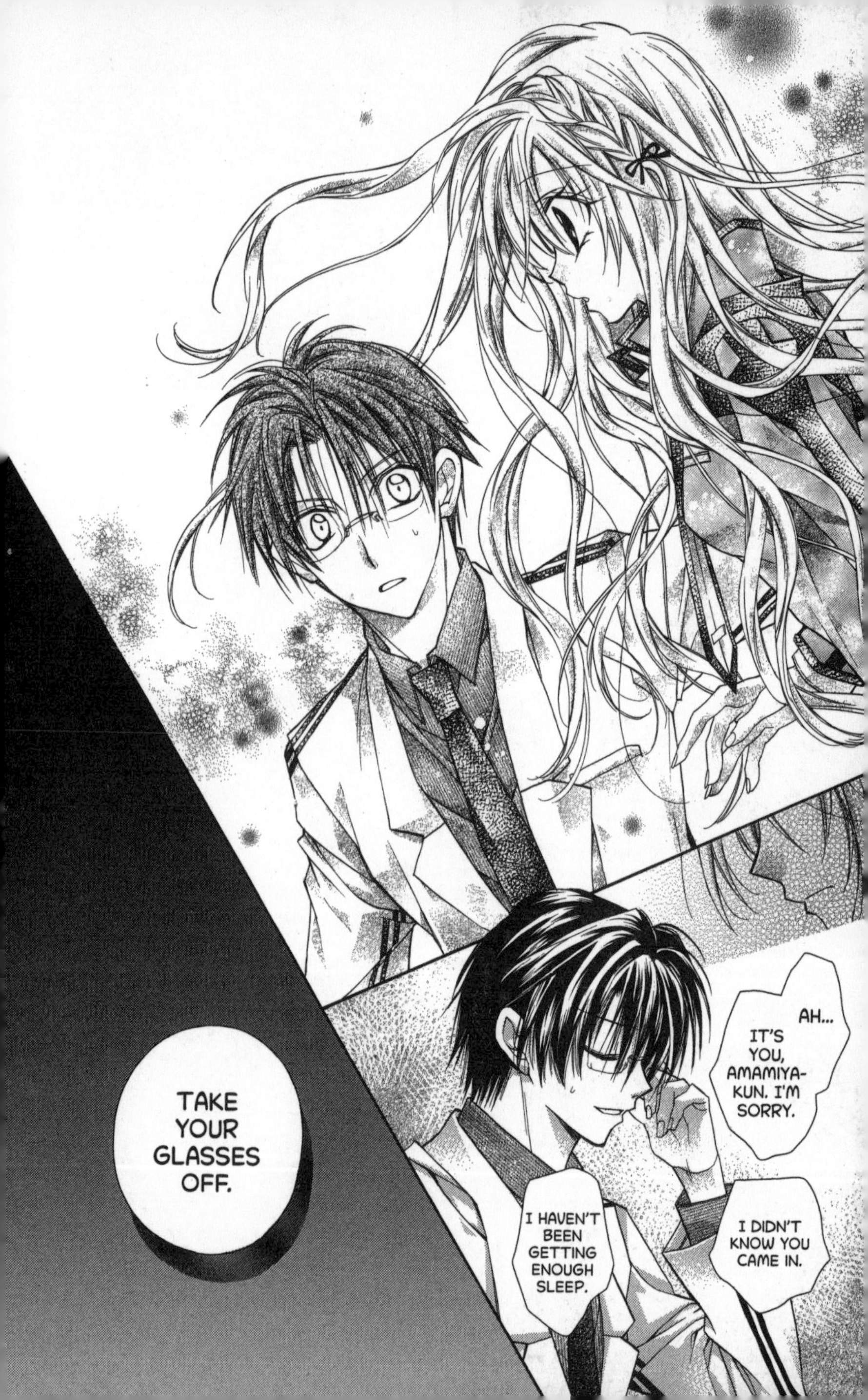
AH... IT'S YOU, AMAMIYA-KUN. I'M SORRY.
I DIDN'T KNOW YOU CAME IN.
I HAVEN'T BEEN GETTING ENOUGH SLEEP.
TAKE YOUR GLASSES OFF.

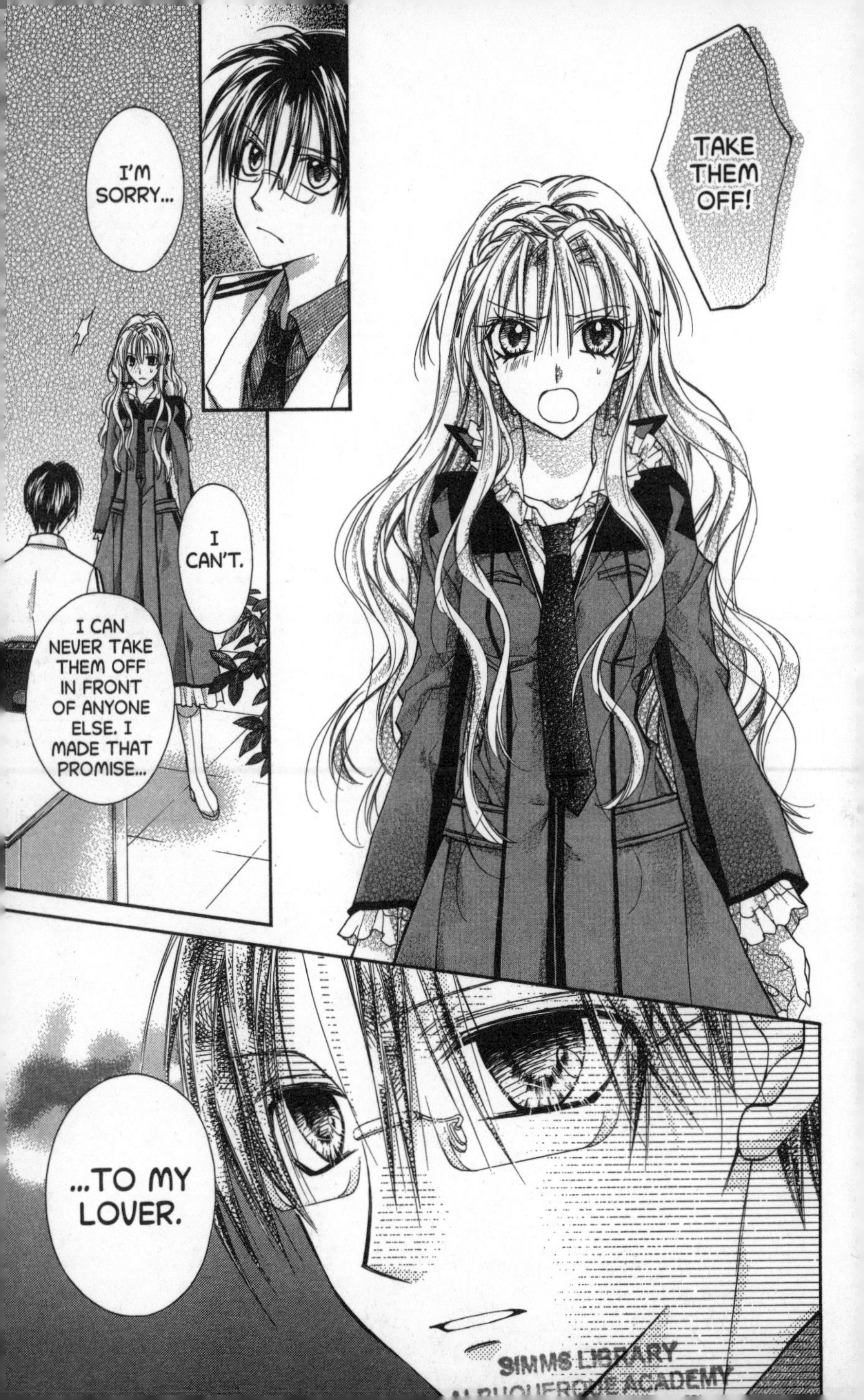
TAKE THEM OFF!
I'M SORRY...
I CAN'T.
I CAN NEVER TAKE THEM OFF IN FRONT OF ANYONE ELSE. I MADE THAT PROMISE...
...TO MY LOVER.

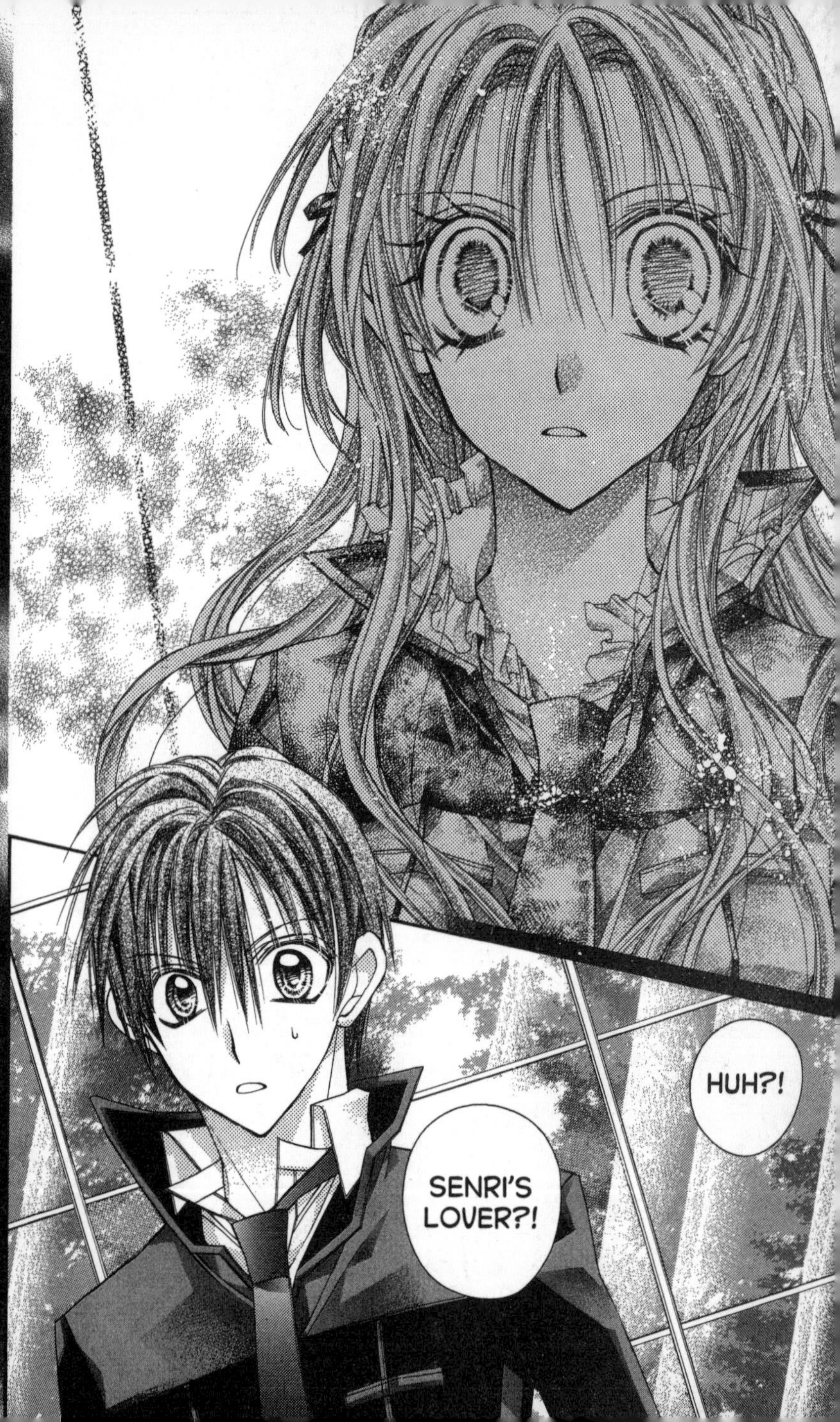
HUH?!
SENRI'S LOVER?!

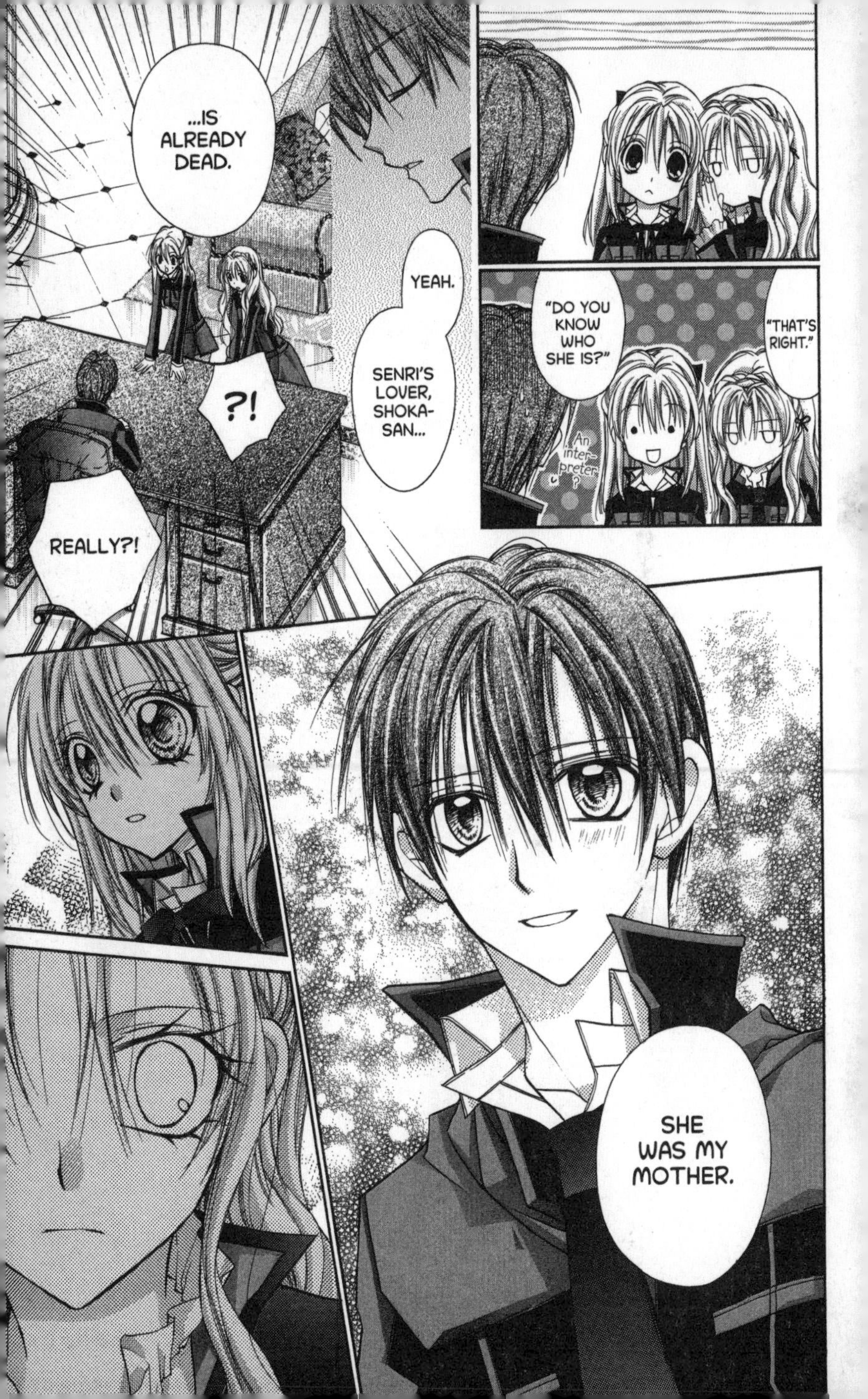
"DO YOU KNOW WHO SHE IS?"
"THAT'S RIGHT."
An interpreter?
YEAH.
SENRI'S LOVER, SHOKA-SAN...
...IS ALREADY DEAD.
?!
REALLY?!
SHE WAS MY MOTHER.

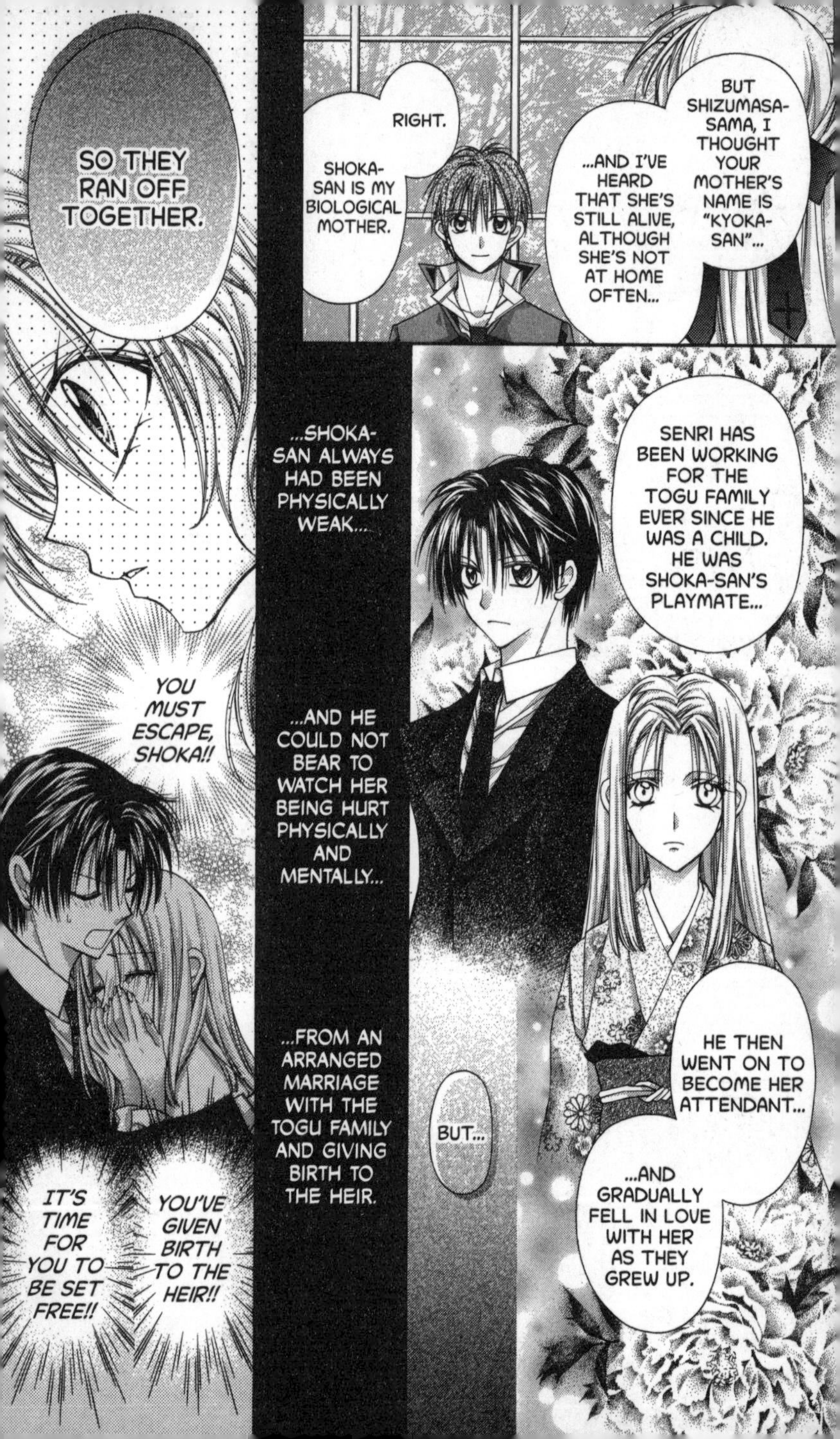
BUT SHIZUMASA-SAMA, I THOUGHT YOUR MOTHER'S NAME IS "KYOKA-SAN"...
...AND I'VE HEARD THAT SHE'S STILL ALIVE, ALTHOUGH SHE'S NOT AT HOME OFTEN...
RIGHT.
SHOKA-SAN IS MY BIOLOGICAL MOTHER.
SENRI HAS BEEN WORKING FOR THE TOGU FAMILY EVER SINCE HE WAS A CHILD. HE WAS SHOKA-SAN'S PLAYMATE...
HE THEN WENT ON TO BECOME HER ATTENDANT...
...AND GRADUALLY FELL IN LOVE WITH HER AS THEY GREW UP.
BUT...
...SHOKA-SAN ALWAYS HAD BEEN PHYSICALLY WEAK...
...AND HE COULD NOT BEAR TO WATCH HER BEING HURT PHYSICALLY AND MENTALLY...
...FROM AN ARRANGED MARRIAGE WITH THE TOGU FAMILY AND GIVING BIRTH TO THE HEIR.
SO THEY RAN OFF TOGETHER.
YOU MUST ESCAPE, SHOKA!!
YOU'VE GIVEN BIRTH TO THE HEIR!!
IT'S TIME FOR YOU TO BE SET FREE!!

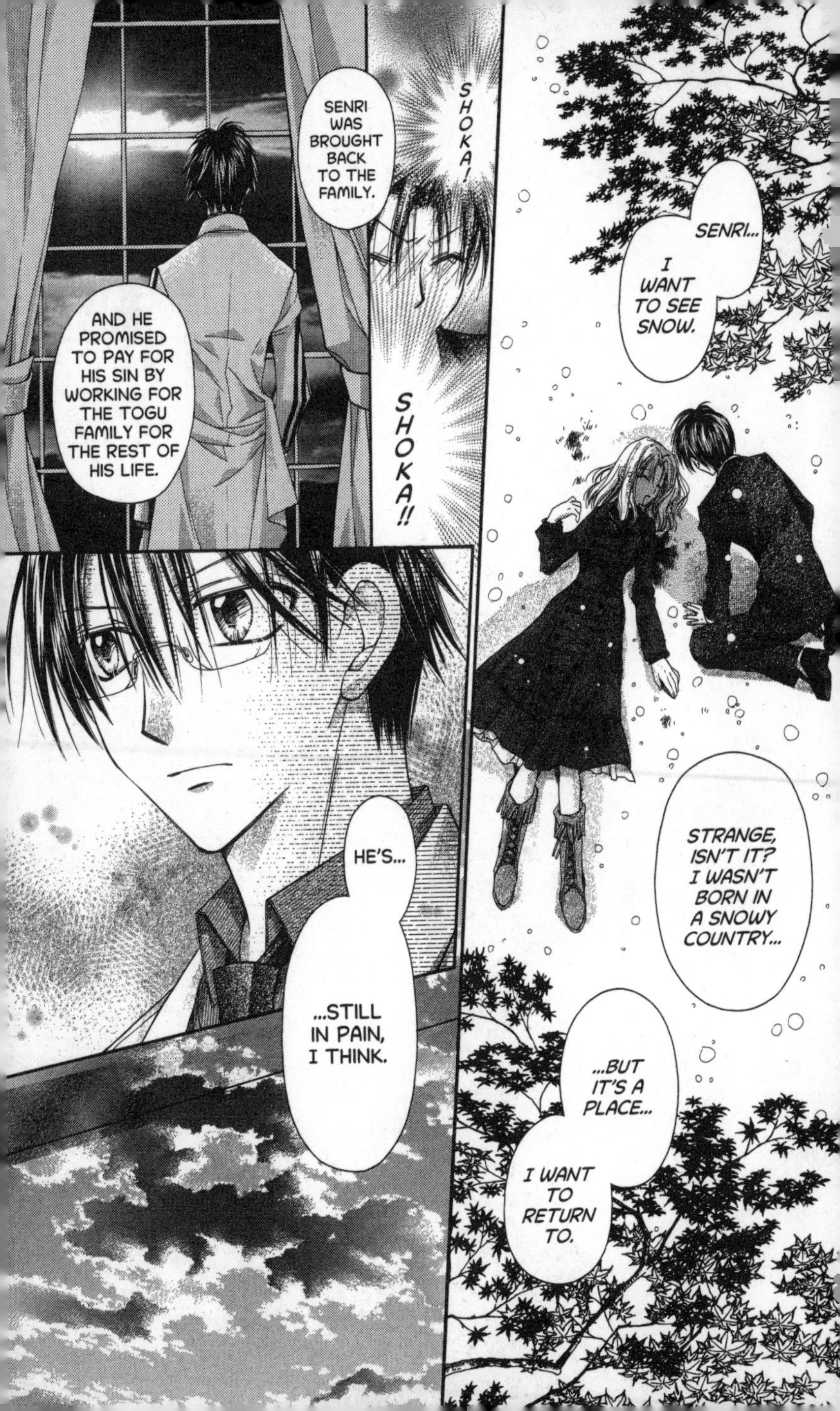
SENRI...
I WANT TO SEE SNOW.
STRANGE, ISN'T IT? I WASN'T BORN IN A SNOWY COUNTRY...
...BUT IT'S A PLACE...
I WANT TO RETURN TO.
SHOKA!
SHOKA!!
SENRI WAS BROUGHT BACK TO THE FAMILY.
AND HE PROMISED TO PAY FOR HIS SIN BY WORKING FOR THE TOGU FAMILY FOR THE REST OF HIS LIFE.
HE'S...
...STILL IN PAIN, I THINK.

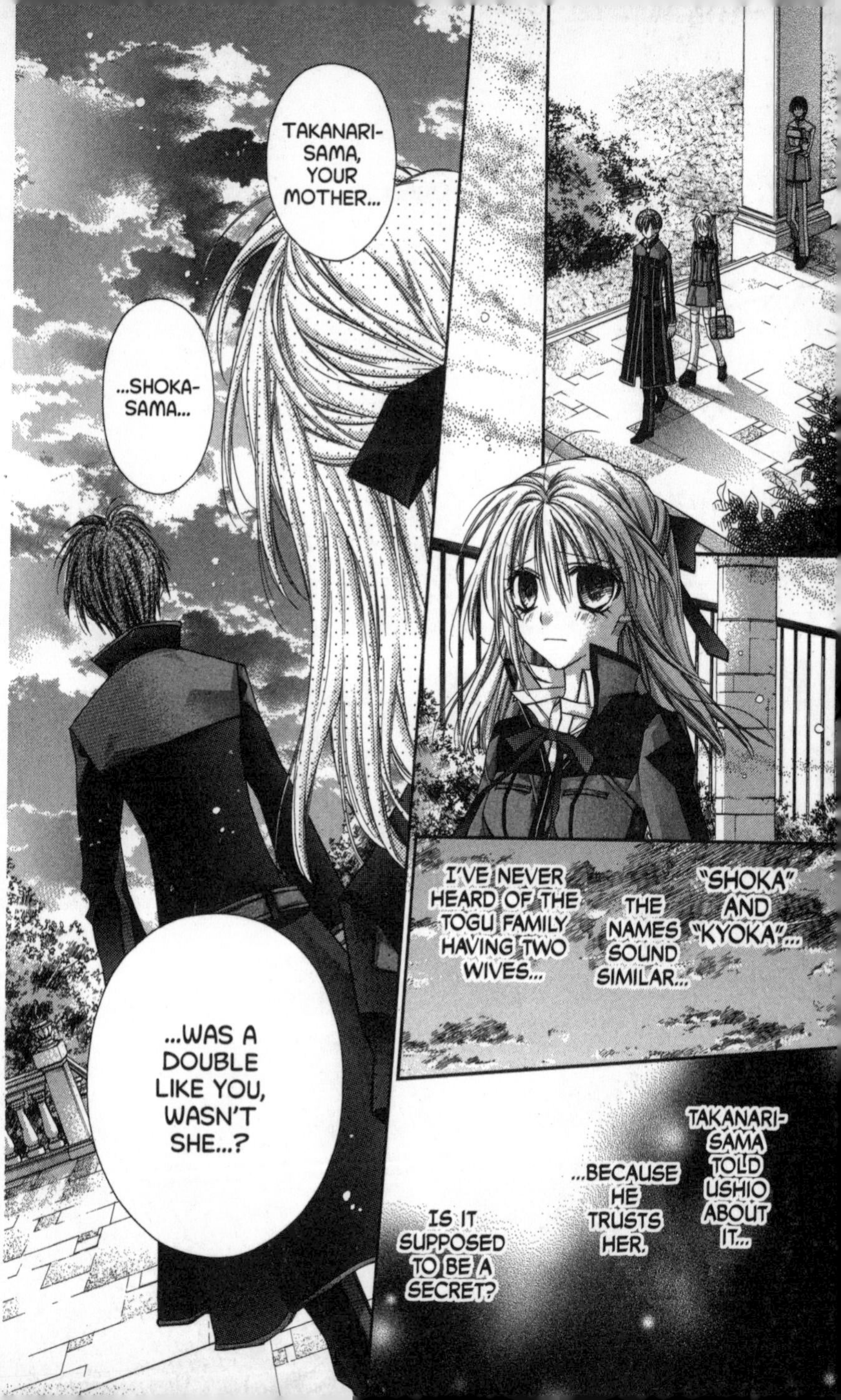
"SHOKA" AND "KYOKA"...
THE NAMES SOUND SIMILAR...
I'VE NEVER HEARD OF THE TOGU FAMILY HAVING TWO WIVES...
TAKANARI-SAMA TOLD USHIO ABOUT IT...
...BECAUSE HE TRUSTS HER.
IS IT SUPPOSED TO BE A SECRET?
TAKANARI-SAMA, YOUR MOTHER...
...SHOKA-SAMA...
...WAS A DOUBLE LIKE YOU, WASN'T SHE...?

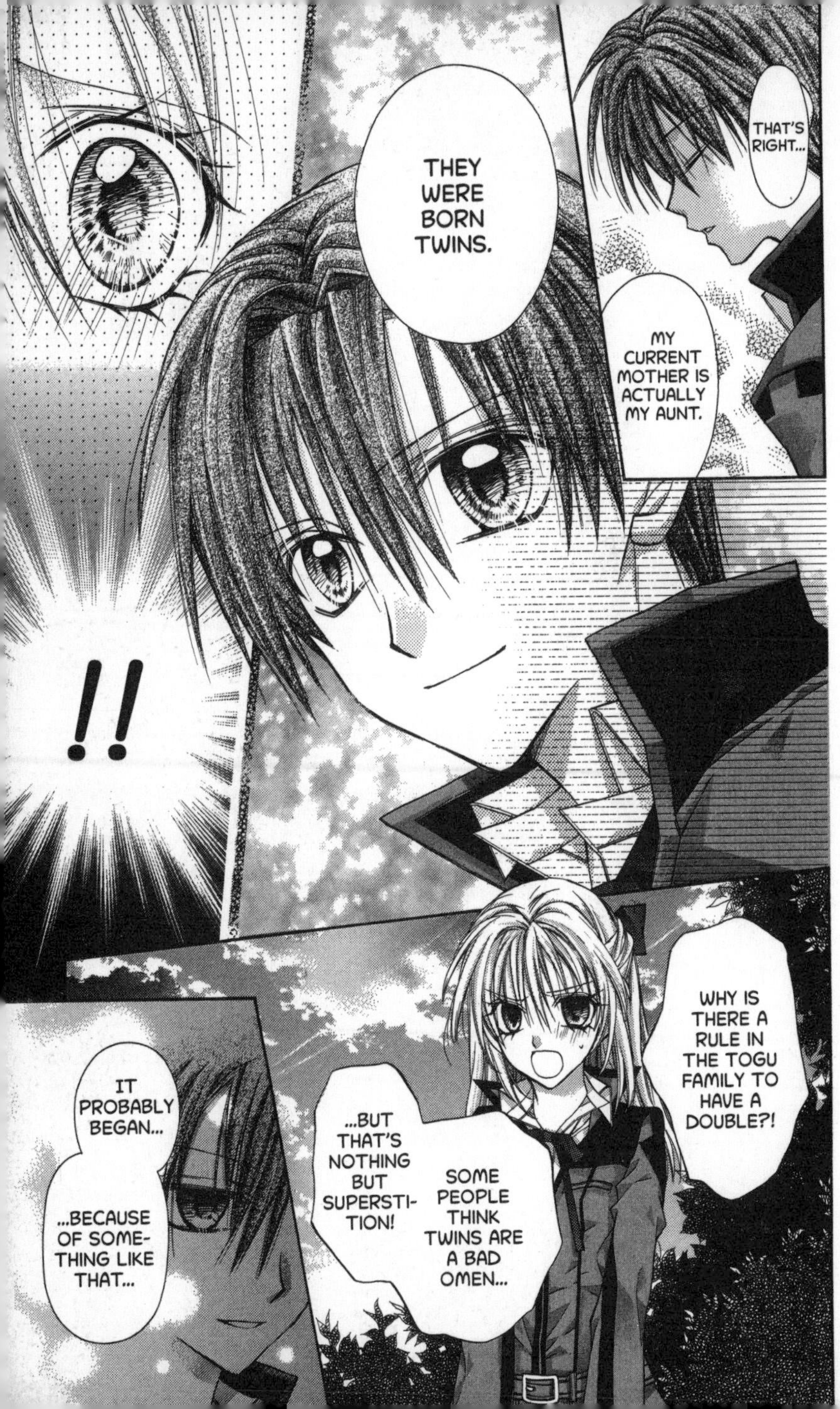
THAT'S RIGHT...
MY CURRENT MOTHER IS ACTUALLY MY AUNT.
THEY WERE BORN TWINS.
!!
WHY IS THERE A RULE IN THE TOGU FAMILY TO HAVE A DOUBLE?!
SOME PEOPLE THINK TWINS ARE A BAD OMEN...
...BUT THAT'S NOTHING BUT SUPERSTI-TION!
IT PROBABLY BEGAN...
...BECAUSE OF SOME-THING LIKE THAT...

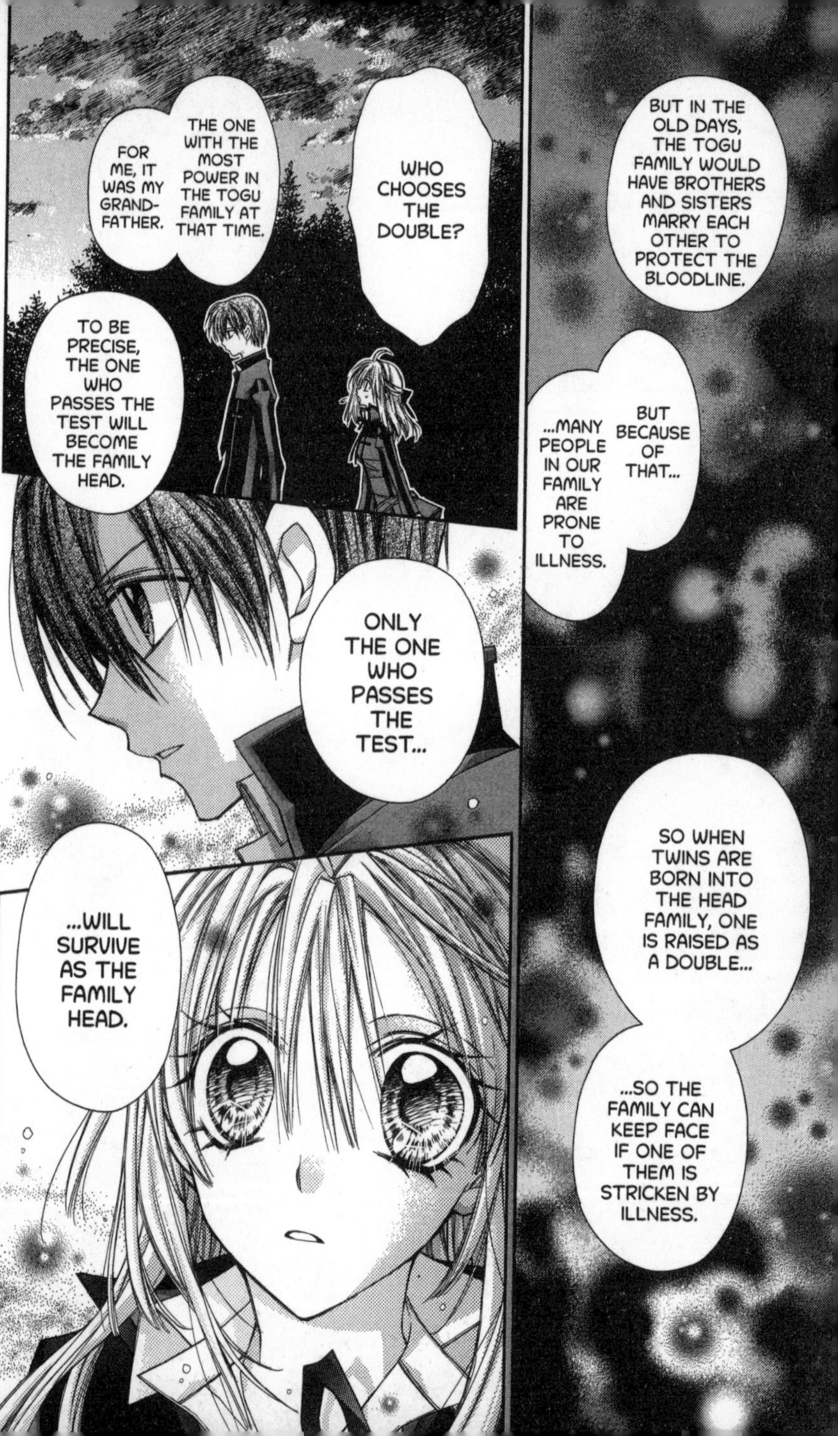
BUT IN THE OLD DAYS, THE TOGU FAMILY WOULD HAVE BROTHERS AND SISTERS MARRY EACH OTHER TO PROTECT THE BLOODLINE.
BUT BECAUSE OF THAT...
...MANY PEOPLE IN OUR FAMILY ARE PRONE TO ILLNESS.
SO WHEN TWINS ARE BORN INTO THE HEAD FAMILY, ONE IS RAISED AS A DOUBLE...
...SO THE FAMILY CAN KEEP FACE IF ONE OF THEM IS STRICKEN BY ILLNESS.
WHO CHOOSES THE DOUBLE?
THE ONE WITH THE MOST POWER IN THE TOGU FAMILY AT THAT TIME.
FOR ME, IT WAS MY GRAND-FATHER.
TO BE PRECISE, THE ONE WHO PASSES THE TEST WILL BECOME THE FAMILY HEAD.
ONLY THE ONE WHO PASSES THE TEST...
...WILL SURVIVE AS THE FAMILY HEAD.

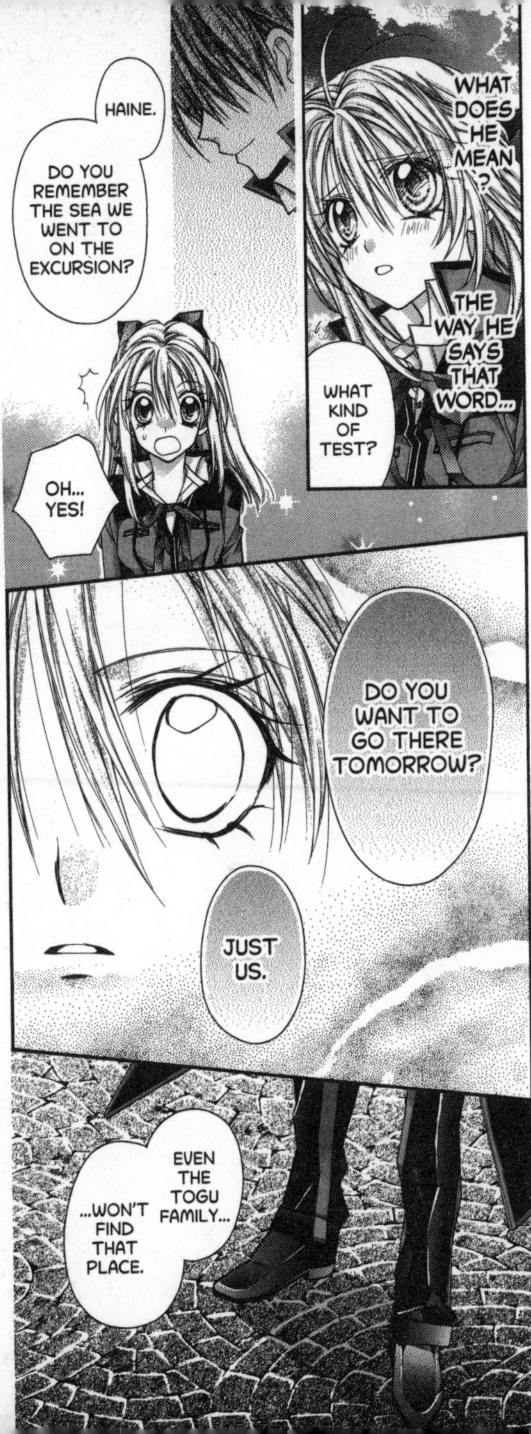
WHAT DOES HE MEAN?
THE WAY HE SAYS THAT WORD...
WHAT KIND OF TEST?
HAINE.
DO YOU REMEMBER THE SEA WE WENT TO ON THE EXCURSION?
OH... YES!
DO YOU WANT TO GO THERE TOMORROW?
JUST US.
EVEN THE TOGU FAMILY...
...WON'T FIND THAT PLACE.

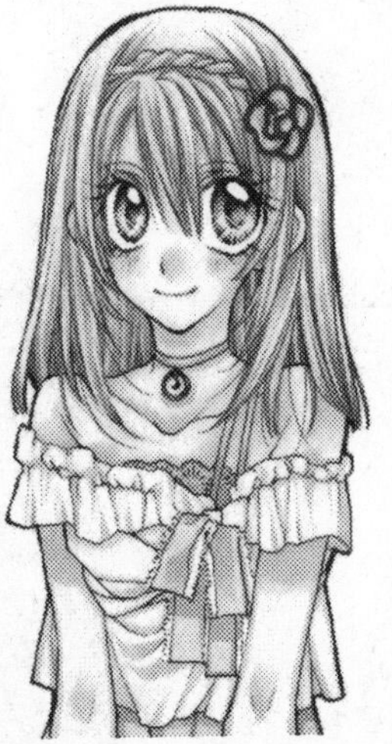

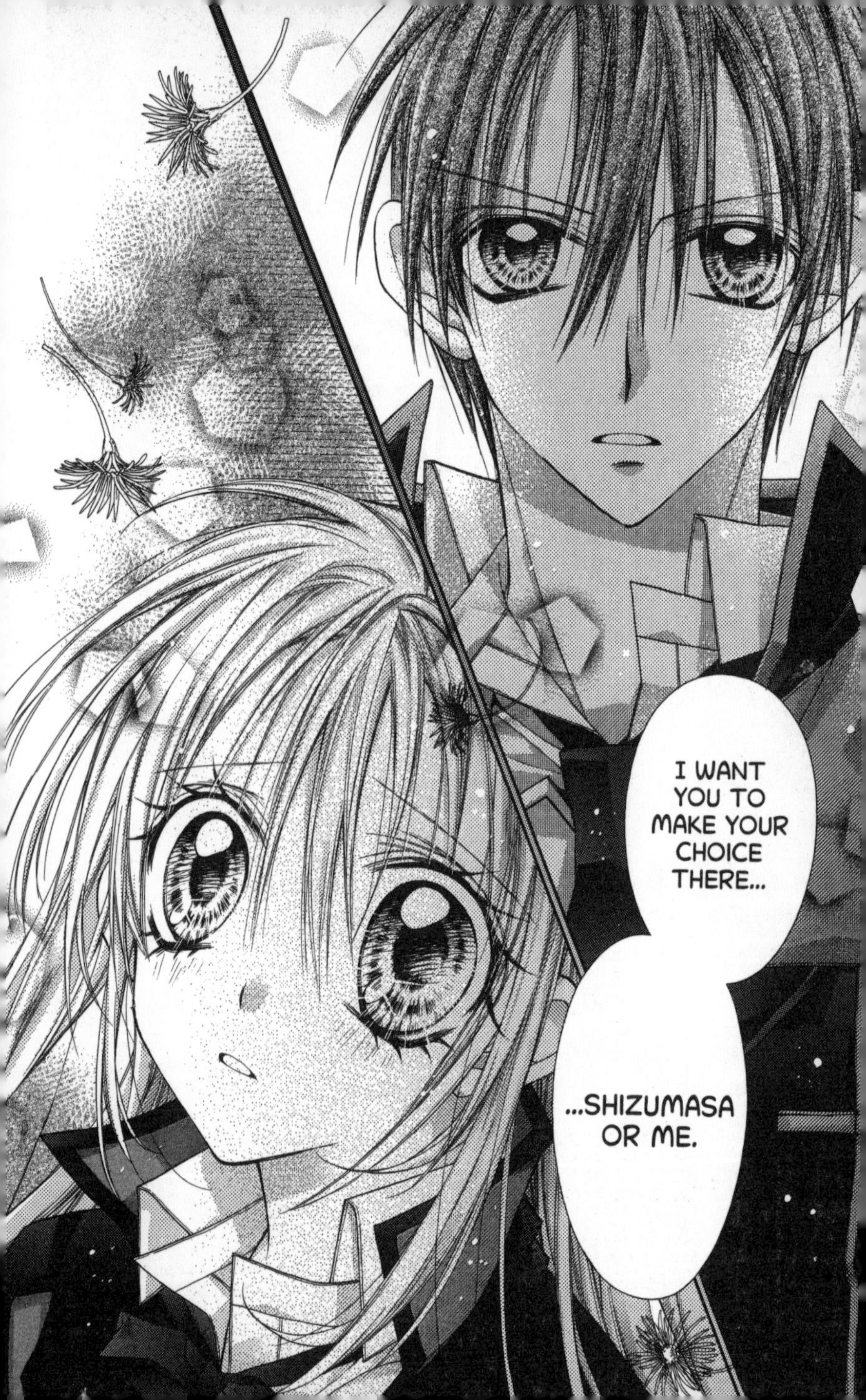
I WANT YOU TO MAKE YOUR CHOICE THERE...
...SHIZUMASA OR ME.

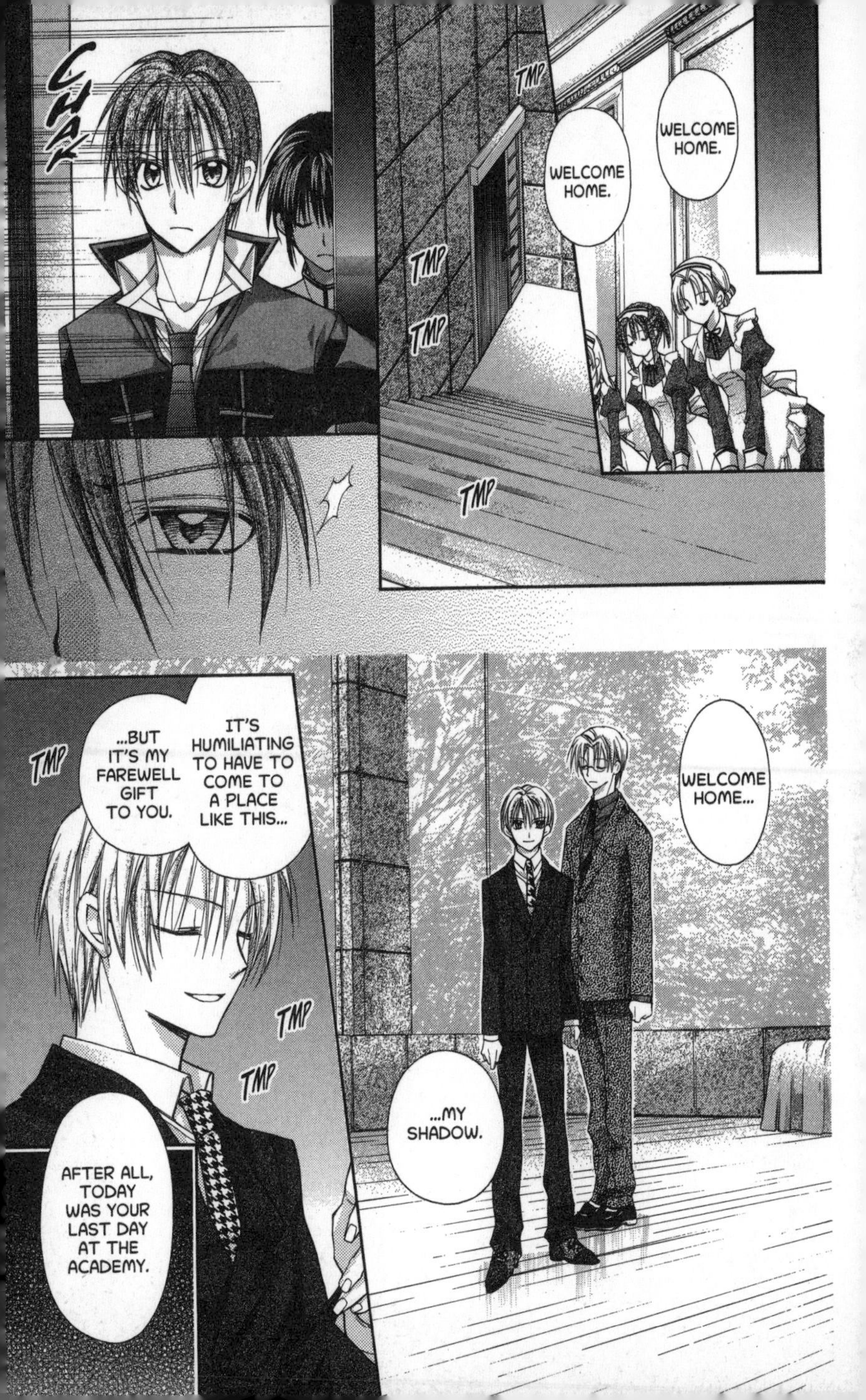
TMP
WELCOME HOME.
WELCOME HOME.
TMP
TMP
TMP
CHAK
WELCOME HOME...
...MY SHADOW.
IT'S HUMILIATING TO HAVE TO COME TO A PLACE LIKE THIS...
...BUT IT'S MY FAREWELL GIFT TO YOU.
TMP
TMP
TMP
AFTER ALL, TODAY WAS YOUR LAST DAY AT THE ACADEMY.

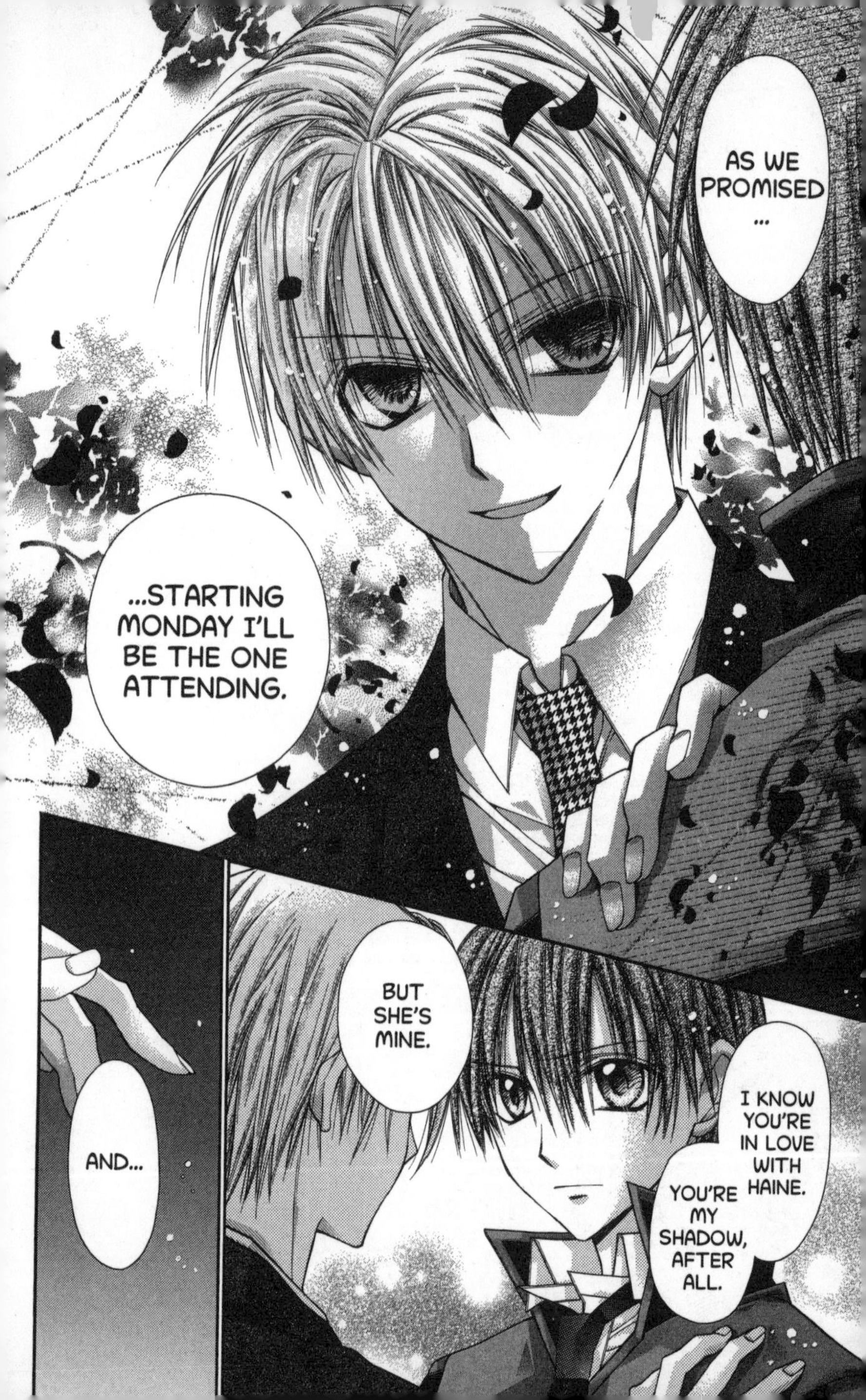
AS WE PROMISED...
...STARTING MONDAY I'LL BE THE ONE ATTENDING.
I KNOW YOU'RE IN LOVE WITH HAINE.
YOU'RE MY SHADOW, AFTER ALL.
BUT SHE'S MINE.
AND...

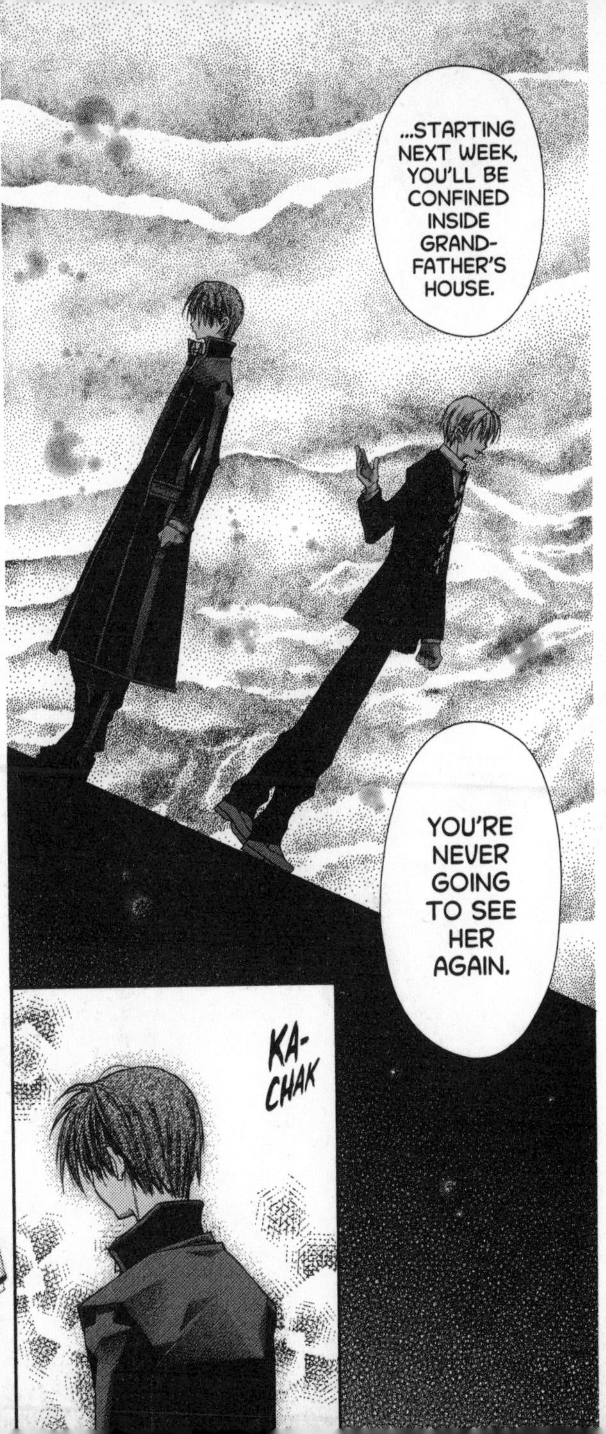
...STARTING NEXT WEEK, YOU'LL BE CONFINED INSIDE GRAND-FATHER'S HOUSE.
YOU'RE NEVER GOING TO SEE HER AGAIN.
KA-CHAK

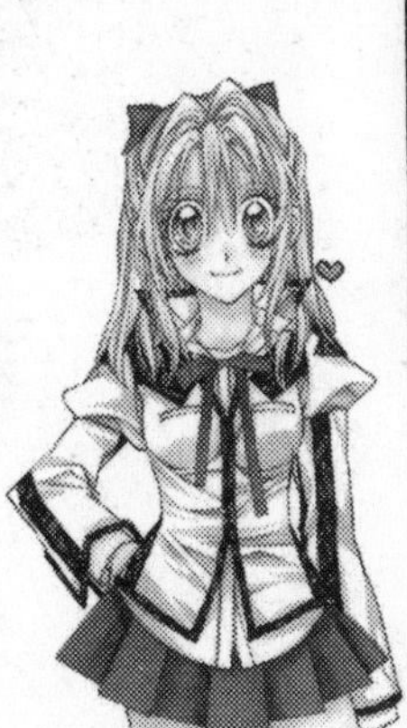

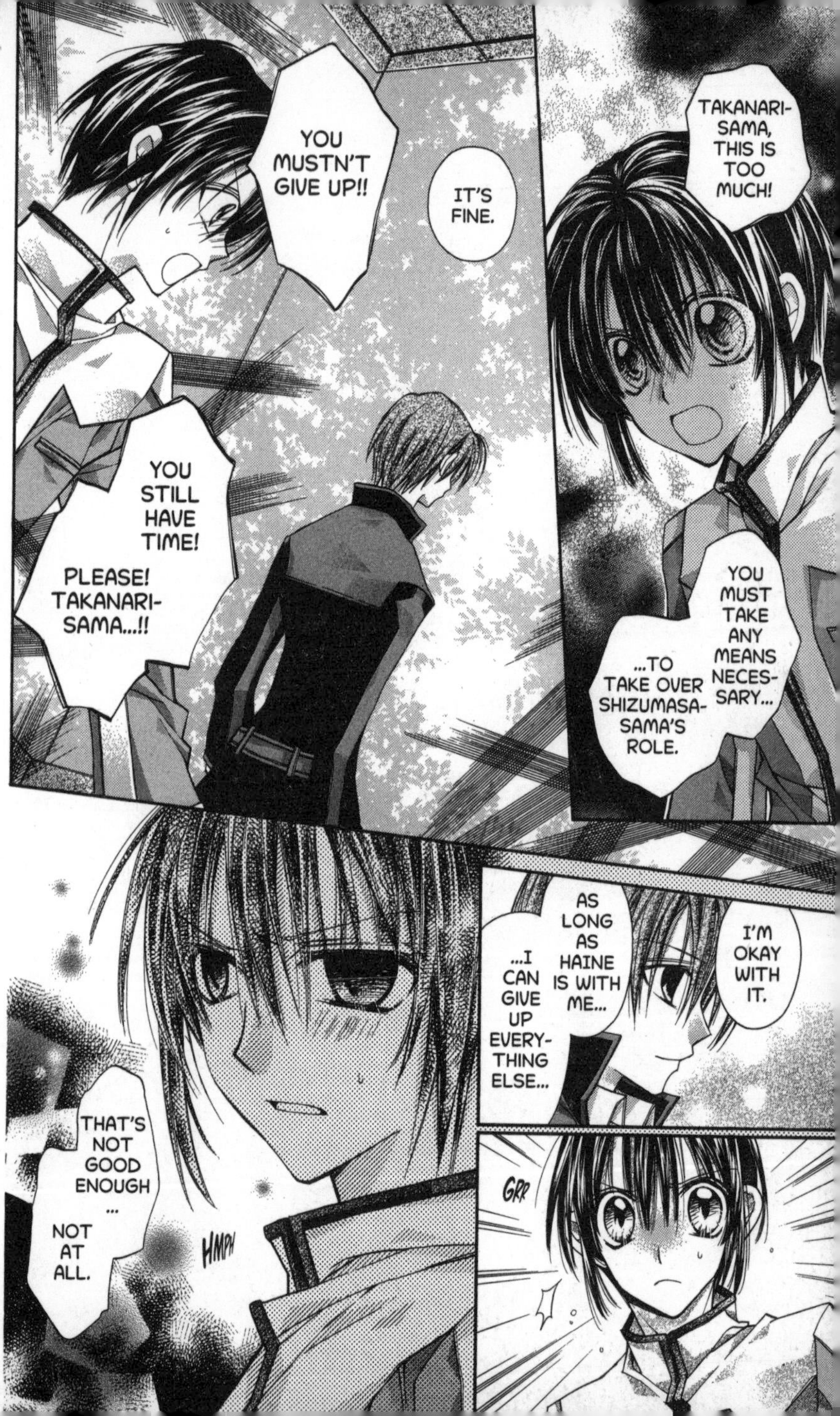
TAKANARI-SAMA, THIS IS TOO MUCH!
YOU MUST TAKE ANY MEANS NECES-SARY...
...TO TAKE OVER SHIZUMASA-SAMA'S ROLE.
IT'S FINE.
YOU MUSTN'T GIVE UP!!
YOU STILL HAVE TIME!
PLEASE! TAKANARI-SAMA...!!
I'M OKAY WITH IT.
AS LONG AS HAINE IS WITH ME...
...I CAN GIVE UP EVERY-THING ELSE...
GRR
HMPH
THAT'S NOT GOOD ENOUGH ...
NOT AT ALL.

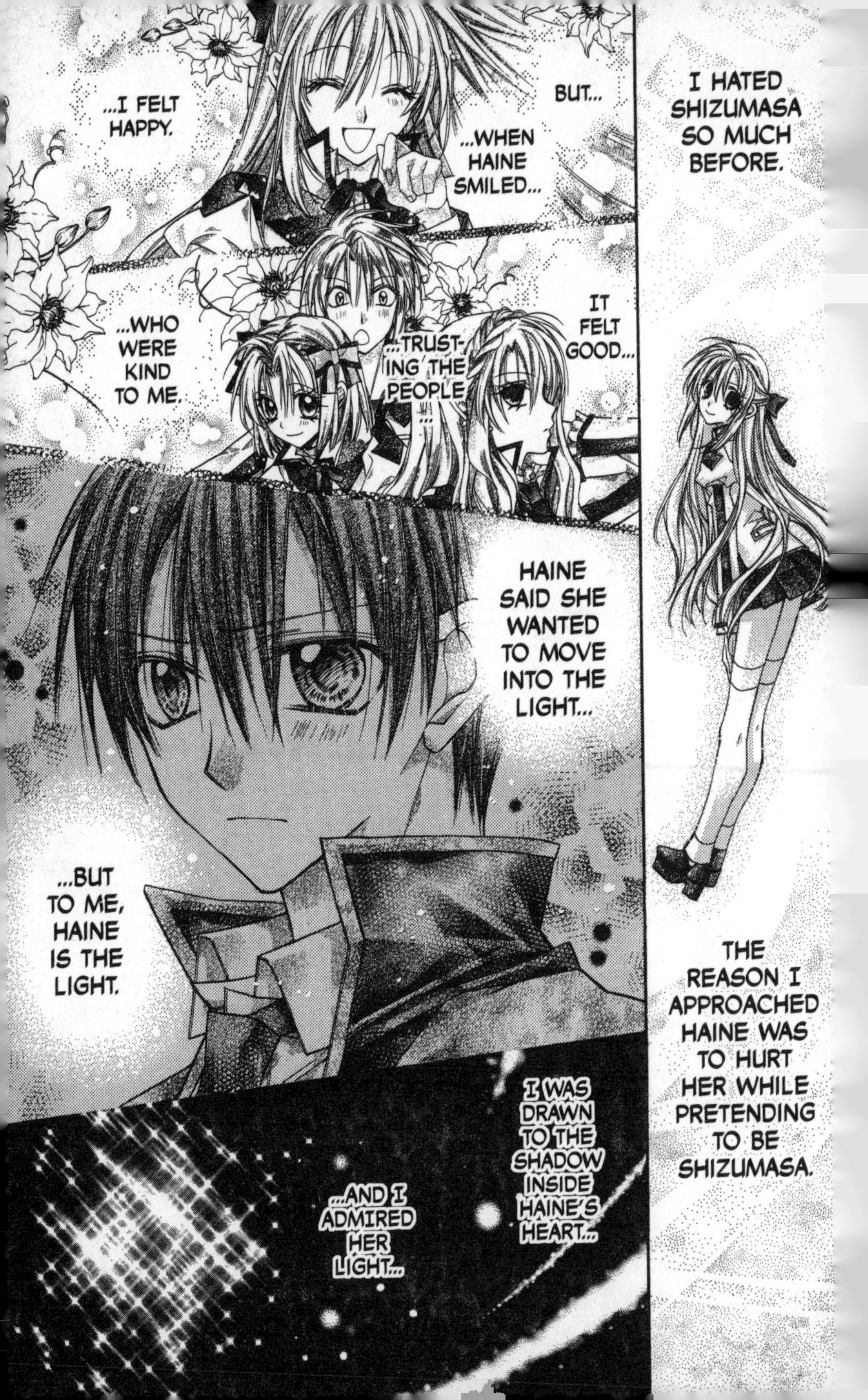
I HATED SHIZUMASA SO MUCH BEFORE.
THE REASON I APPROACHED HAINE WAS TO HURT HER WHILE PRETENDING TO BE SHIZUMASA.
BUT...
...WHEN HAINE SMILED...
...I FELT HAPPY.
IT FELT GOOD...
...TRUSTING THE PEOPLE...
...WHO WERE KIND TO ME.
HAINE SAID SHE WANTED TO MOVE INTO THE LIGHT...
...BUT TO ME, HAINE IS THE LIGHT.
I WAS DRAWN TO THE SHADOW INSIDE HAINE'S HEART...
...AND I ADMIRED HER LIGHT...

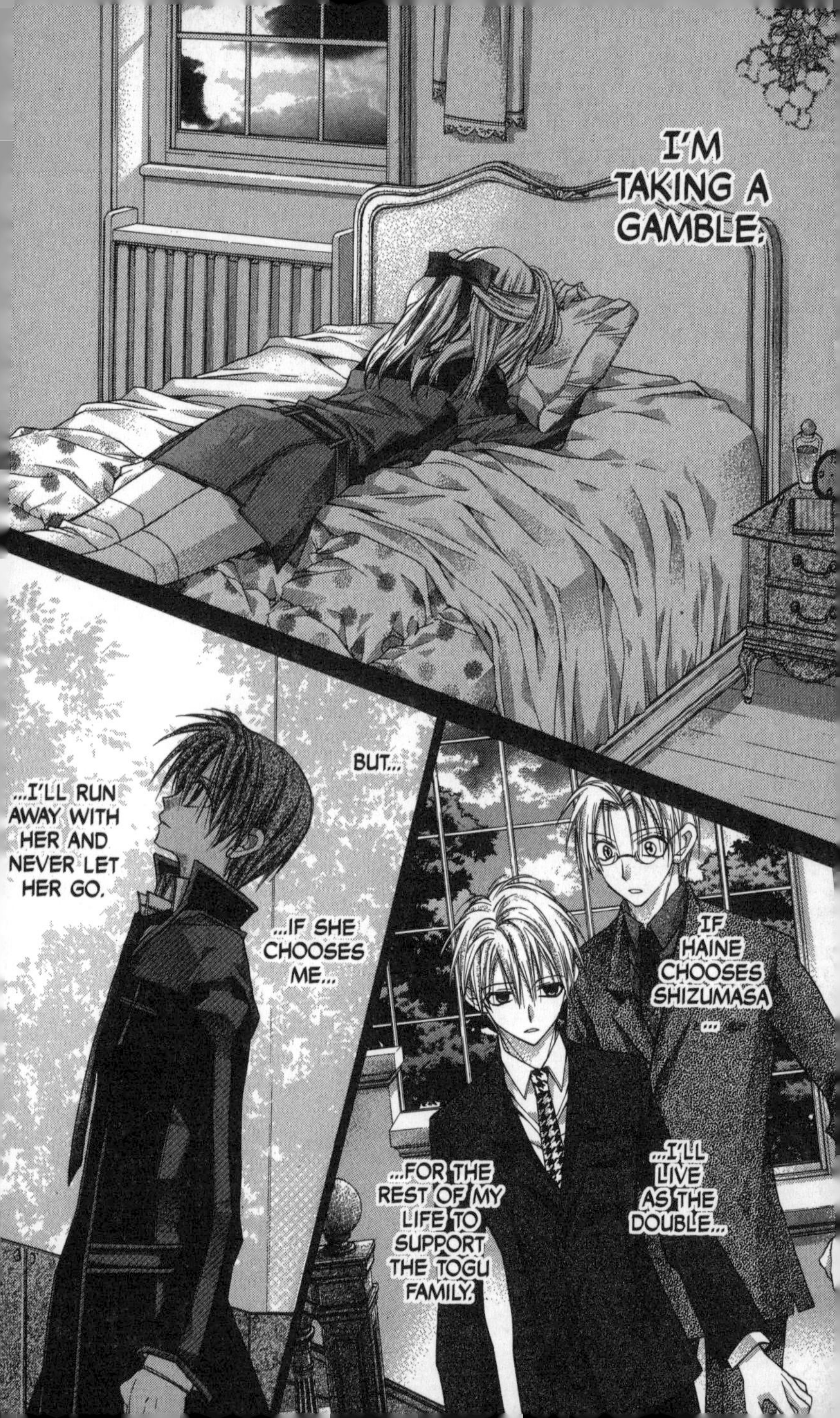
I'M TAKING A GAMBLE.
IF HAINE CHOOSES SHIZUMASA...
...I'LL LIVE AS THE DOUBLE...
...FOR THE REST OF MY LIFE TO SUPPORT THE TOGU FAMILY.
BUT...
...IF SHE CHOOSES ME...
...I'LL RUN AWAY WITH HER AND NEVER LET HER GO.

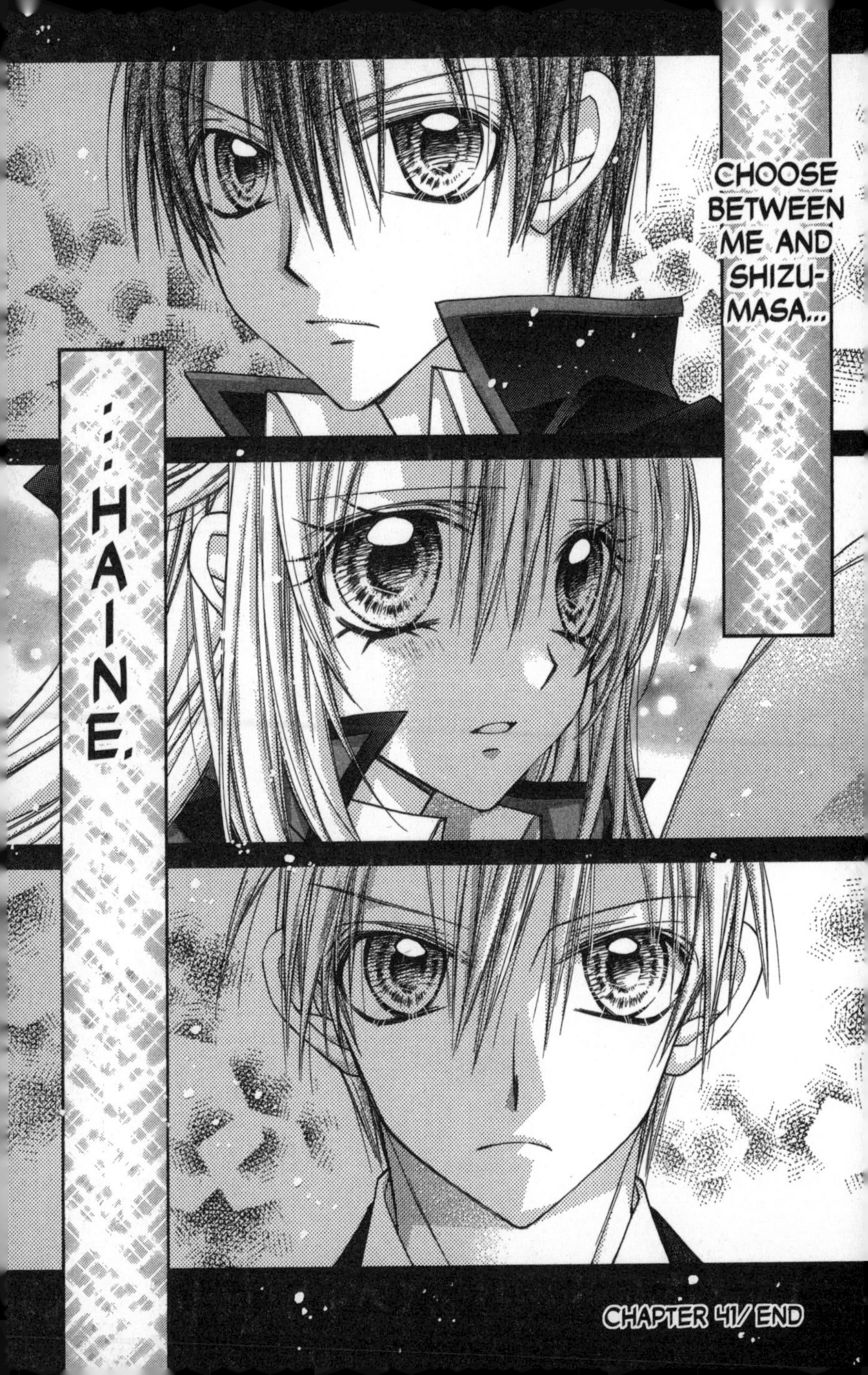
CHOOSE BETWEEN ME AND SHIZU-MASA...
...HAINE.
CHAPTER 41/ END

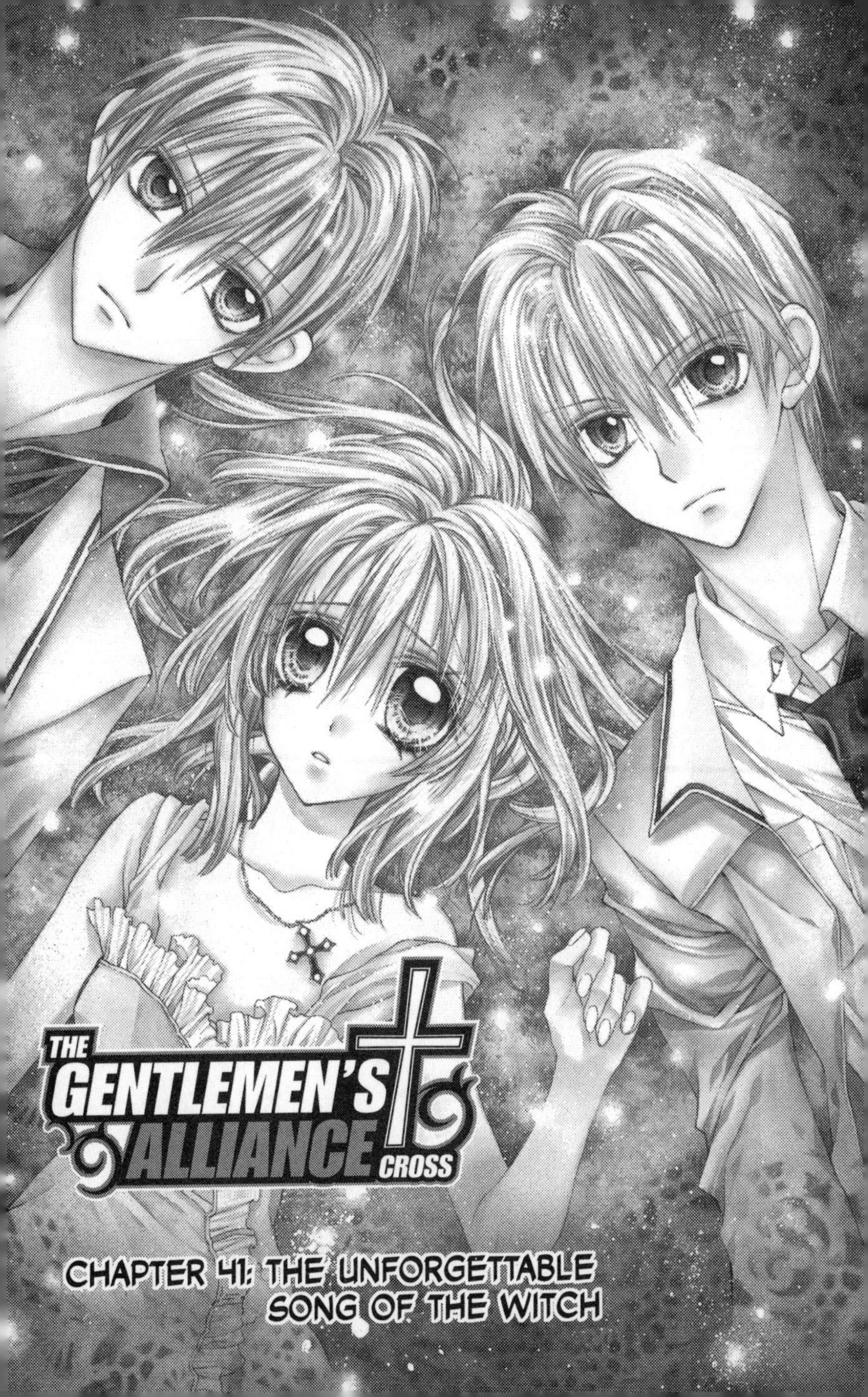
THE GENTLEMEN'S ALLIANCE CROSS
CHAPTER 41: THE UNFORGETTABLE SONG OF THE WITCH

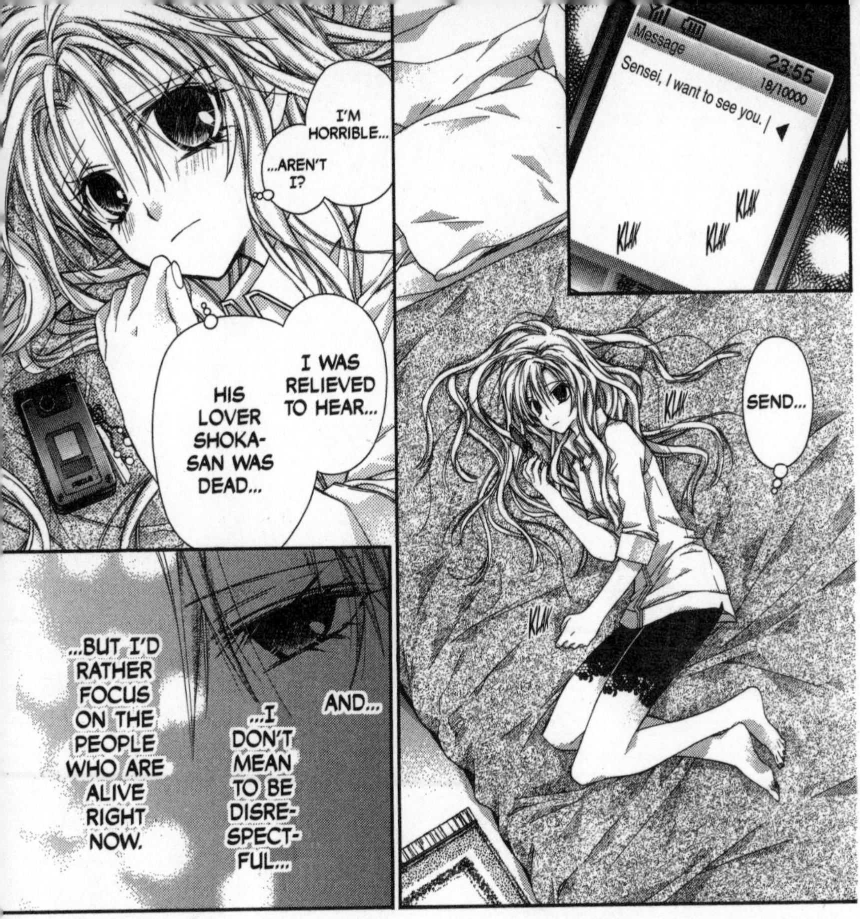
Message
23:55
18/10000
Sensei, I want to see you. |
KLAK
KLAK
KLAK
I'M HORRIBLE...
...AREN'T I?
I WAS RELIEVED TO HEAR...
HIS LOVER SHOKA-SAN WAS DEAD...
SEND...
KLAK
KLAK
AND...
...I DON'T MEAN TO BE DISRESPECTFUL...
...BUT I'D RATHER FOCUS ON THE PEOPLE WHO ARE ALIVE RIGHT NOW.

Chapter 41: The Unforgettable Song of the Witch Lead-in Don't let the fire of love...burn out.

※ I'm giving away the story.

This is the second date between Takanari and Haine. I like to draw date scenes. The picture book from this story has been included in the special edition of volume 10 in Japan. Did any of you get hold of it?

I may have said this before, but I used one of my unreleased stories from a different series of mine and changed it into the picture book. (It was about Yami-chan from *Time Stranger Kyoko*.)

Toya-Kun starts to barge into the spotlight in this chapter, but to me, he is like Haine's shadow, so he has an important role to play at the end.

Anyway... *The Gentlemen's Alliance* is long, isn't it?
I don't know if I'll ever create another series with so many characters.
I may never again do a series this long either.
That's how I feel right now.

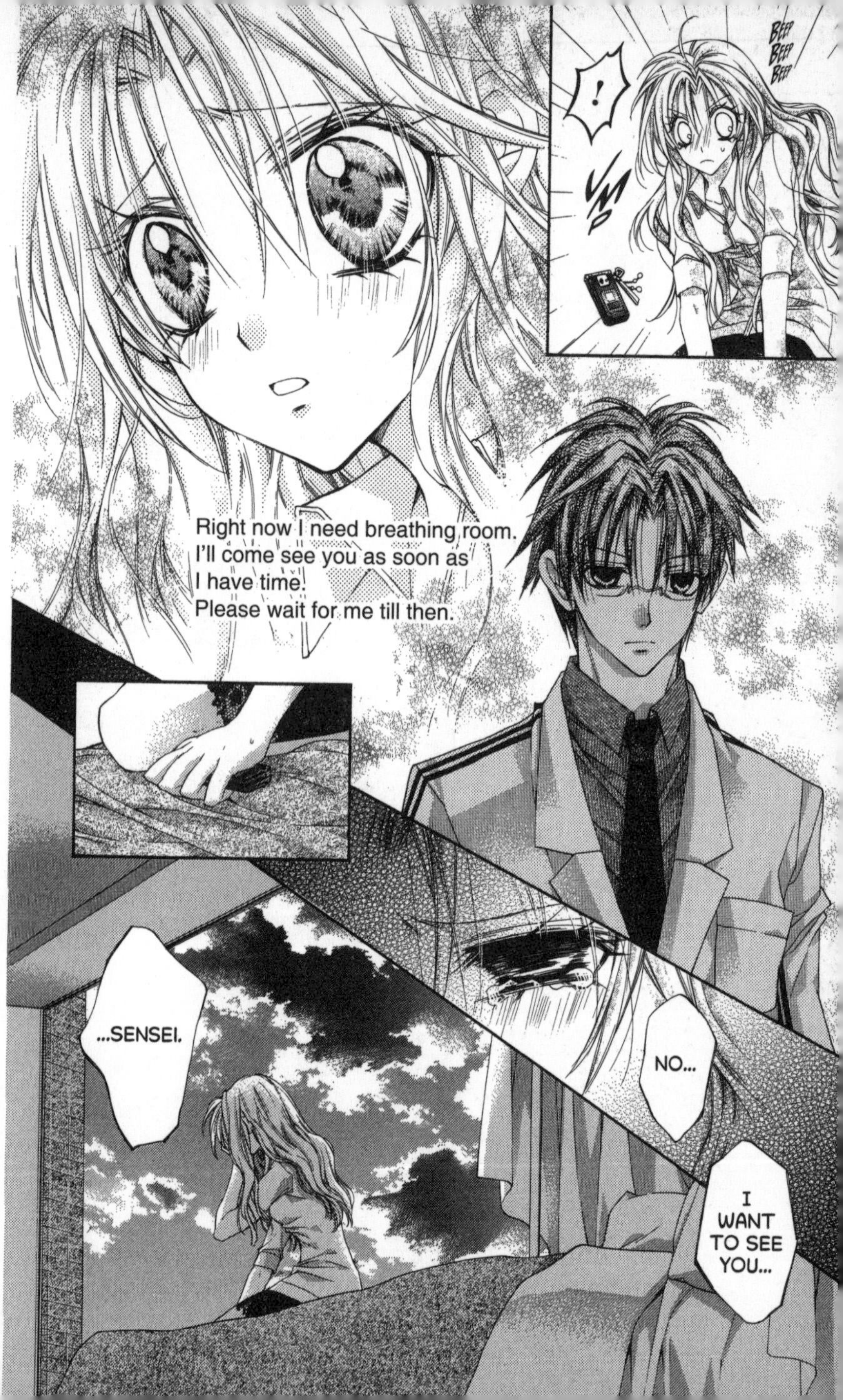
BEEP BEEP BEEP
!
Right now I need breathing room.
I'll come see you as soon as
I have time.
Please wait for me till then.
NO...
I WANT TO SEE YOU...
...SENSEI.

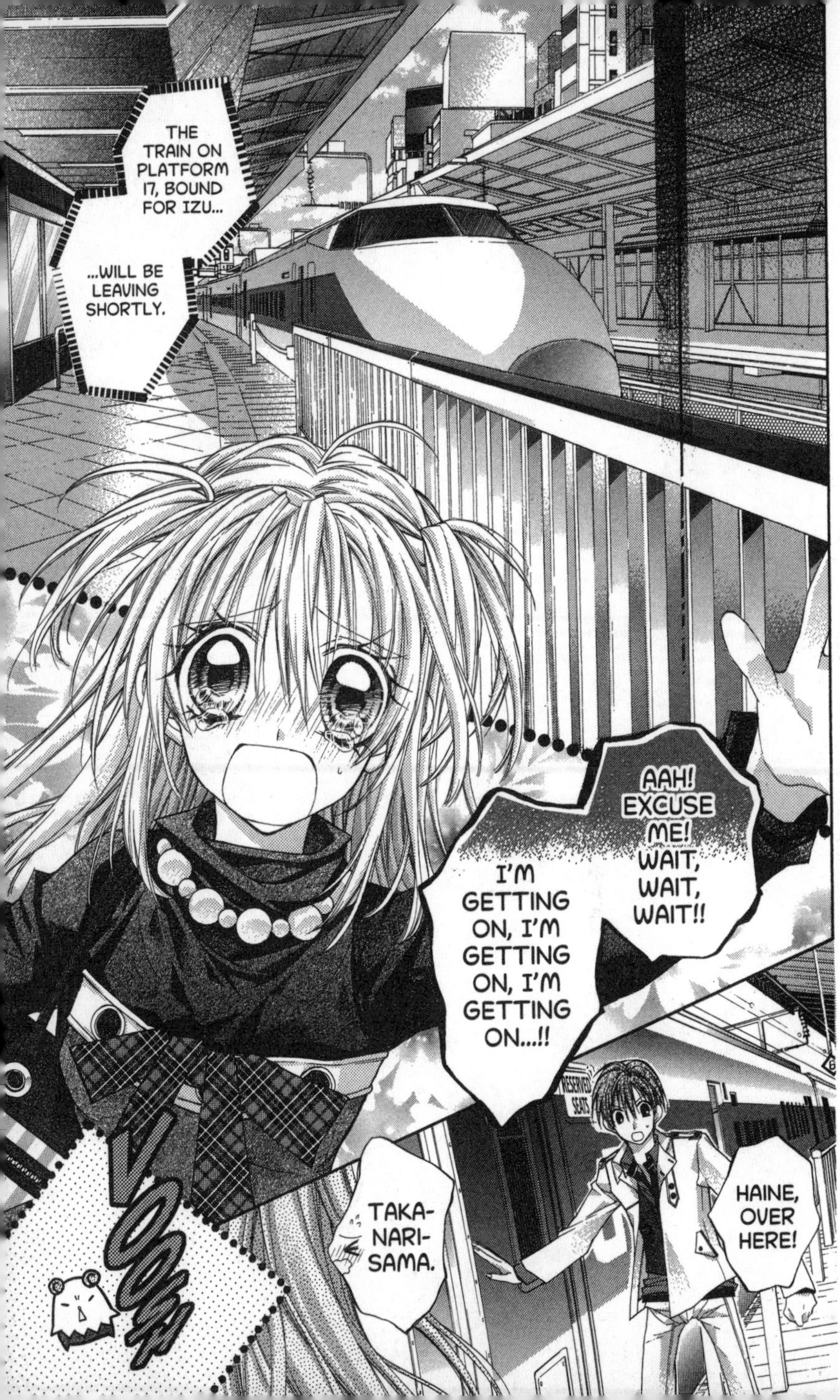
THE TRAIN ON PLATFORM 17, BOUND FOR IZU...
...WILL BE LEAVING SHORTLY.
AAH! EXCUSE ME! WAIT, WAIT, WAIT!!
I'M GETTING ON, I'M GETTING ON, I'M GETTING ON...!!
RESERVED SEATS
HAINE, OVER HERE!
TAKA-NARI-SAMA.

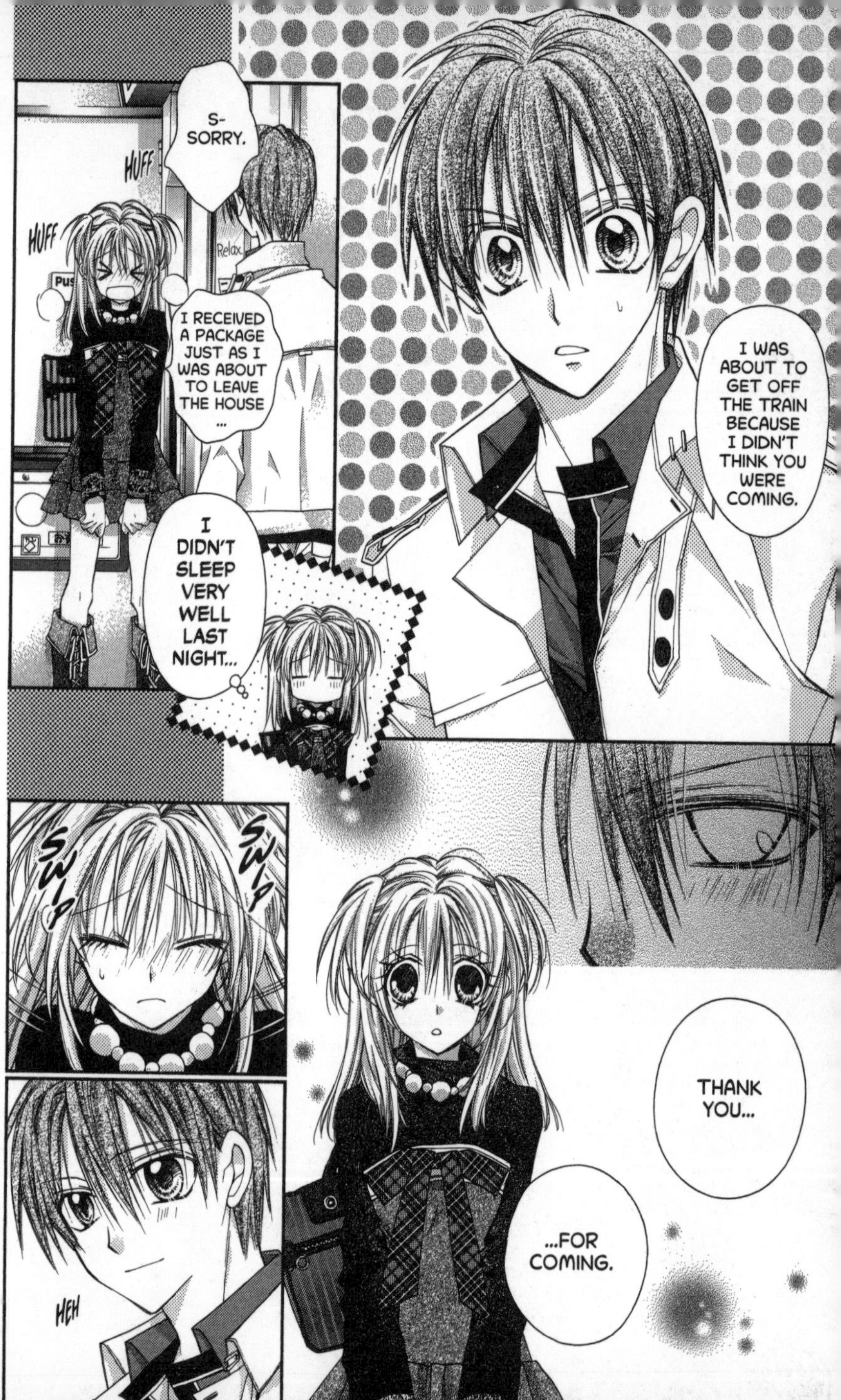
I WAS ABOUT TO GET OFF THE TRAIN BECAUSE I DIDN'T THINK YOU WERE COMING.
S-SORRY.
HUFF
HUFF
Relax.
I RECEIVED A PACKAGE JUST AS I WAS ABOUT TO LEAVE THE HOUSE ...
I DIDN'T SLEEP VERY WELL LAST NIGHT...
THANK YOU...
...FOR COMING.
SWIP
SWIP
HEH

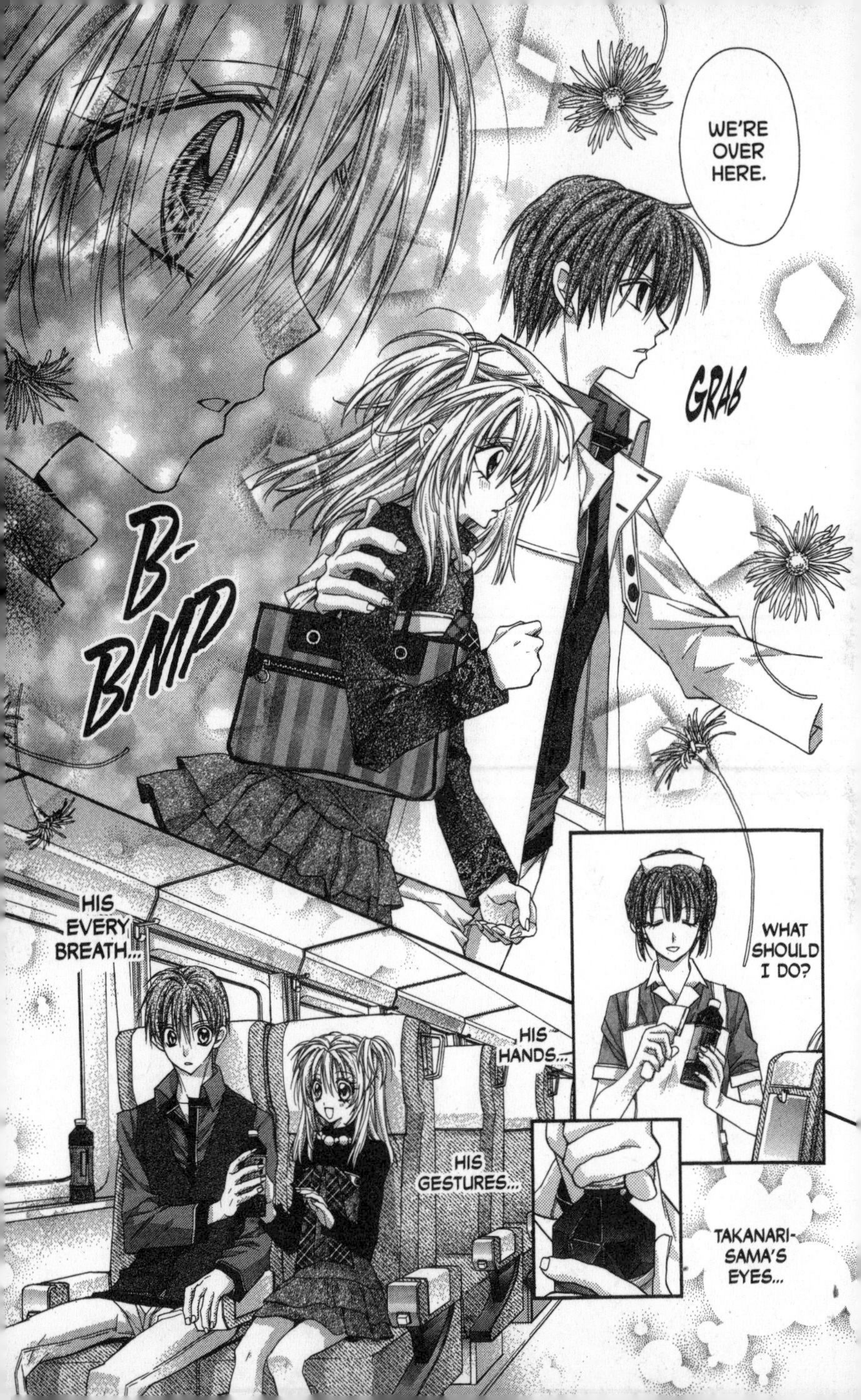
WE'RE OVER HERE.
GRAB
B-BMP
WHAT SHOULD I DO?
TAKANARI-SAMA'S EYES...
HIS GESTURES...
HIS HANDS...
HIS EVERY BREATH...

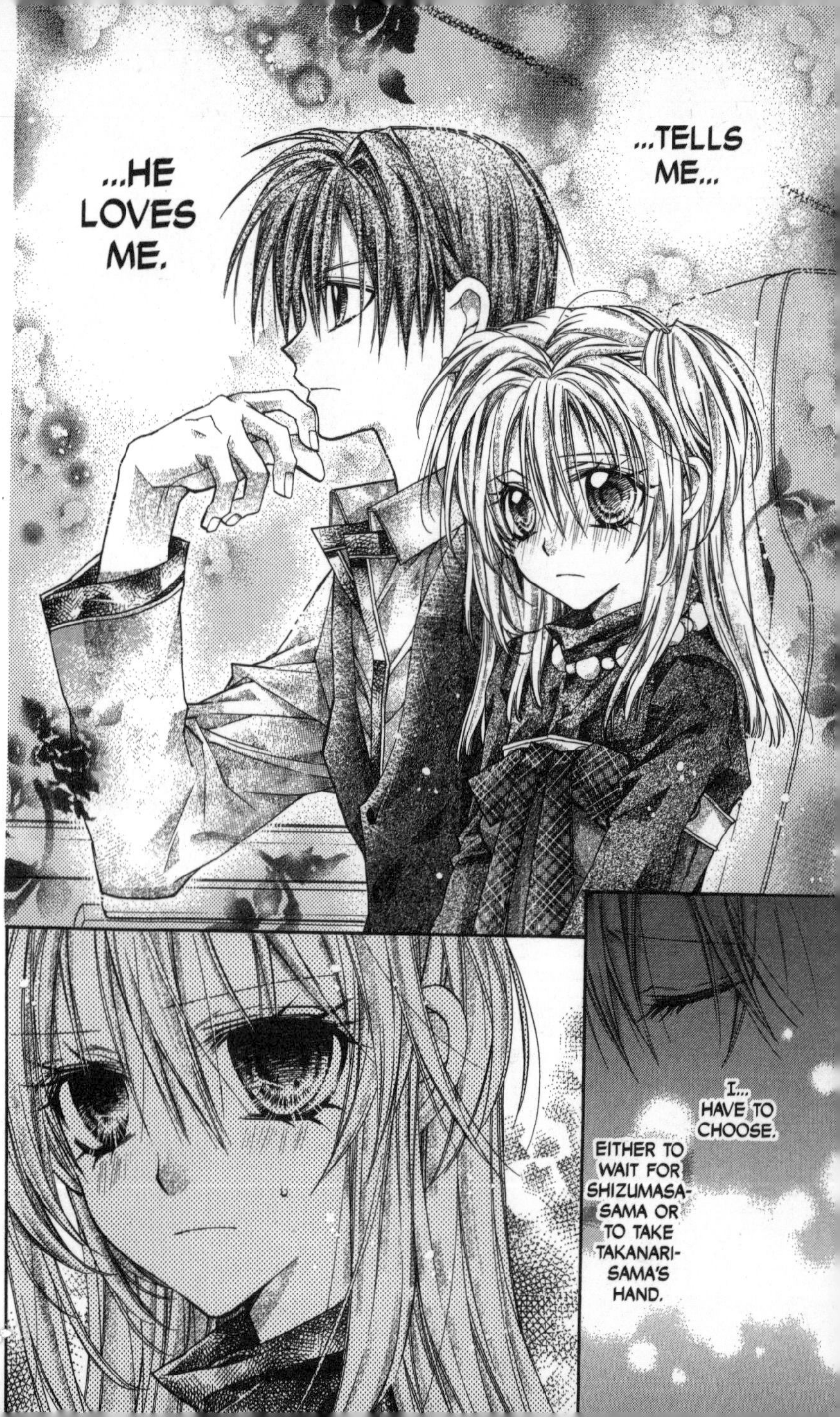
...TELLS ME...
...HE LOVES ME.
I... HAVE TO CHOOSE.
EITHER TO WAIT FOR SHIZUMASA-SAMA OR TO TAKE TAKANARI-SAMA'S HAND.

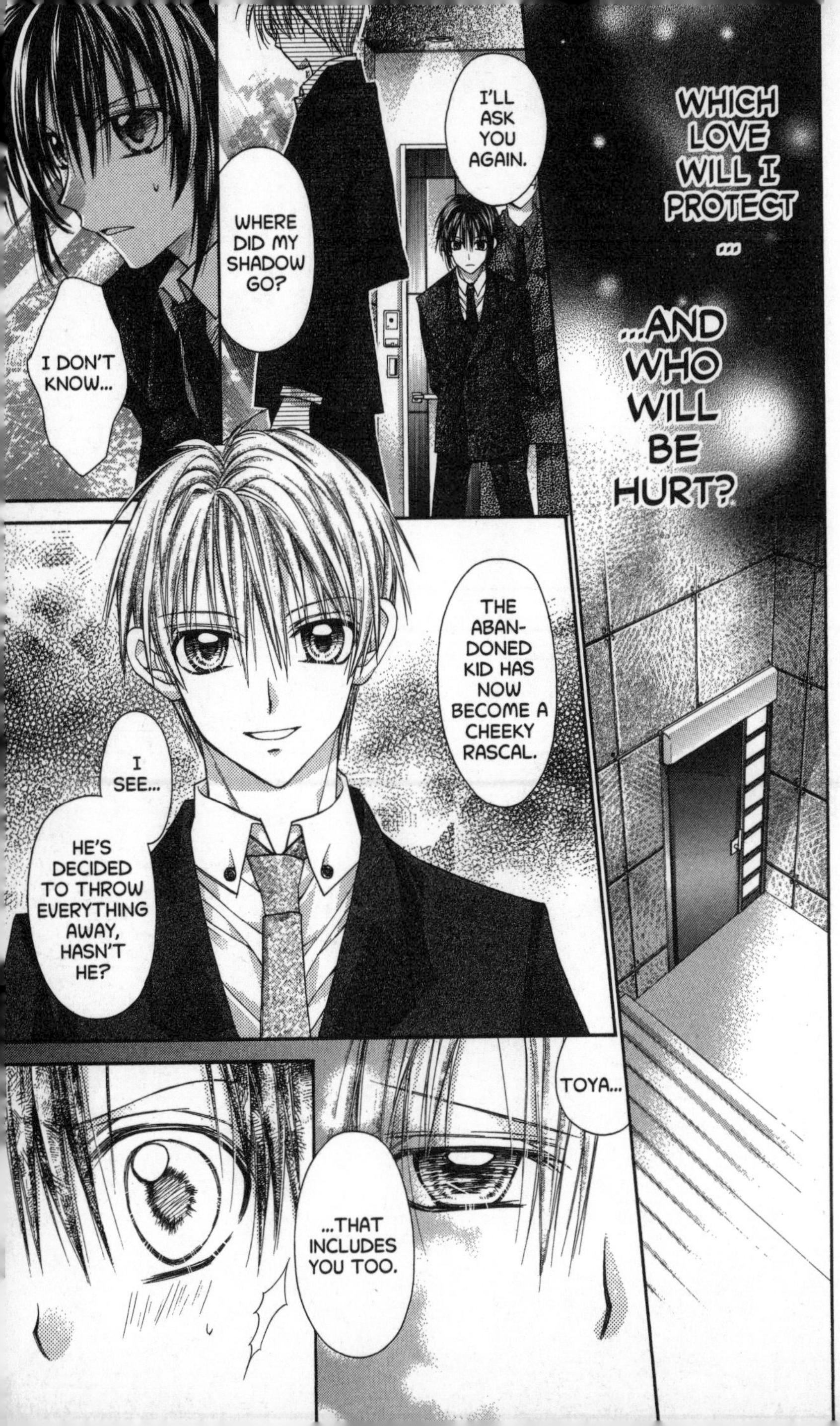
WHICH LOVE WILL I PROTECT ...
...AND WHO WILL BE HURT?
I'LL ASK YOU AGAIN.
WHERE DID MY SHADOW GO?
I DON'T KNOW...
THE ABAN-DONED KID HAS NOW BECOME A CHEEKY RASCAL.
I SEE...
HE'S DECIDED TO THROW EVERYTHING AWAY, HASN'T HE?
TOYA...
...THAT INCLUDES YOU TOO.

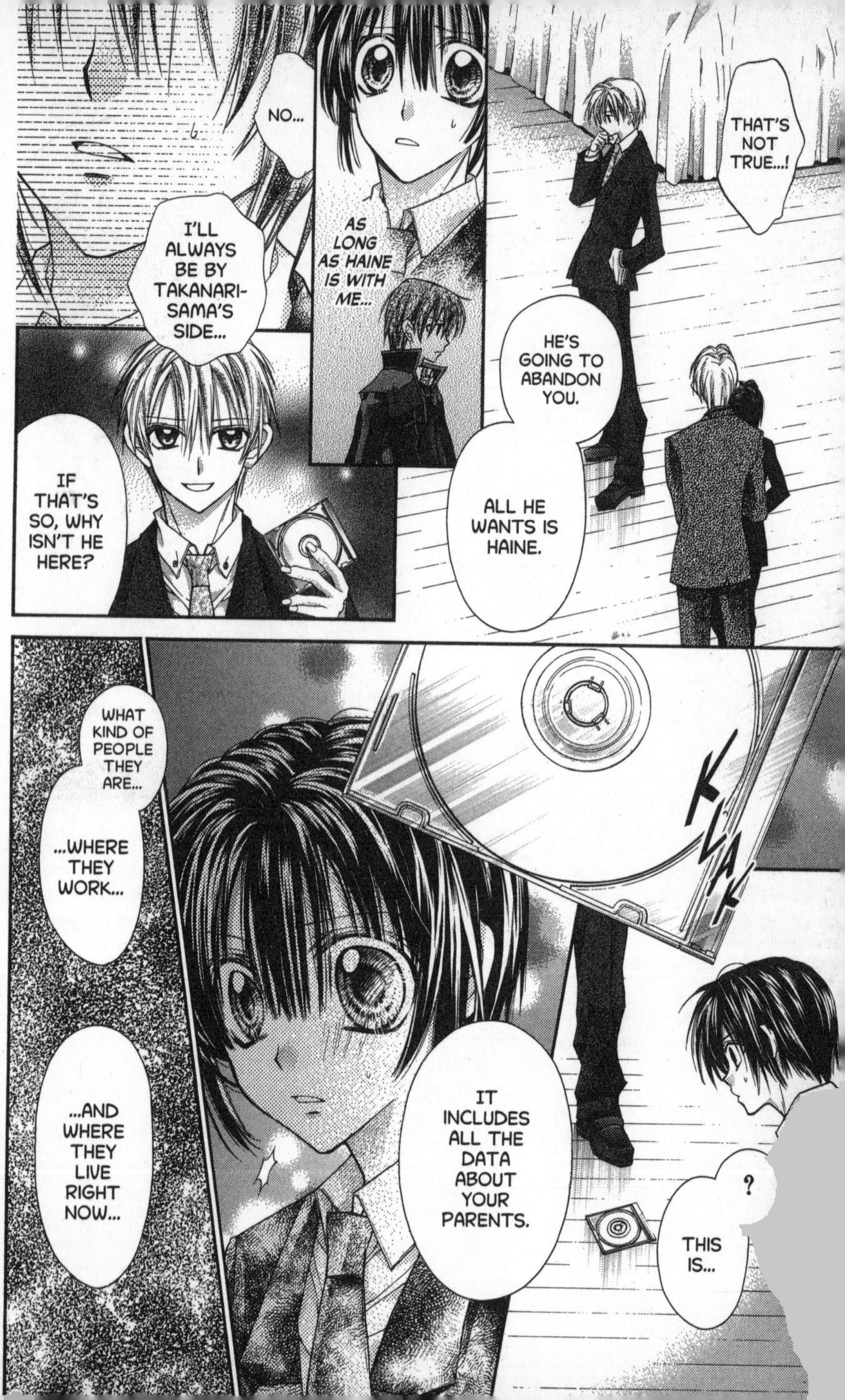
THAT'S NOT TRUE...!
HE'S GOING TO ABANDON YOU.
ALL HE WANTS IS HAINE.
NO...
AS LONG AS HAINE IS WITH ME...
I'LL ALWAYS BE BY TAKANARI-SAMA'S SIDE...
IF THAT'S SO, WHY ISN'T HE HERE?
KLAK
?
THIS IS...
IT INCLUDES ALL THE DATA ABOUT YOUR PARENTS.
WHAT KIND OF PEOPLE THEY ARE...
...WHERE THEY WORK...
...AND WHERE THEY LIVE RIGHT NOW...

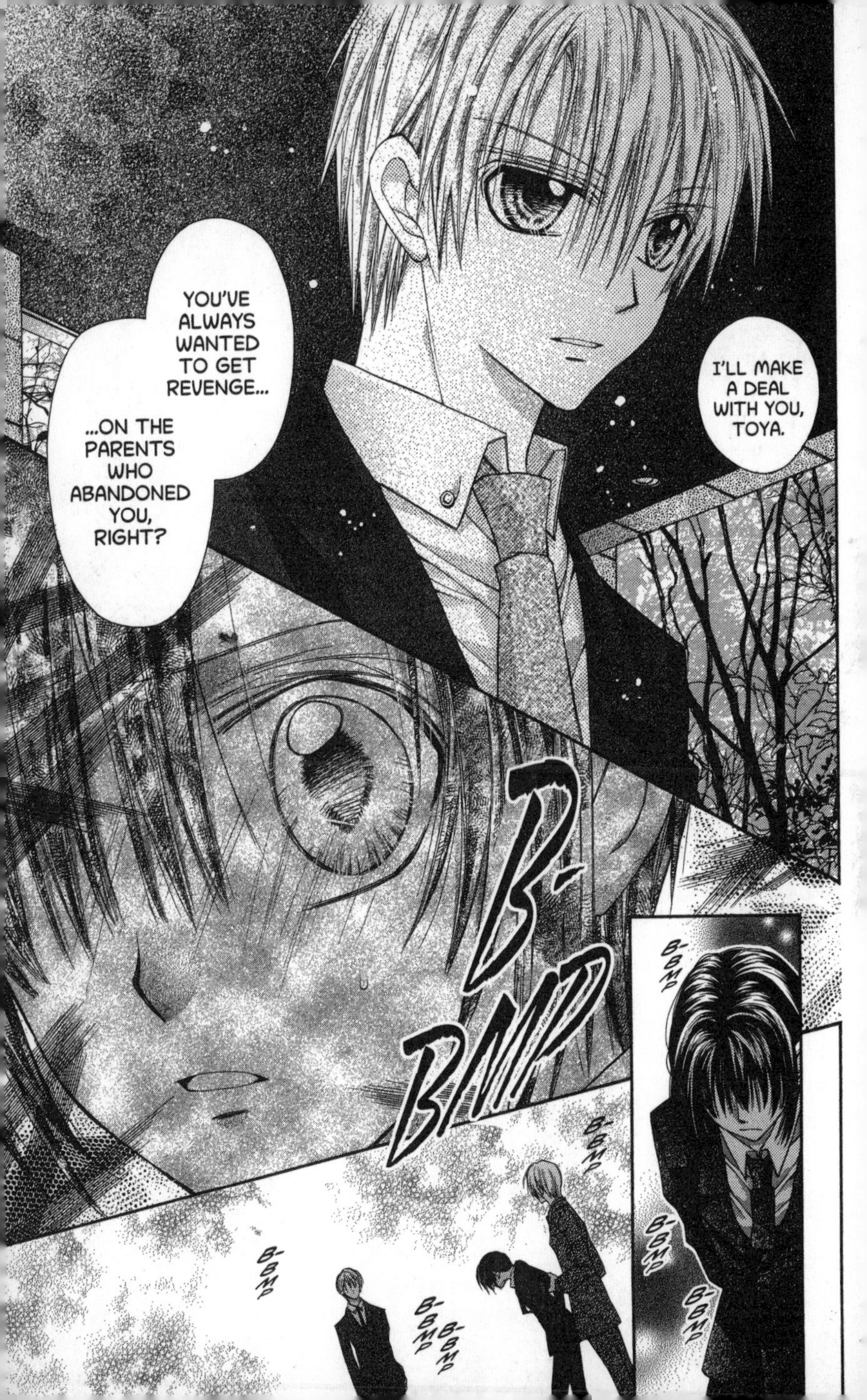
I'LL MAKE A DEAL WITH YOU, TOYA.
YOU'VE ALWAYS WANTED TO GET REVENGE...
...ON THE PARENTS WHO ABANDONED YOU, RIGHT?
B-BMP
B-BMP
B-BMP
B-BMP
B-BMP
B-BMP
B-BMP
B-BMP

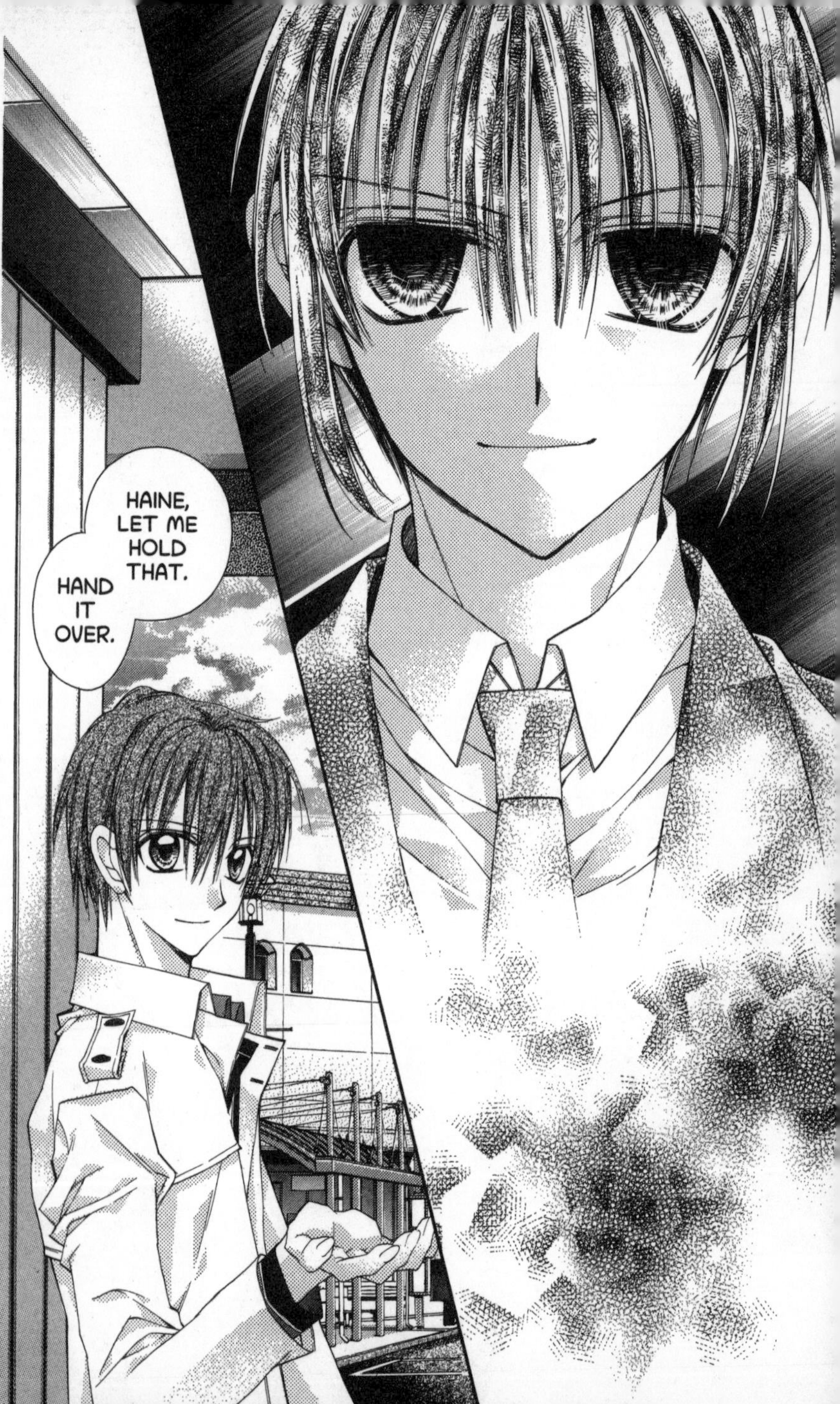
HAINE, LET ME HOLD THAT.
HAND IT OVER.

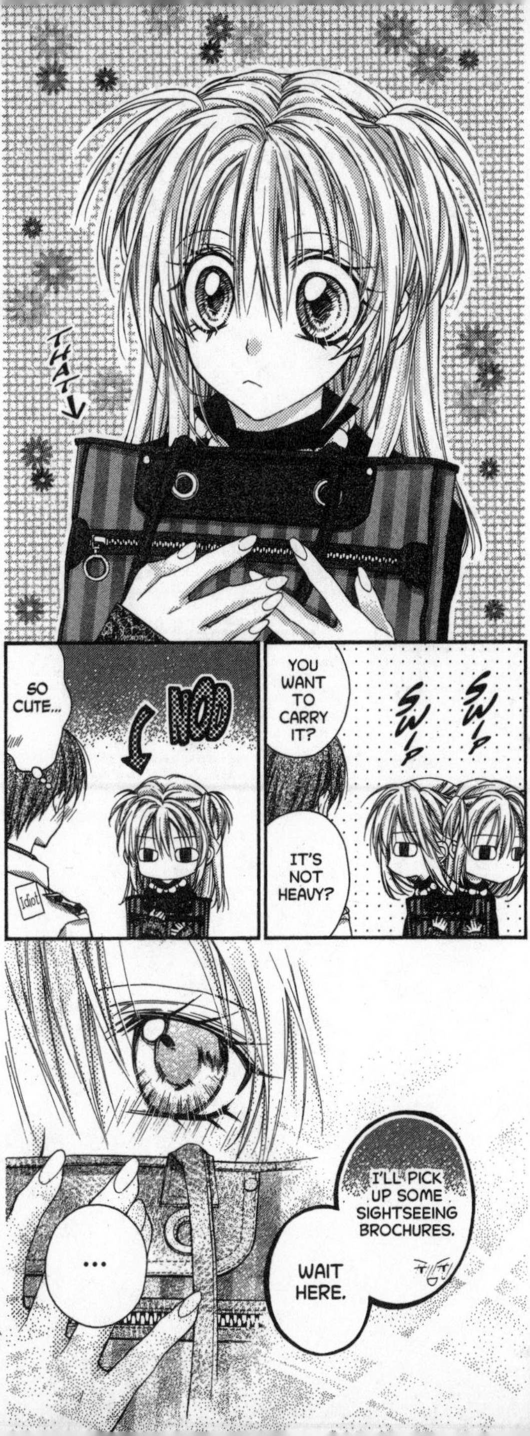
THAT
YOU WANT TO CARRY IT?
SWIP
SWIP
IT'S NOT HEAVY?
SO CUTE...
NOD
Idiot
I'LL PICK UP SOME SIGHTSEEING BROCHURES.
WAIT HERE.
...

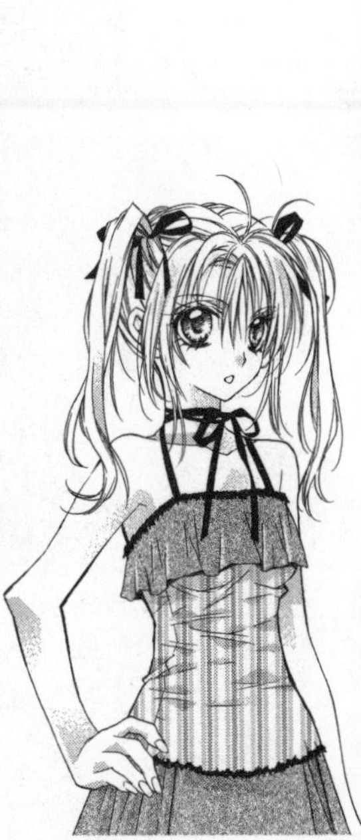

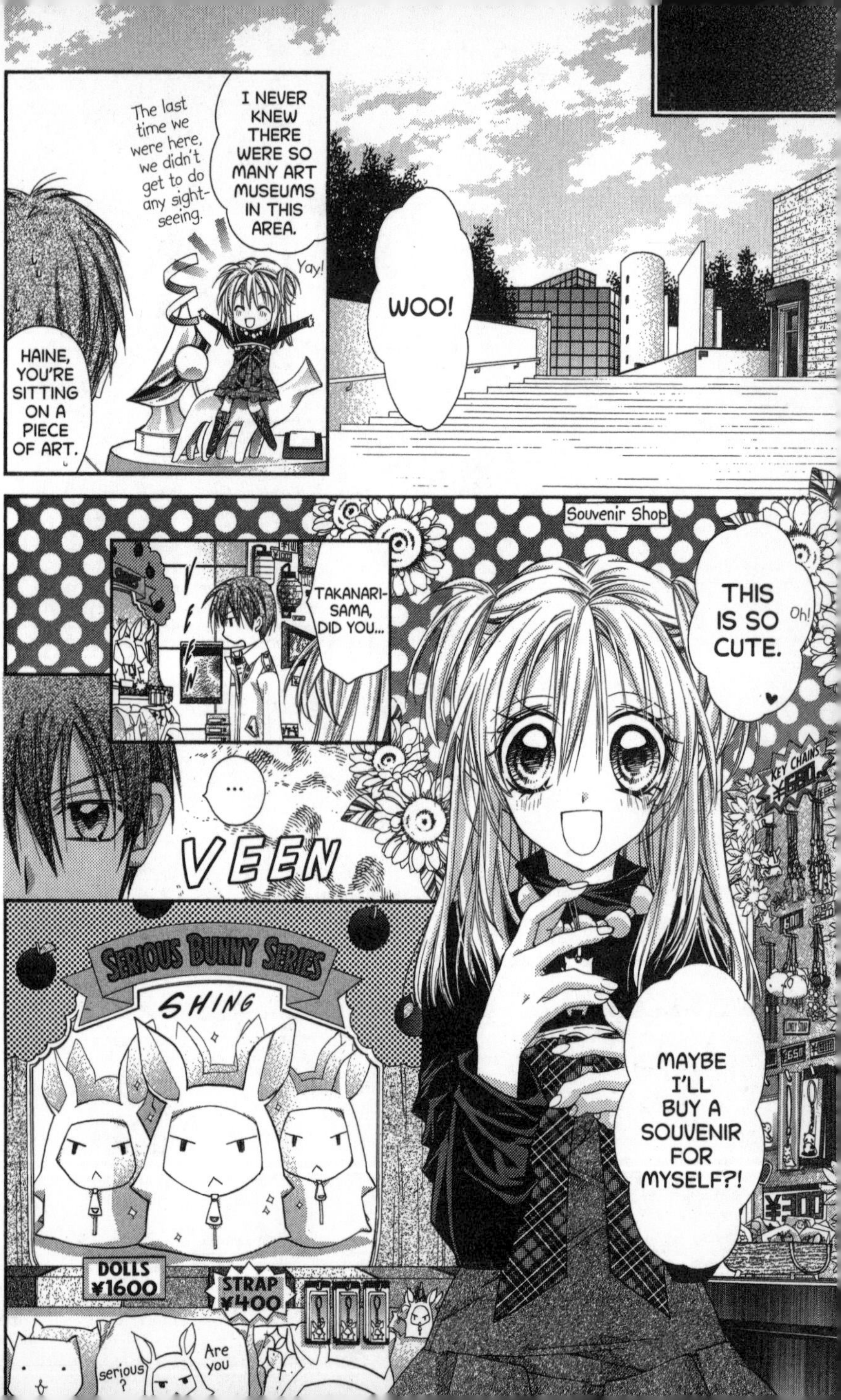
WOO!
I NEVER KNEW THERE WERE SO MANY ART MUSEUMS IN THIS AREA.
The last time we were here, we didn't get to do any sight-seeing.
Yay!
HAINE, YOU'RE SITTING ON A PIECE OF ART.
Souvenir Shop
THIS IS SO CUTE.
Oh!
KEY CHAINS
MAYBE I'LL BUY A SOUVENIR FOR MYSELF?!
TAKANARI-SAMA, DID YOU...
...
VEEN
SERIOUS BUNNY SERIES
SHING
DOLLS ¥1600
STRAP ¥400
Are you serious?

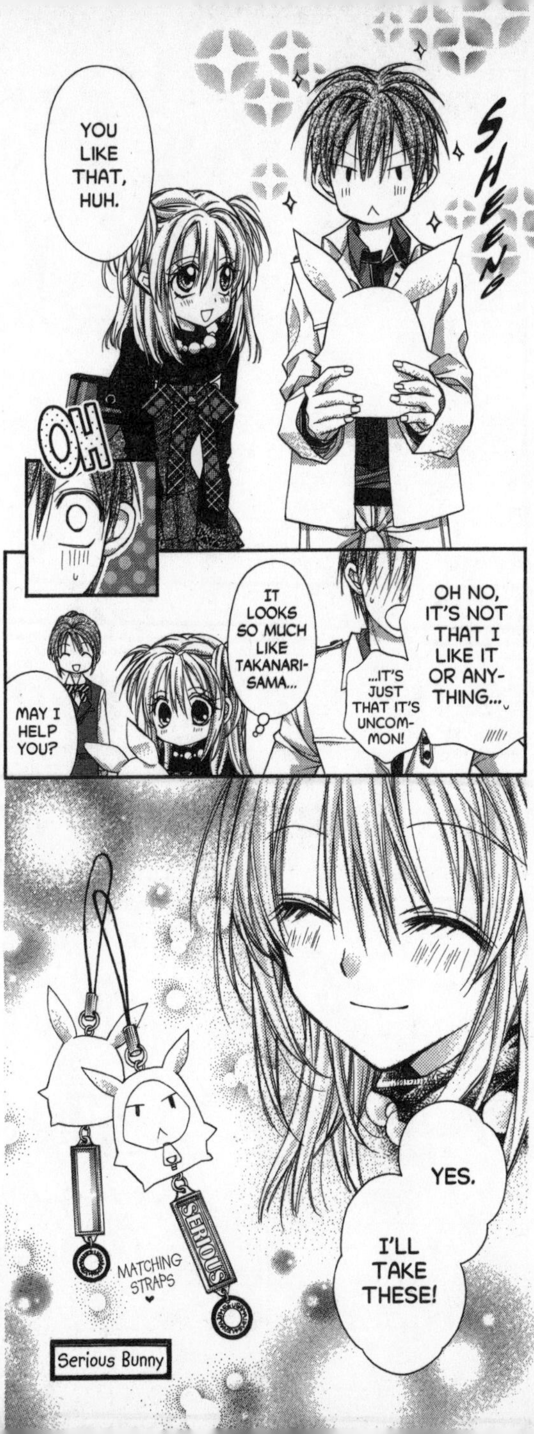
SHEEN
YOU LIKE THAT, HUH.
OH
OH NO, IT'S NOT THAT I LIKE IT OR ANYTHING...
...IT'S JUST THAT IT'S UNCOMMON!
IT LOOKS SO MUCH LIKE TAKANARI-SAMA...
MAY I HELP YOU?
YES.
I'LL TAKE THESE!
SERIOUS
MATCHING STRAPS
Serious Bunny
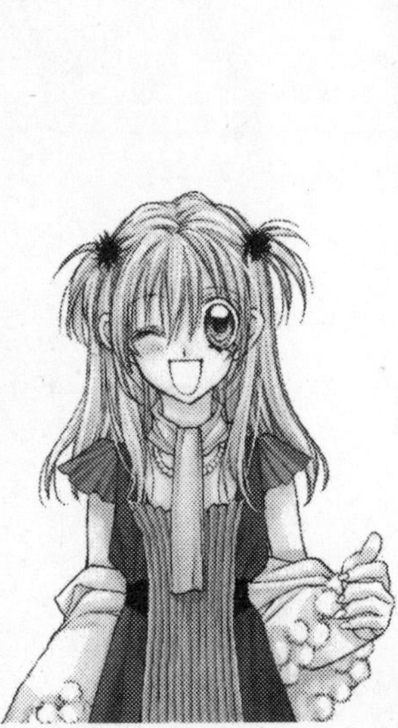

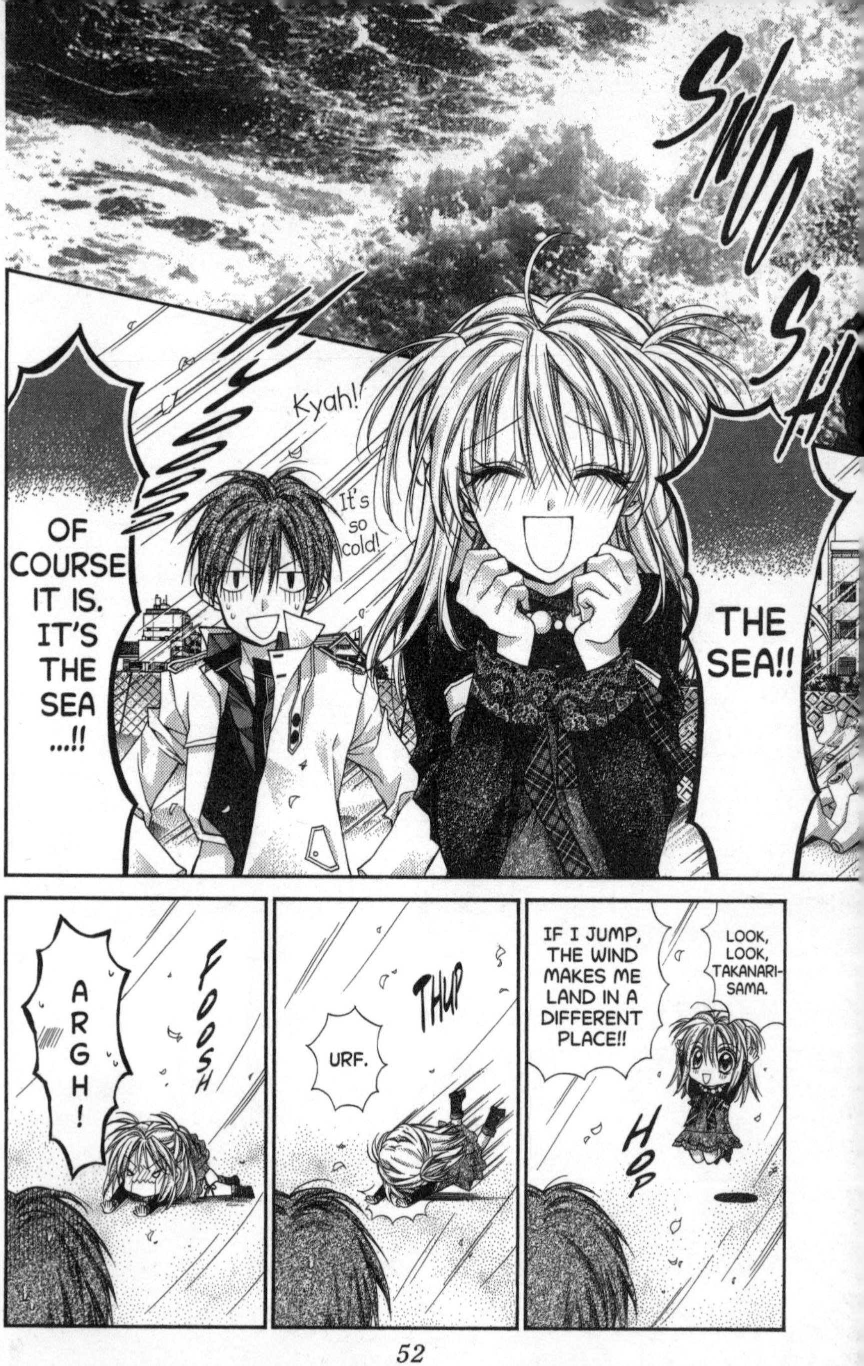
SWOOSH
THE SEA!!
Kyah!
It's so cold!
HWOOOOO
OF COURSE IT IS. IT'S THE SEA ...!!
LOOK, LOOK, TAKANARI-SAMA.
IF I JUMP, THE WIND MAKES ME LAND IN A DIFFERENT PLACE!!
HOP
THUP
URF.
FOOOSH
ARGH!

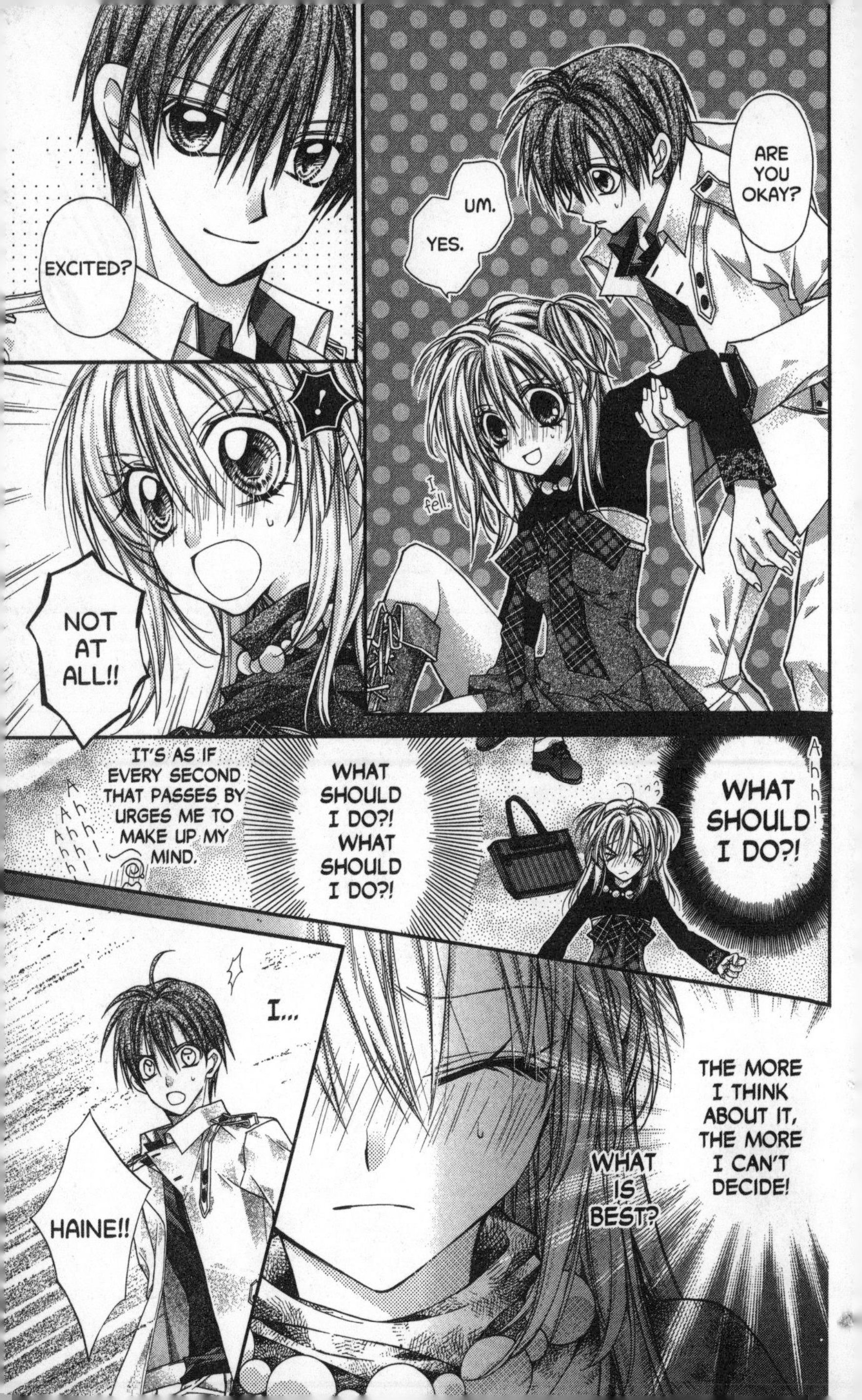

ARE YOU OKAY?
UM.
YES.
I fell.
EXCITED?
NOT AT ALL!!
Ahh!
WHAT SHOULD I DO?!
WHAT SHOULD I DO?! WHAT SHOULD I DO?!
IT'S AS IF EVERY SECOND THAT PASSES BY URGES ME TO MAKE UP MY MIND.
THE MORE I THINK ABOUT IT, THE MORE I CAN'T DECIDE!
WHAT IS BEST?
I...
HAINE!!

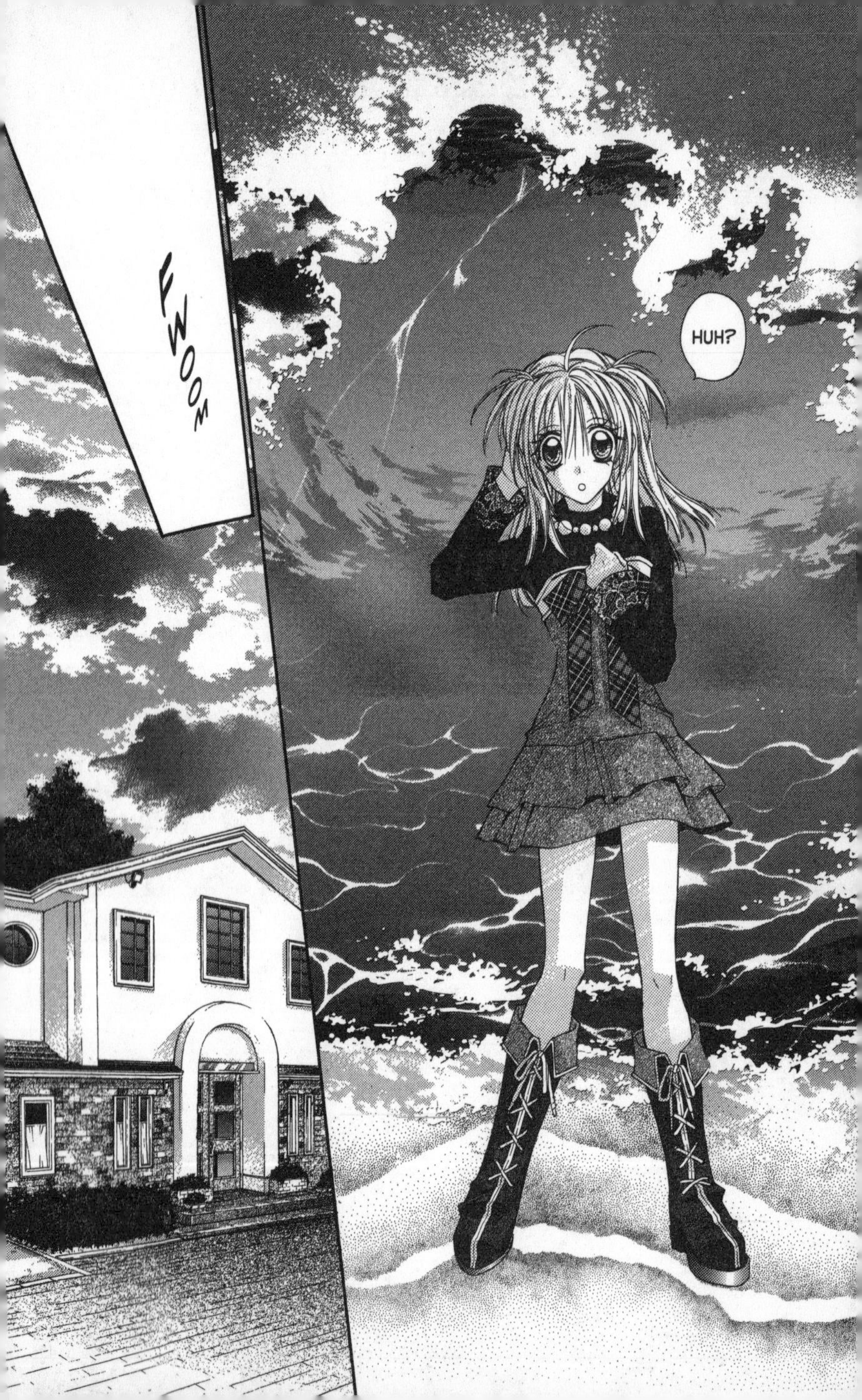
HUH?
FWOOM

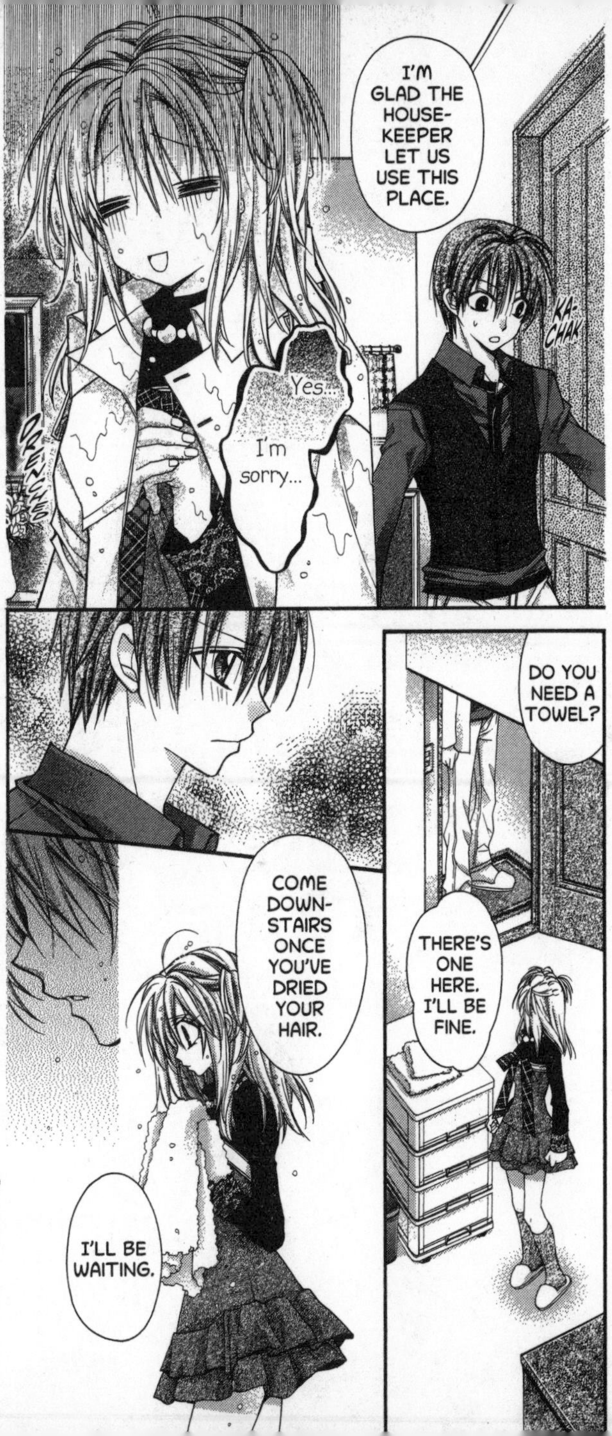
I'M GLAD THE HOUSE-KEEPER LET US USE THIS PLACE.
KA-CHAK
Yes... I'm sorry...
DRENCHED
DO YOU NEED A TOWEL?
THERE'S ONE HERE. I'LL BE FINE.
COME DOWN-STAIRS ONCE YOU'VE DRIED YOUR HAIR.
I'LL BE WAITING.

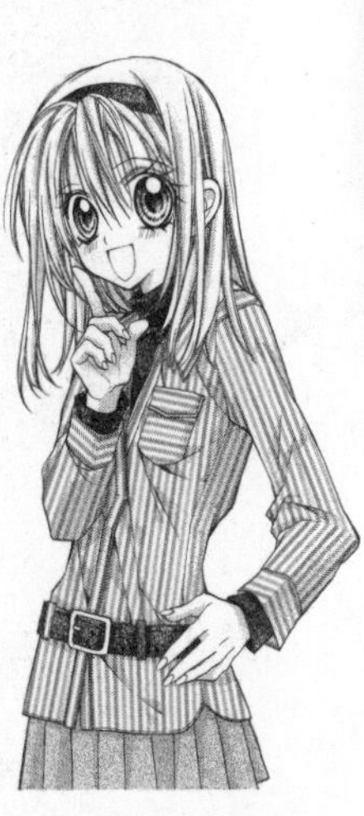

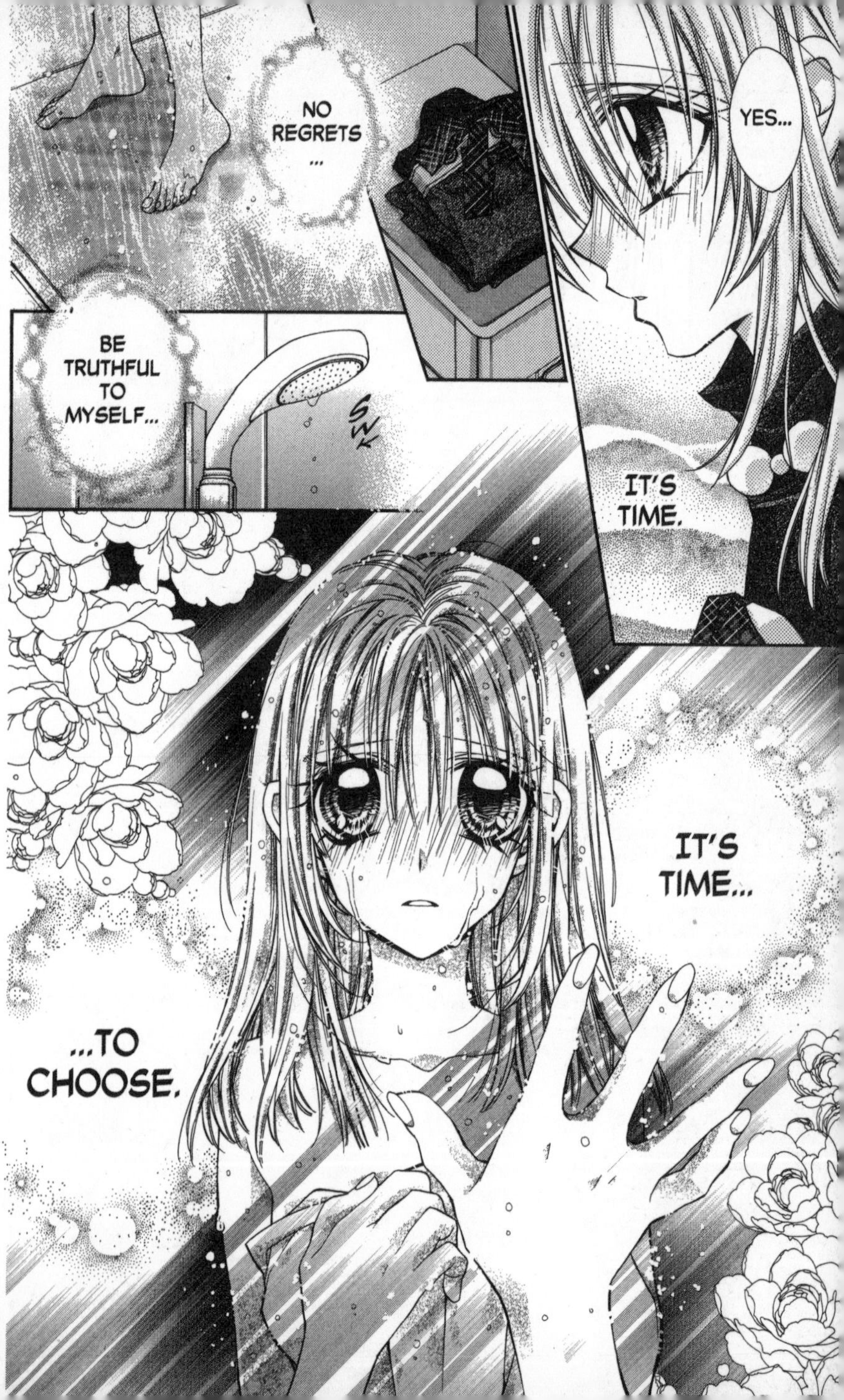
YES...
NO REGRETS ...
IT'S TIME.
BE TRUTHFUL TO MYSELF...
SWK
IT'S TIME...
...TO CHOOSE.

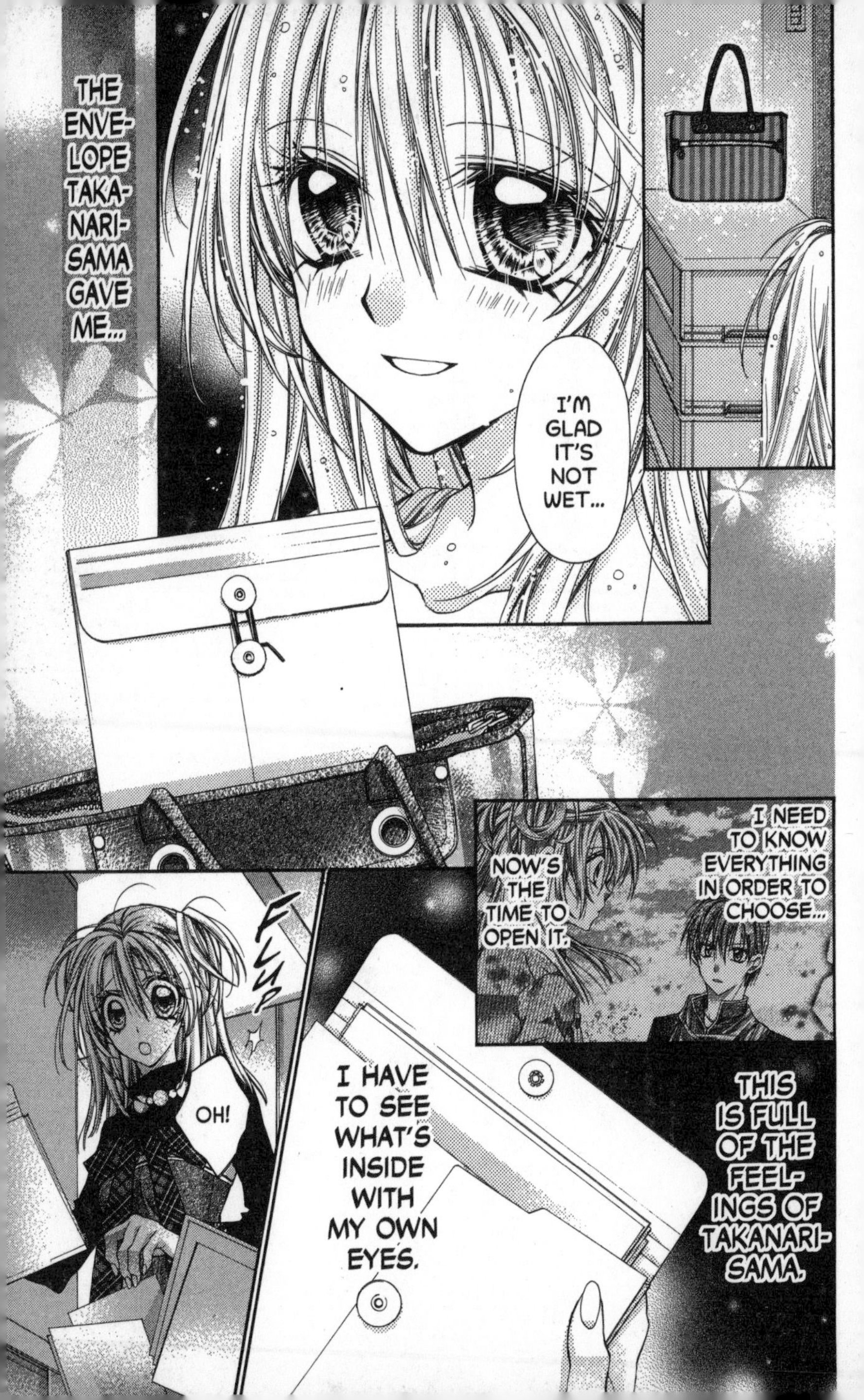
THE ENVELOPE TAKANARI-SAMA GAVE ME...
I'M GLAD IT'S NOT WET...
I NEED TO KNOW EVERYTHING IN ORDER TO CHOOSE...
NOW'S THE TIME TO OPEN IT.
THIS IS FULL OF THE FEELINGS OF TAKANARI-SAMA.
I HAVE TO SEE WHAT'S INSIDE WITH MY OWN EYES.
FLUP
OH!

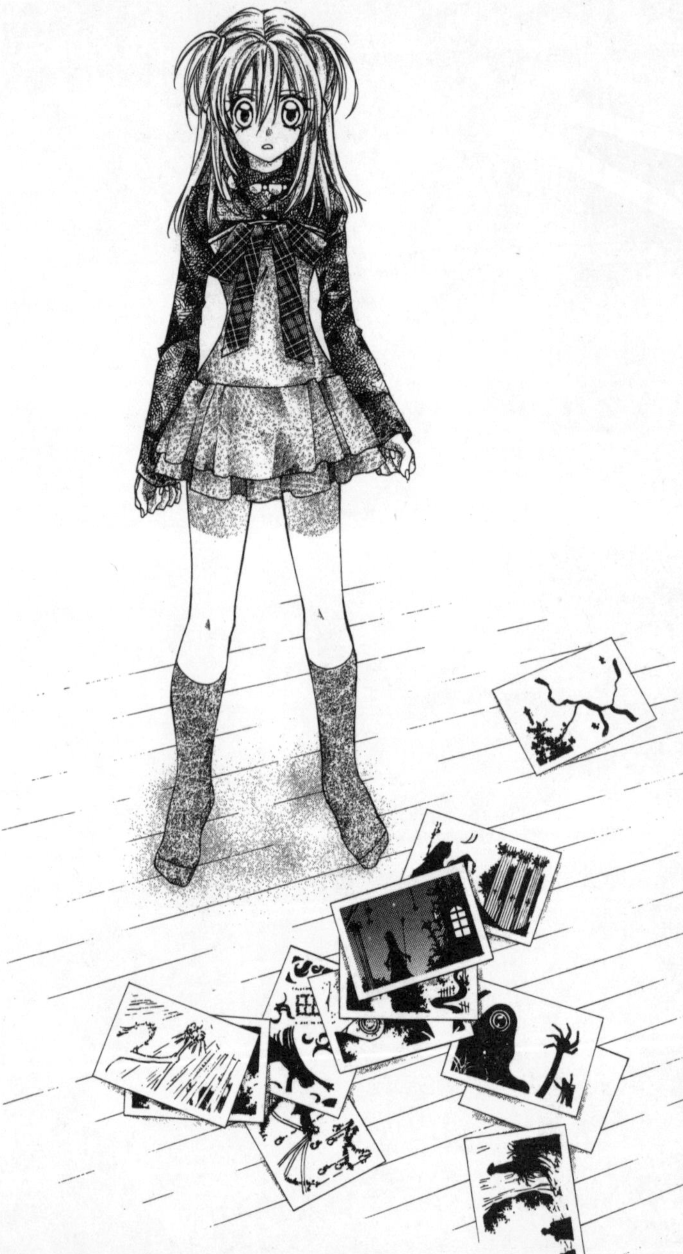

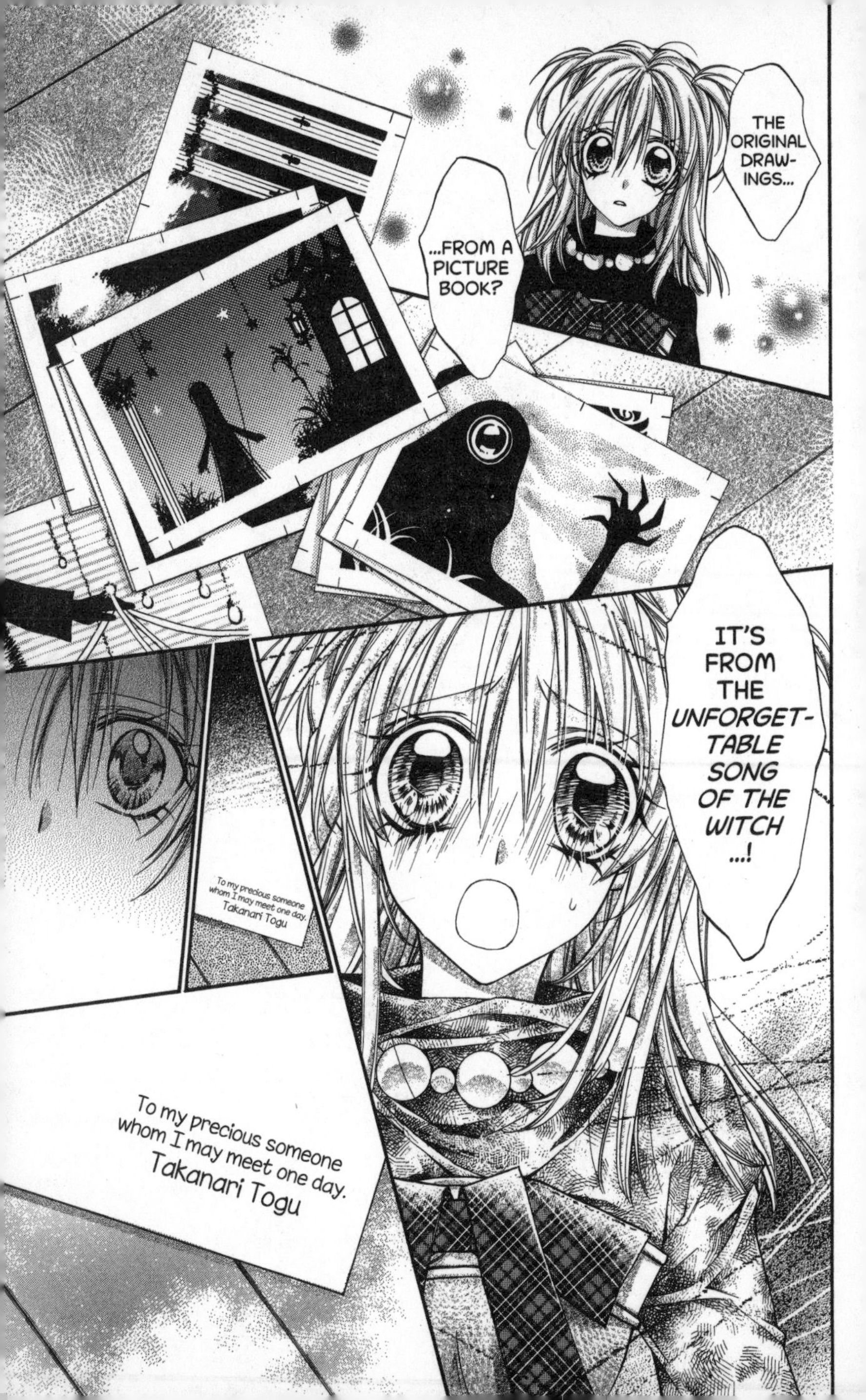
THE ORIGINAL DRAW-INGS...
...FROM A PICTURE BOOK?
IT'S FROM THE UNFORGET-TABLE SONG OF THE WITCH ...!
To my precious someone whom I may meet one day. Takanari Togu
To my precious someone whom I may meet one day. Takanari Togu

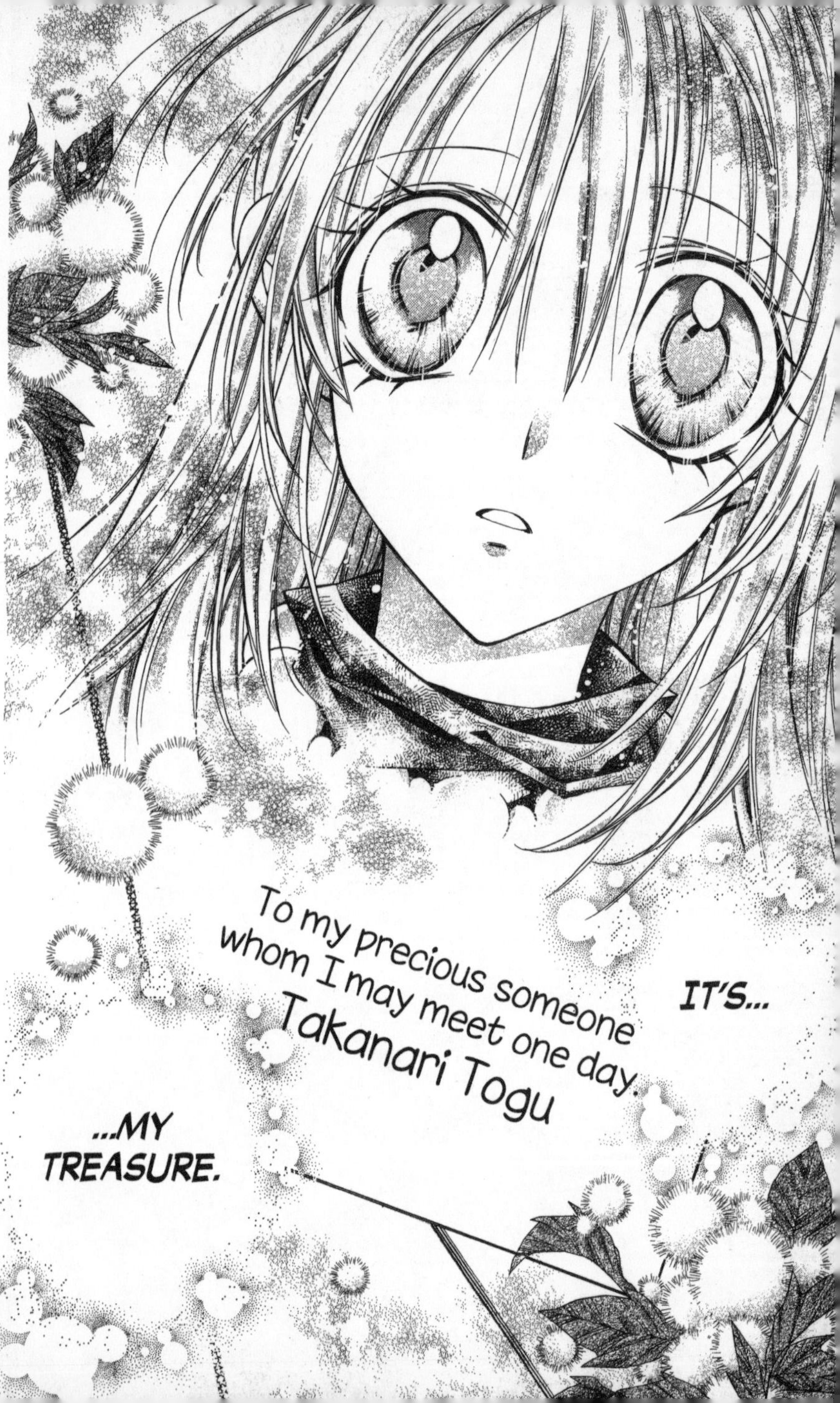
IT'S...
...MY TREASURE.
To my precious someone whom I may meet one day.
Takanari Togu

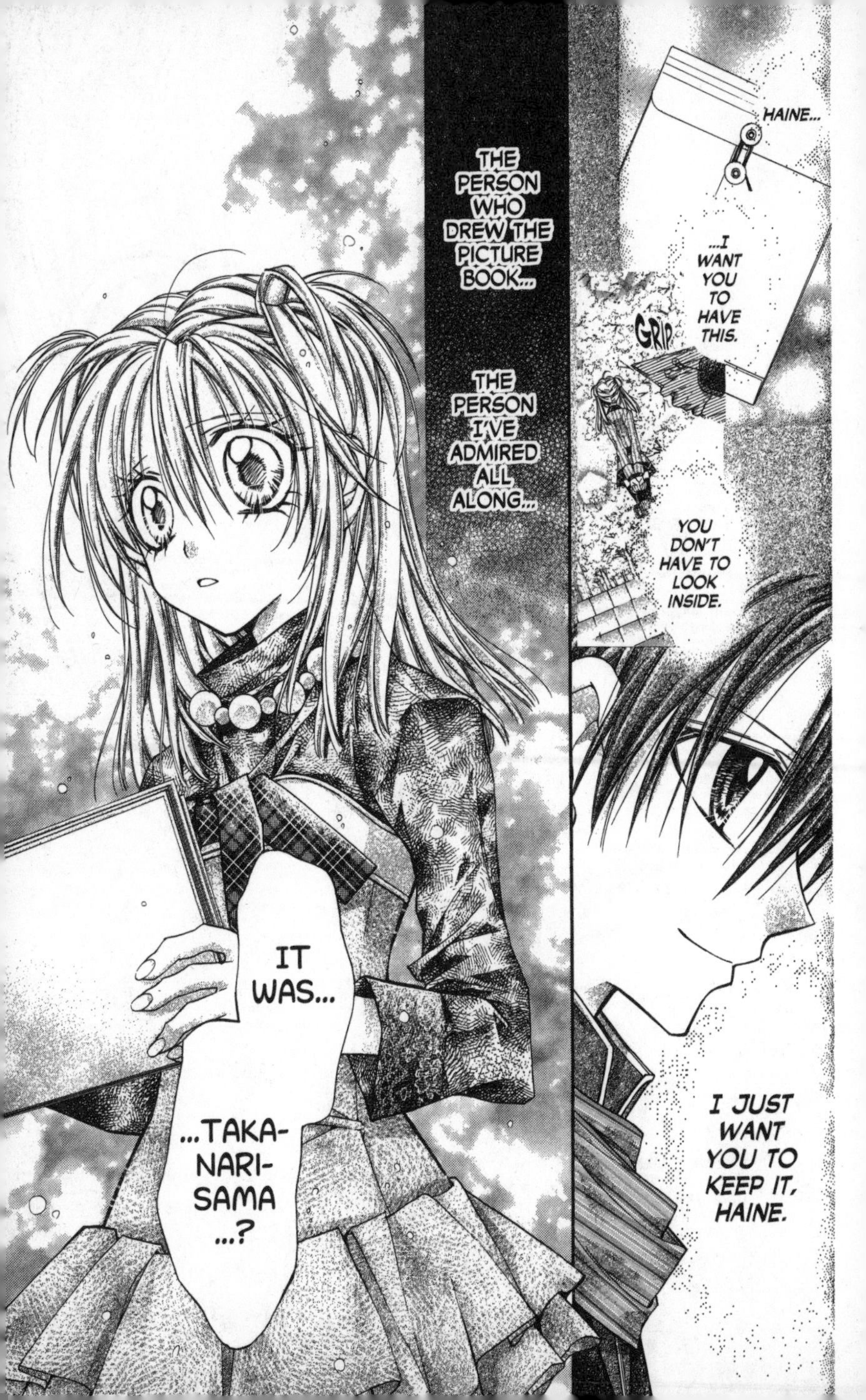
HAINE...
...I WANT YOU TO HAVE THIS.
GRIP
YOU DON'T HAVE TO LOOK INSIDE.
I JUST WANT YOU TO KEEP IT, HAINE.
THE PERSON WHO DREW THE PICTURE BOOK...
THE PERSON I'VE ADMIRED ALL ALONG...
IT WAS...
...TAKA-NARI-SAMA...?

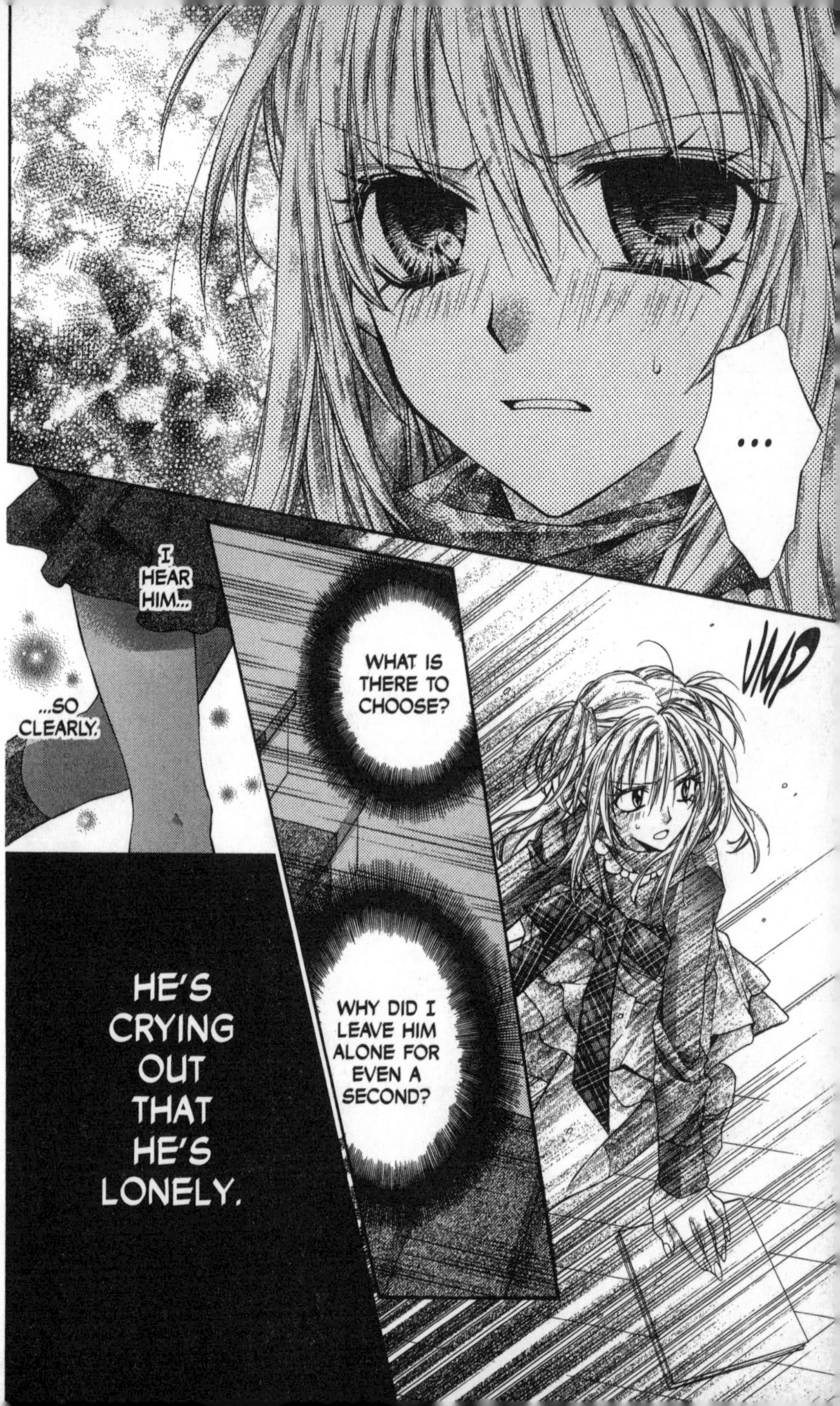
...
UMP
WHAT IS THERE TO CHOOSE?
WHY DID I LEAVE HIM ALONE FOR EVEN A SECOND?
I HEAR HIM...
...SO CLEARLY.
HE'S CRYING OUT THAT HE'S LONELY.

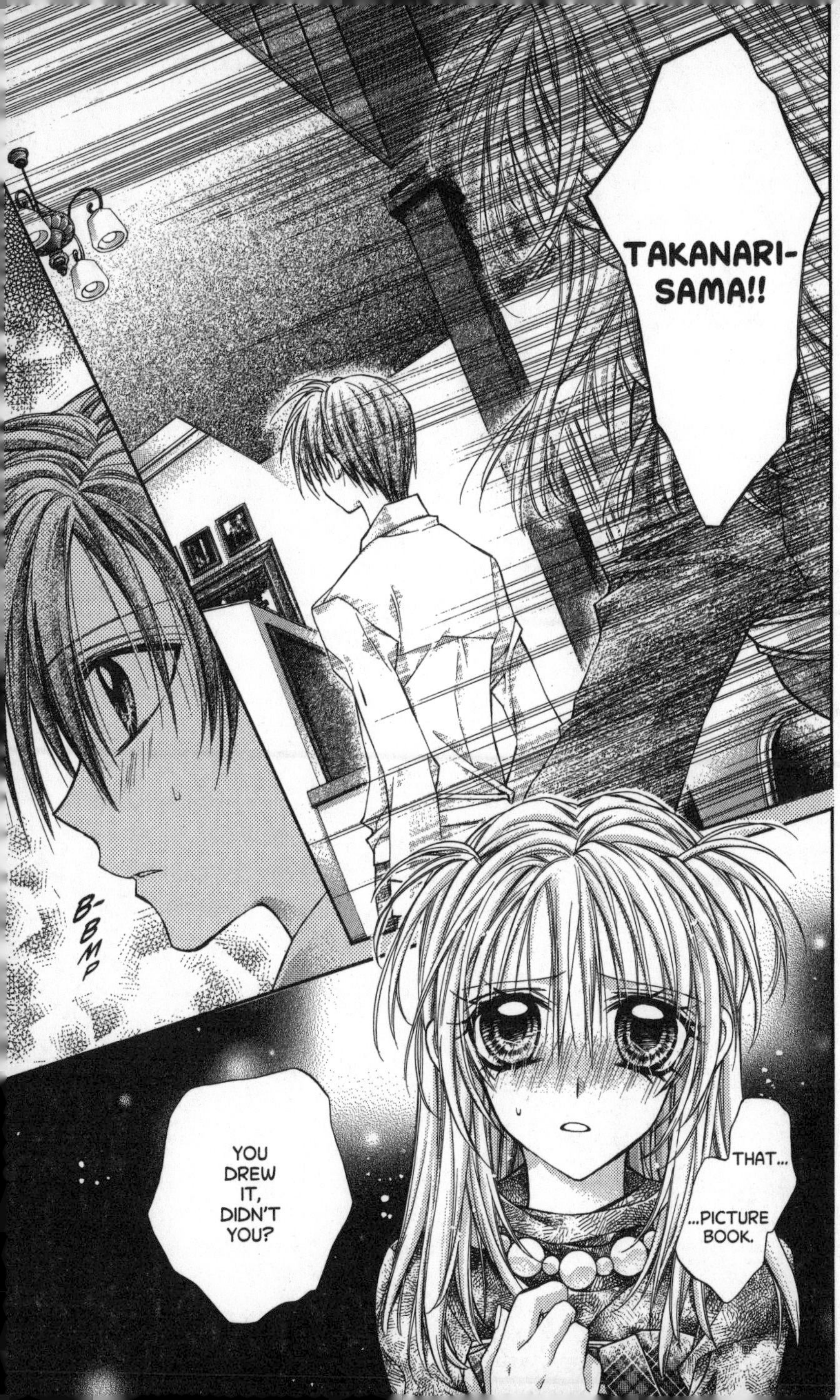
TAKANARI-SAMA!!
B-BMP
THAT...
...PICTURE BOOK.
YOU DREW IT, DIDN'T YOU?

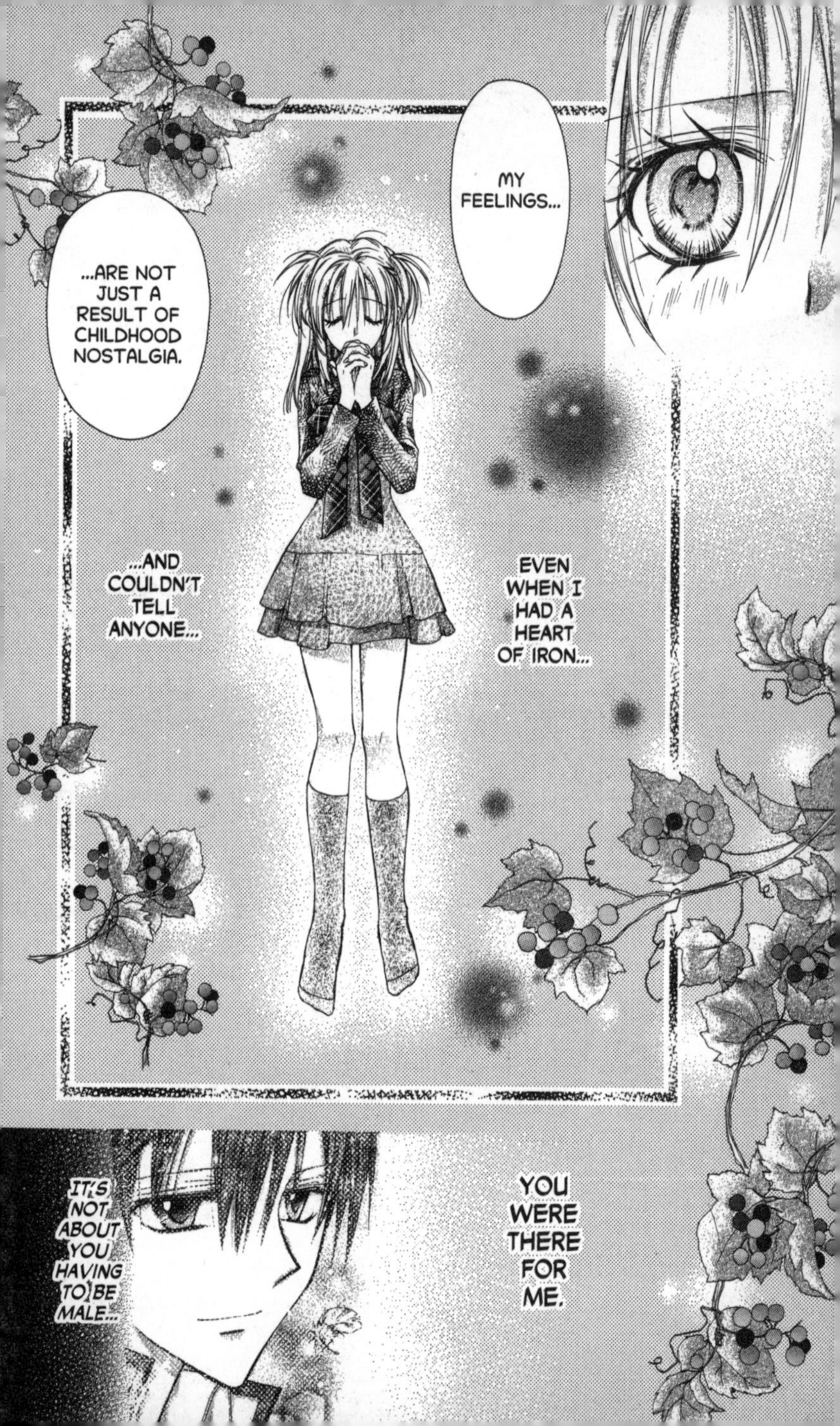
MY FEELINGS...
...ARE NOT JUST A RESULT OF CHILDHOOD NOSTALGIA.
EVEN WHEN I HAD A HEART OF IRON...
...AND COULDN'T TELL ANYONE...
YOU WERE THERE FOR ME.
IT'S NOT ABOUT YOU HAVING TO BE MALE...

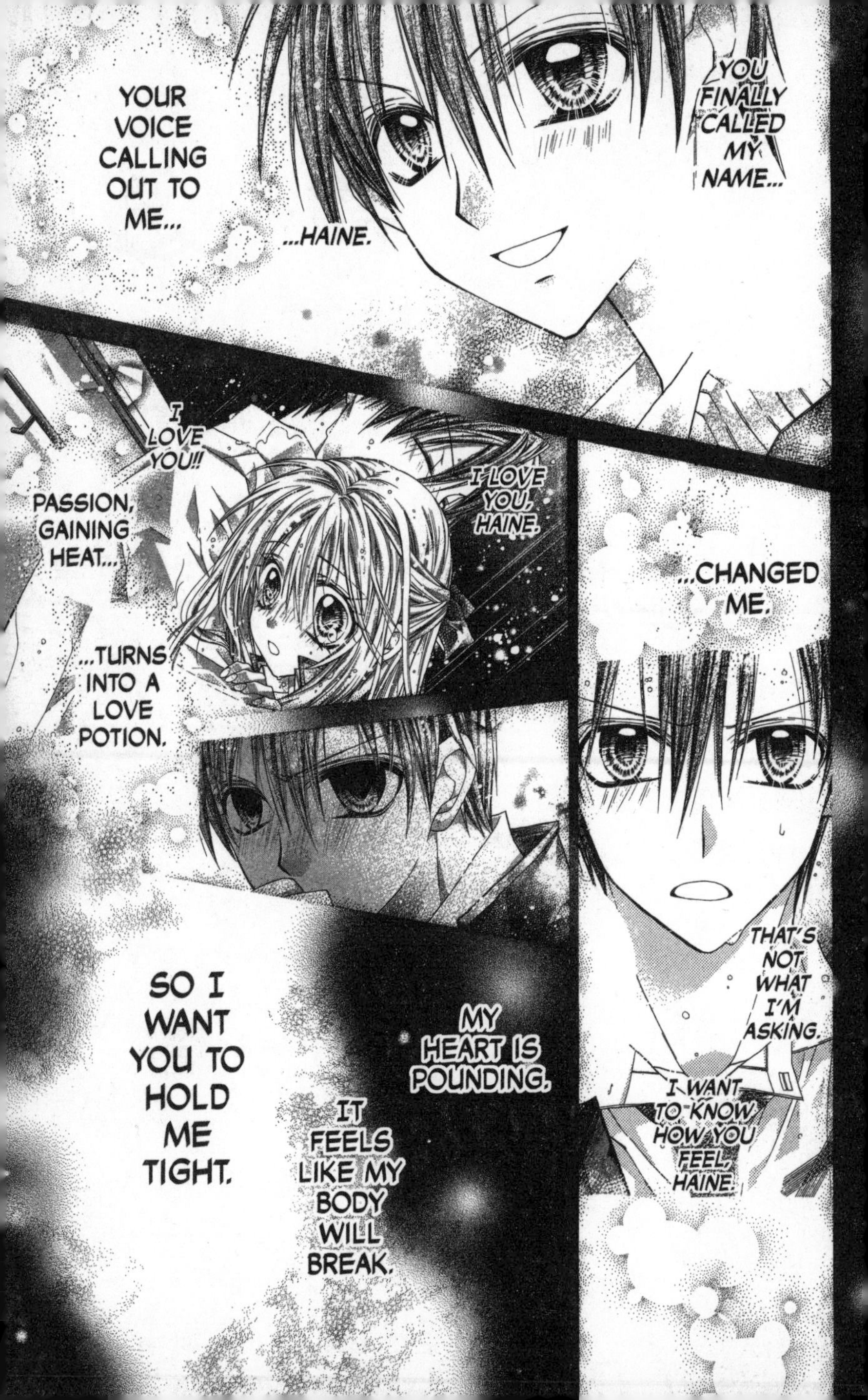
YOU FINALLY CALLED MY NAME...
...HAINE.
YOUR VOICE CALLING OUT TO ME...
...CHANGED ME.
THAT'S NOT WHAT I'M ASKING.
I WANT TO KNOW HOW YOU FEEL, HAINE.
I LOVE YOU, HAINE.
I LOVE YOU!!
PASSION, GAINING HEAT...
...TURNS INTO A LOVE POTION.
MY HEART IS POUNDING.
IT FEELS LIKE MY BODY WILL BREAK.
SO I WANT YOU TO HOLD ME TIGHT.

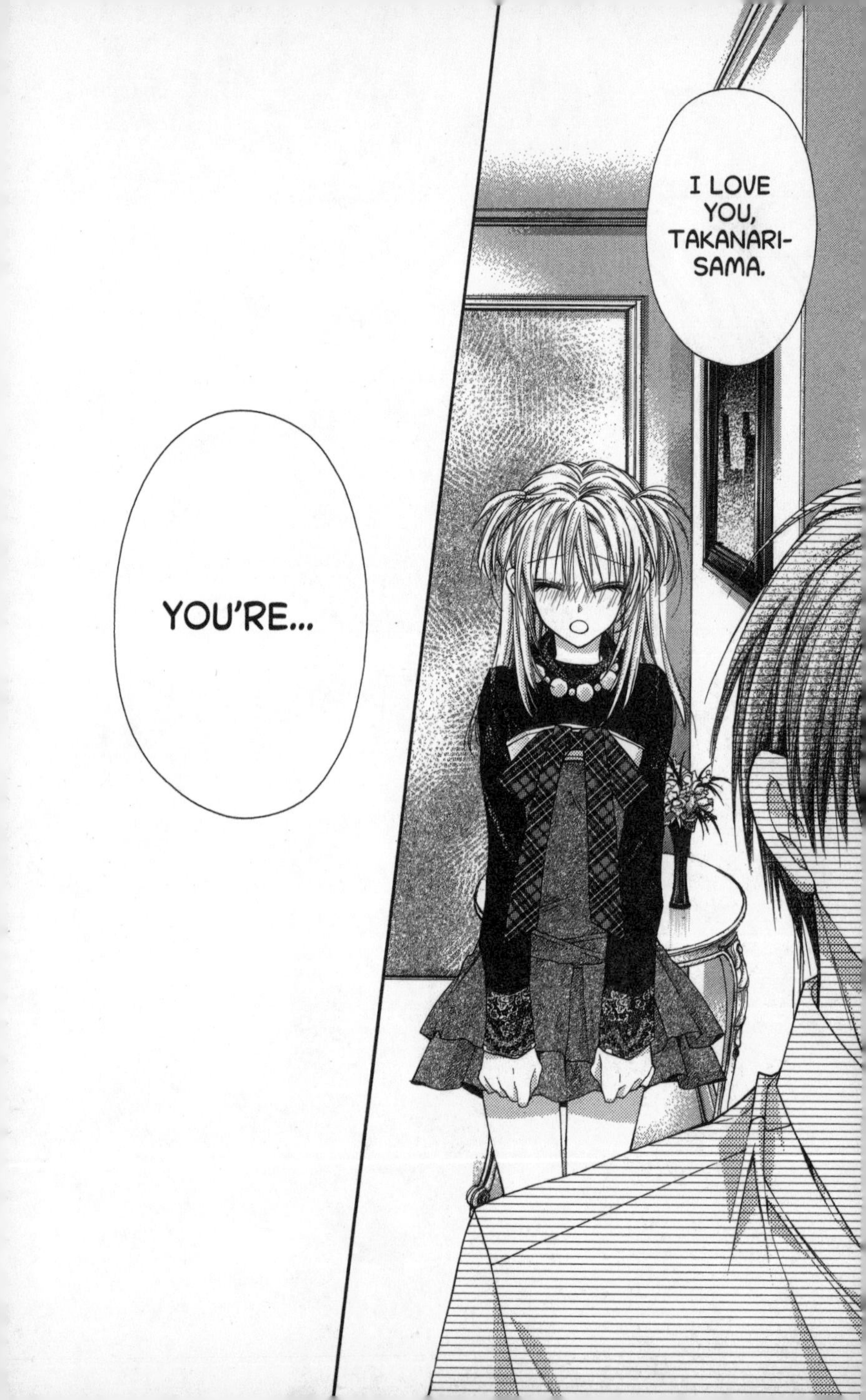
I LOVE YOU, TAKANARI-SAMA.
YOU'RE...

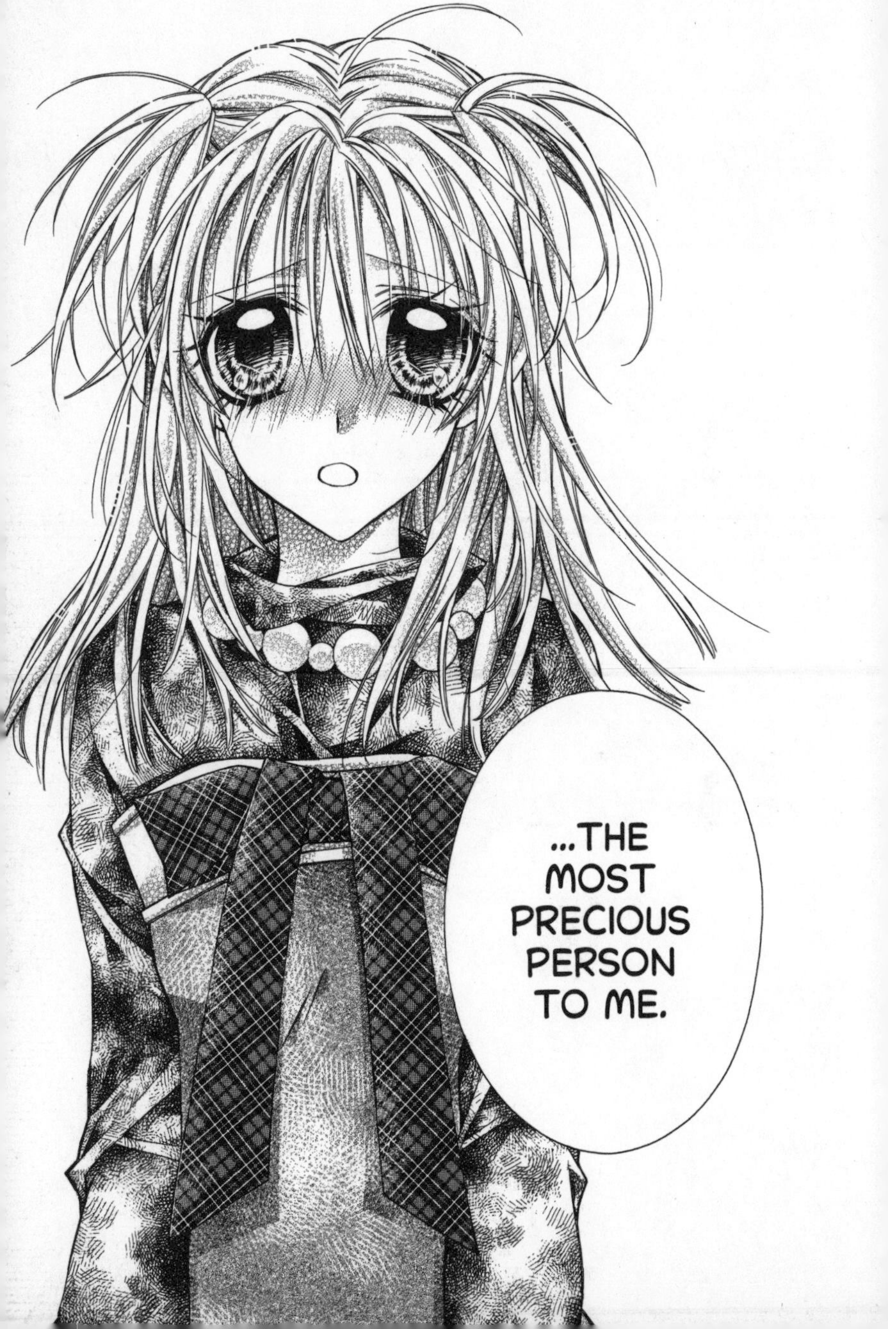
...THE MOST PRECIOUS PERSON TO ME.

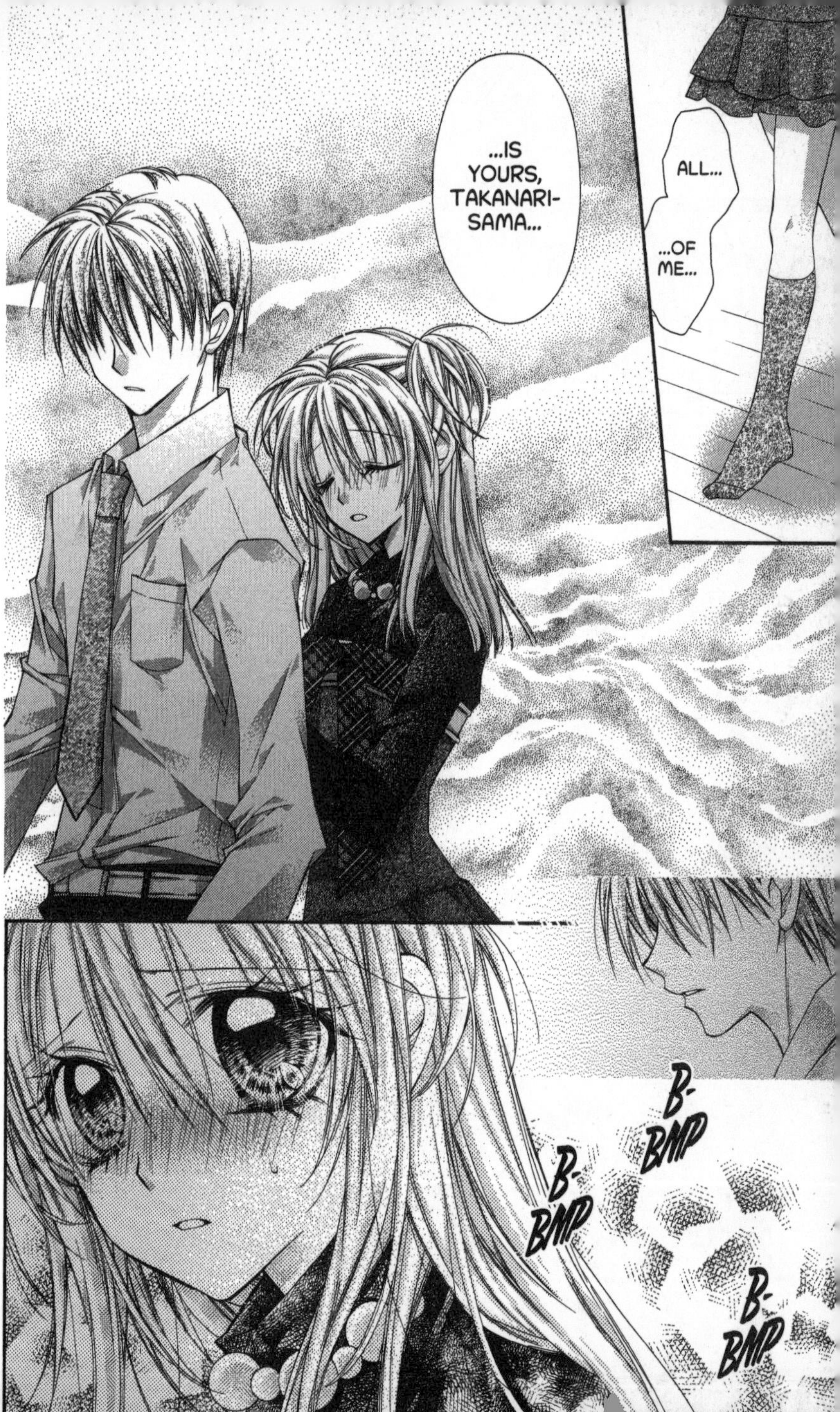
ALL...
...OF ME...
...IS YOURS, TAKANARI-SAMA...
B-BMP
B-BMP
B-BMP

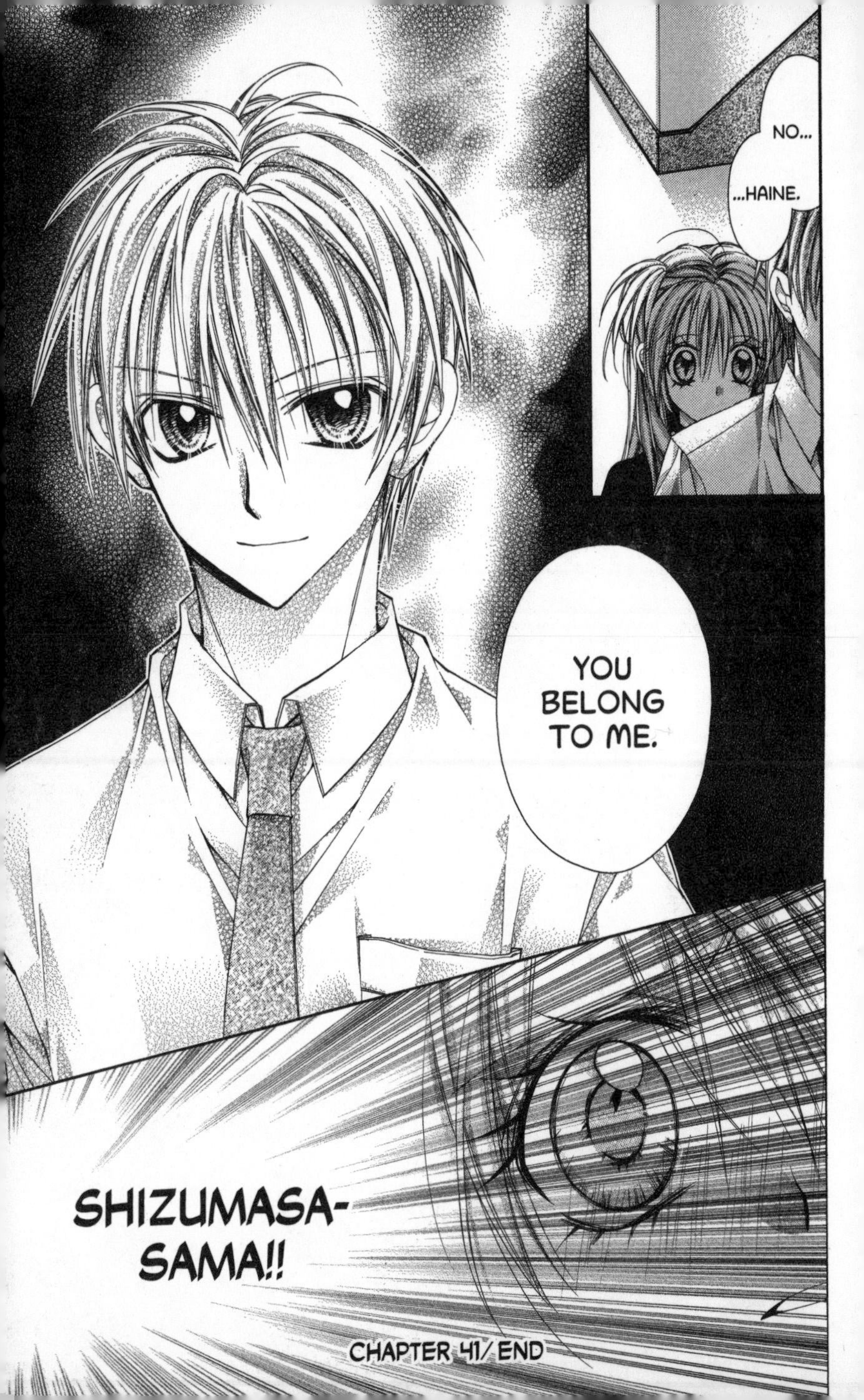
NO...
...HAINE.
YOU BELONG TO ME.
SHIZUMASA-SAMA!!
CHAPTER 41/ END

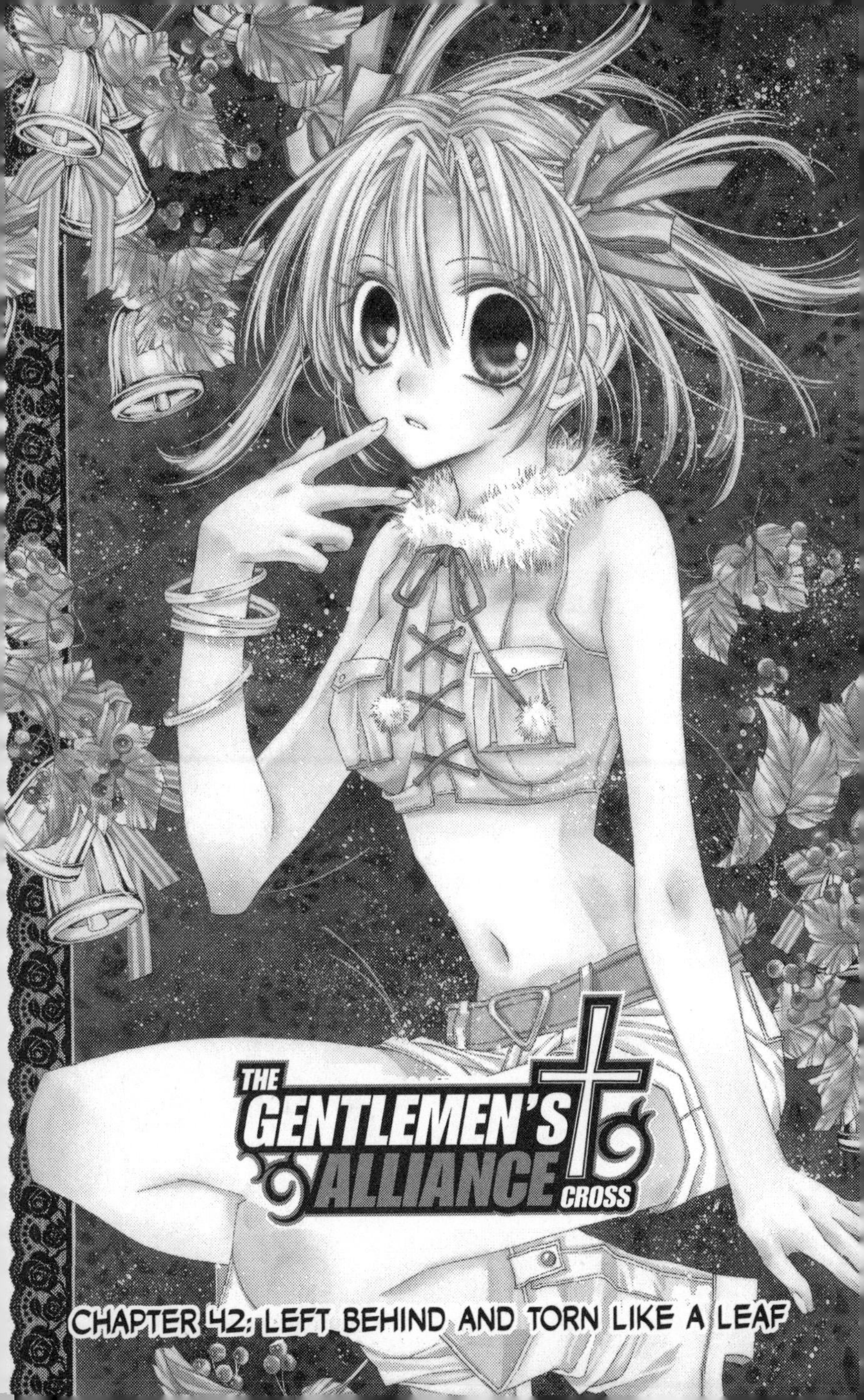
THE GENTLEMEN'S ALLIANCE CROSS
CHAPTER 42: LEFT BEHIND AND TORN LIKE A LEAF

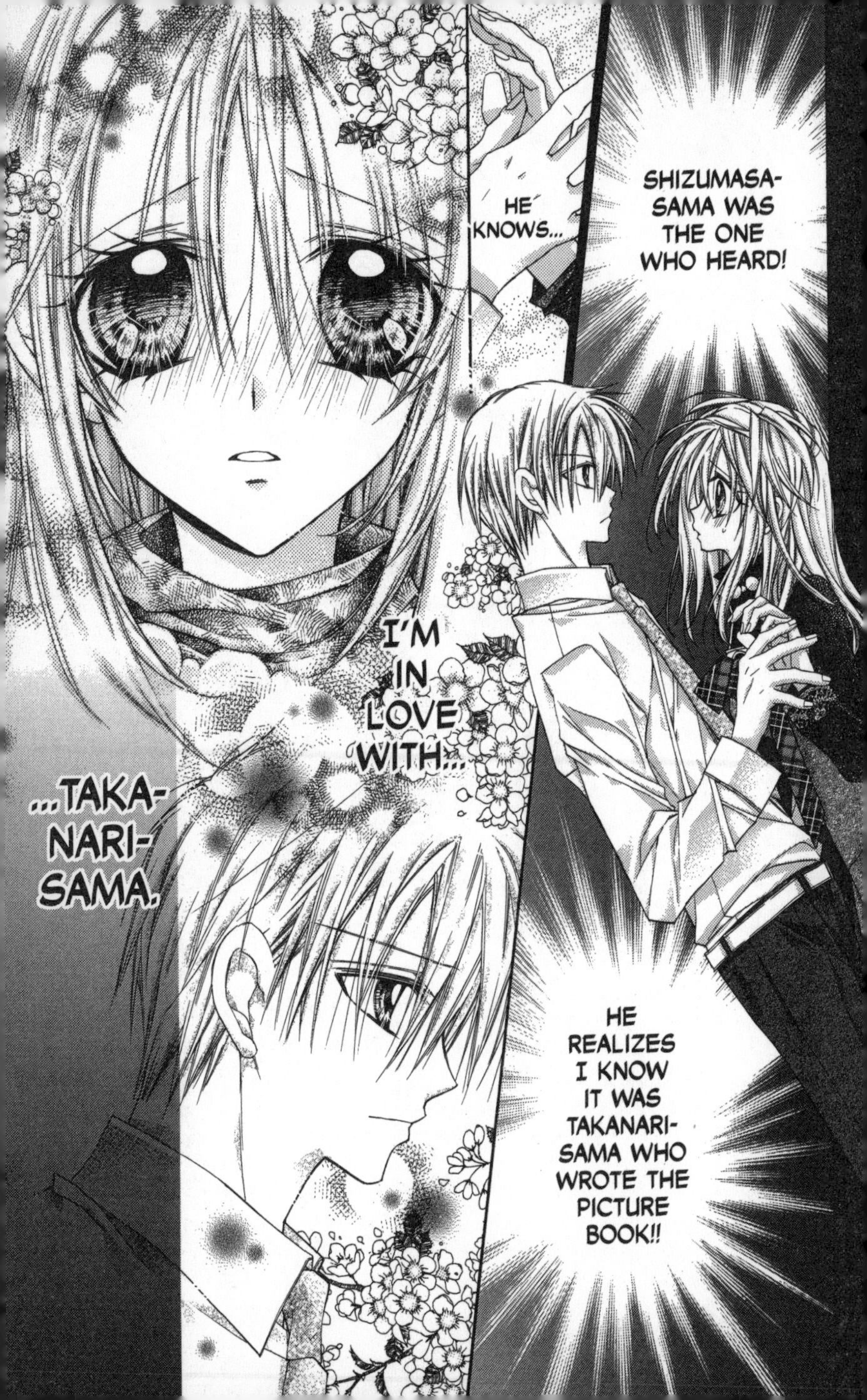
SHIZUMASA-SAMA WAS THE ONE WHO HEARD!
HE KNOWS...
HE REALIZES I KNOW IT WAS TAKANARI-SAMA WHO WROTE THE PICTURE BOOK!!
I'M IN LOVE WITH...
...TAKANARI-SAMA.

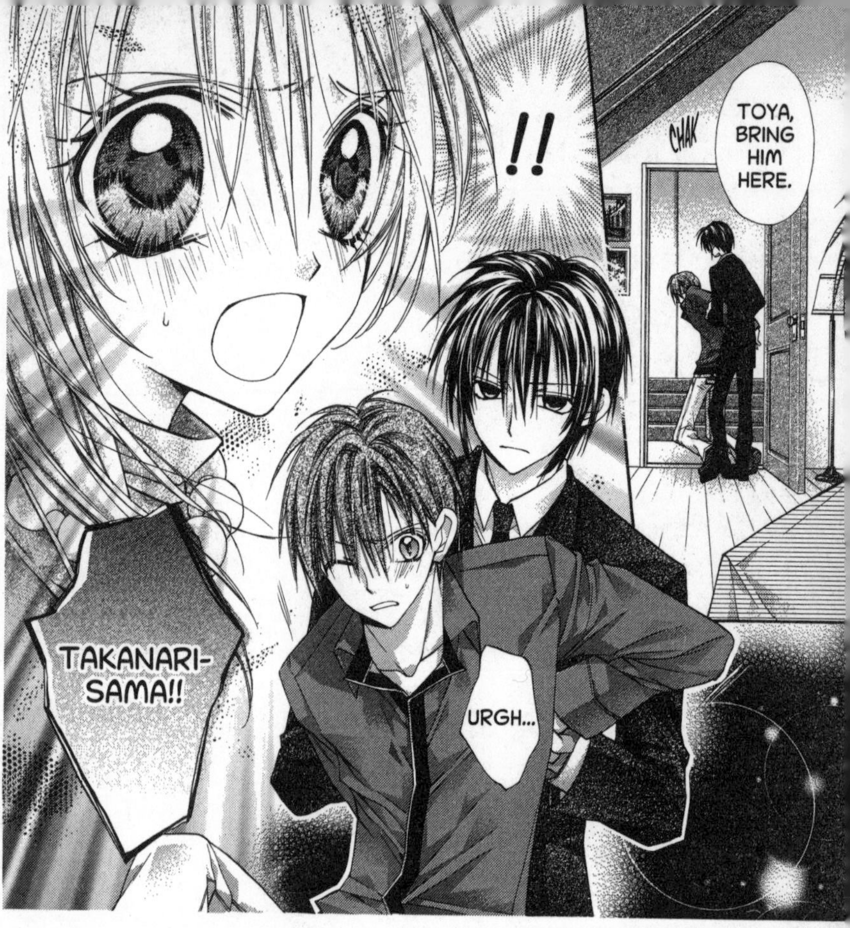
TOYA, BRING HIM HERE.
CHAK
!!
URGH...
TAKANARI-SAMA!!

Chapter 42: Left Behind and Torn Like a Leaf Lead-in Haine confessed she was in love with Takanari. But it was Shizumasa standing there...?!

※ I'm giving away the story.

This chapter was filled with all sorts of no-nos for me, like in many of the other chapters.
First: A guy hits a girl. Second: A male character cries. Waah.
But "drawing what I'm not good at drawing" is my hidden agenda behind the *Gentlemen's Alliance*.

I think the must-see in this chapter is how much Ushio-chan has grown. She's become so expressive. And in the scene with the four of them together, she happens to be the one who is trying to calm everyone down...yet she hated other people so much to begin with... I'm so glad.

Haine-chan is a huge crybaby in this chapter. I wish she'd become a little stronger. As least so she wouldn't cry this much.

I didn't do it intentionally, but this chapter was drawn when my motivation was at an all-time low, so maybe that's showing in the expressions of the characters??

I never intended it to be like that, but...I guess I've still got a lot to learn.
I'm a feeling a bit better now.

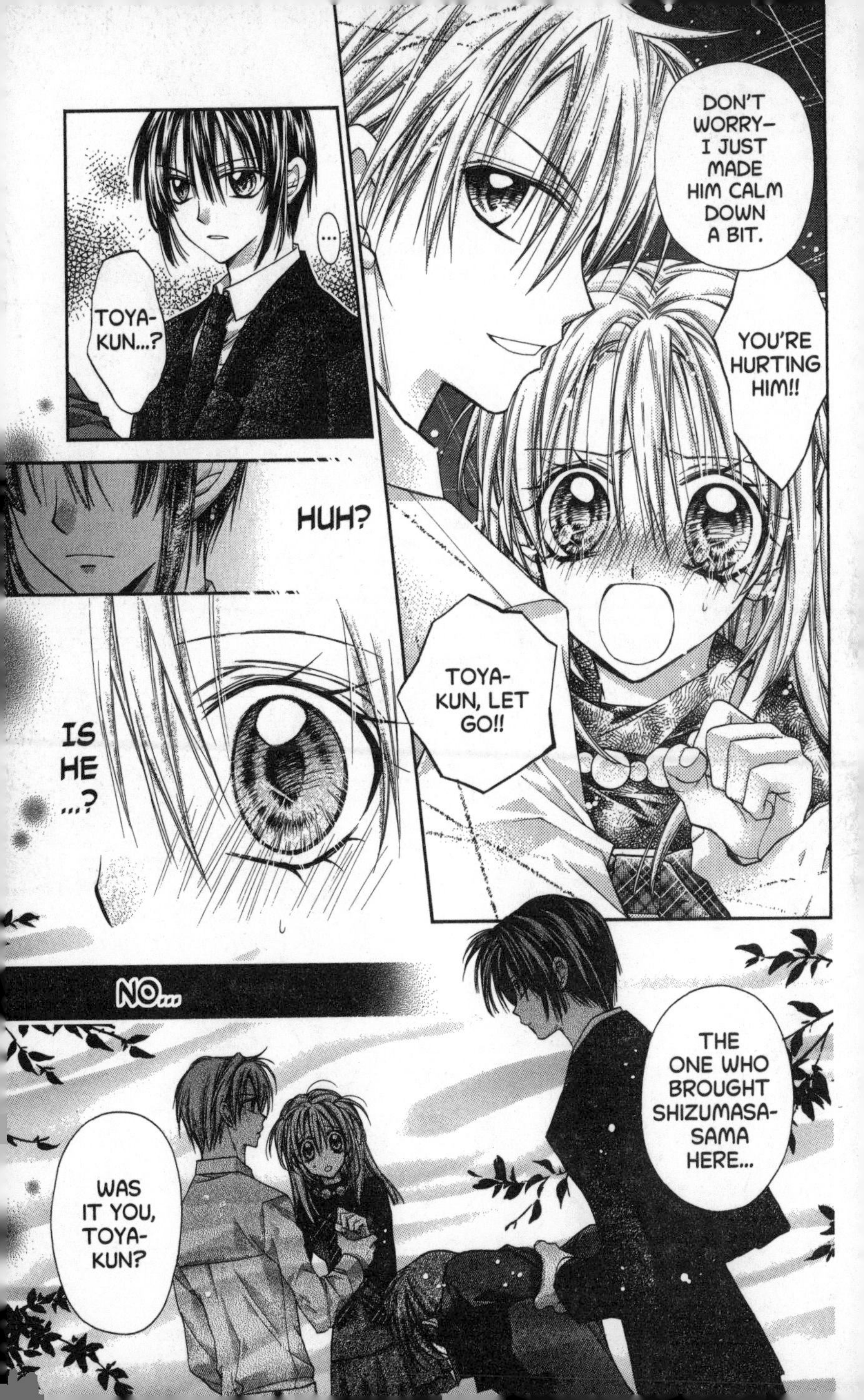
DON'T WORRY— I JUST MADE HIM CALM DOWN A BIT.
YOU'RE HURTING HIM!!
TOYA-KUN, LET GO!!
...
TOYA-KUN...?
HUH?
IS HE ...?
NO...
THE ONE WHO BROUGHT SHIZUMASA-SAMA HERE...
WAS IT YOU, TOYA-KUN?

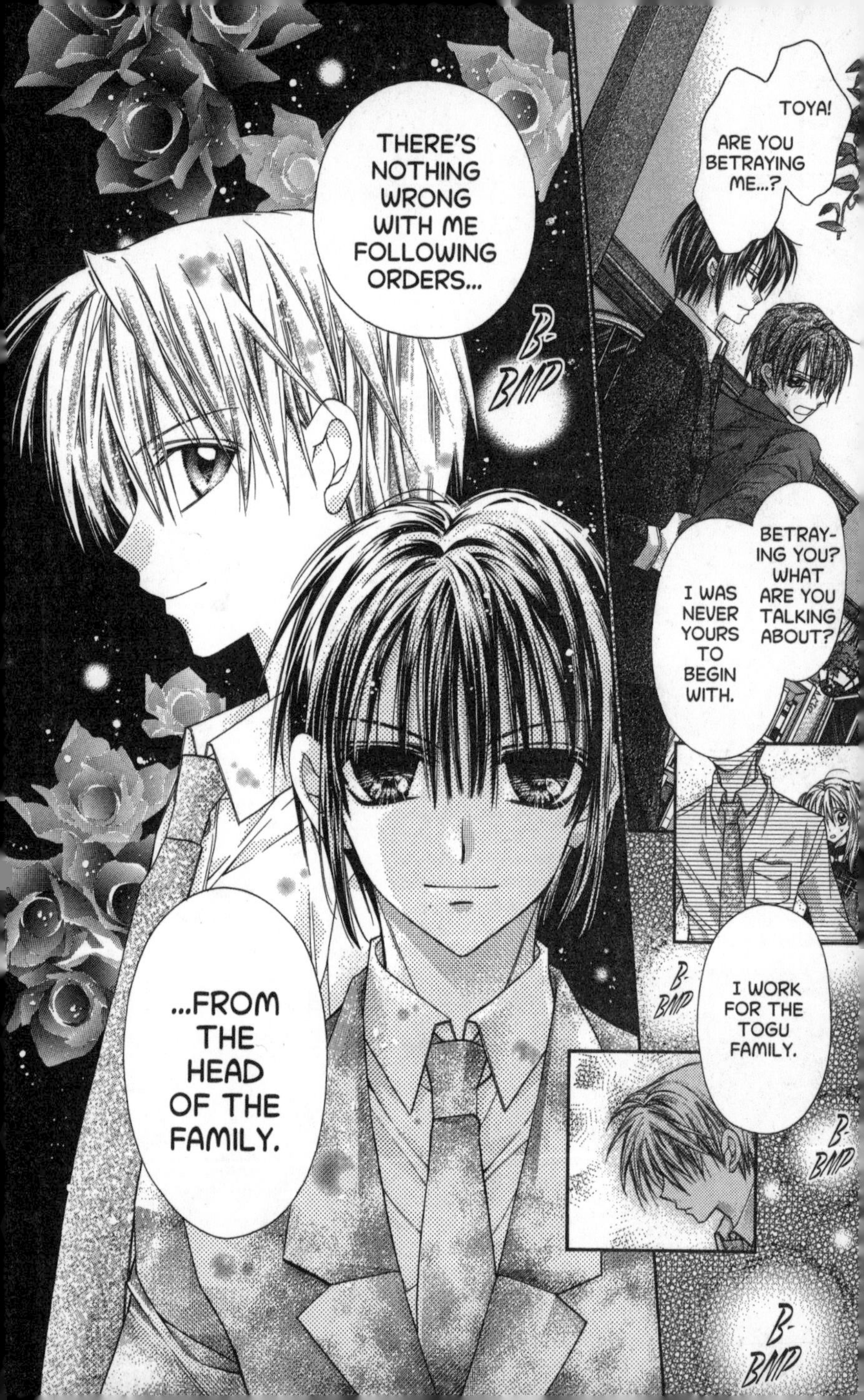
TOYA!
ARE YOU BETRAYING ME...?
BETRAYING YOU? WHAT ARE YOU TALKING ABOUT?
I WAS NEVER YOURS TO BEGIN WITH.
B-BMP
I WORK FOR THE TOGU FAMILY.
B-BMP
B-BMP
THERE'S NOTHING WRONG WITH ME FOLLOWING ORDERS...
B-BMP
...FROM THE HEAD OF THE FAMILY.

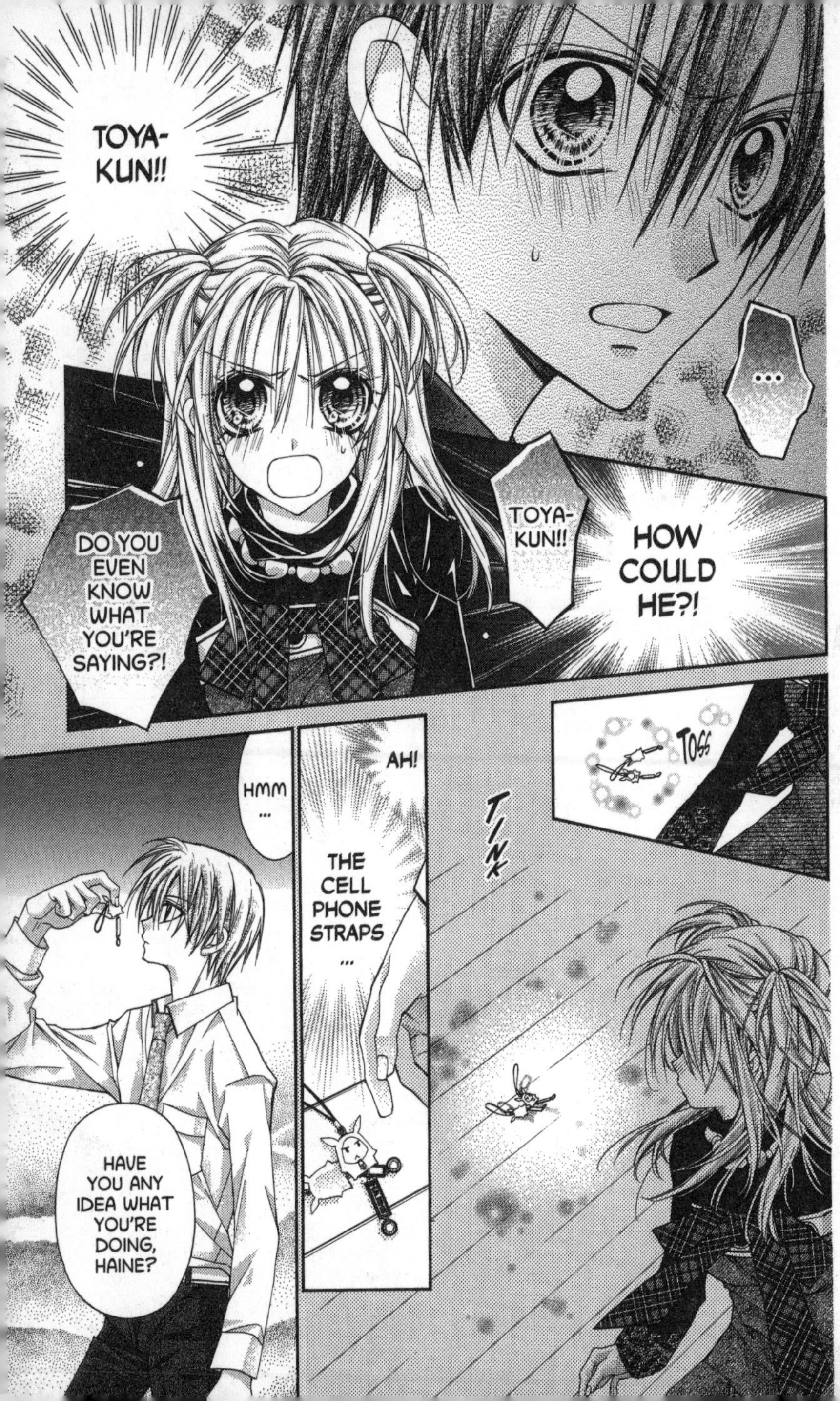
TOYA-KUN!!
...
HOW COULD HE?!
TOYA-KUN!!
DO YOU EVEN KNOW WHAT YOU'RE SAYING?!
TOSS
TINK
AH!
THE CELL PHONE STRAPS...
HMM...
HAVE YOU ANY IDEA WHAT YOU'RE DOING, HAINE?

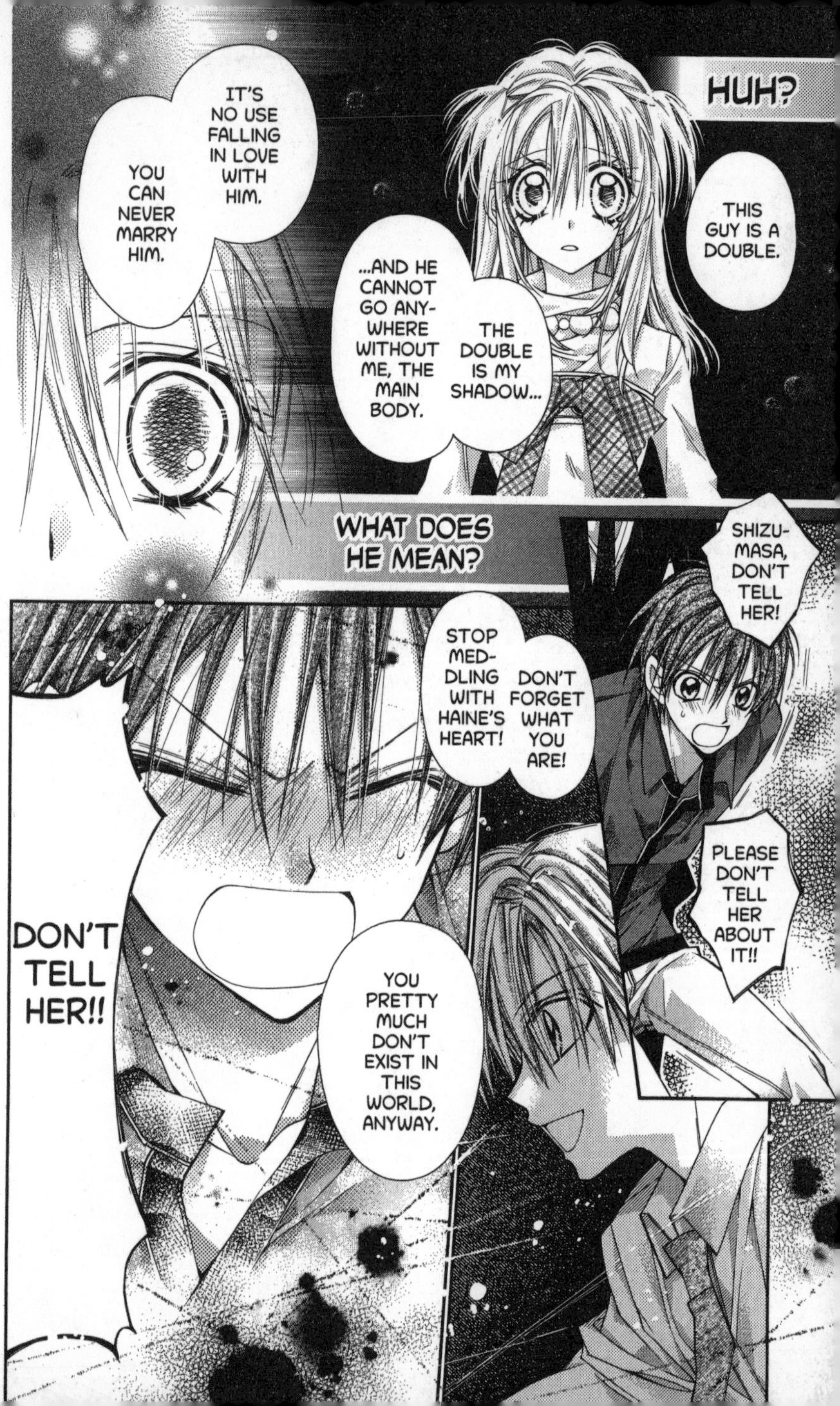
HUH?
THIS GUY IS A DOUBLE.
THE DOUBLE IS MY SHADOW...
...AND HE CANNOT GO ANYWHERE WITHOUT ME, THE MAIN BODY.
IT'S NO USE FALLING IN LOVE WITH HIM.
YOU CAN NEVER MARRY HIM.
WHAT DOES HE MEAN?
SHIZUMASA, DON'T TELL HER!
DON'T FORGET WHAT YOU ARE!
STOP MEDDLING WITH HAINE'S HEART!
PLEASE DON'T TELL HER ABOUT IT!!
YOU PRETTY MUCH DON'T EXIST IN THIS WORLD, ANYWAY.
DON'T TELL HER!!

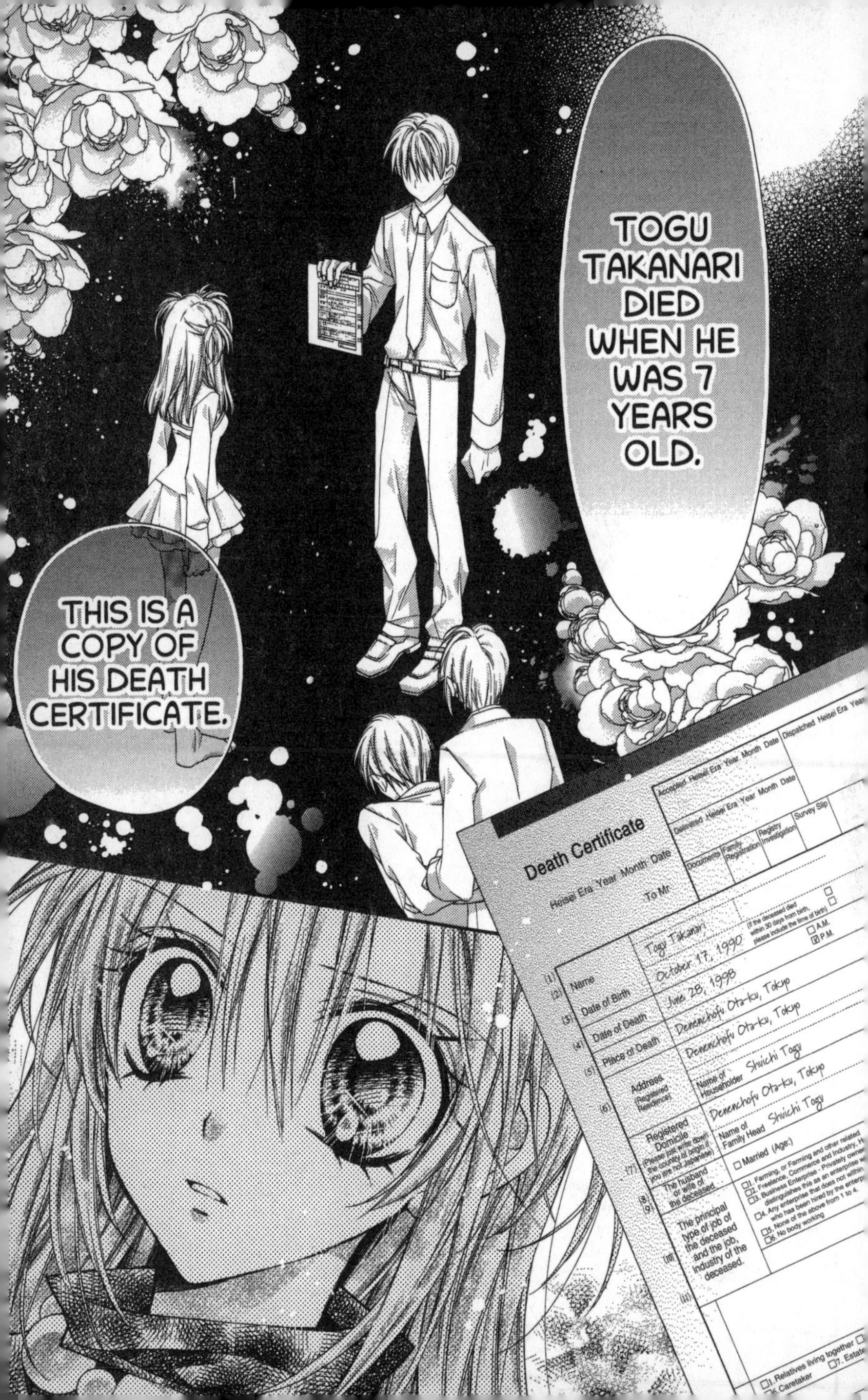
TOGU TAKANARI DIED WHEN HE WAS 7 YEARS OLD.
THIS IS A COPY OF HIS DEATH CERTIFICATE.
Death Certificate
Heisei Era Year Month Date
To Mr.
Accepted Heisei Era Year Month Date
Delivered Heisei Era Year Month Date
Documents
Family Registration
Registry Investigation
Survey Slip
(If the deceased died within 30 days from birth, please include the time of birth)
A.M.
P.M.
Name Togu Takanari
Date of Birth October 17, 1990
Date of Death June 28, 1998
Place of Death Denenchofu Ota-ku, Tokyo
Address (Registered Residence) Denenchofu Ota-ku, Tokyo
Name of Householder Shuichi Togu
Registered Domicile Denenchofu Ota-ku, Tokyo
Name of Family Head Shuichi Togu
The husband or wife of the deceased
Married (Age:)
The principal type of job of the deceased and the job, industry of the deceased.
5. None of the above from 1 to 4.
6. No body working

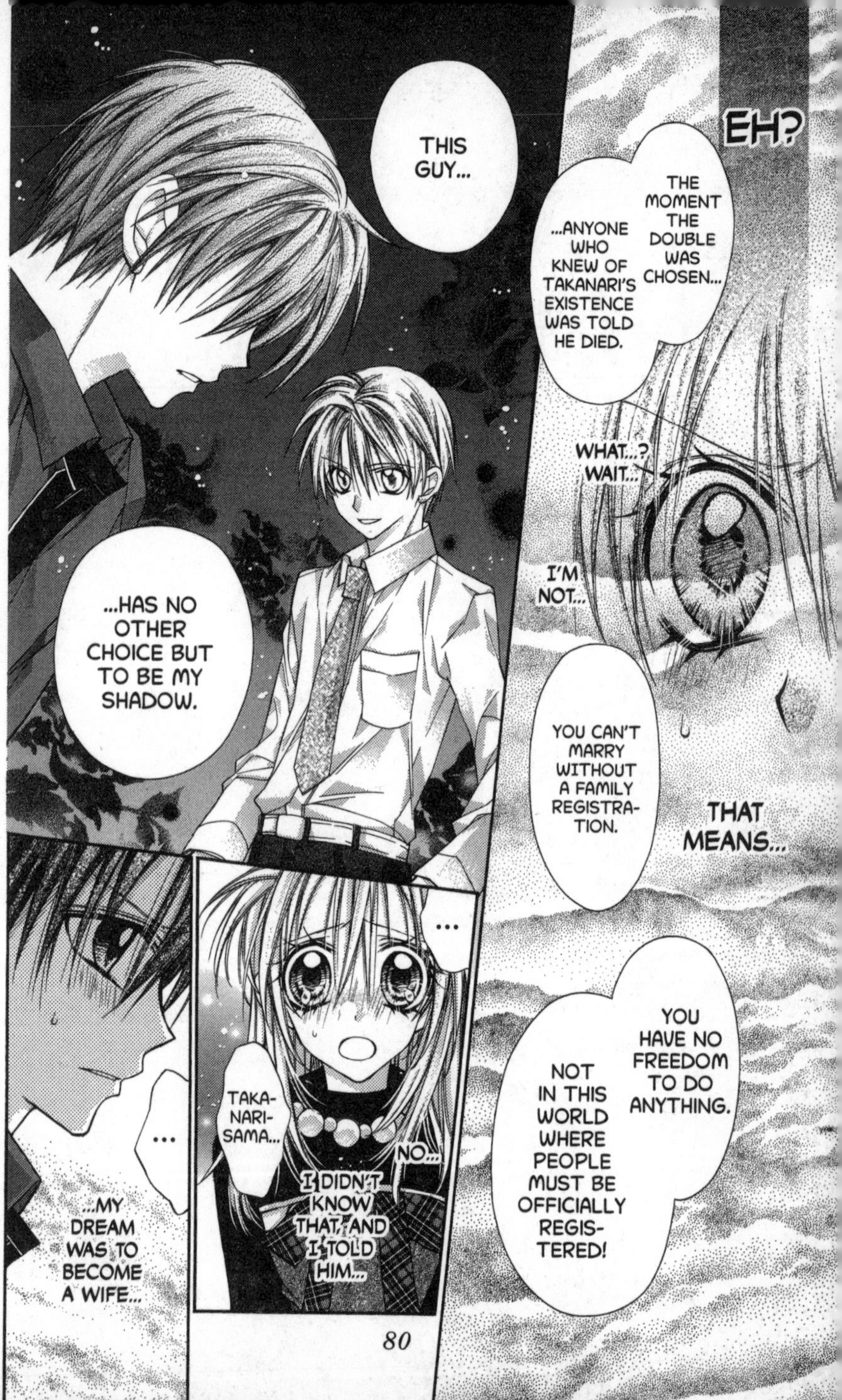
EH?
THE MOMENT THE DOUBLE WAS CHOSEN...
...ANYONE WHO KNEW OF TAKANARI'S EXISTENCE WAS TOLD HE DIED.
WHAT...? WAIT...
I'M NOT...
YOU CAN'T MARRY WITHOUT A FAMILY REGISTRATION.
THAT MEANS...
YOU HAVE NO FREEDOM TO DO ANYTHING.
NOT IN THIS WORLD WHERE PEOPLE MUST BE OFFICIALLY REGISTERED!
THIS GUY...
...HAS NO OTHER CHOICE BUT TO BE MY SHADOW.
...
TAKANARI-SAMA...
NO...
I DIDN'T KNOW THAT AND I TOLD HIM...
...
...MY DREAM WAS TO BECOME A WIFE...

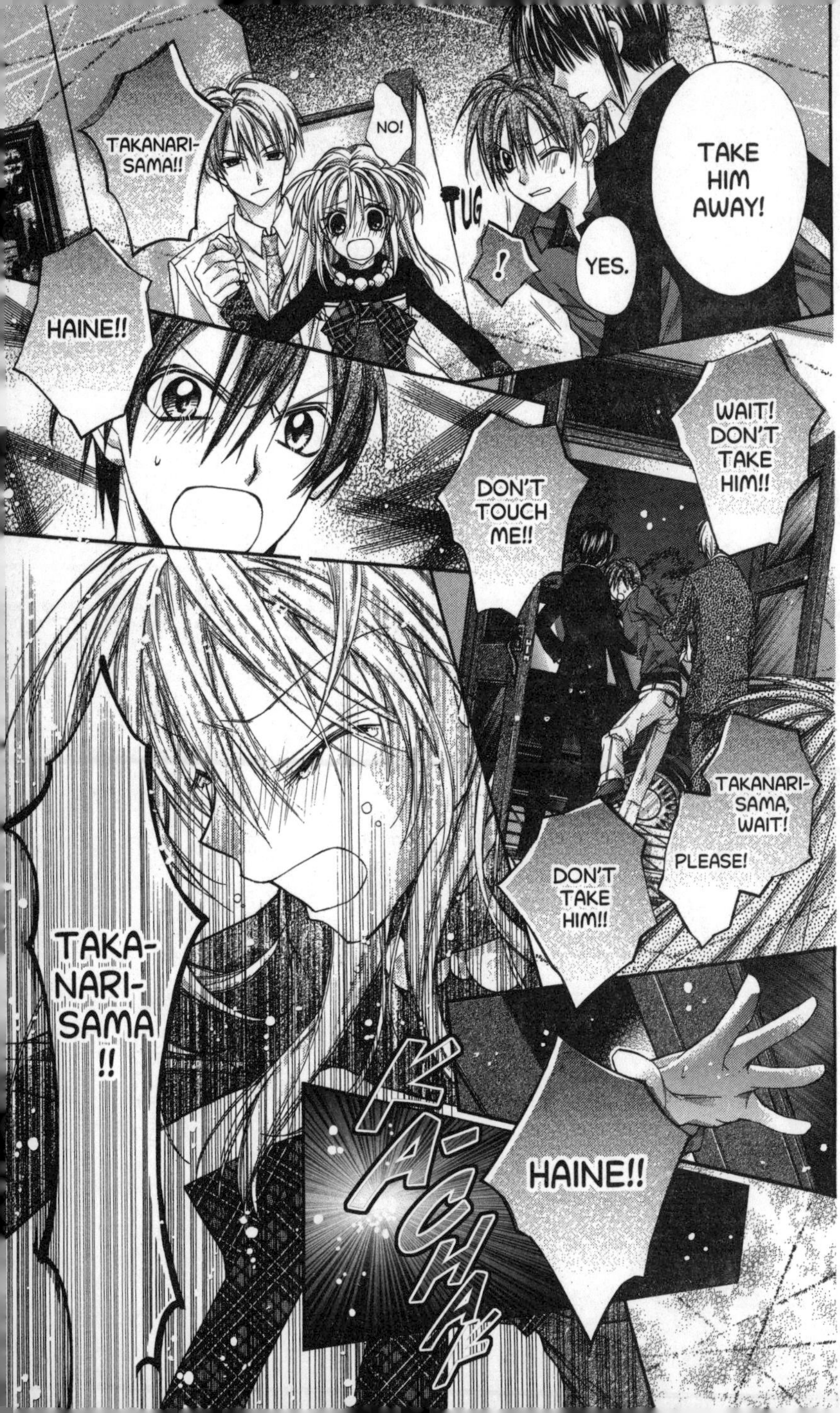
TAKE HIM AWAY!
YES.
!
TUG
NO!
TAKANARI-SAMA!!
WAIT! DON'T TAKE HIM!!
DON'T TOUCH ME!!
HAINE!!
TAKANARI-SAMA, WAIT!
PLEASE!
DON'T TAKE HIM!!
TAKA-NARI-SAMA!!
HAINE!!
KA-CHAK

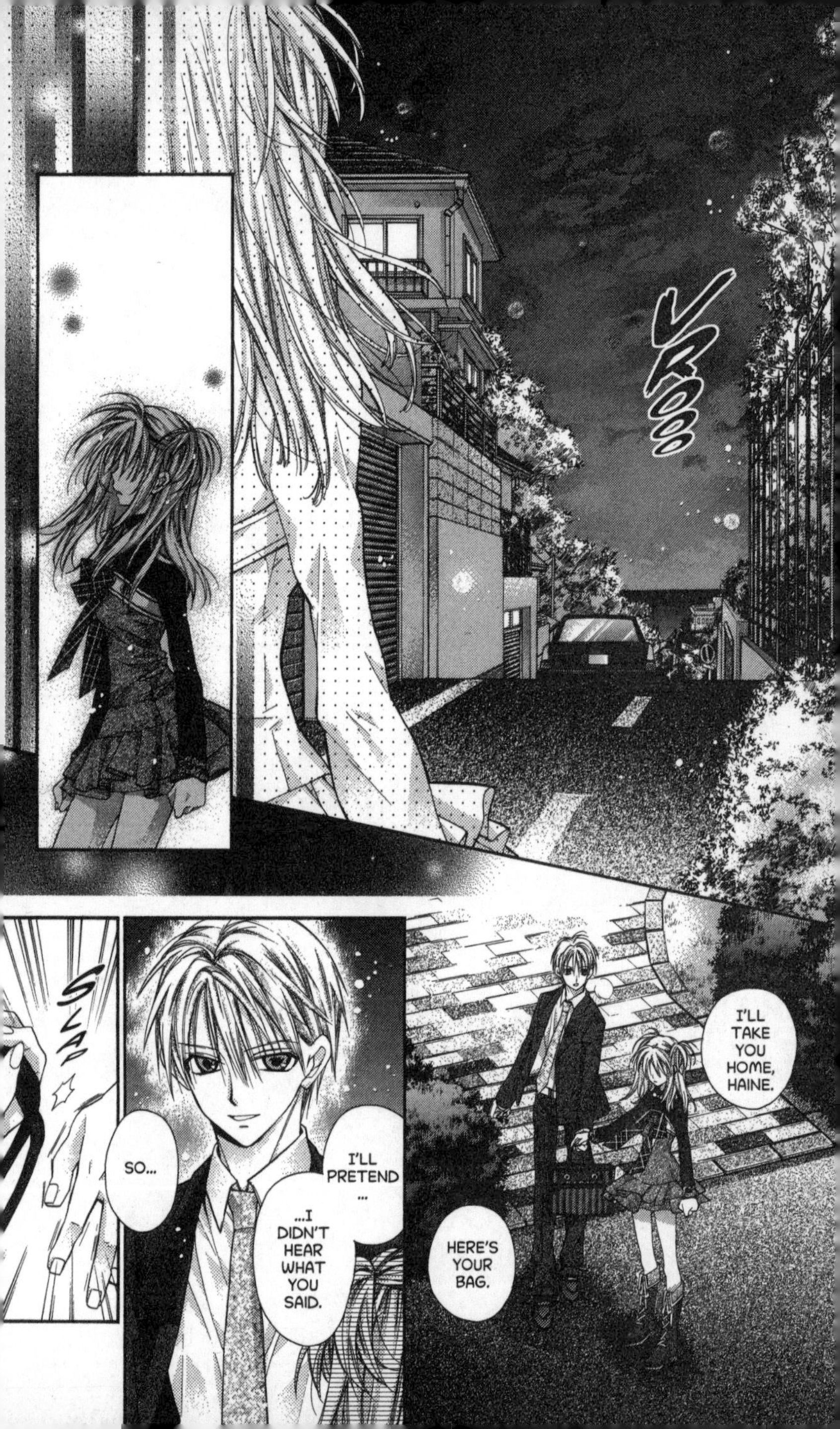
VROOOO
I'LL TAKE YOU HOME, HAINE.
HERE'S YOUR BAG.
I'LL PRETEND ...
SO...
...I DIDN'T HEAR WHAT YOU SAID.
SLAP

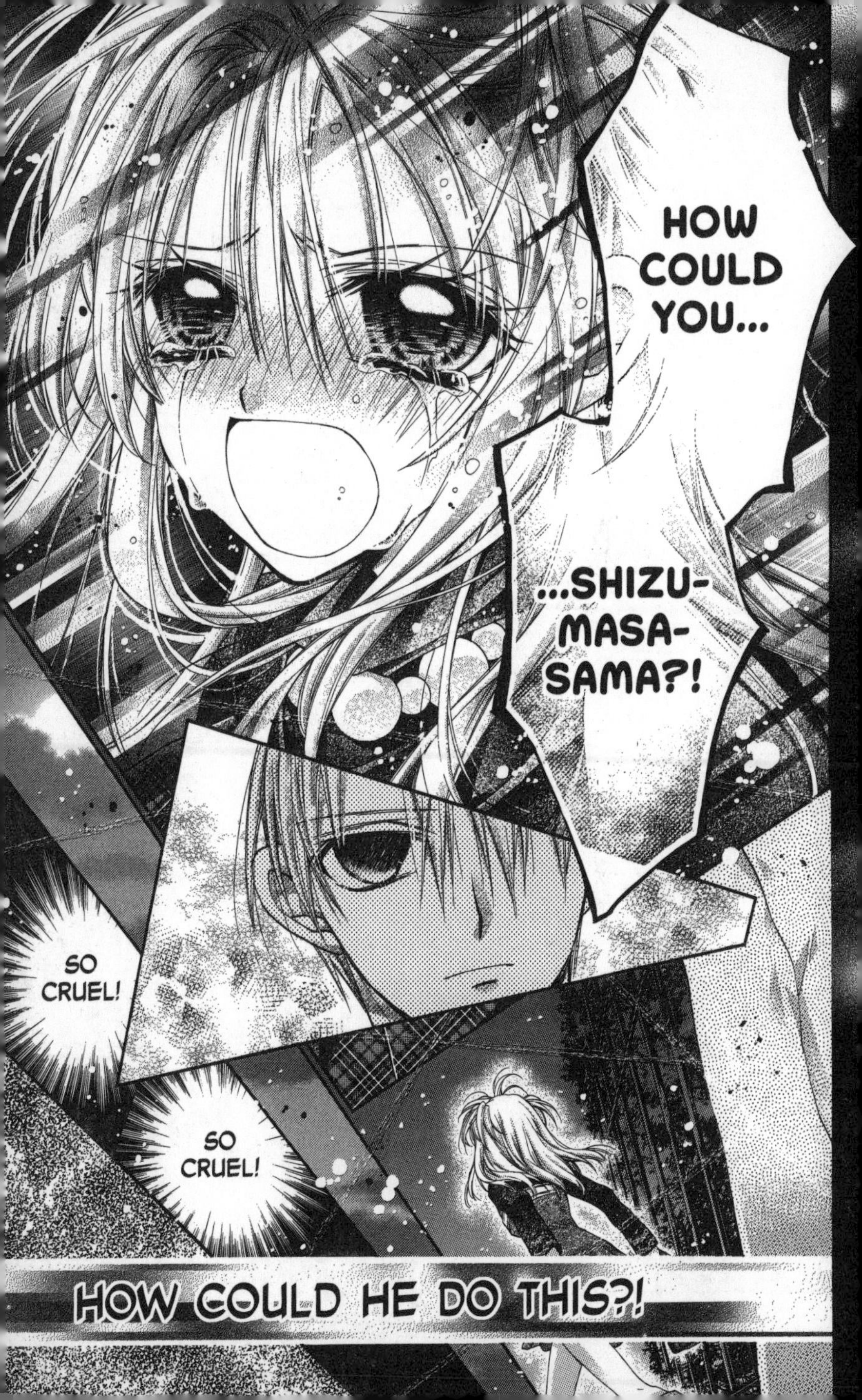
HOW COULD YOU...
...SHIZU-MASA-SAMA?!
SO CRUEL!
SO CRUEL!
HOW COULD HE DO THIS?!

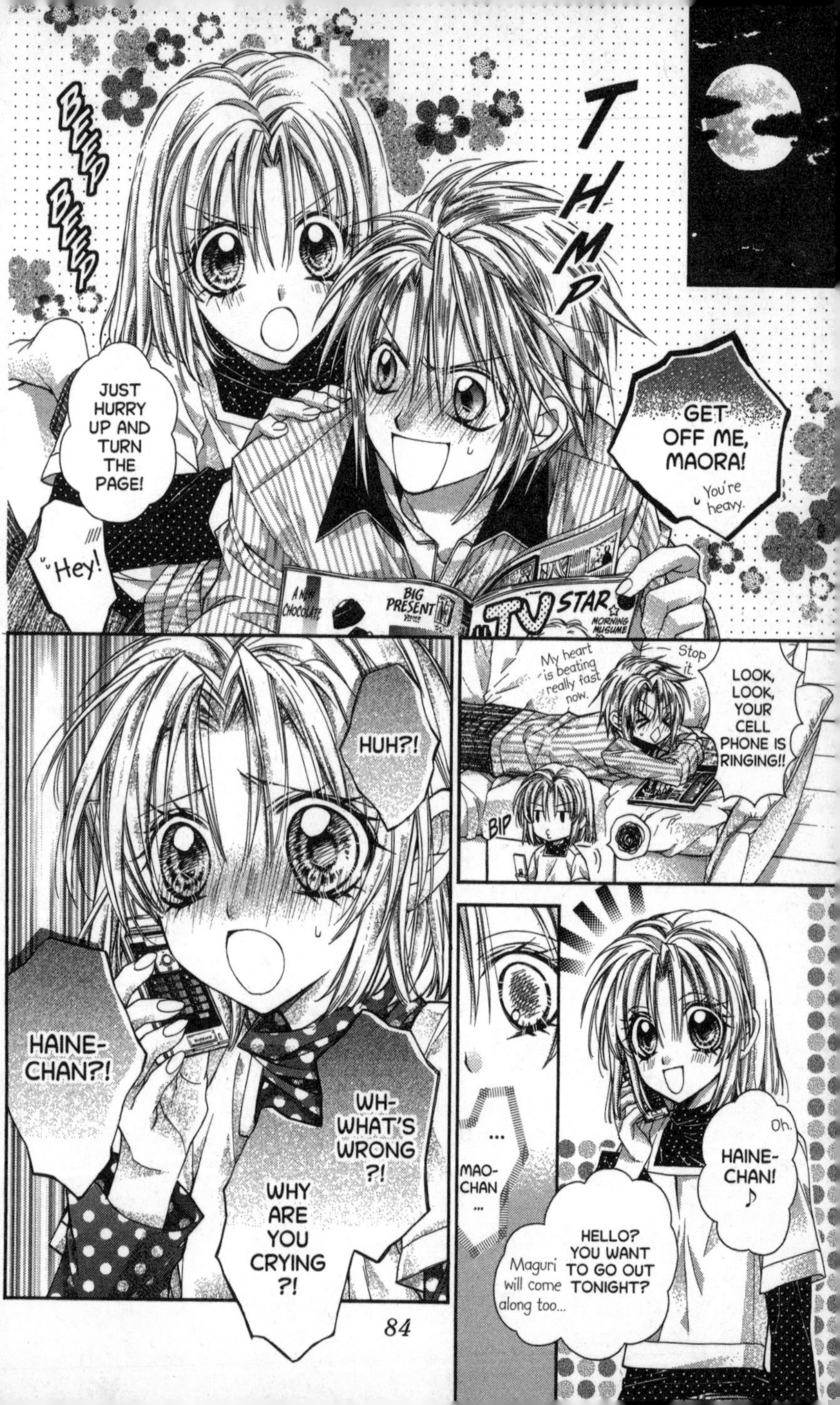

THMP
GET OFF ME, MAORA!
You're heavy.
BEEP BEEP
JUST HURRY UP AND TURN THE PAGE!
Hey!
BIG PRESENT
TV STAR
MORNING MUSUME
LOOK, LOOK, YOUR CELL PHONE IS RINGING!!
Stop it.
My heart is beating really fast now.
BIP
Oh.
HAINE-CHAN! ♪
HELLO? YOU WANT TO GO OUT TONIGHT?
Maguri will come along too...
... MAO-CHAN ...
HUH?!
HAINE-CHAN?!
WH-WHAT'S WRONG?!
WHY ARE YOU CRYING?!

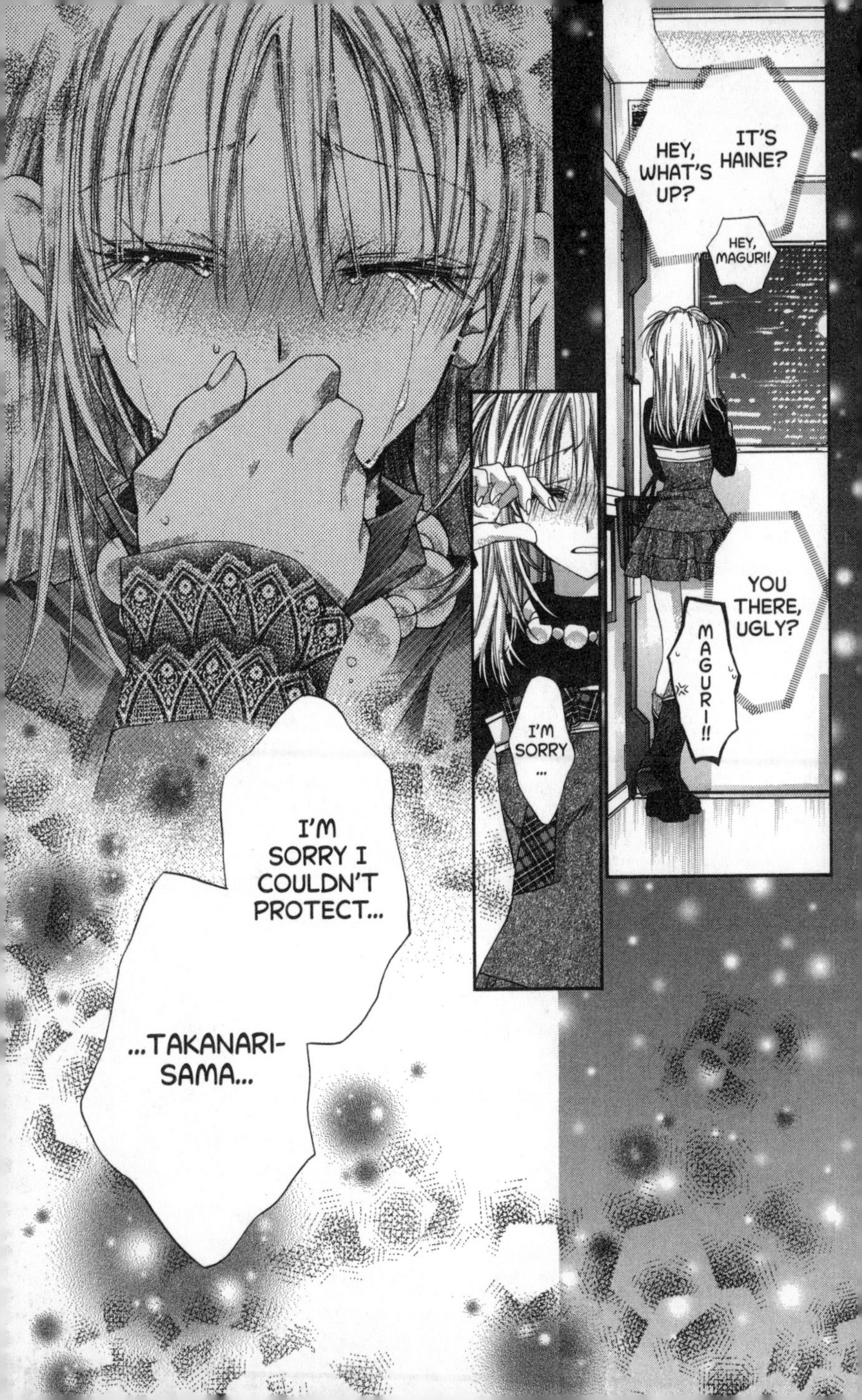
IT'S HAINE?
HEY, WHAT'S UP?
HEY, MAGURI!
YOU THERE, UGLY?
MAGURI!!
I'M SORRY ...
I'M SORRY I COULDN'T PROTECT...
...TAKANARI-SAMA...

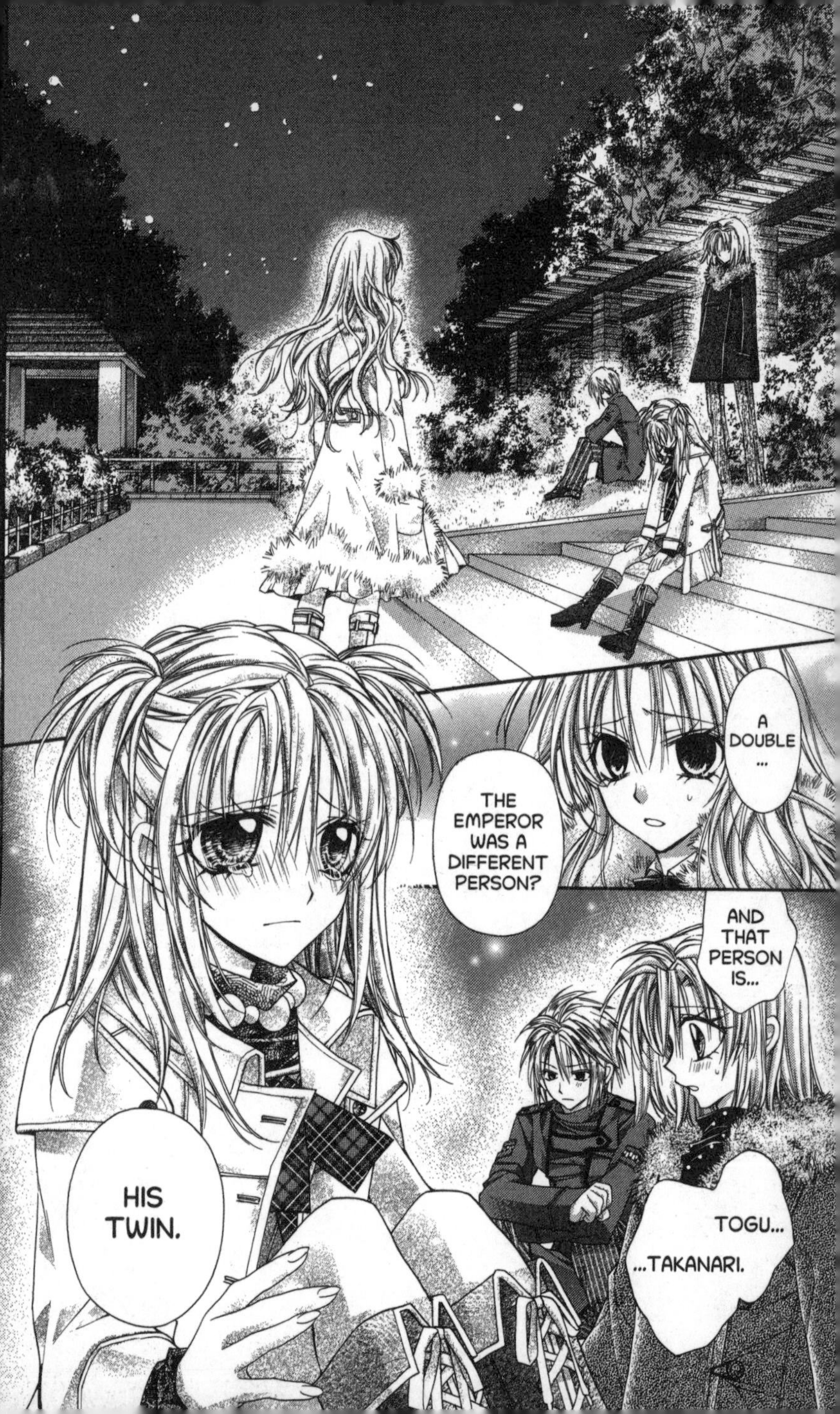
A DOUBLE...
THE EMPEROR WAS A DIFFERENT PERSON?
AND THAT PERSON IS...
TOGU...
...TAKANARI.
HIS TWIN.

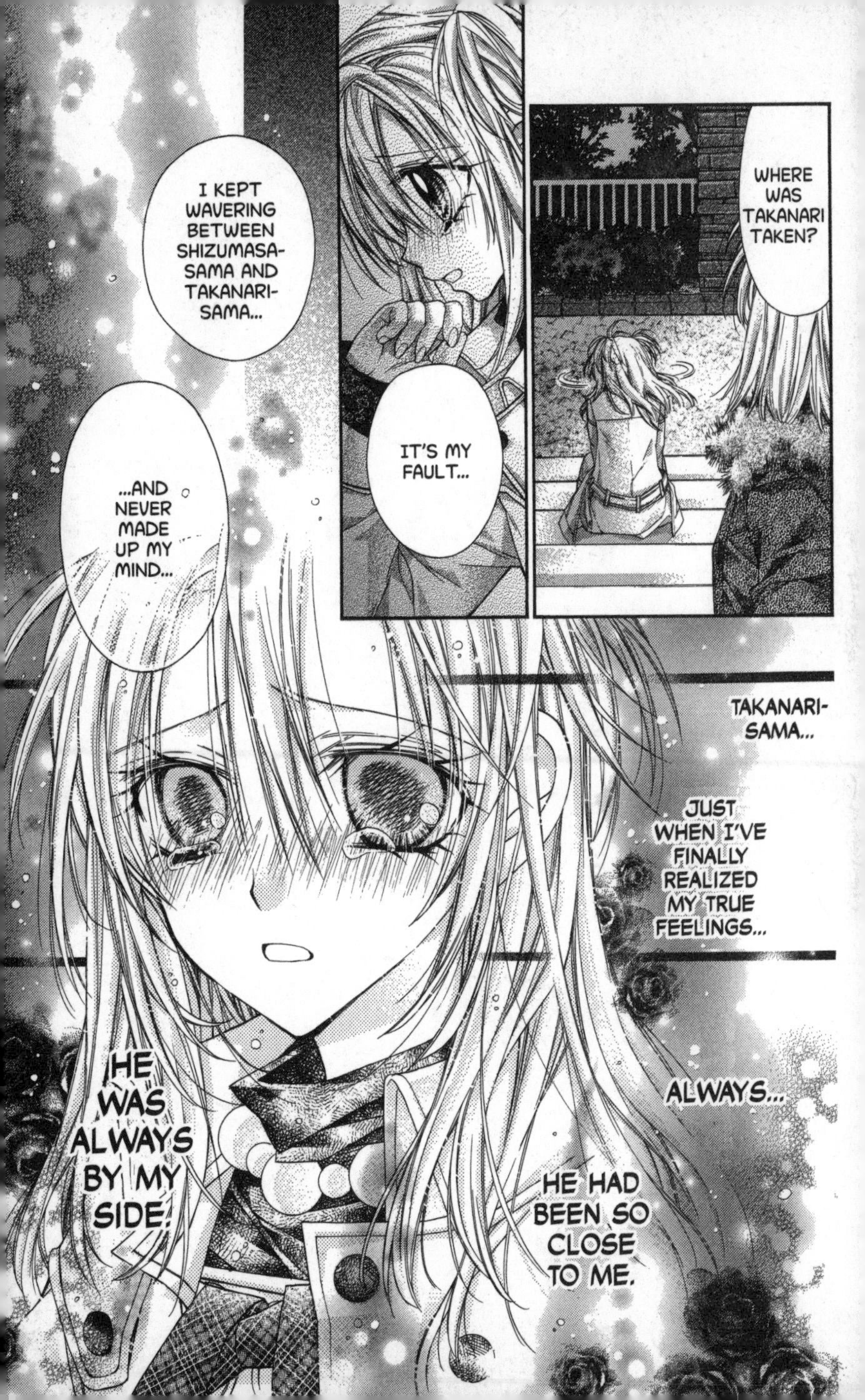
WHERE WAS TAKANARI TAKEN?
IT'S MY FAULT...
I KEPT WAVERING BETWEEN SHIZUMASA-SAMA AND TAKANARI-SAMA...
...AND NEVER MADE UP MY MIND...
TAKANARI-SAMA...
JUST WHEN I'VE FINALLY REALIZED MY TRUE FEELINGS...
ALWAYS...
HE HAD BEEN SO CLOSE TO ME.
HE WAS ALWAYS BY MY SIDE.

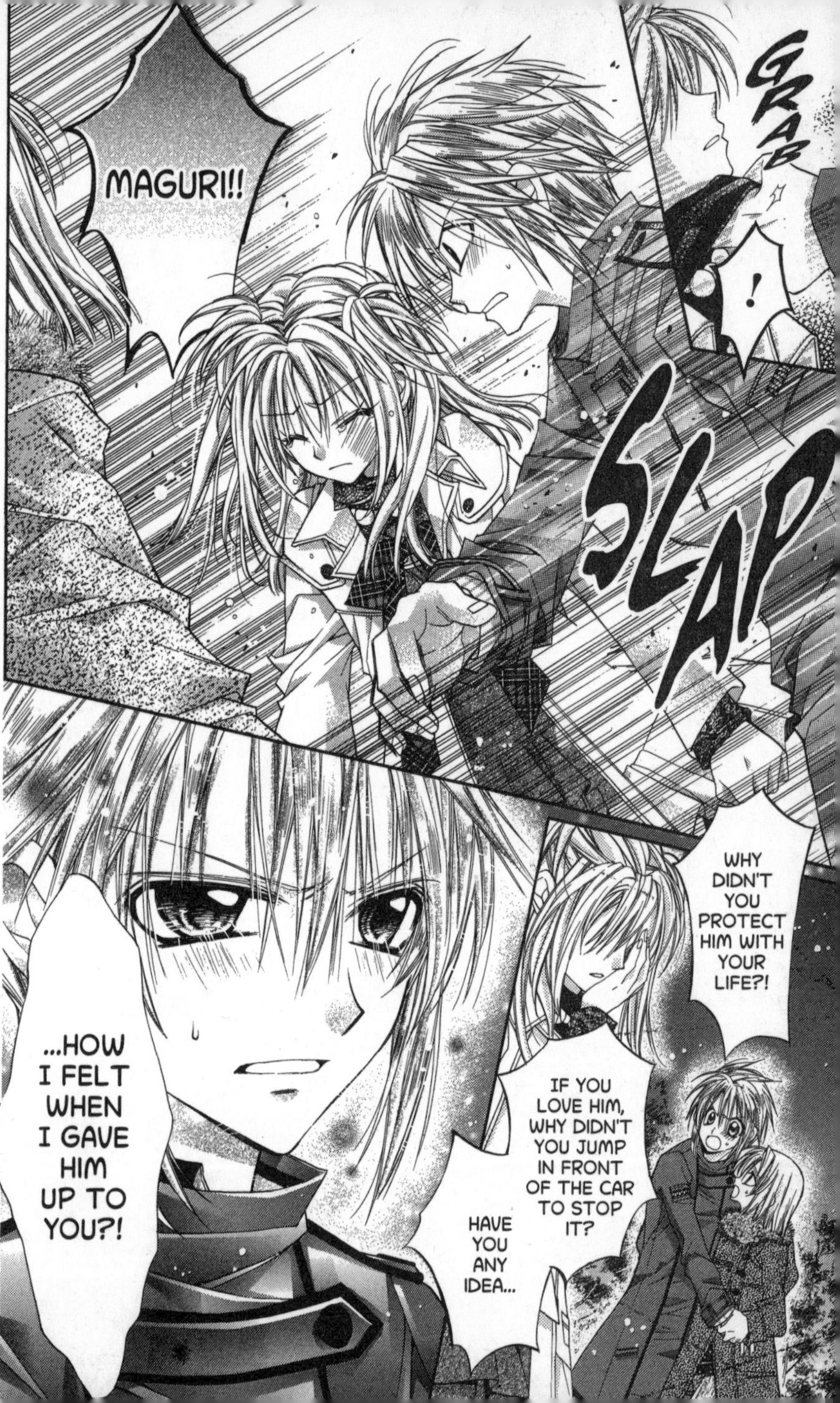
GRAB
!
MAGURI!!
SLAP
WHY DIDN'T YOU PROTECT HIM WITH YOUR LIFE?!
IF YOU LOVE HIM, WHY DIDN'T YOU JUMP IN FRONT OF THE CAR TO STOP IT?
HAVE YOU ANY IDEA...
...HOW I FELT WHEN I GAVE HIM UP TO YOU?!

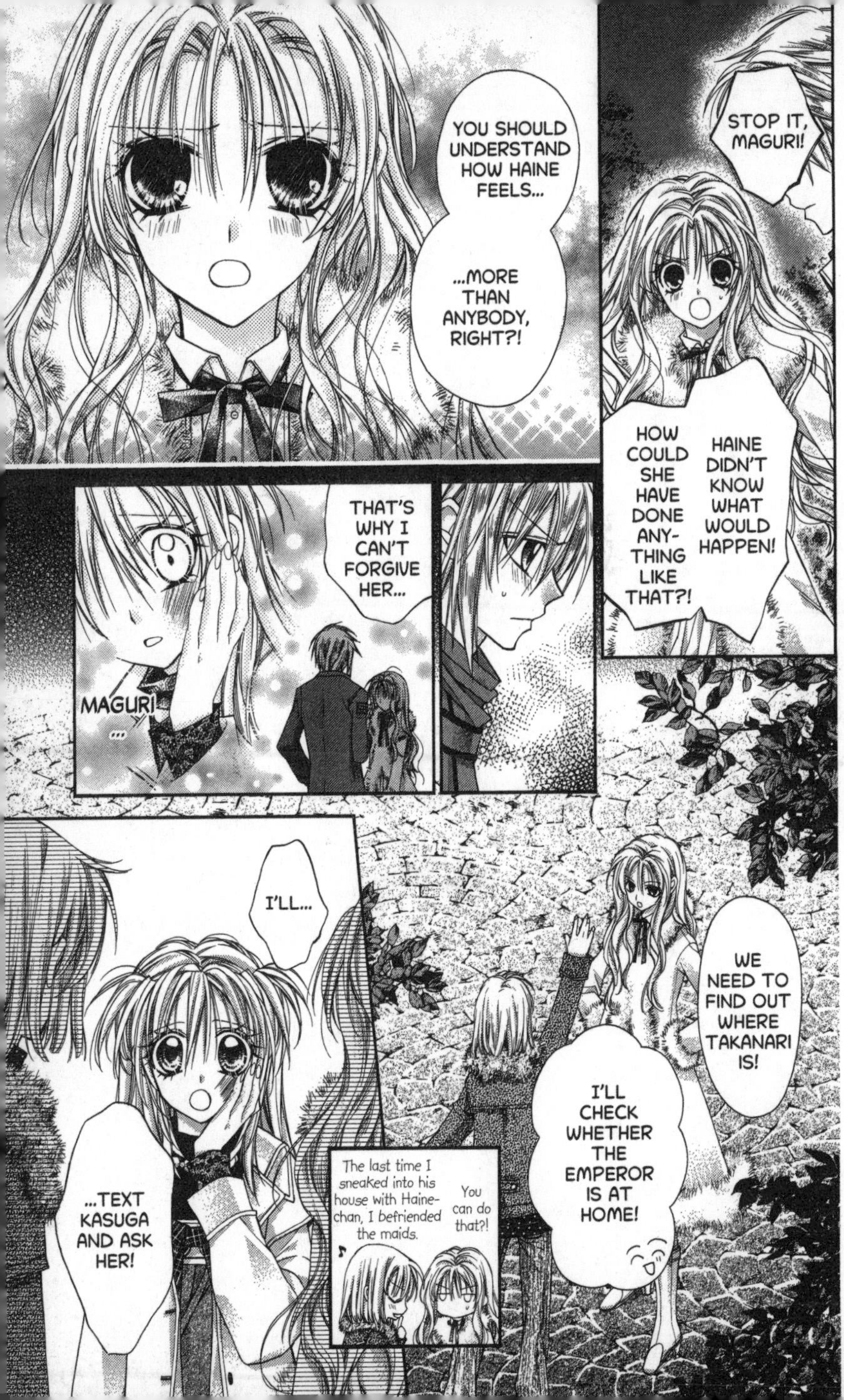
STOP IT, MAGURI!
HAINE DIDN'T KNOW WHAT WOULD HAPPEN!
HOW COULD SHE HAVE DONE ANY-THING LIKE THAT?!
YOU SHOULD UNDERSTAND HOW HAINE FEELS...
...MORE THAN ANYBODY, RIGHT?!
THAT'S WHY I CAN'T FORGIVE HER...
MAGURI...
WE NEED TO FIND OUT WHERE TAKANARI IS!
I'LL CHECK WHETHER THE EMPEROR IS AT HOME!
You can do that?!
The last time I sneaked into his house with Haine-chan, I befriended the maids.
I'LL...
...TEXT KASUGA AND ASK HER!

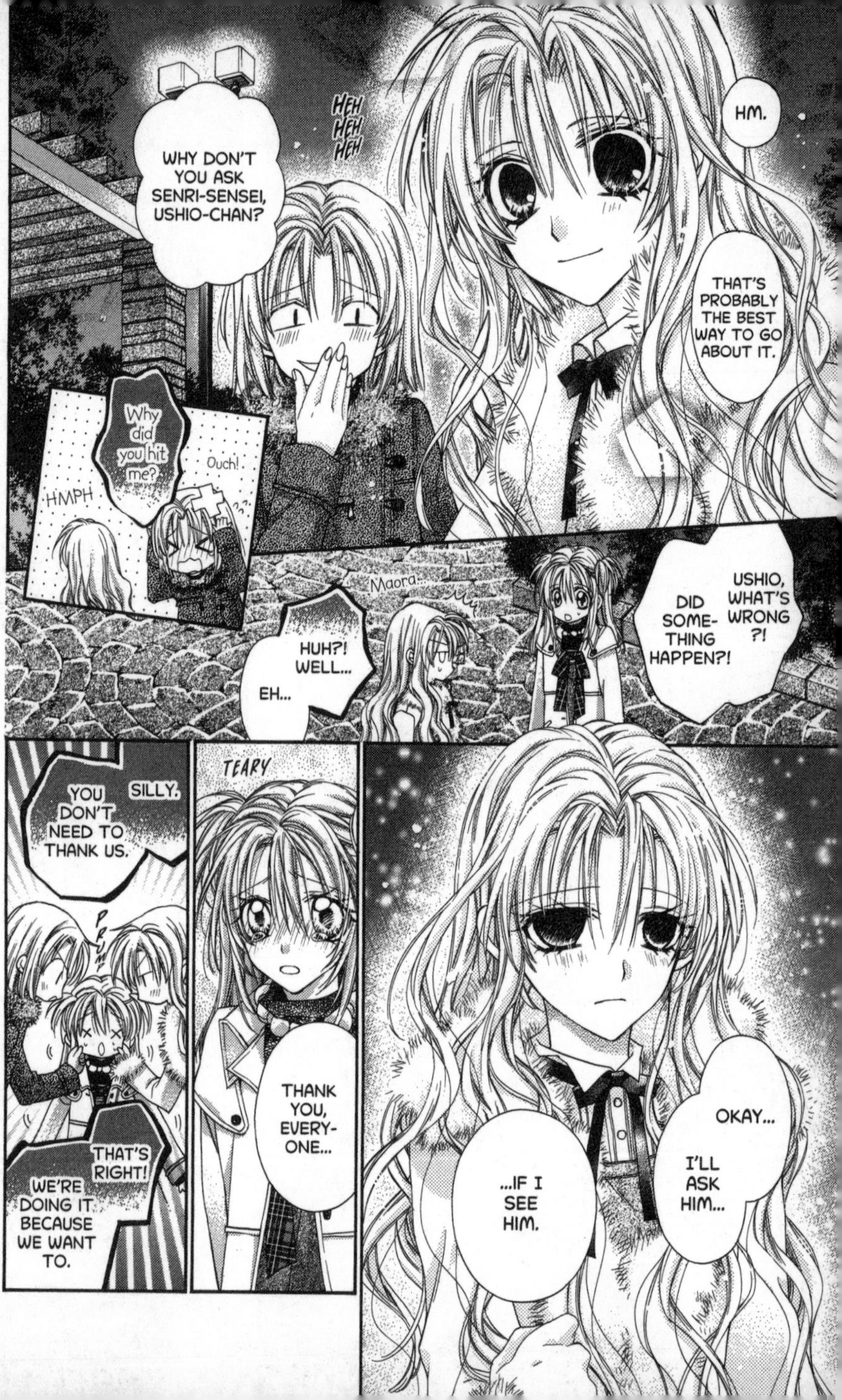
HM.
HEH HEH HEH
WHY DON'T YOU ASK SENRI-SENSEI, USHIO-CHAN?
THAT'S PROBABLY THE BEST WAY TO GO ABOUT IT.
Why did you hit me?
Ouch!
HMPH
USHIO, WHAT'S WRONG?!
DID SOMETHING HAPPEN?!
Maora...
HUH?! WELL...
EH...
OKAY...
I'LL ASK HIM...
...IF I SEE HIM.
TEARY
THANK YOU, EVERYONE...
SILLY.
YOU DON'T NEED TO THANK US.
THAT'S RIGHT!
WE'RE DOING IT BECAUSE WE WANT TO.

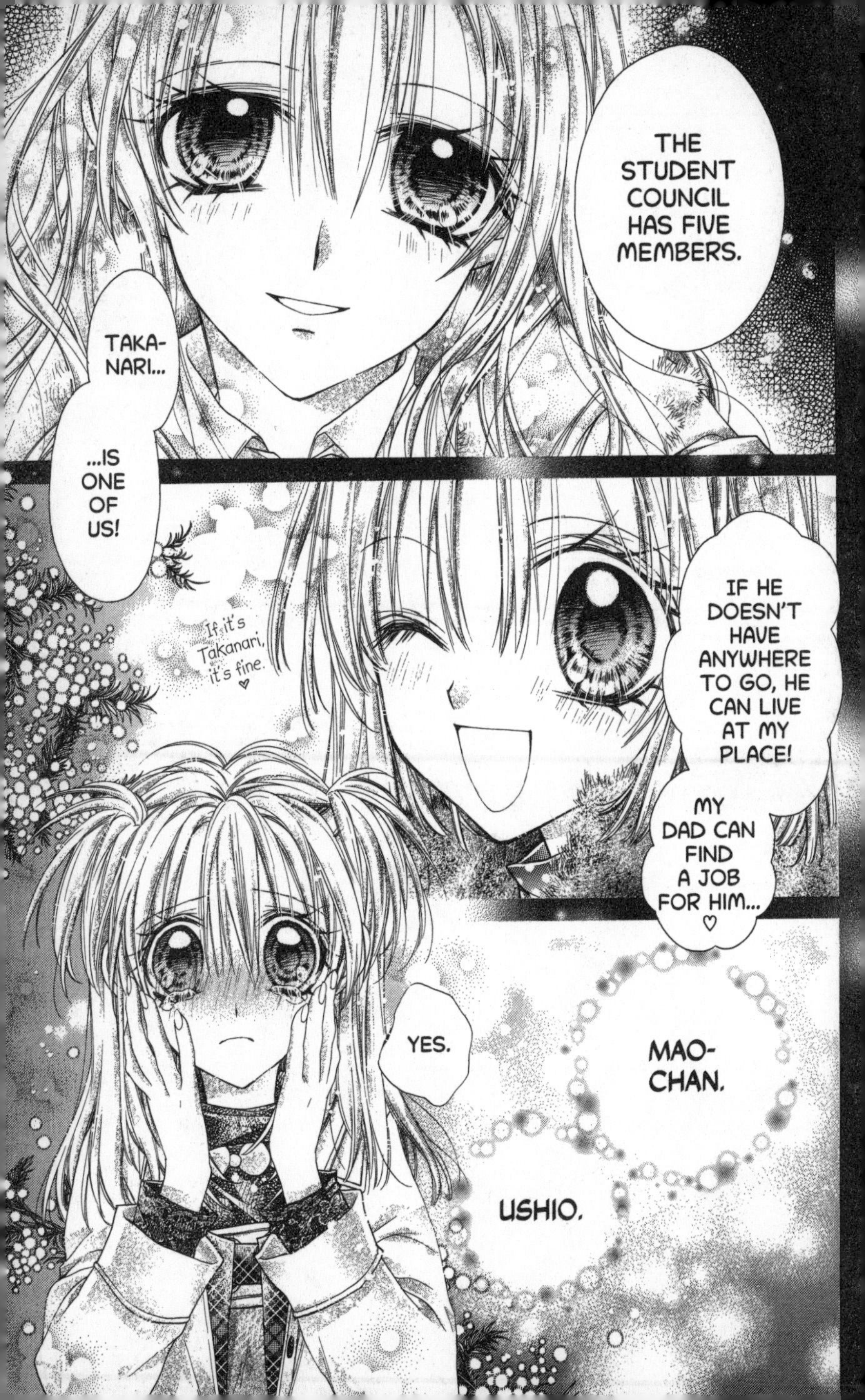
THE STUDENT COUNCIL HAS FIVE MEMBERS.
TAKA-NARI...
...IS ONE OF US!
IF HE DOESN'T HAVE ANYWHERE TO GO, HE CAN LIVE AT MY PLACE!
If it's Takanari, it's fine. ♡
MY DAD CAN FIND A JOB FOR HIM... ♡
MAO-CHAN.
USHIO.
YES.

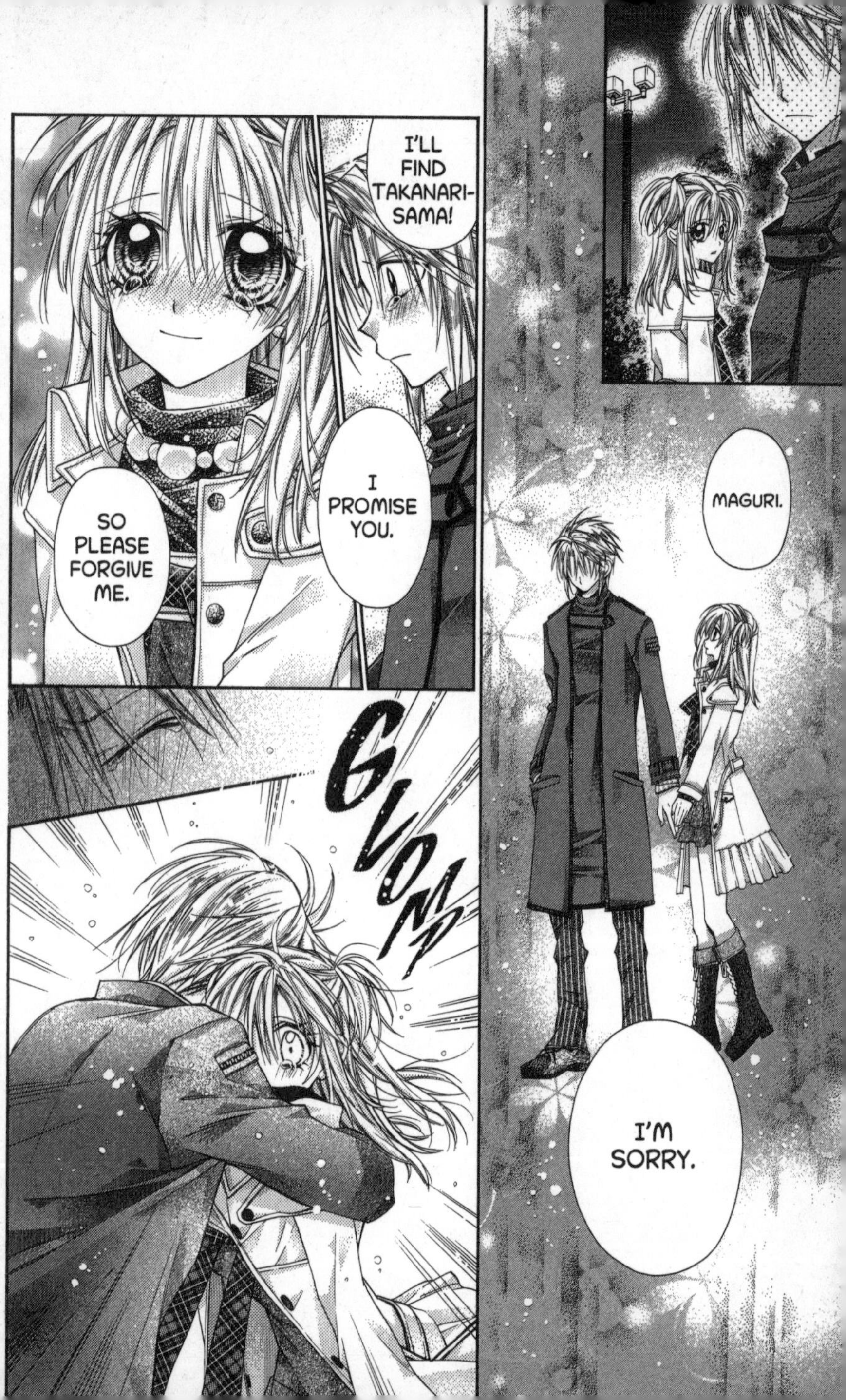
MAGURI.
I'M SORRY.
I'LL FIND TAKANARI-SAMA!
I PROMISE YOU.
SO PLEASE FORGIVE ME.
GYUM

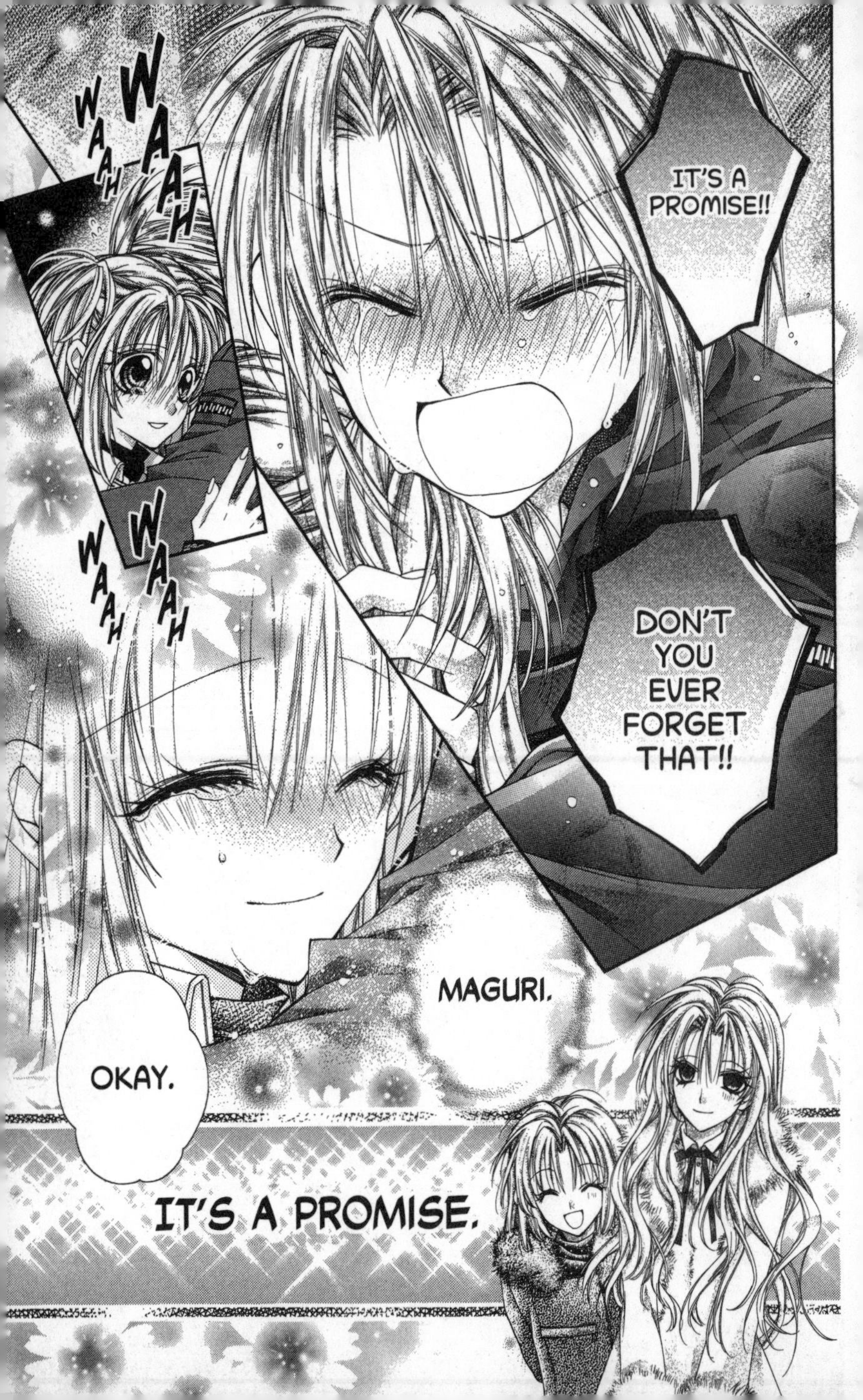
IT'S A PROMISE!!
DON'T YOU EVER FORGET THAT!!
WAAH WAAH
WAAH WAAH
MAGURI.
OKAY.
IT'S A PROMISE.

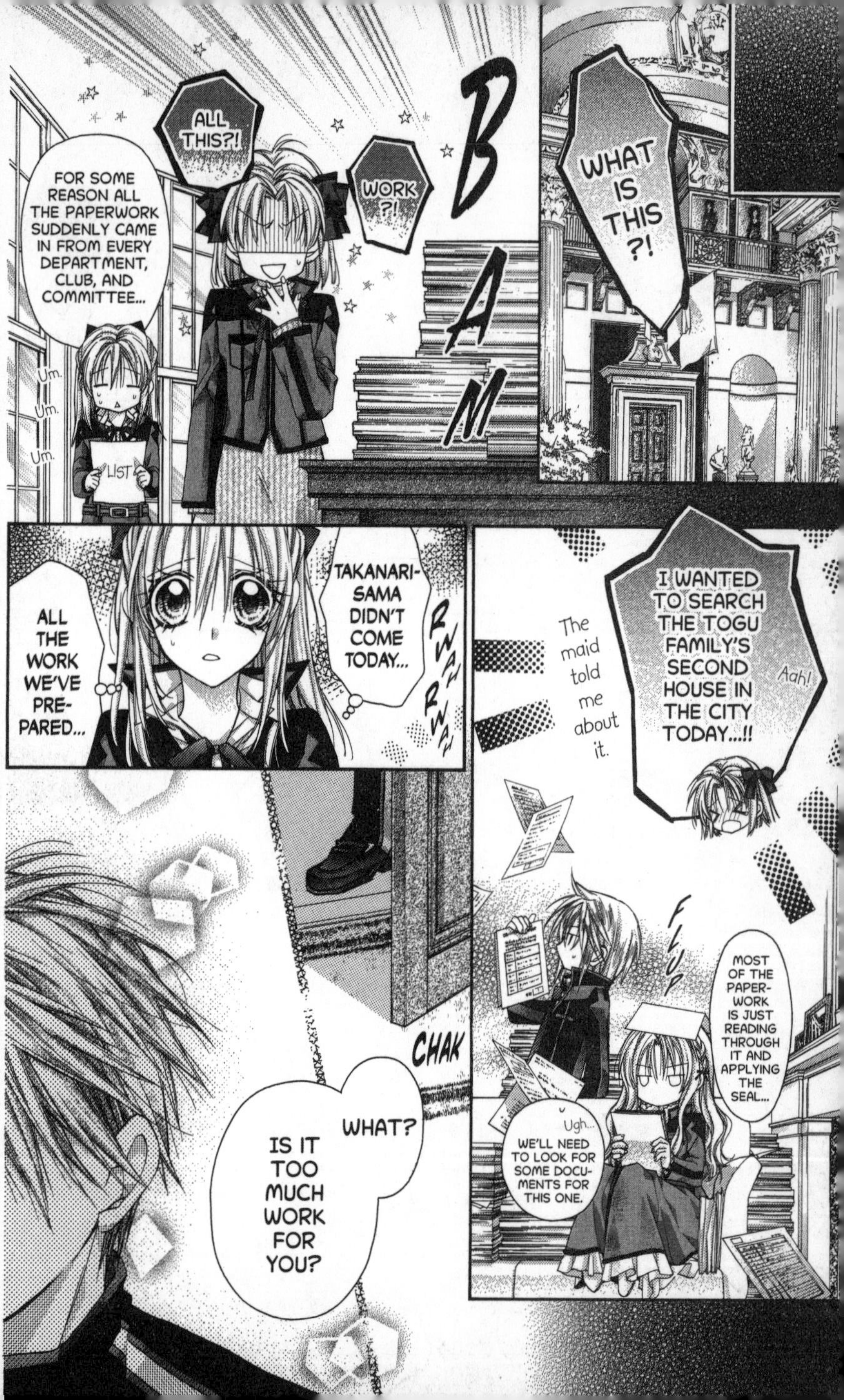
WHAT IS THIS?!
BAM
WORK?!
ALL THIS?!
FOR SOME REASON ALL THE PAPERWORK SUDDENLY CAME IN FROM EVERY DEPARTMENT, CLUB, AND COMMITTEE...
Um.
Um.
Um.
LIST
I WANTED TO SEARCH THE TOGU FAMILY'S SECOND HOUSE IN THE CITY TODAY...!!
Aah!
The maid told me about it.
FLUP
MOST OF THE PAPERWORK IS JUST READING THROUGH IT AND APPLYING THE SEAL...
Ugh...
WE'LL NEED TO LOOK FOR SOME DOCUMENTS FOR THIS ONE.
TAKANARI-SAMA DIDN'T COME TODAY...
RWAH RWAH
ALL THE WORK WE'VE PREPARED...
CHAK
WHAT?
IS IT TOO MUCH WORK FOR YOU?

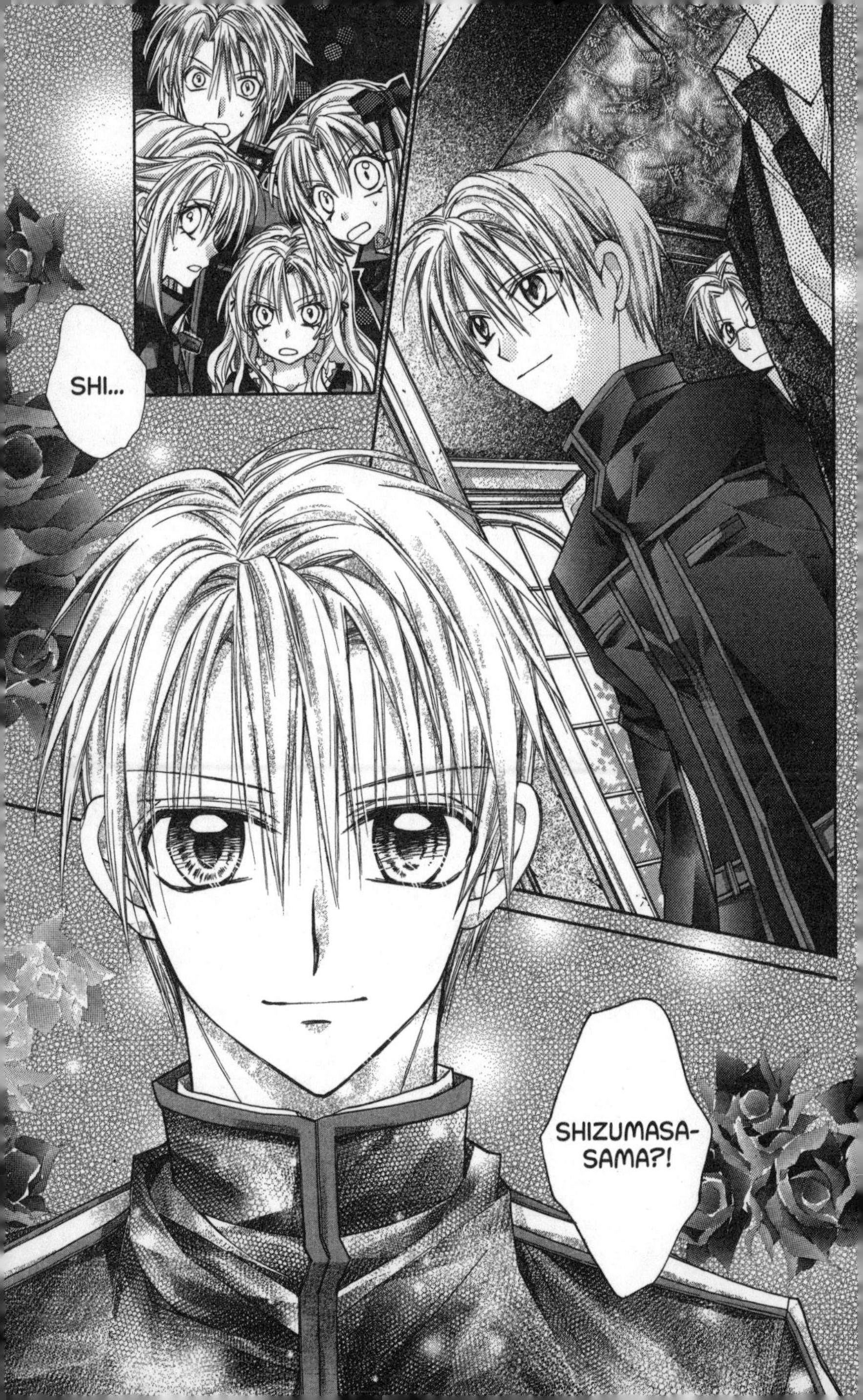
SHI...
SHIZUMASA-SAMA?!

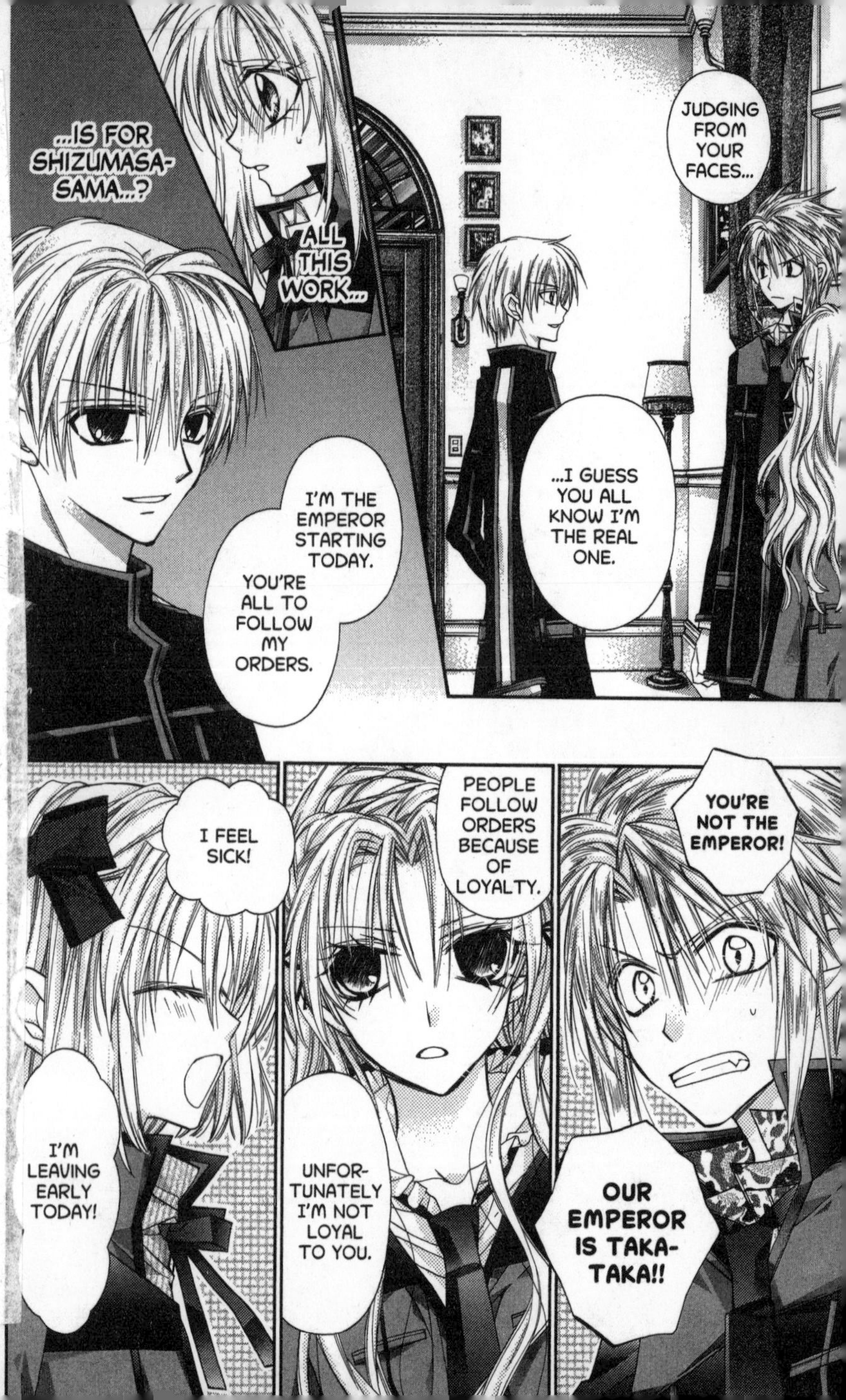
JUDGING FROM YOUR FACES...
...I GUESS YOU ALL KNOW I'M THE REAL ONE.
ALL THIS WORK...
...IS FOR SHIZUMASA-SAMA...?
I'M THE EMPEROR STARTING TODAY.
YOU'RE ALL TO FOLLOW MY ORDERS.
YOU'RE NOT THE EMPEROR!
OUR EMPEROR IS TAKA-TAKA!!
PEOPLE FOLLOW ORDERS BECAUSE OF LOYALTY.
UNFOR-TUNATELY I'M NOT LOYAL TO YOU.
I FEEL SICK!
I'M LEAVING EARLY TODAY!

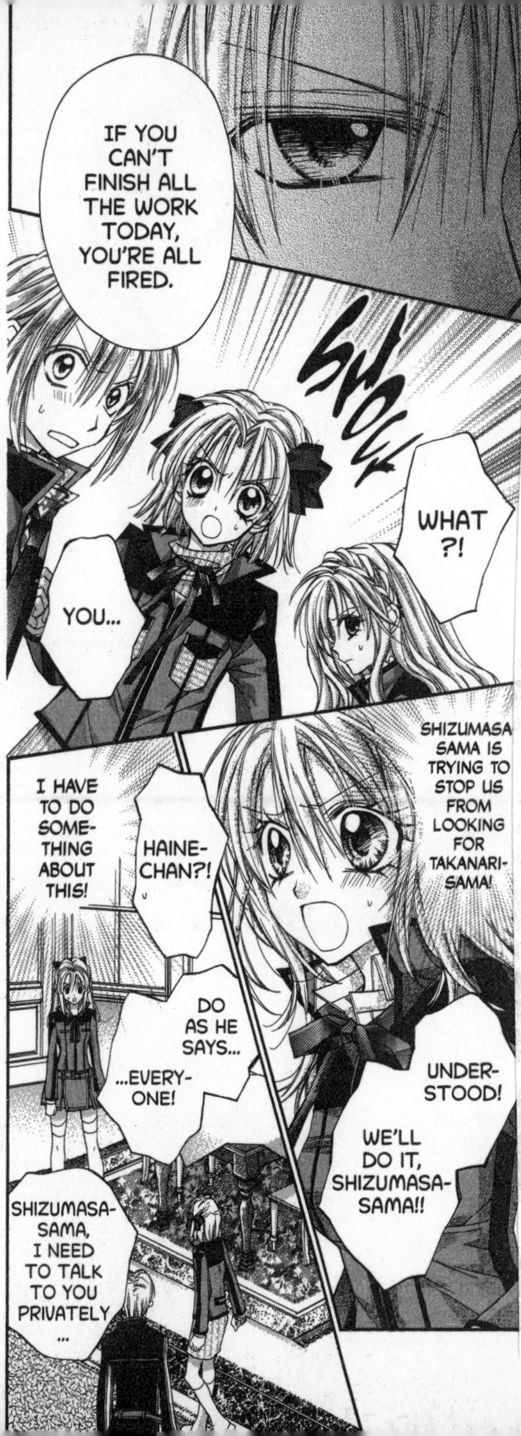
IF YOU CAN'T FINISH ALL THE WORK TODAY, YOU'RE ALL FIRED.
SHOCK
WHAT?!
YOU...
SHIZUMASA SAMA IS TRYING TO STOP US FROM LOOKING FOR TAKANARI-SAMA!
UNDER-STOOD!
WE'LL DO IT, SHIZUMASA-SAMA!!
I HAVE TO DO SOME-THING ABOUT THIS!
HAINE-CHAN?!
DO AS HE SAYS...
...EVERY-ONE!
SHIZUMASA-SAMA, I NEED TO TALK TO YOU PRIVATELY ...

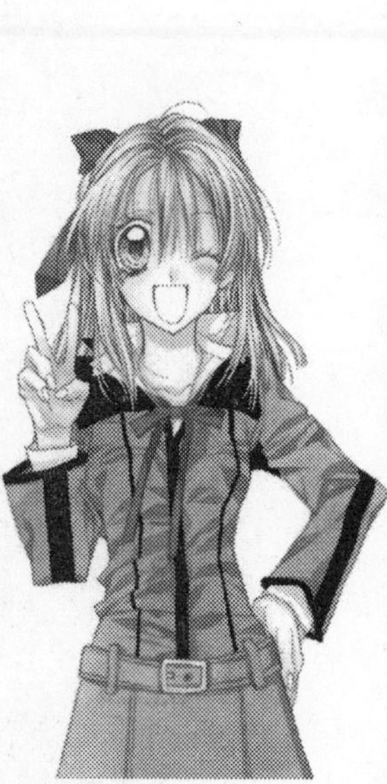

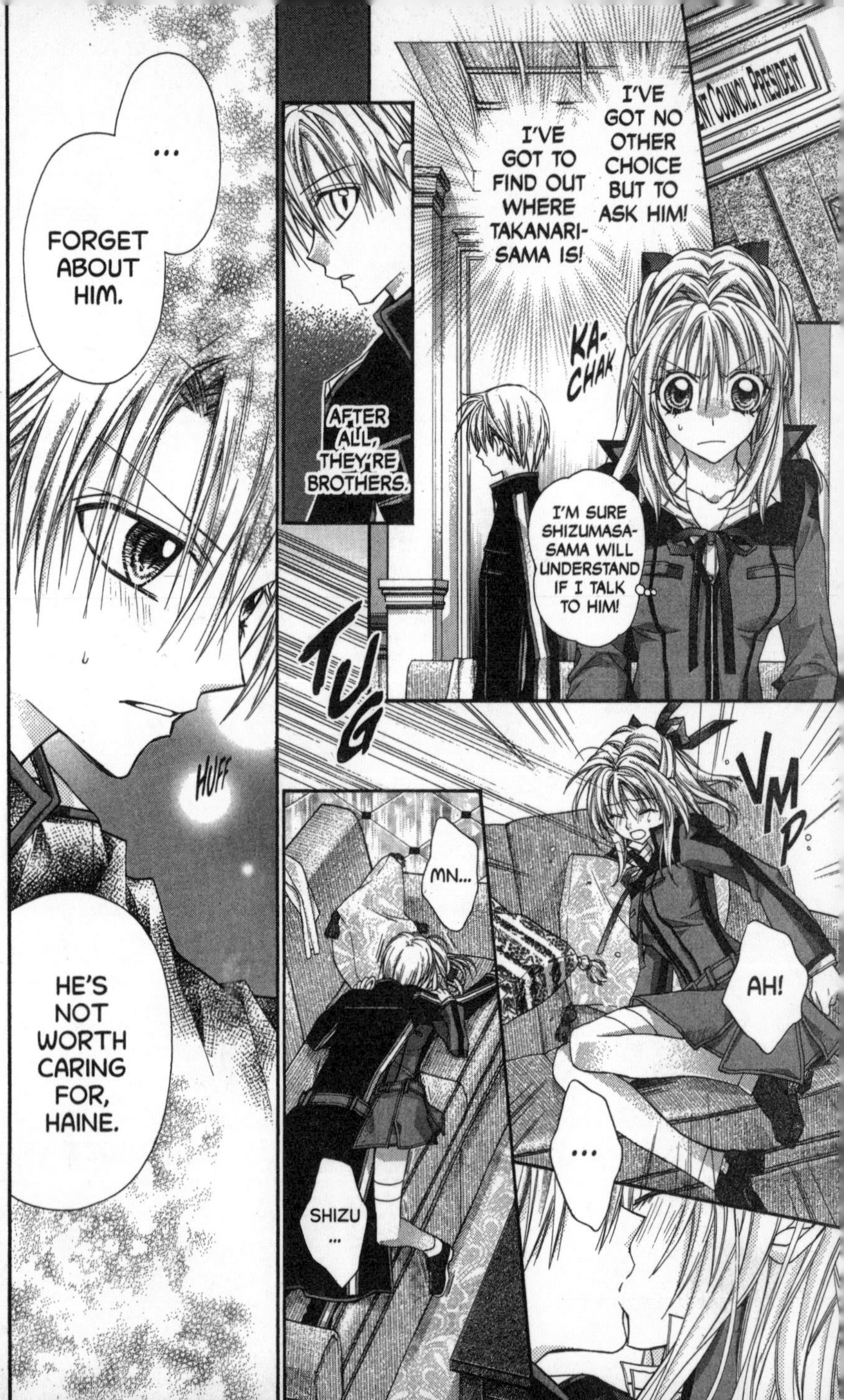
NT COUNCIL PRESIDENT
I'VE GOT NO OTHER CHOICE BUT TO ASK HIM!
I'VE GOT TO FIND OUT WHERE TAKANARI-SAMA IS!
KA-CHAK
I'M SURE SHIZUMASA-SAMA WILL UNDERSTAND IF I TALK TO HIM!
AFTER ALL, THEY'RE BROTHERS.
TUG
VMP
AH!
...
MN...
SHIZU...
...
FORGET ABOUT HIM.
HUFF
HE'S NOT WORTH CARING FOR, HAINE.

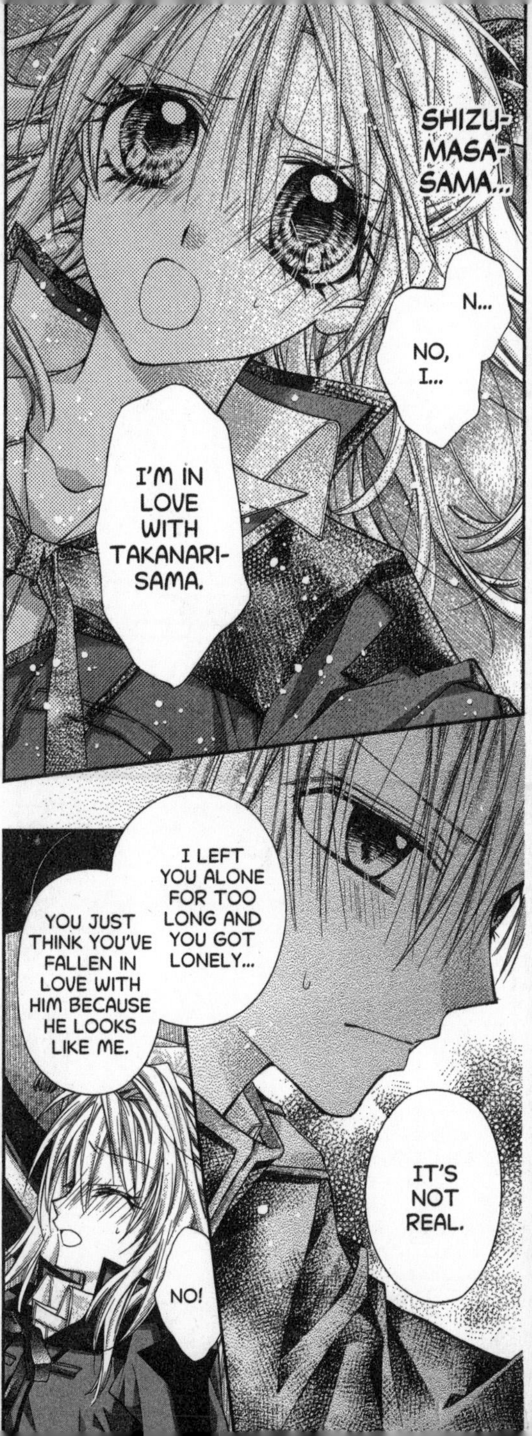
SHIZU-MASA-SAMA...
N...
NO, I...
I'M IN LOVE WITH TAKANARI-SAMA.
I LEFT YOU ALONE FOR TOO LONG AND YOU GOT LONELY...
YOU JUST THINK YOU'VE FALLEN IN LOVE WITH HIM BECAUSE HE LOOKS LIKE ME.
IT'S NOT REAL.
NO!

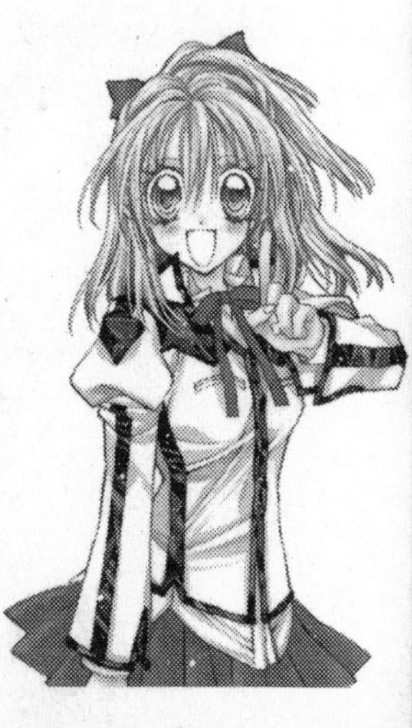

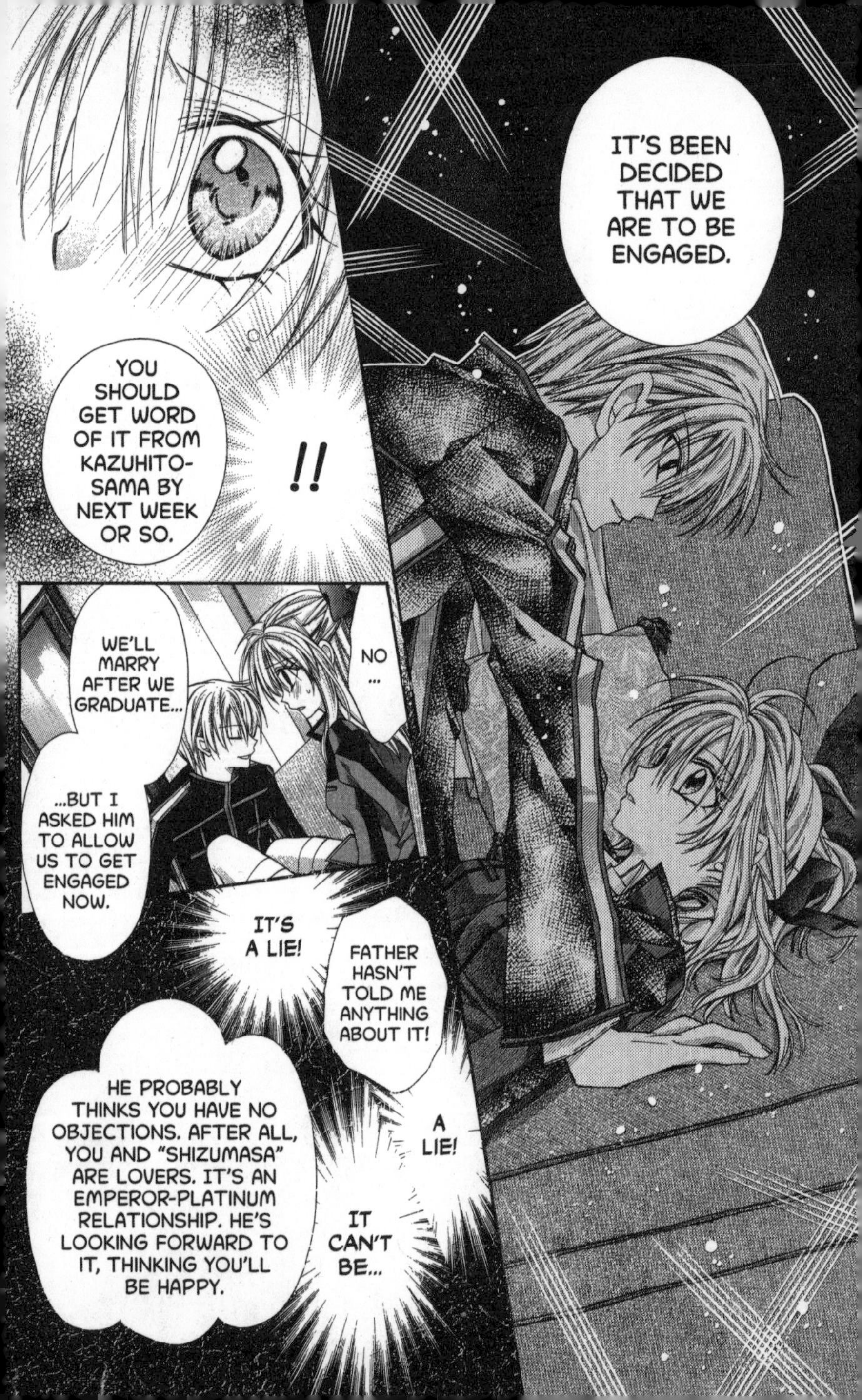
IT'S BEEN DECIDED THAT WE ARE TO BE ENGAGED.
YOU SHOULD GET WORD OF IT FROM KAZUHITO-SAMA BY NEXT WEEK OR SO.
!!
NO...
WE'LL MARRY AFTER WE GRADUATE...
...BUT I ASKED HIM TO ALLOW US TO GET ENGAGED NOW.
IT'S A LIE!
FATHER HASN'T TOLD ME ANYTHING ABOUT IT!
A LIE!
HE PROBABLY THINKS YOU HAVE NO OBJECTIONS. AFTER ALL, YOU AND "SHIZUMASA" ARE LOVERS. IT'S AN EMPEROR-PLATINUM RELATIONSHIP. HE'S LOOKING FORWARD TO IT, THINKING YOU'LL BE HAPPY.
IT CAN'T BE...

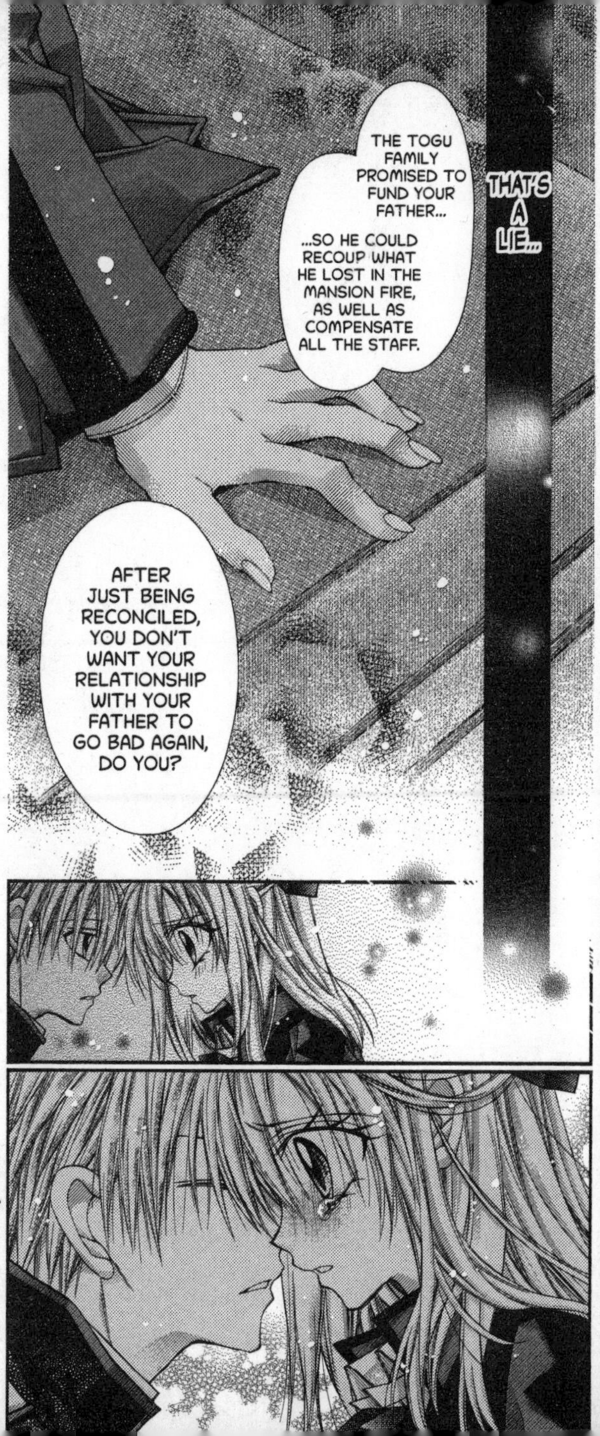
THAT'S A LIE...
THE TOGU FAMILY PROMISED TO FUND YOUR FATHER...
...SO HE COULD RECOUP WHAT HE LOST IN THE MANSION FIRE, AS WELL AS COMPENSATE ALL THE STAFF.
AFTER JUST BEING RECONCILED, YOU DON'T WANT YOUR RELATIONSHIP WITH YOUR FATHER TO GO BAD AGAIN, DO YOU?

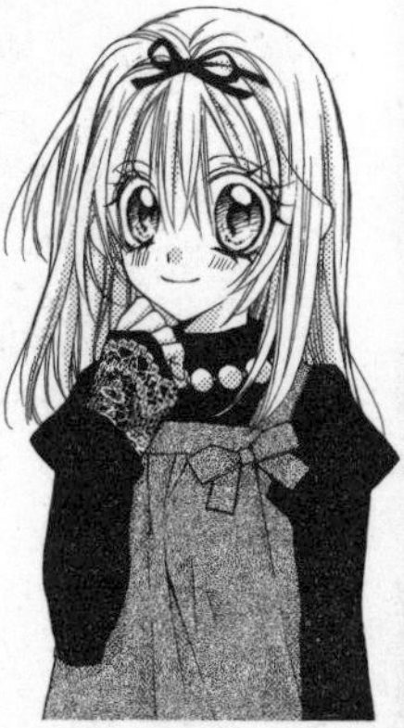

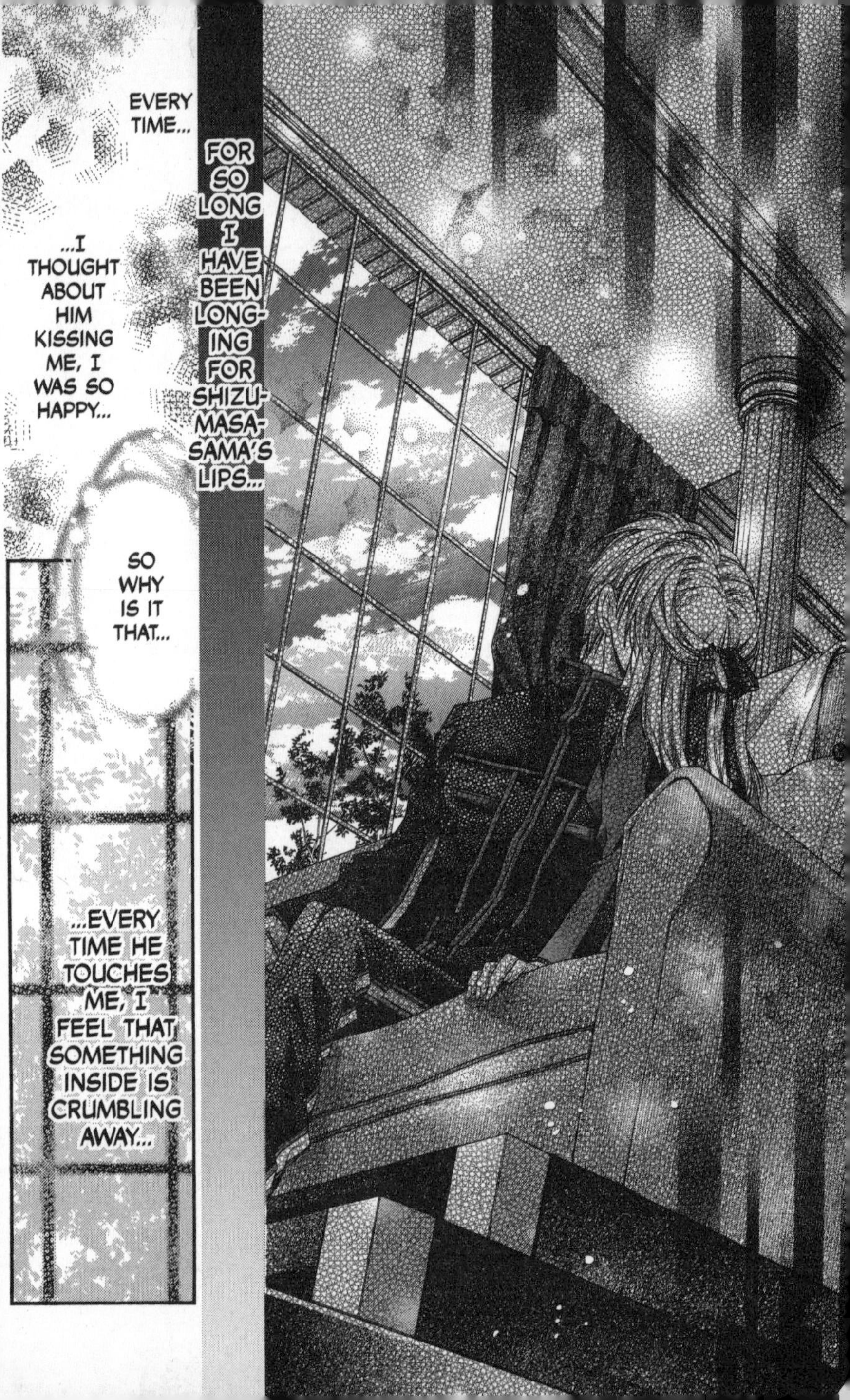
FOR SO LONG I HAVE BEEN LONG-ING FOR SHIZU-MASA-SAMA'S LIPS...
EVERY TIME...
...I THOUGHT ABOUT HIM KISSING ME, I WAS SO HAPPY...
SO WHY IS IT THAT...
...EVERY TIME HE TOUCHES ME, I FEEL THAT SOMETHING INSIDE IS CRUMBLING AWAY...

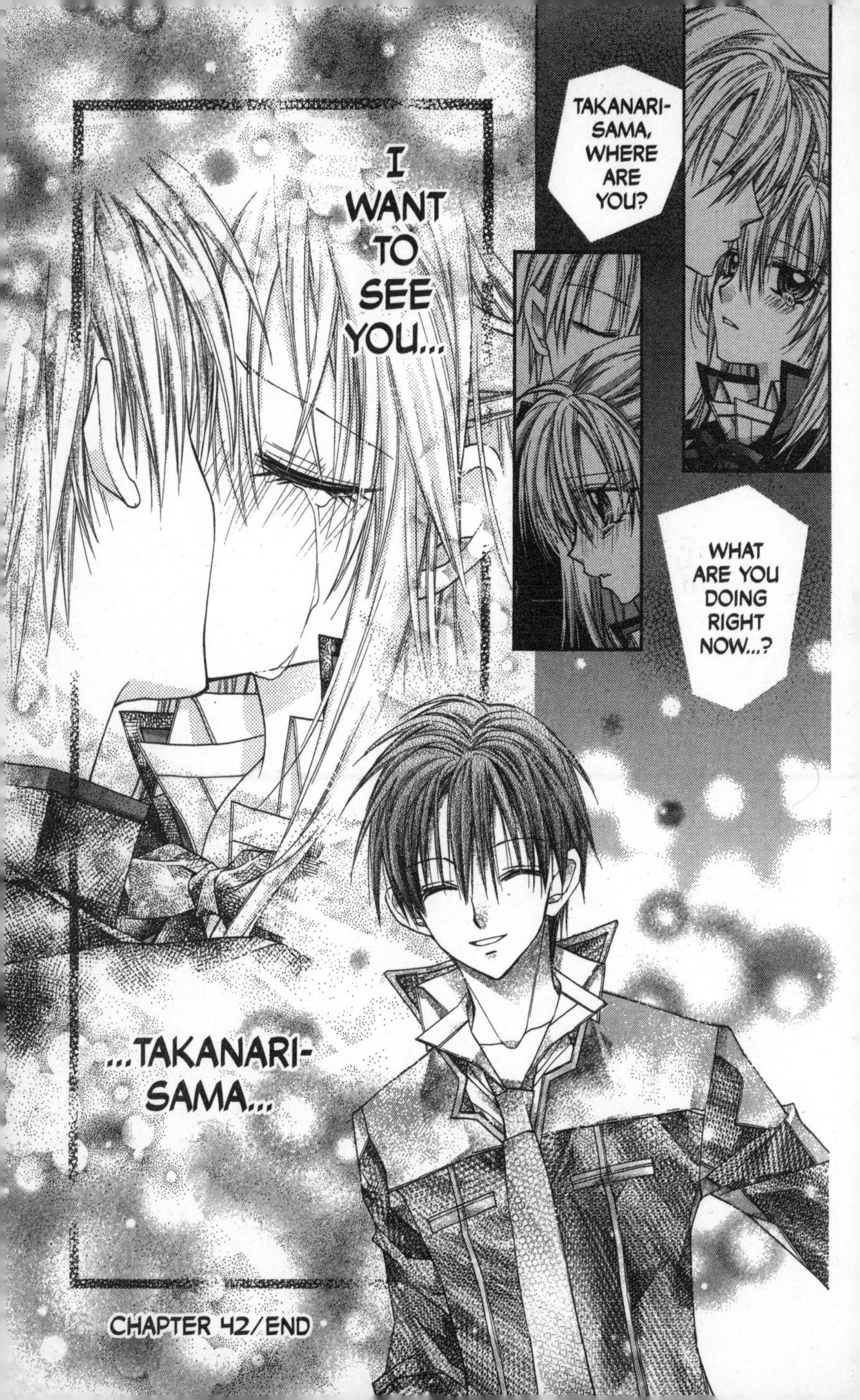
TAKANARI-SAMA, WHERE ARE YOU?
WHAT ARE YOU DOING RIGHT NOW...?
I WANT TO SEE YOU...
...TAKANARI-SAMA...

CHAPTER 42/END

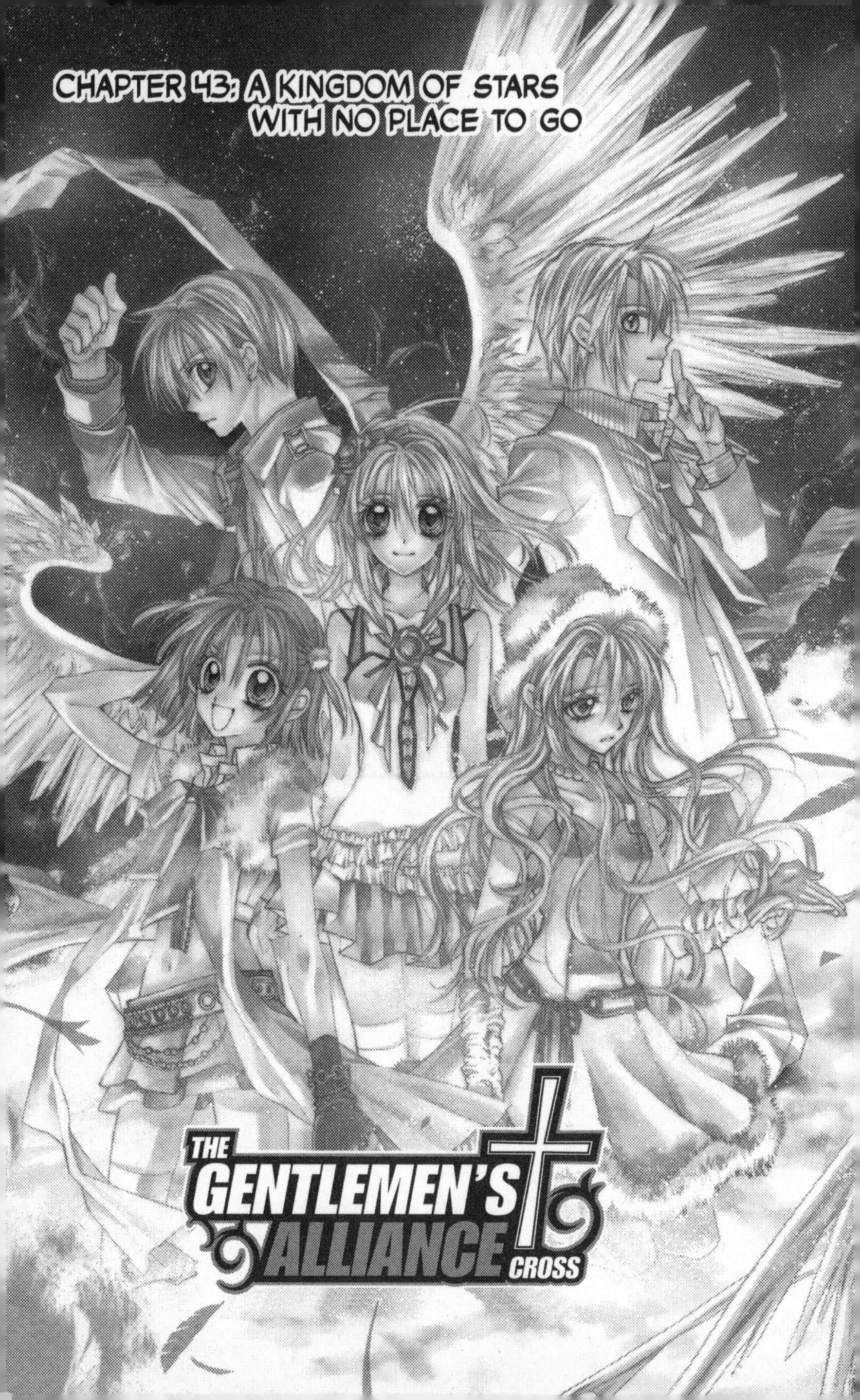
CHAPTER 43: A KINGDOM OF STARS WITH NO PLACE TO GO
THE GENTLEMEN'S ALLIANCE CROSS

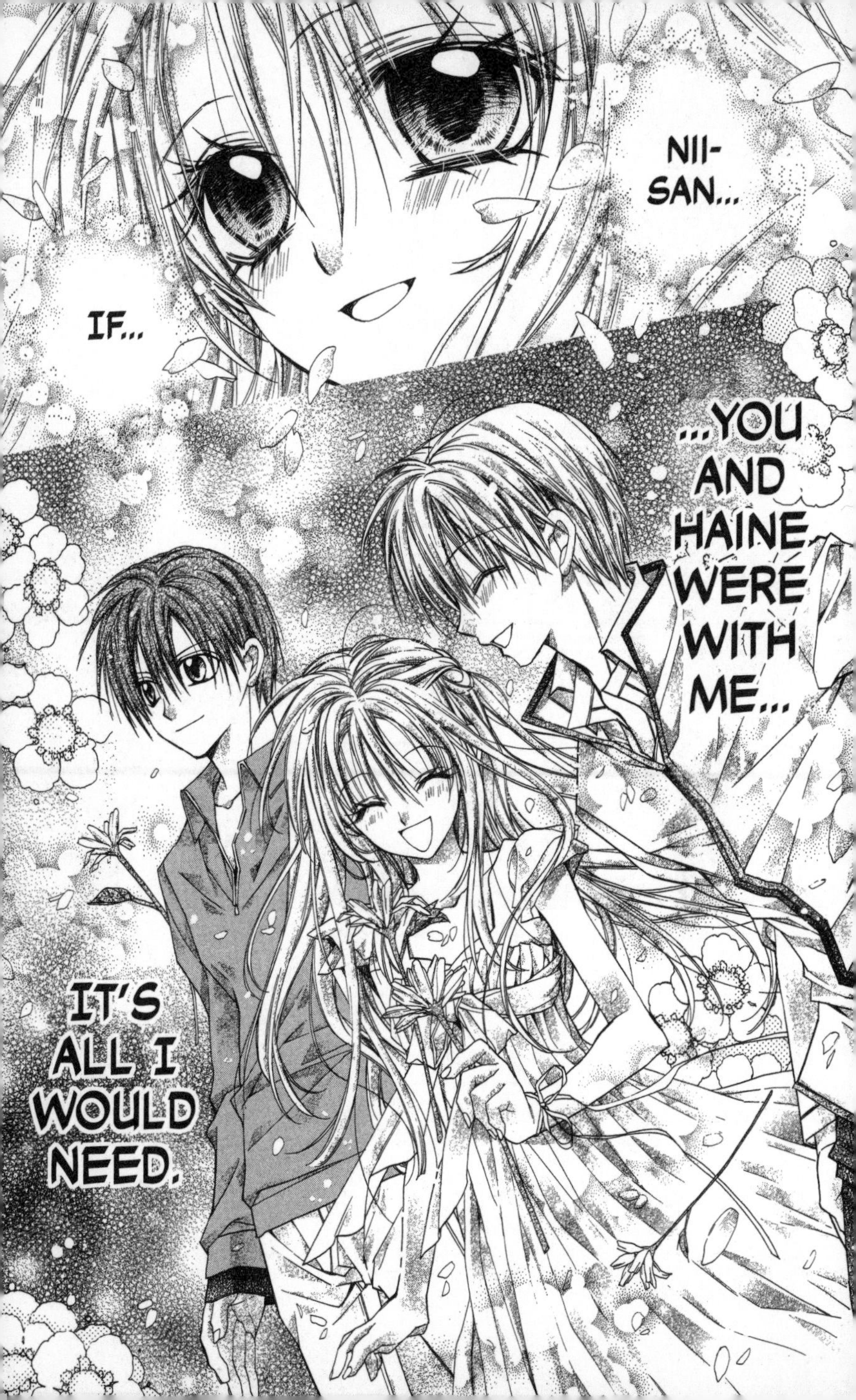
NII-SAN...
IF...
...YOU AND HAINE WERE WITH ME...
IT'S ALL I WOULD NEED.

Chapter 43: A Kingdom of Stars with No Place to Go [Lead-in] Ask someone someday... ...what your value is...

※ I'm giving away the story.

The title is obviously in reference to Shizumasa-sama. This chapter was very popular in the magazine. (Even though Haine-chan was hardly in it!)

It was fun to draw the young twins when they got along with each other. Takanari has the "big brother" image, and Shizumasa seems to be a lot more active now?!

They were still kids, so I guess they didn't know how to convey their feelings to each other. They actually respect each other... Tough, isn't it?

In the fourth panel on page 129, I tried to reproduce the "eye" Takanari had when he was reunited with Shizumasa after the accident for the "Of course I do."

I got many responses like "So Shizumasa-sama was a nice person after all!" but I'm not too sure about that... ᵕᵕ?? He abandoned his big brother, you know...??? ᵕᵕ You're the nice person for being able to forgive him for doing something like that!

Well, he's been regretting it all this time. Hmm. ᵕ But I think it's a bit too self-centered to be fretting over something like this by yourself?? ᵕᵕ You know? There's no reason to go to the grave with it! I'm sure the others will understand!

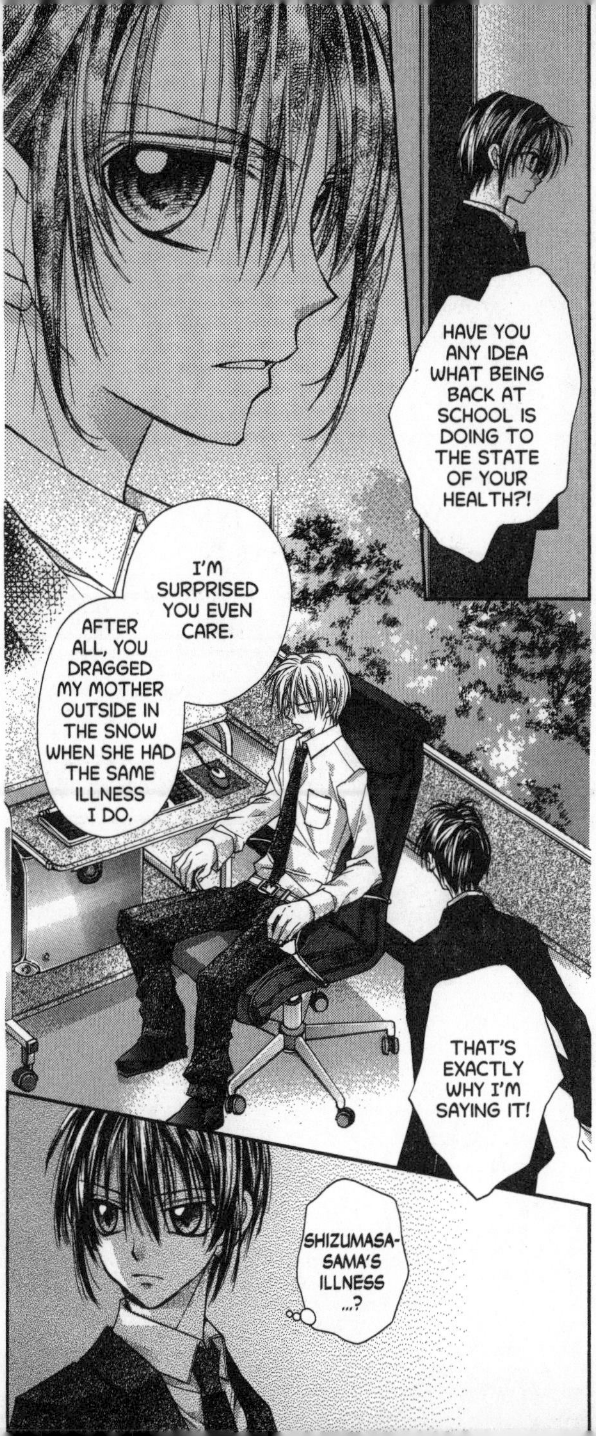
HAVE YOU ANY IDEA WHAT BEING BACK AT SCHOOL IS DOING TO THE STATE OF YOUR HEALTH?!
I'M SURPRISED YOU EVEN CARE.
AFTER ALL, YOU DRAGGED MY MOTHER OUTSIDE IN THE SNOW WHEN SHE HAD THE SAME ILLNESS I DO.
THAT'S EXACTLY WHY I'M SAYING IT!
SHIZUMASA-SAMA'S ILLNESS ...?

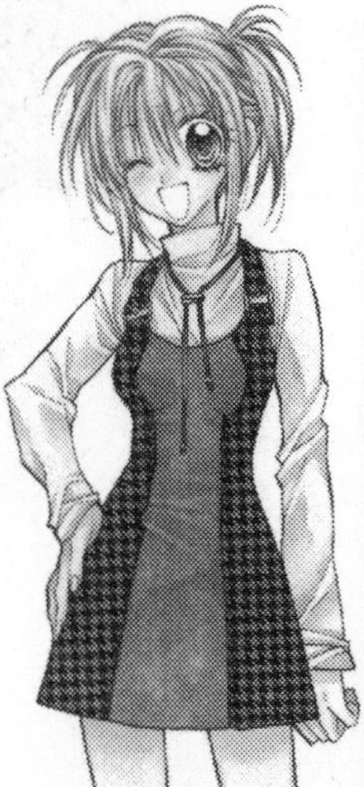

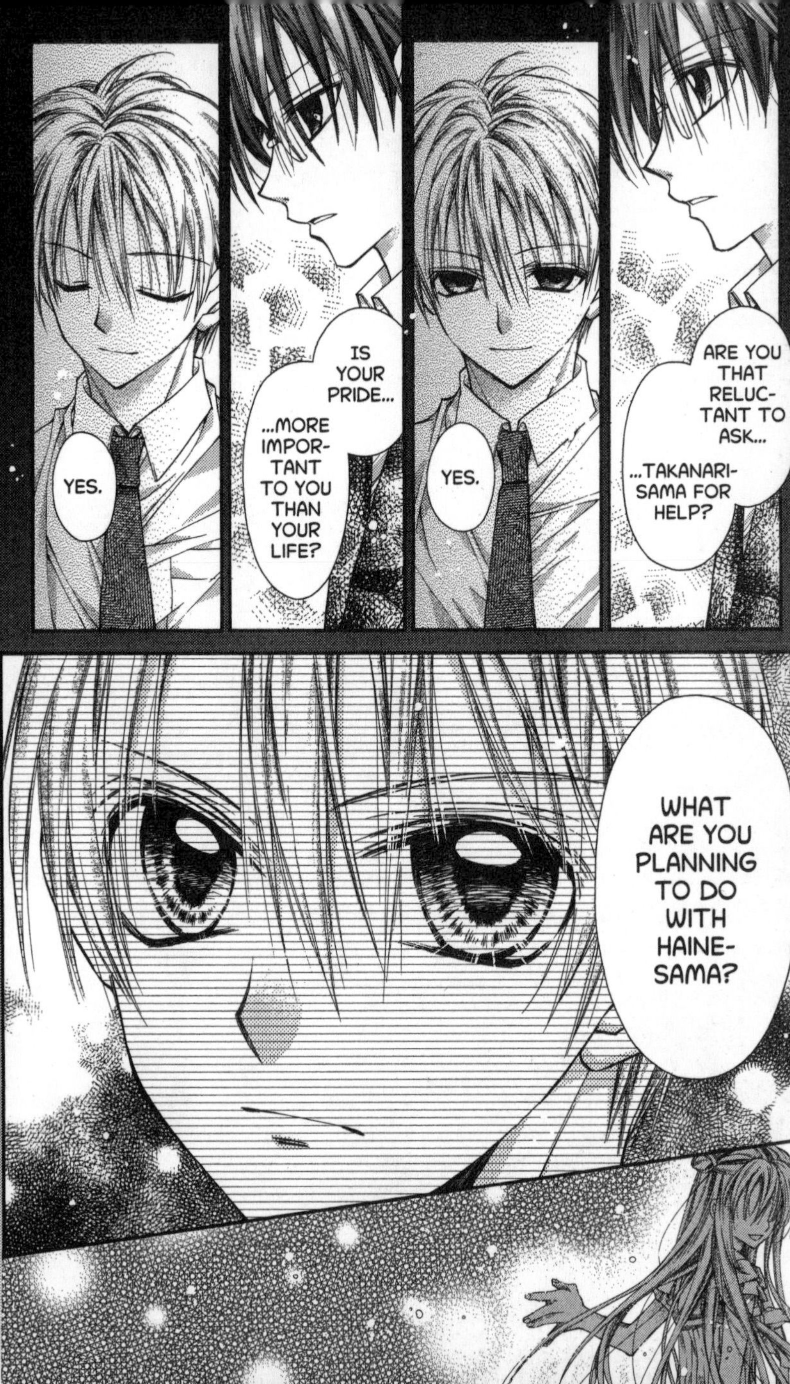
ARE YOU THAT RELUCTANT TO ASK...
...TAKANARI-SAMA FOR HELP?
YES.
IS YOUR PRIDE...
...MORE IMPORTANT TO YOU THAN YOUR LIFE?
YES.
WHAT ARE YOU PLANNING TO DO WITH HAINE-SAMA?

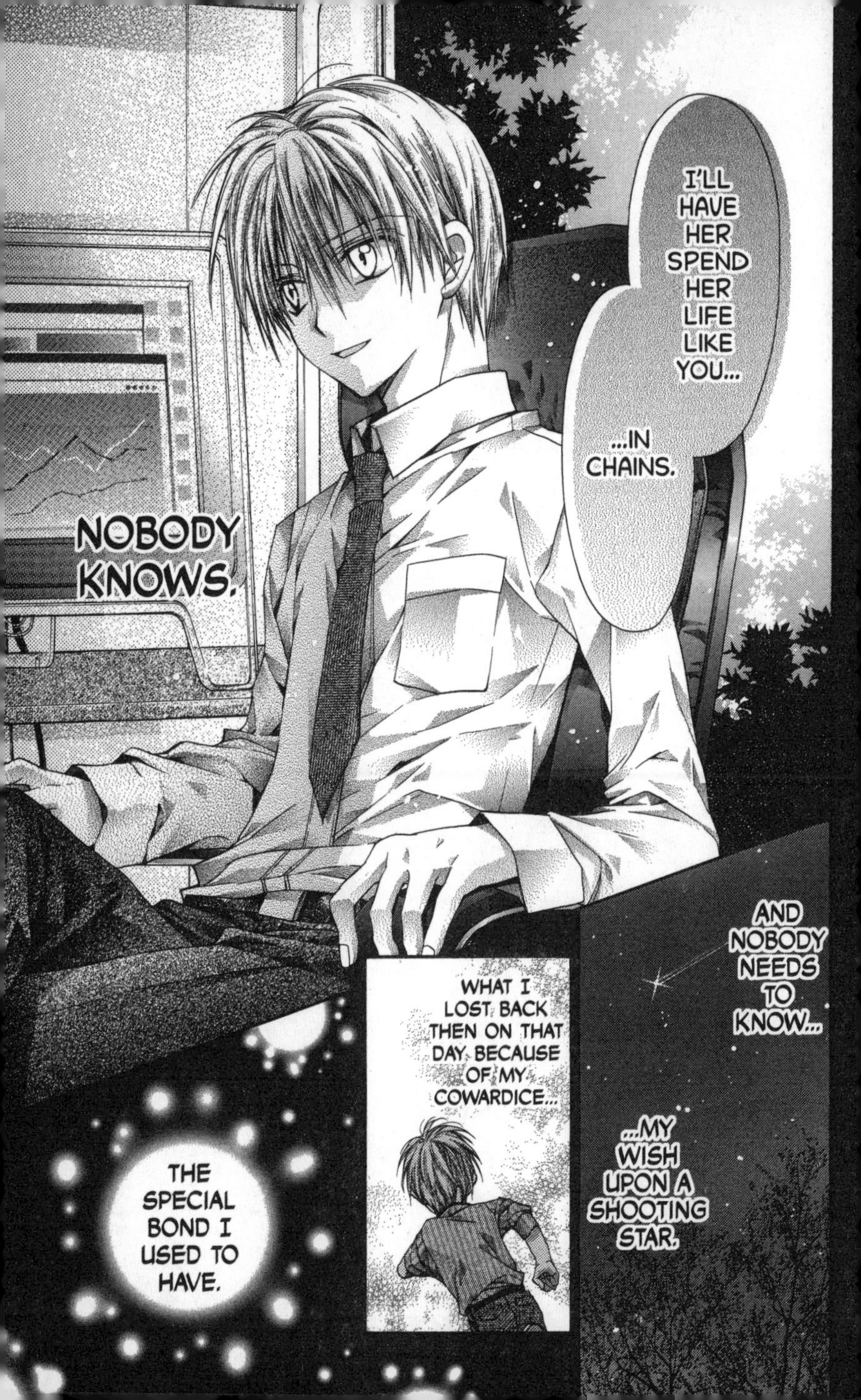
I'LL HAVE HER SPEND HER LIFE LIKE YOU...
...IN CHAINS.
NOBODY KNOWS.
AND NOBODY NEEDS TO KNOW...
...MY WISH UPON A SHOOTING STAR.
WHAT I LOST BACK THEN ON THAT DAY BECAUSE OF MY COWARDICE...
THE SPECIAL BOND I USED TO HAVE.

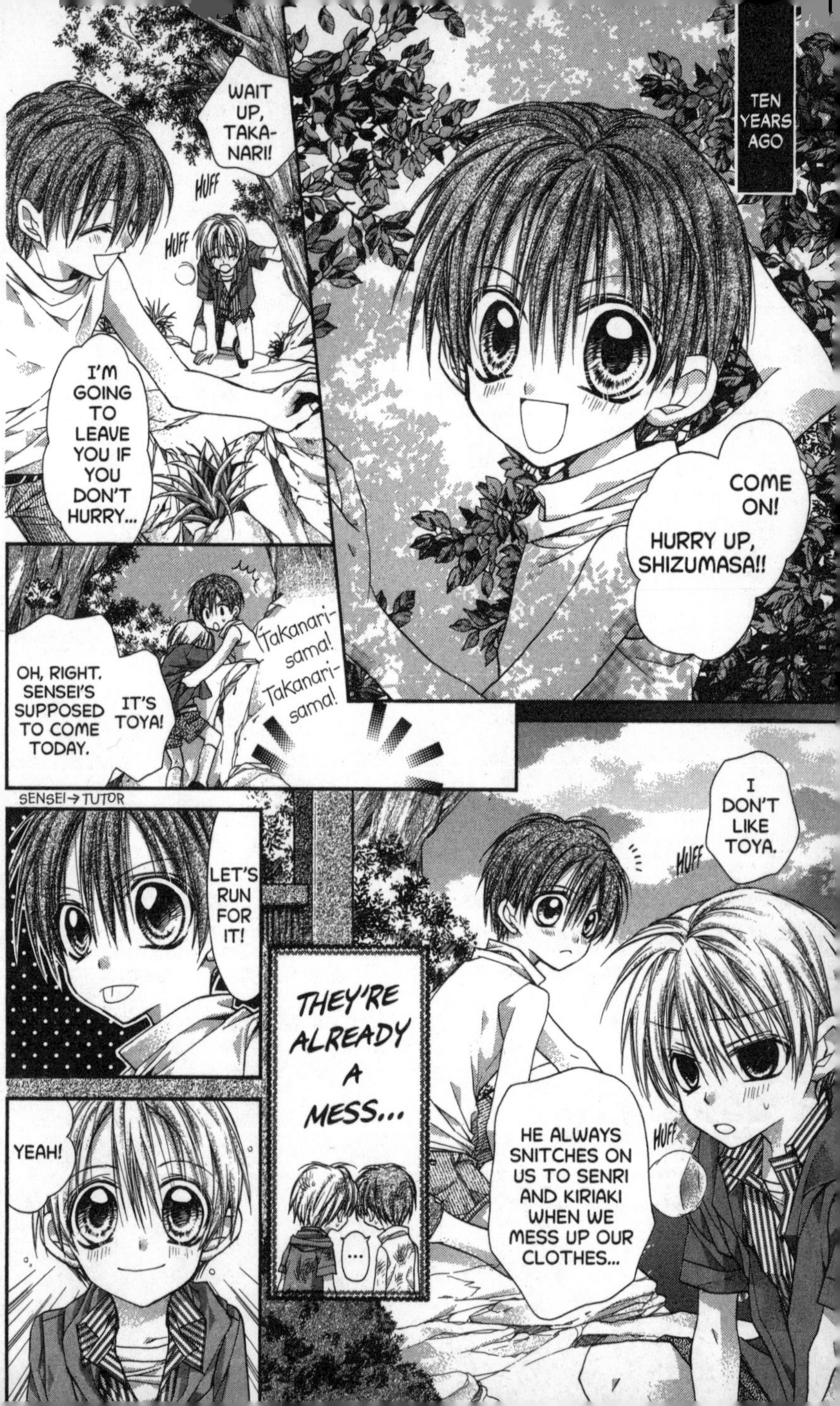
TEN YEARS AGO
COME ON!
HURRY UP, SHIZUMASA!!
WAIT UP, TAKA-NARI!
HUFF
HUFF
I'M GOING TO LEAVE YOU IF YOU DON'T HURRY...
Takanari-sama! Takanari-sama!
IT'S TOYA!
OH, RIGHT. SENSEI'S SUPPOSED TO COME TODAY.
SENSEI→TUTOR
I DON'T LIKE TOYA.
HUFF
HUFF
HE ALWAYS SNITCHES ON US TO SENRI AND KIRIAKI WHEN WE MESS UP OUR CLOTHES...
THEY'RE ALREADY A MESS...
...
LET'S RUN FOR IT!
YEAH!

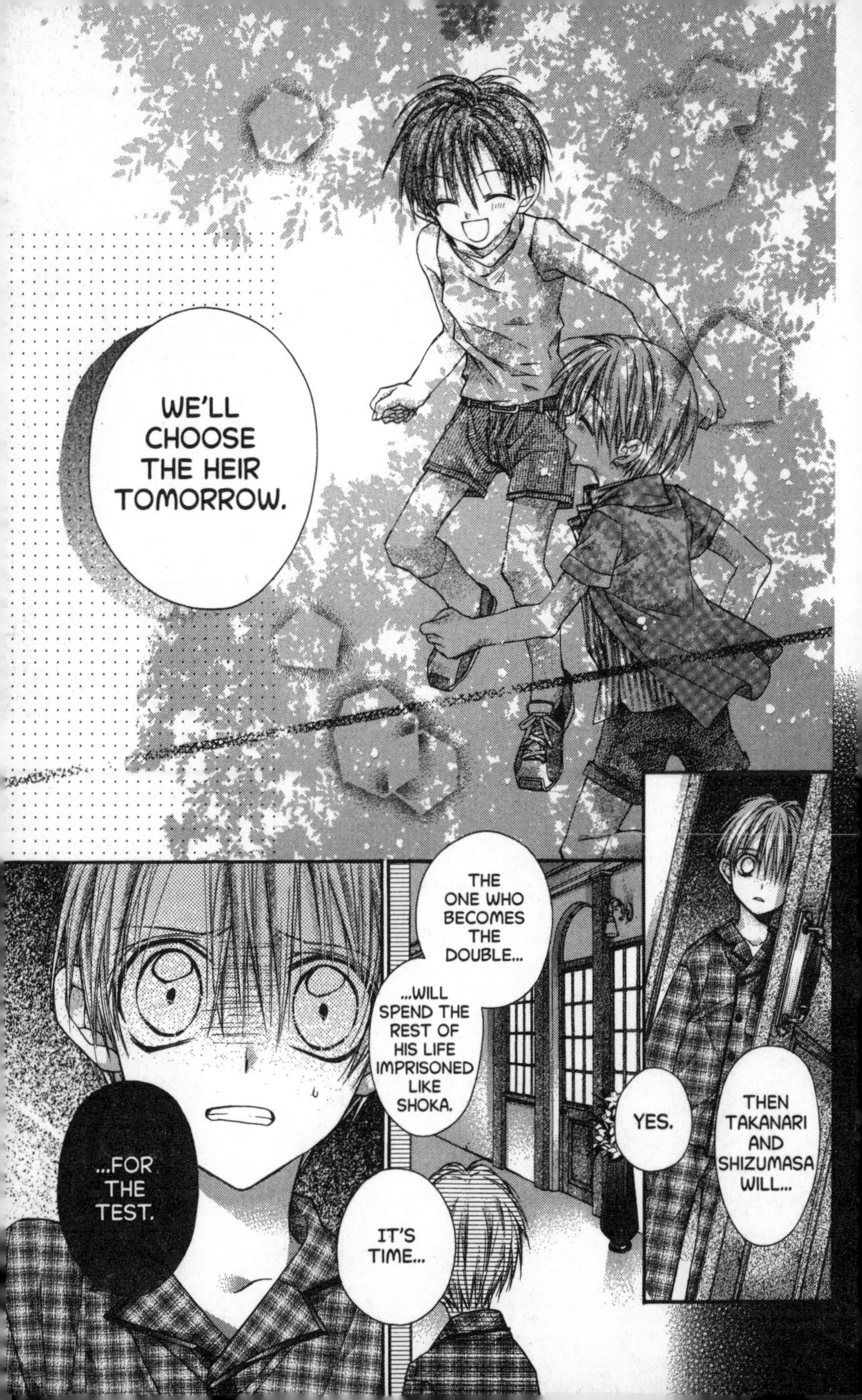
WE'LL CHOOSE THE HEIR TOMORROW.
THEN TAKANARI AND SHIZUMASA WILL...
YES.
THE ONE WHO BECOMES THE DOUBLE...
...WILL SPEND THE REST OF HIS LIFE IMPRISONED LIKE SHOKA.
IT'S TIME...
...FOR THE TEST.

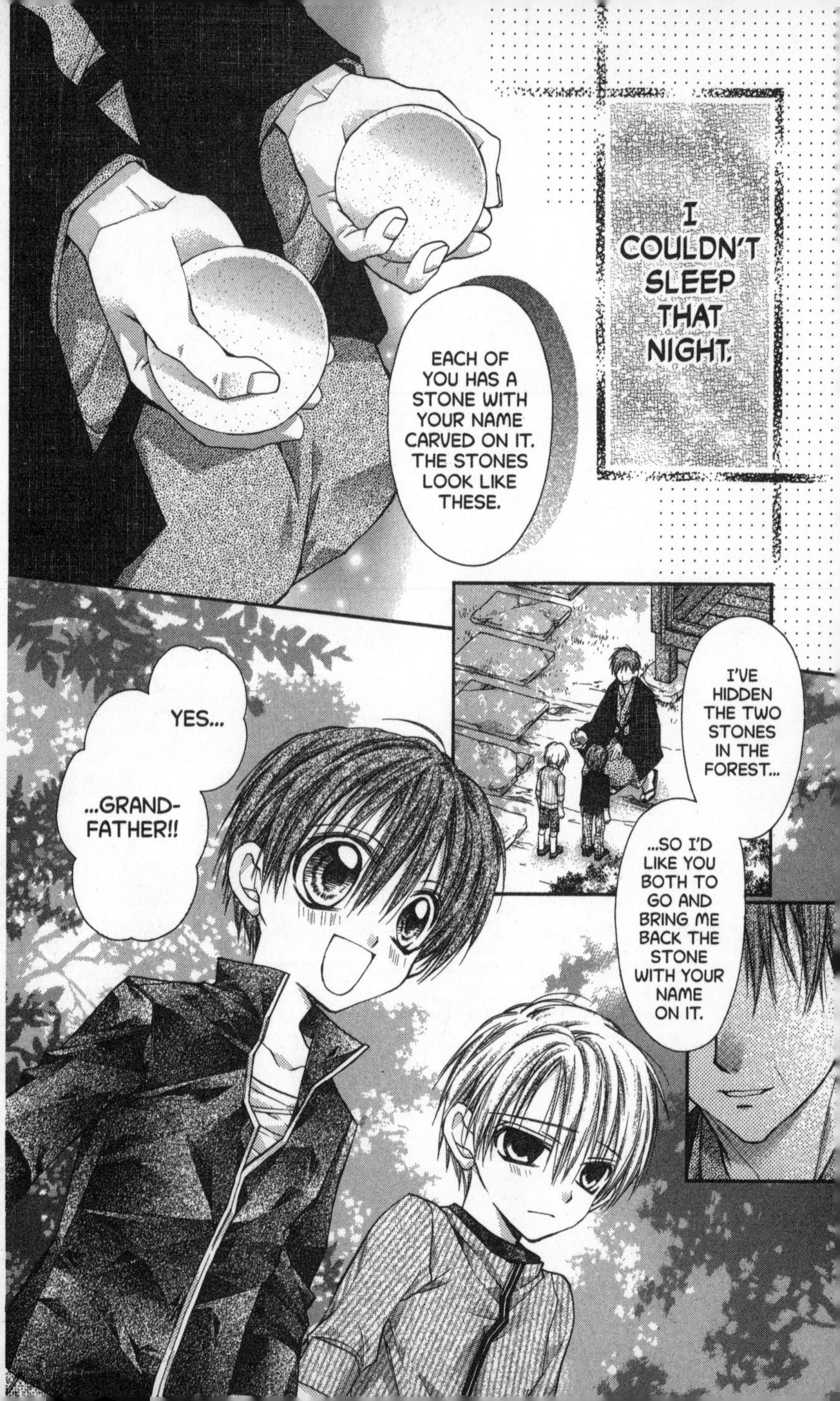
I COULDN'T SLEEP THAT NIGHT.
EACH OF YOU HAS A STONE WITH YOUR NAME CARVED ON IT. THE STONES LOOK LIKE THESE.
I'VE HIDDEN THE TWO STONES IN THE FOREST...
...SO I'D LIKE YOU BOTH TO GO AND BRING ME BACK THE STONE WITH YOUR NAME ON IT.
YES...
...GRAND-FATHER!!

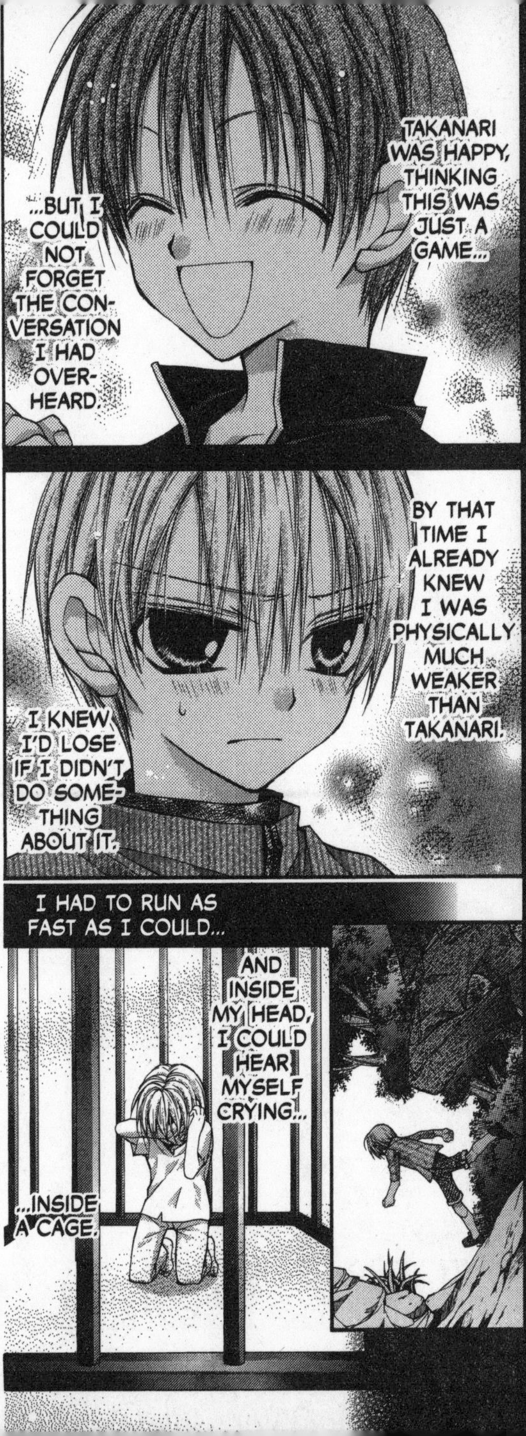
TAKANARI WAS HAPPY, THINKING THIS WAS JUST A GAME...
...BUT I COULD NOT FORGET THE CON-VERSATION I HAD OVER-HEARD.
BY THAT TIME I ALREADY KNEW I WAS PHYSICALLY MUCH WEAKER THAN TAKANARI.
I KNEW I'D LOSE IF I DIDN'T DO SOME-THING ABOUT IT.
I HAD TO RUN AS FAST AS I COULD...
AND INSIDE MY HEAD, I COULD HEAR MYSELF CRYING...
...INSIDE A CAGE.
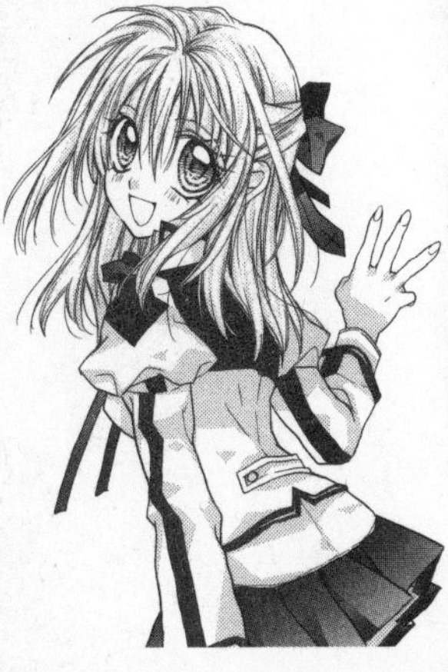

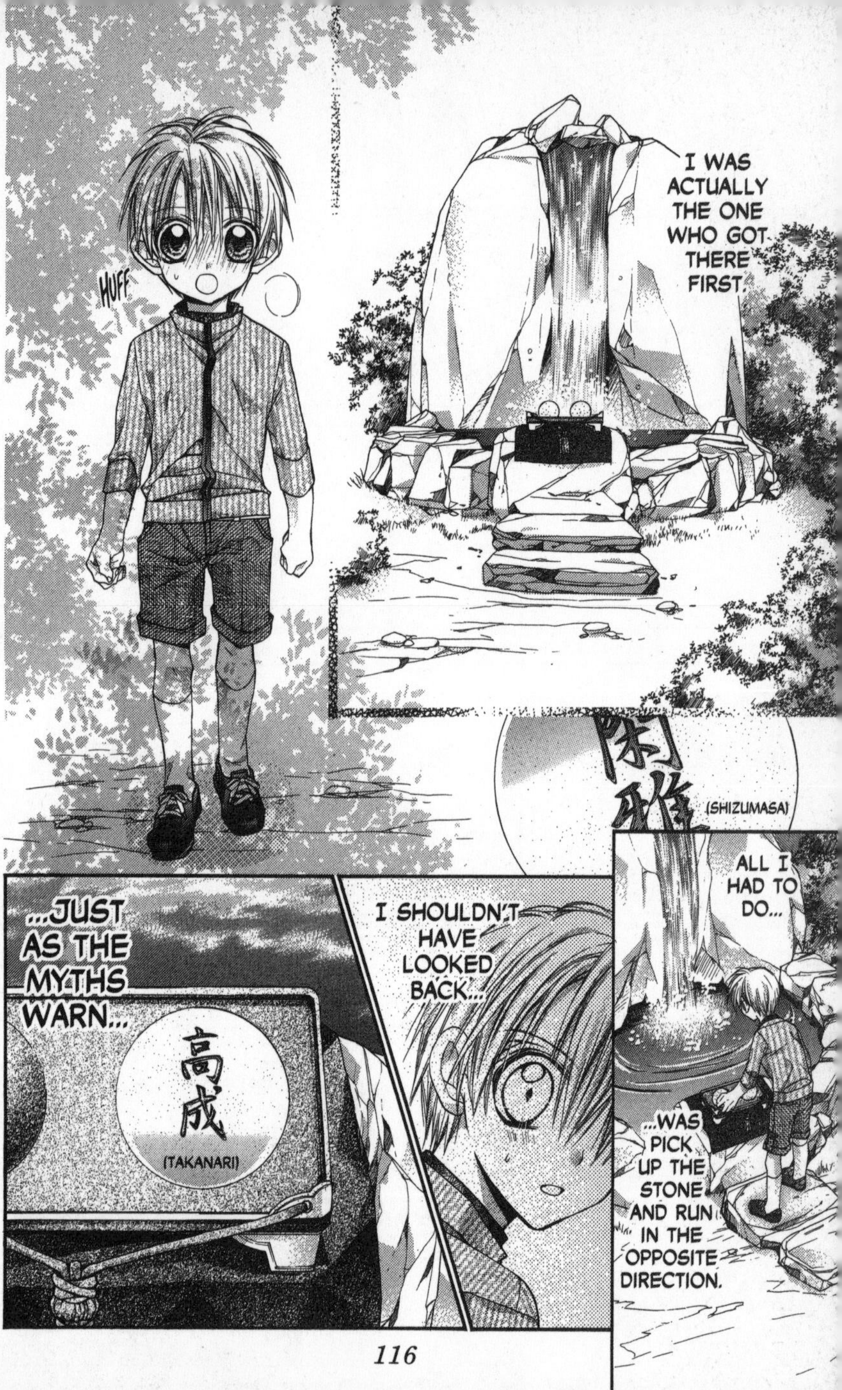
I WAS ACTUALLY THE ONE WHO GOT THERE FIRST.
HUFF
(SHIZUMASA)
ALL I HAD TO DO...
...WAS PICK UP THE STONE AND RUN IN THE OPPOSITE DIRECTION.
I SHOULDN'T HAVE LOOKED BACK...
...JUST AS THE MYTHS WARN...
高成
(TAKANARI)

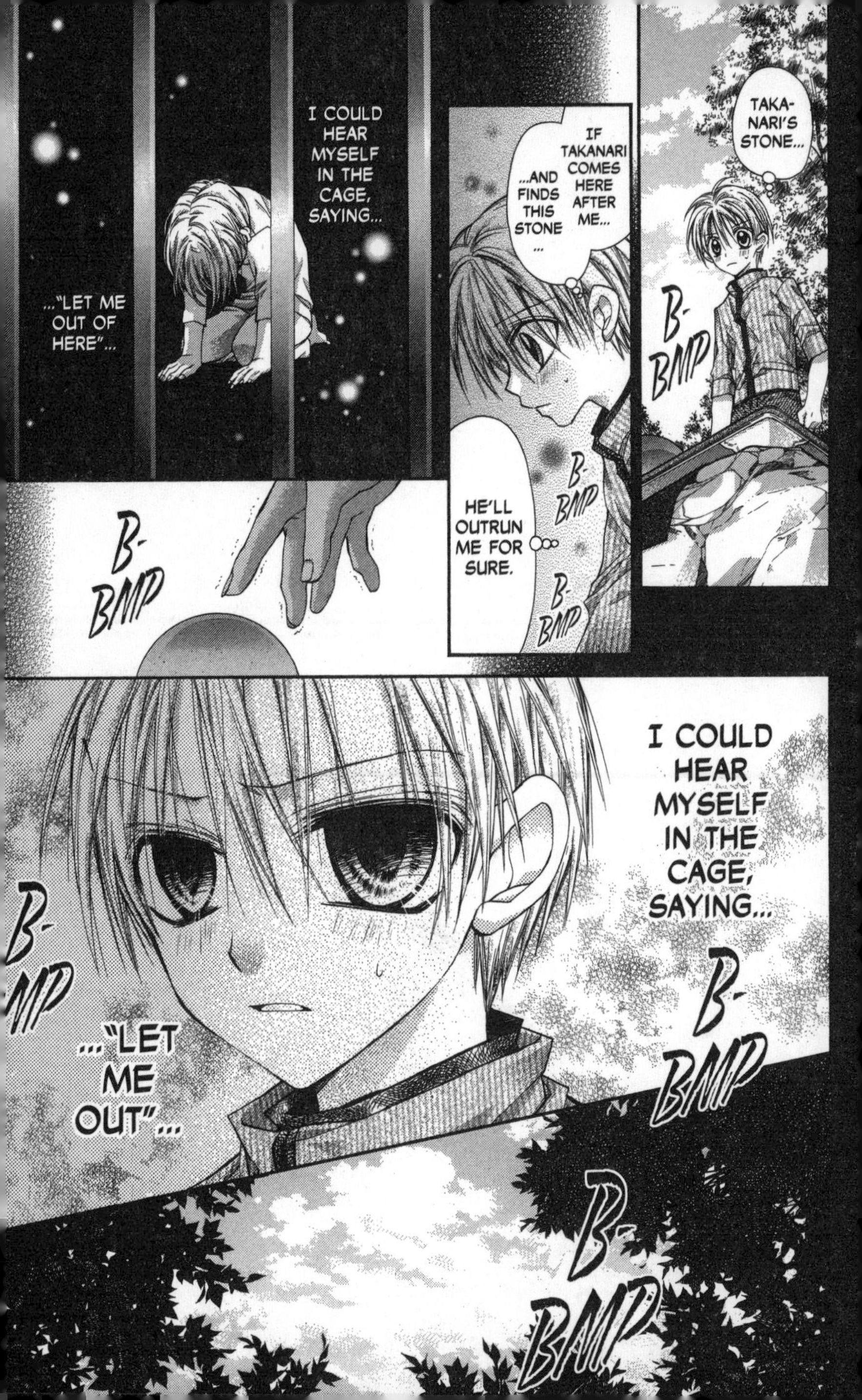
TAKA-NARI'S STONE...
B-BMP
IF TAKANARI COMES HERE AFTER ME...
...AND FINDS THIS STONE...
HE'LL OUTRUN ME FOR SURE.
B-BMP
B-BMP
I COULD HEAR MYSELF IN THE CAGE, SAYING...
..."LET ME OUT OF HERE"...
B-BMP
I COULD HEAR MYSELF IN THE CAGE, SAYING...
B-BMP
..."LET ME OUT"...
B-BMP
B-BMP

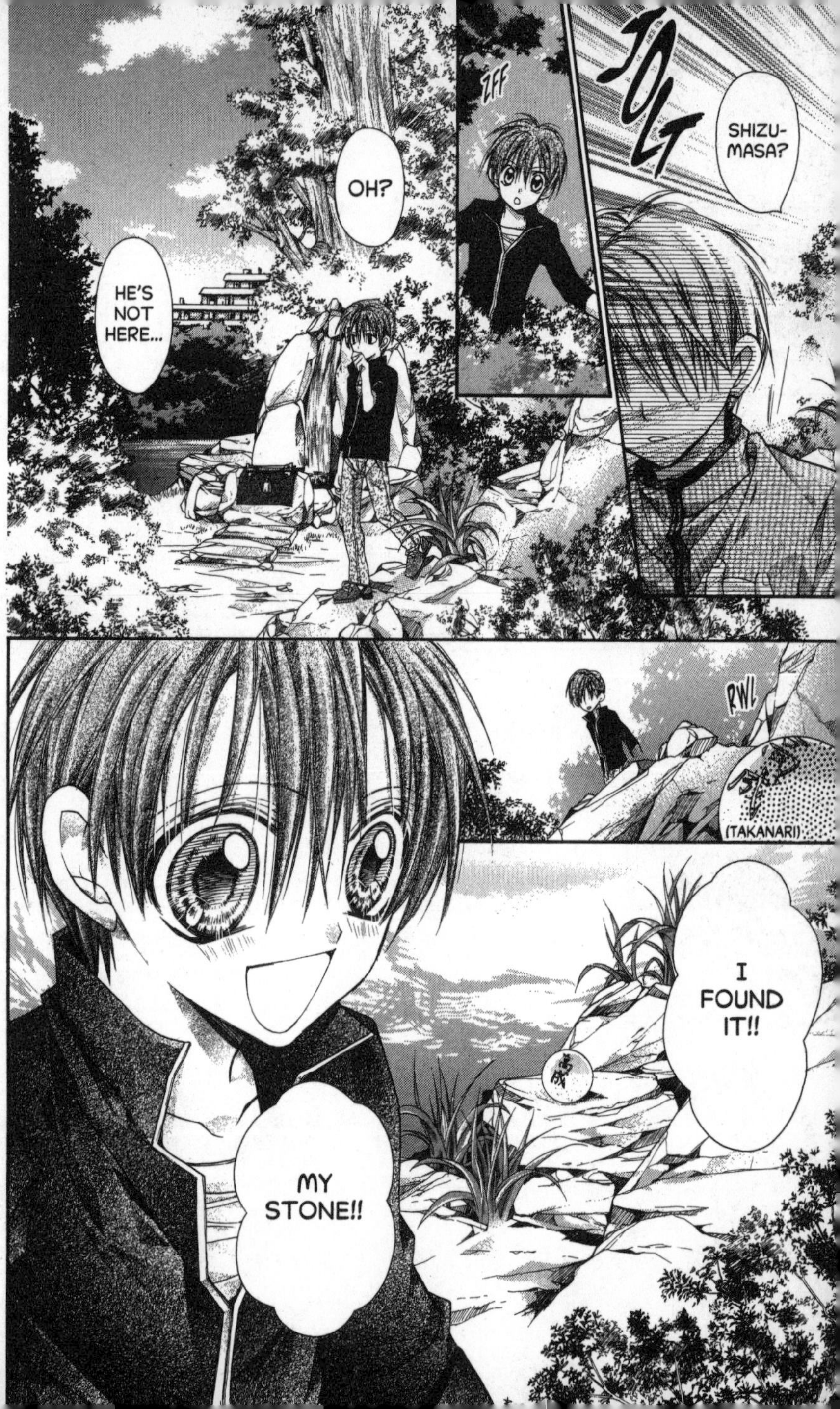
JOLT
SHIZU-MASA?
ZFF
OH?
HE'S NOT HERE...
RWL
(TAKANARI)
I FOUND IT!!
MY STONE!!

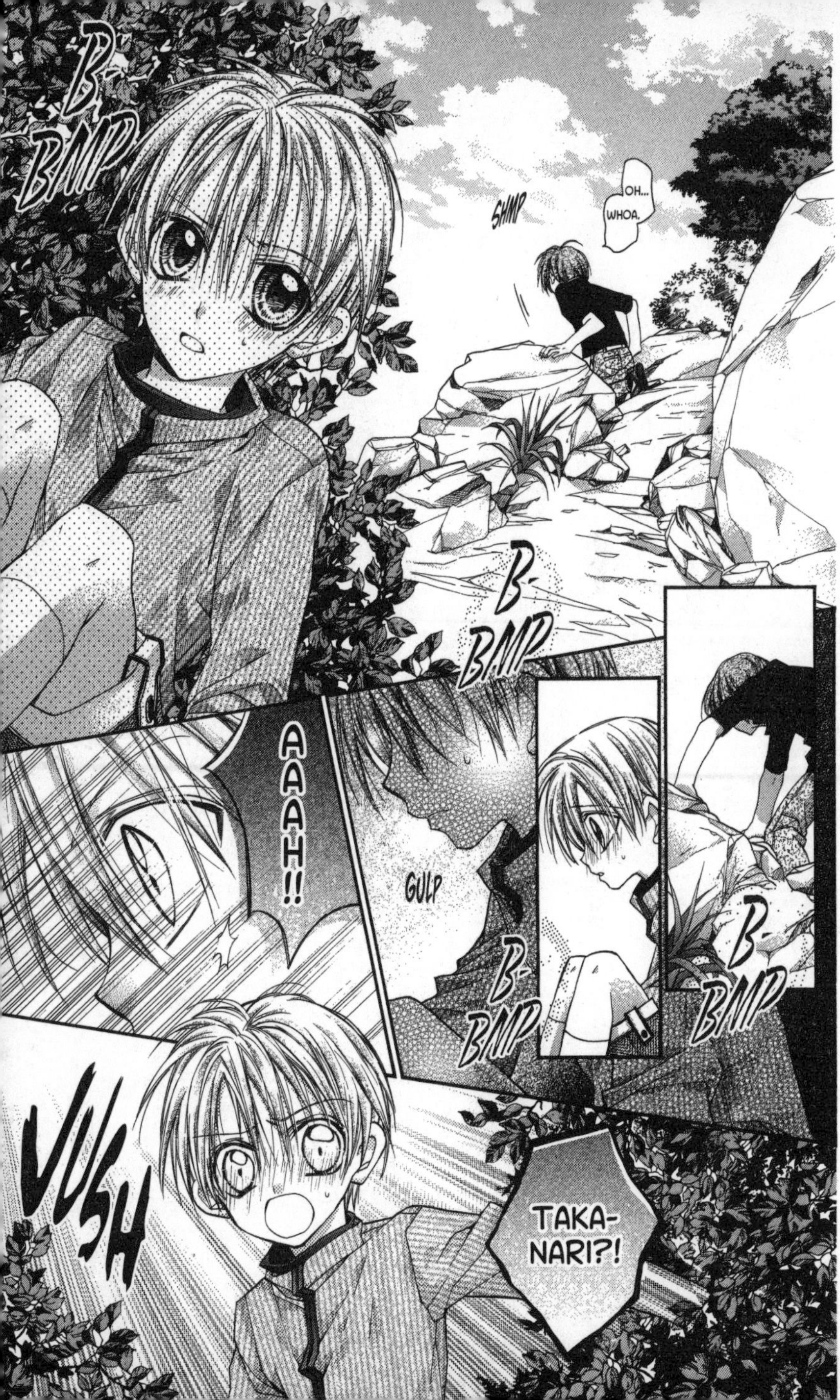
OH... WHOA.
SHMP
B-BMP
B-BMP
B-BMP
B-BMP
GULP
AAAAH!!
TAKA-NARI?!
VUSH

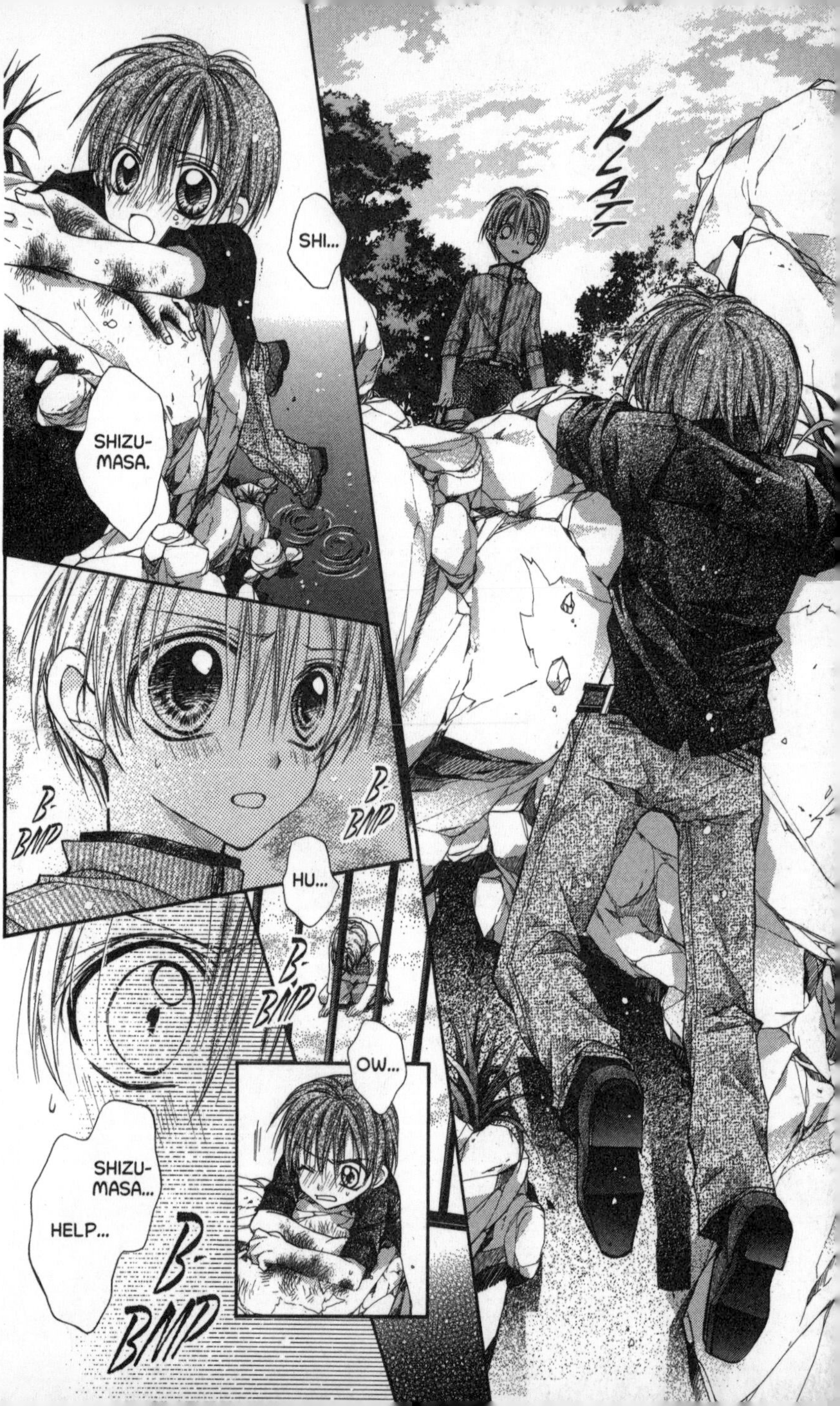
KLAKK
SHI...
SHIZU-MASA.
B-BMP
B-BMP
HU...
B-BMP
OW...
SHIZU-MASA... HELP...
B-BMP

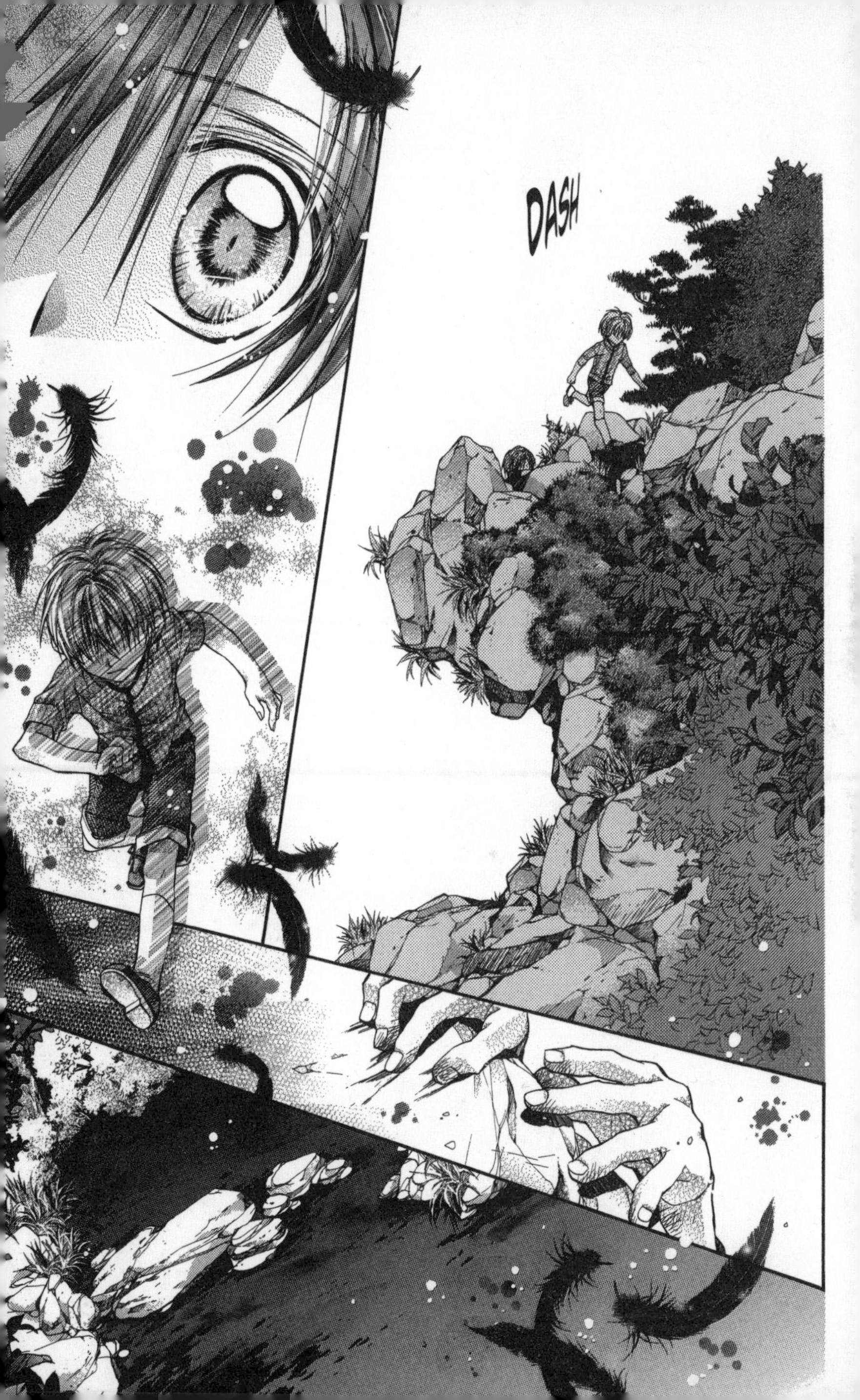
DASH

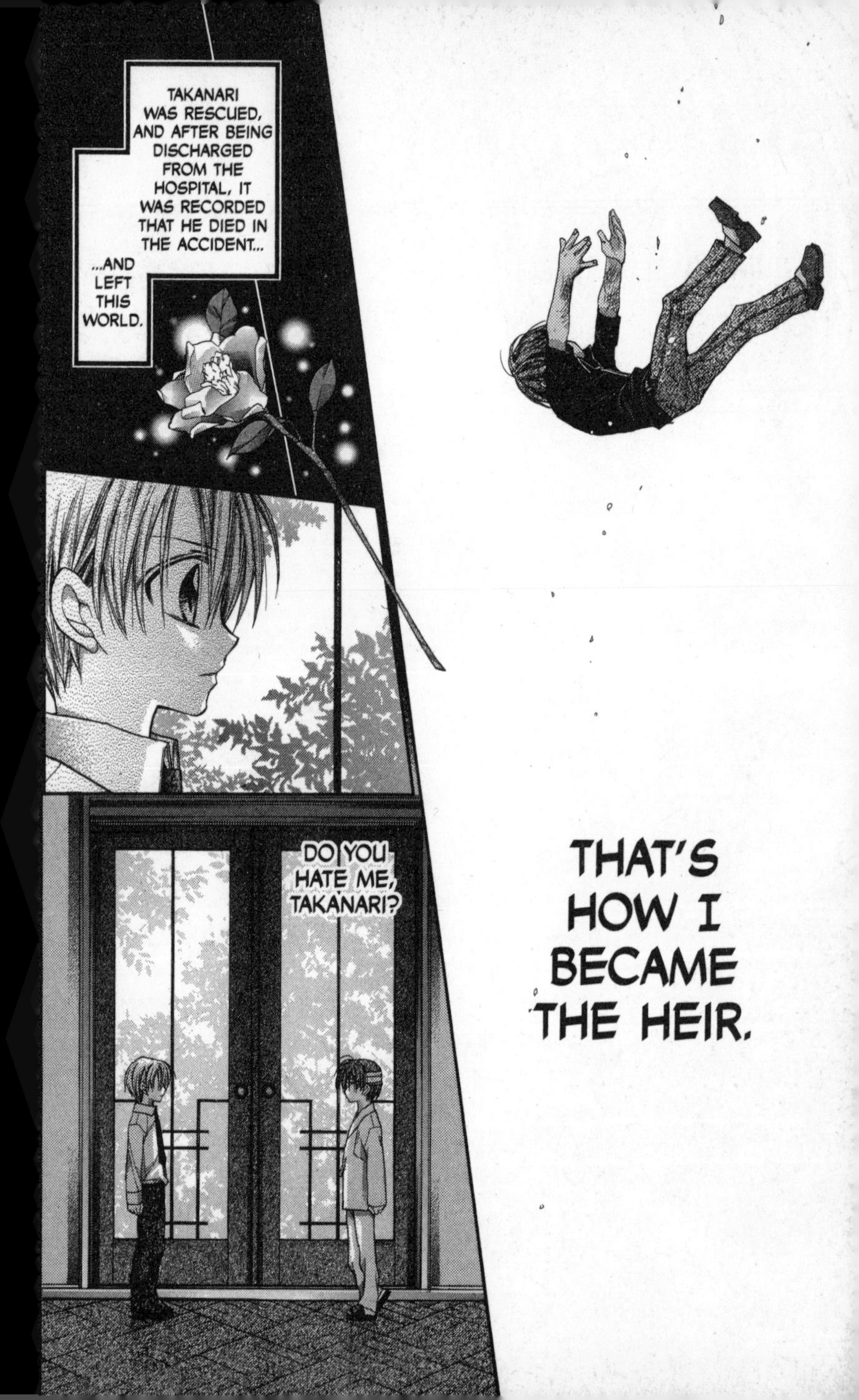
THAT'S HOW I BECAME THE HEIR.
TAKANARI WAS RESCUED, AND AFTER BEING DISCHARGED FROM THE HOSPITAL, IT WAS RECORDED THAT HE DIED IN THE ACCIDENT...
...AND LEFT THIS WORLD.
DO YOU HATE ME, TAKANARI?

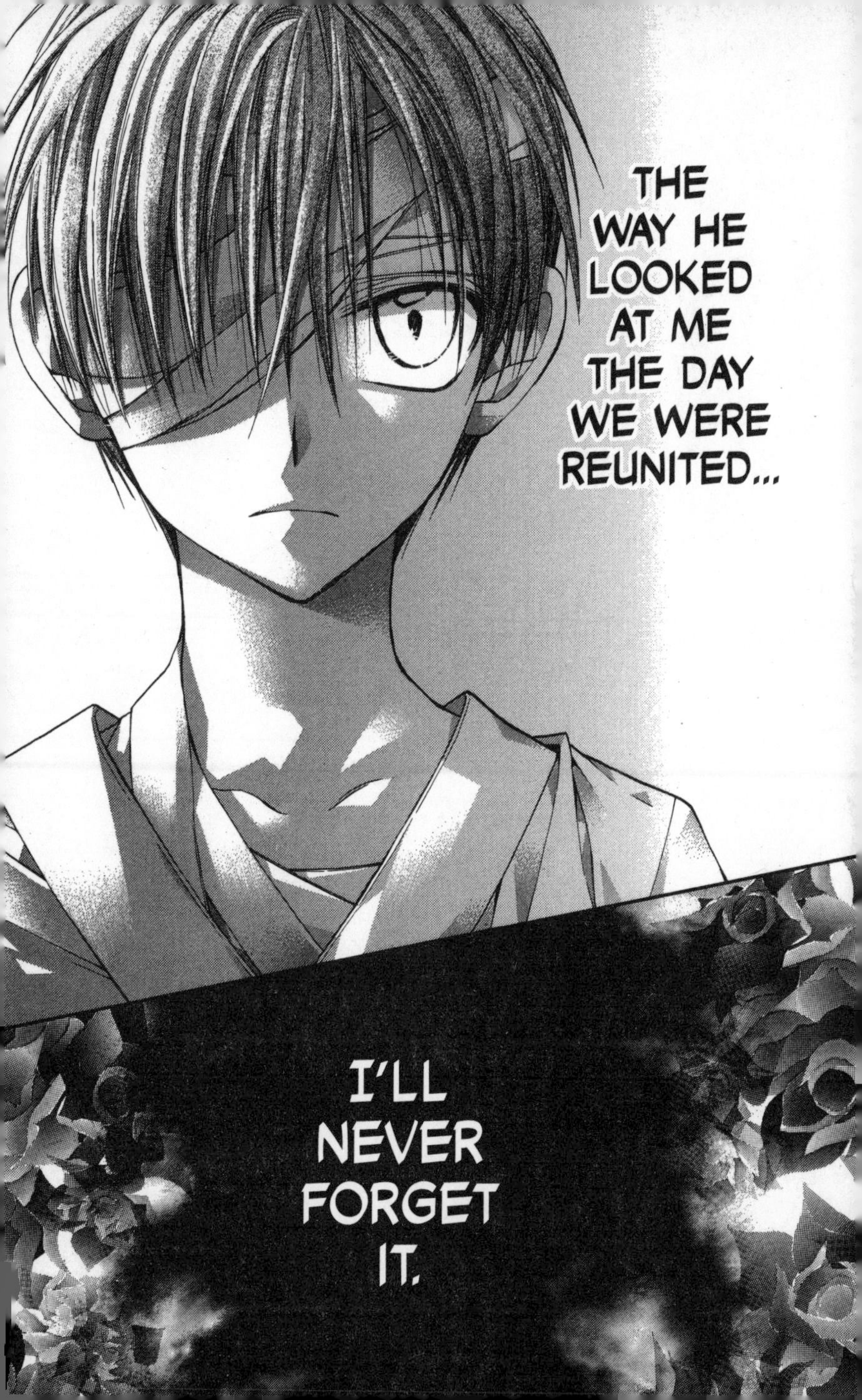
THE WAY HE LOOKED AT ME THE DAY WE WERE REUNITED...
I'LL NEVER FORGET IT.

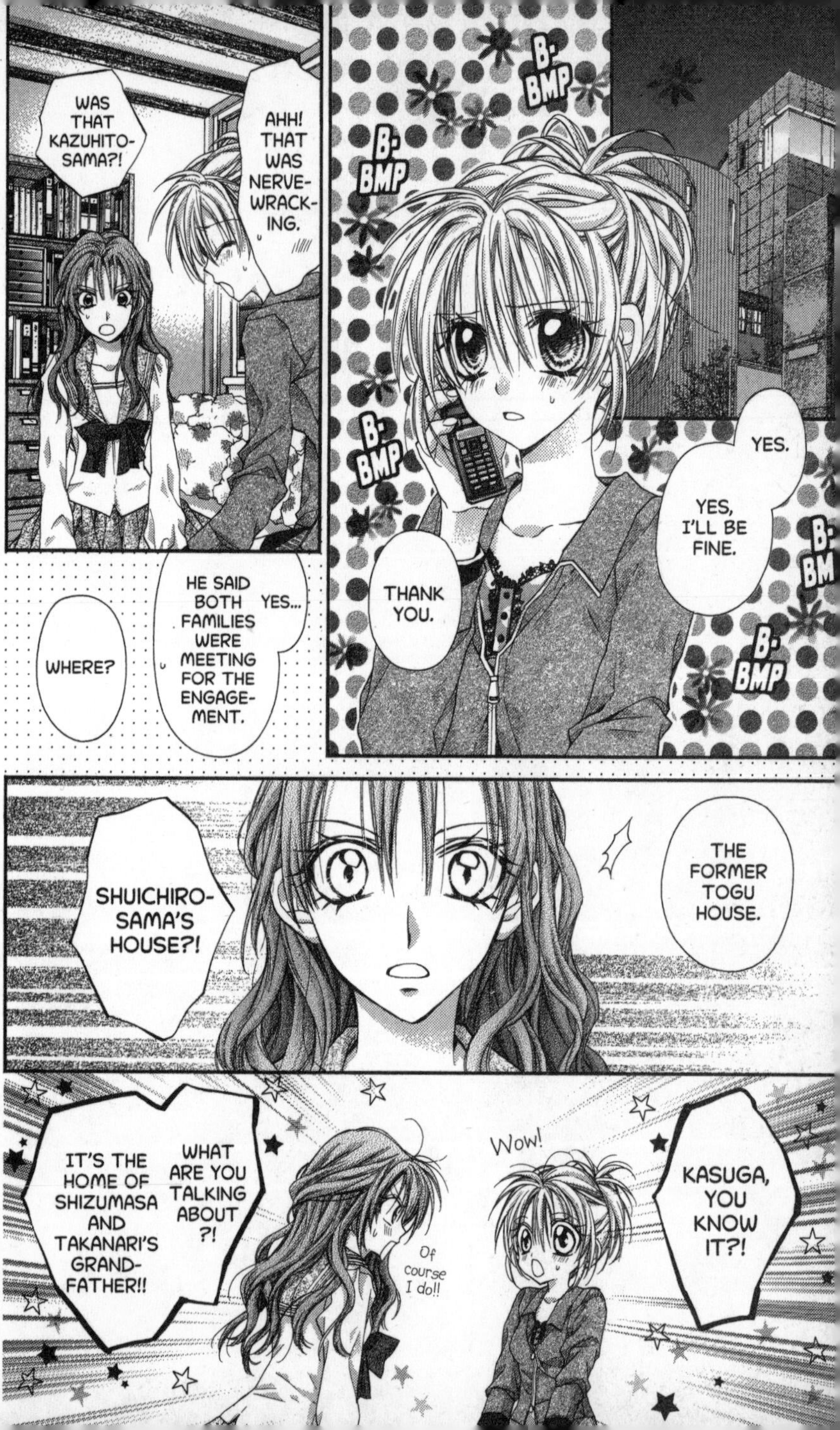
B-BMP
B-BMP
B-BMP
YES.
YES, I'LL BE FINE.
B-BM
B-BMP
THANK YOU.
AHH! THAT WAS NERVE-WRACKING.
WAS THAT KAZUHITO-SAMA?!
YES...
HE SAID BOTH FAMILIES WERE MEETING FOR THE ENGAGEMENT.
WHERE?
THE FORMER TOGU HOUSE.
SHUICHIRO-SAMA'S HOUSE?!
KASUGA, YOU KNOW IT?!
Wow!
Of course I do!!
WHAT ARE YOU TALKING ABOUT?!
IT'S THE HOME OF SHIZUMASA AND TAKANARI'S GRANDFATHER!!

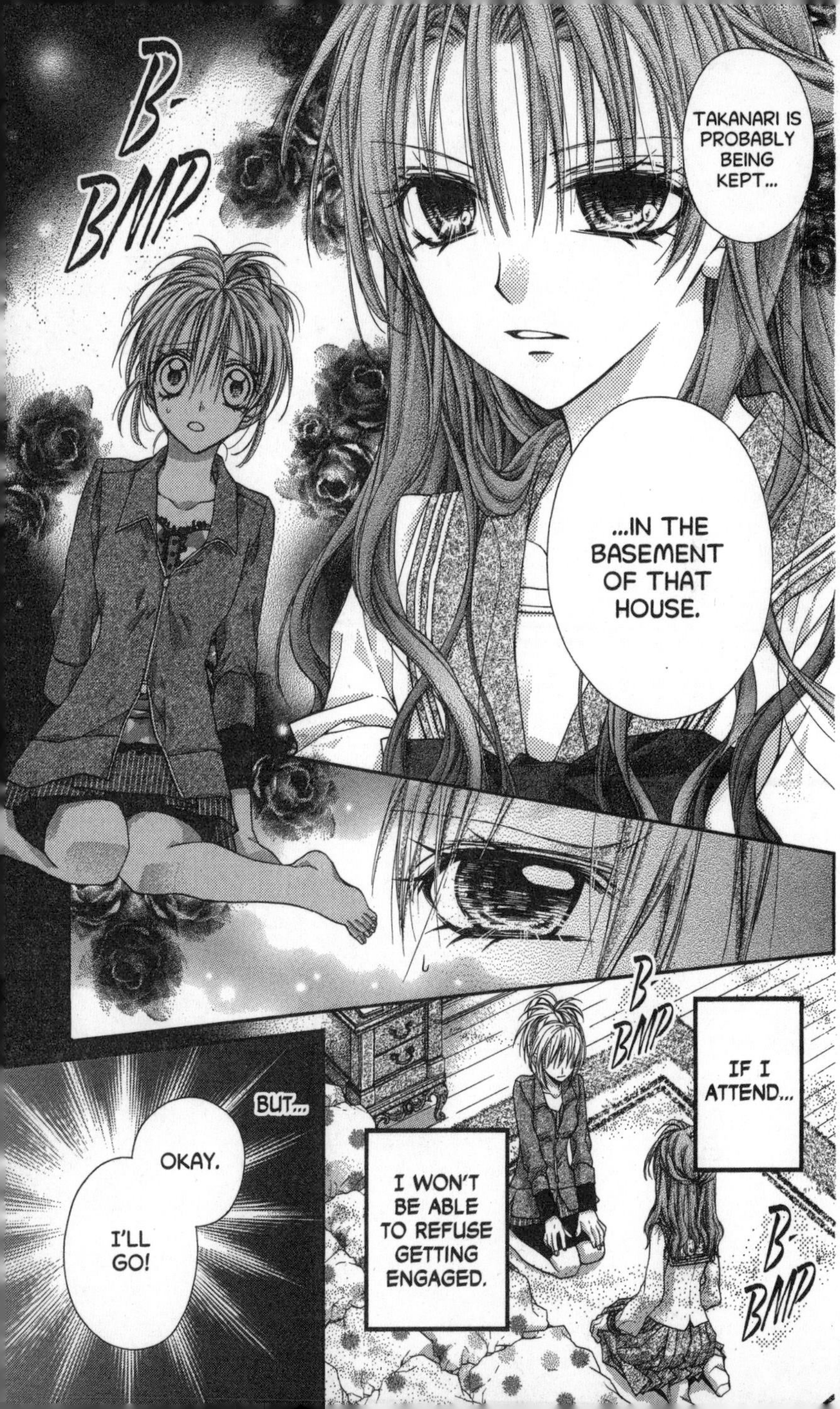
TAKANARI IS PROBABLY BEING KEPT...
...IN THE BASEMENT OF THAT HOUSE.
B-BMP
B-BMP
IF I ATTEND...
I WON'T BE ABLE TO REFUSE GETTING ENGAGED.
B-BMP
BUT...
OKAY. I'LL GO!

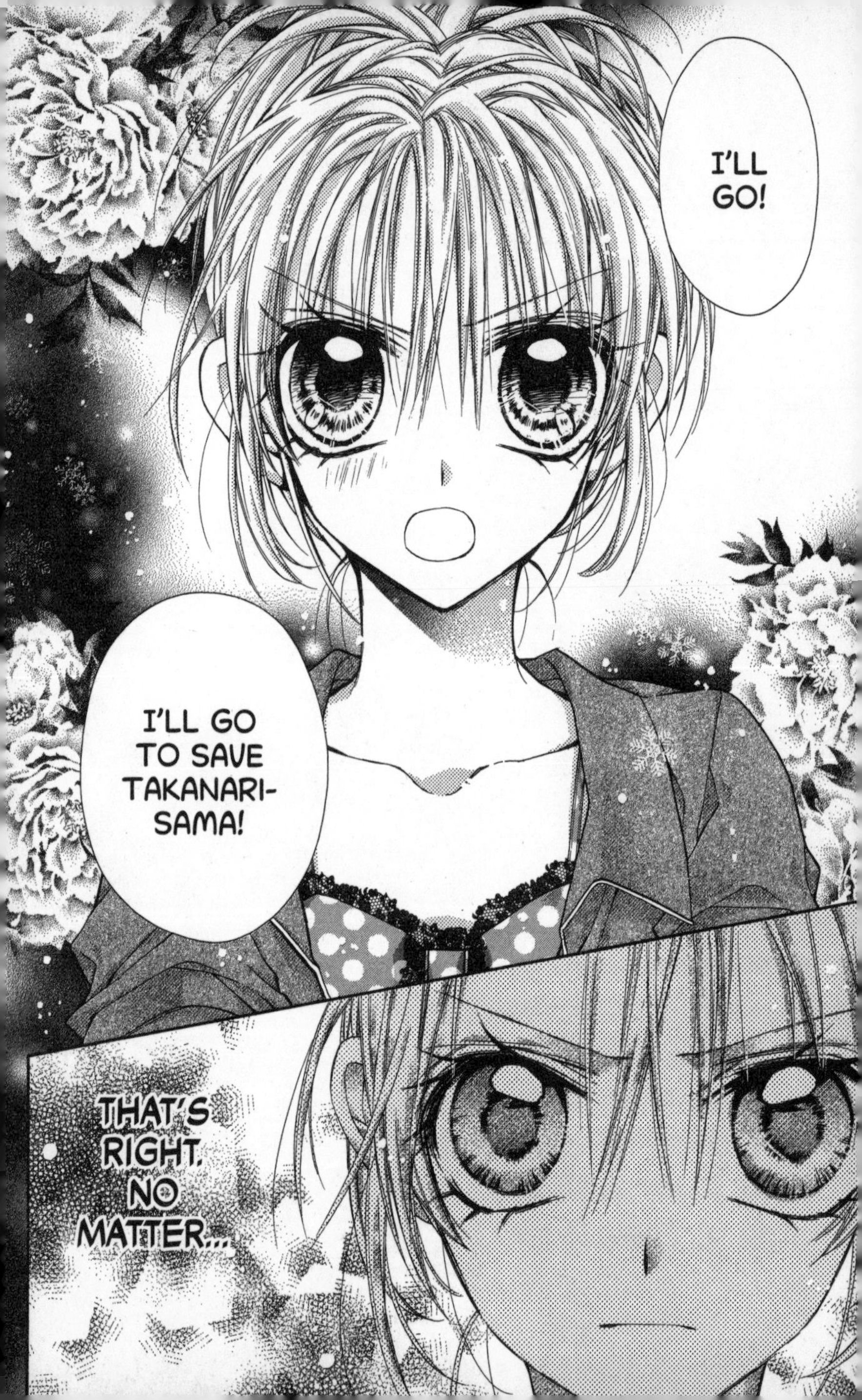
I'LL GO!
I'LL GO TO SAVE TAKANARI-SAMA!
THAT'S RIGHT. NO MATTER...

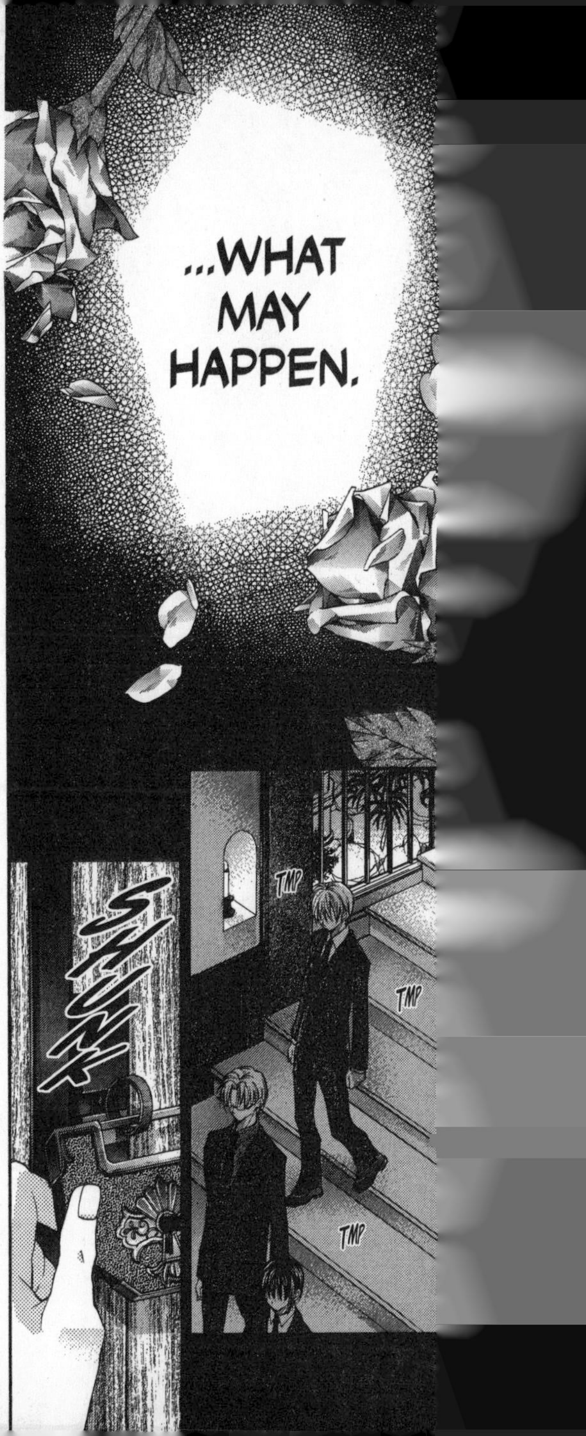
...WHAT MAY HAPPEN.
TMP
TMP
TMP
SHUNK
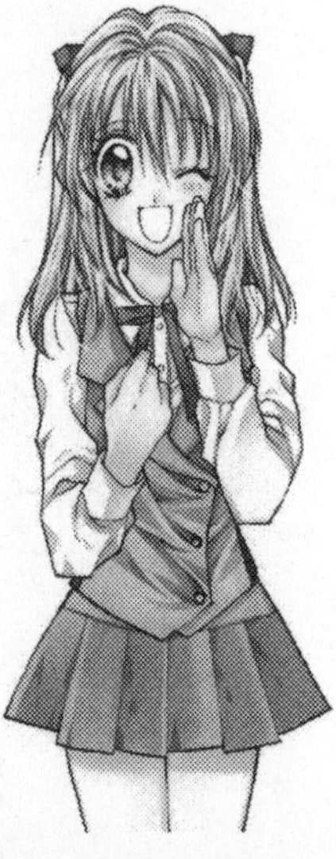

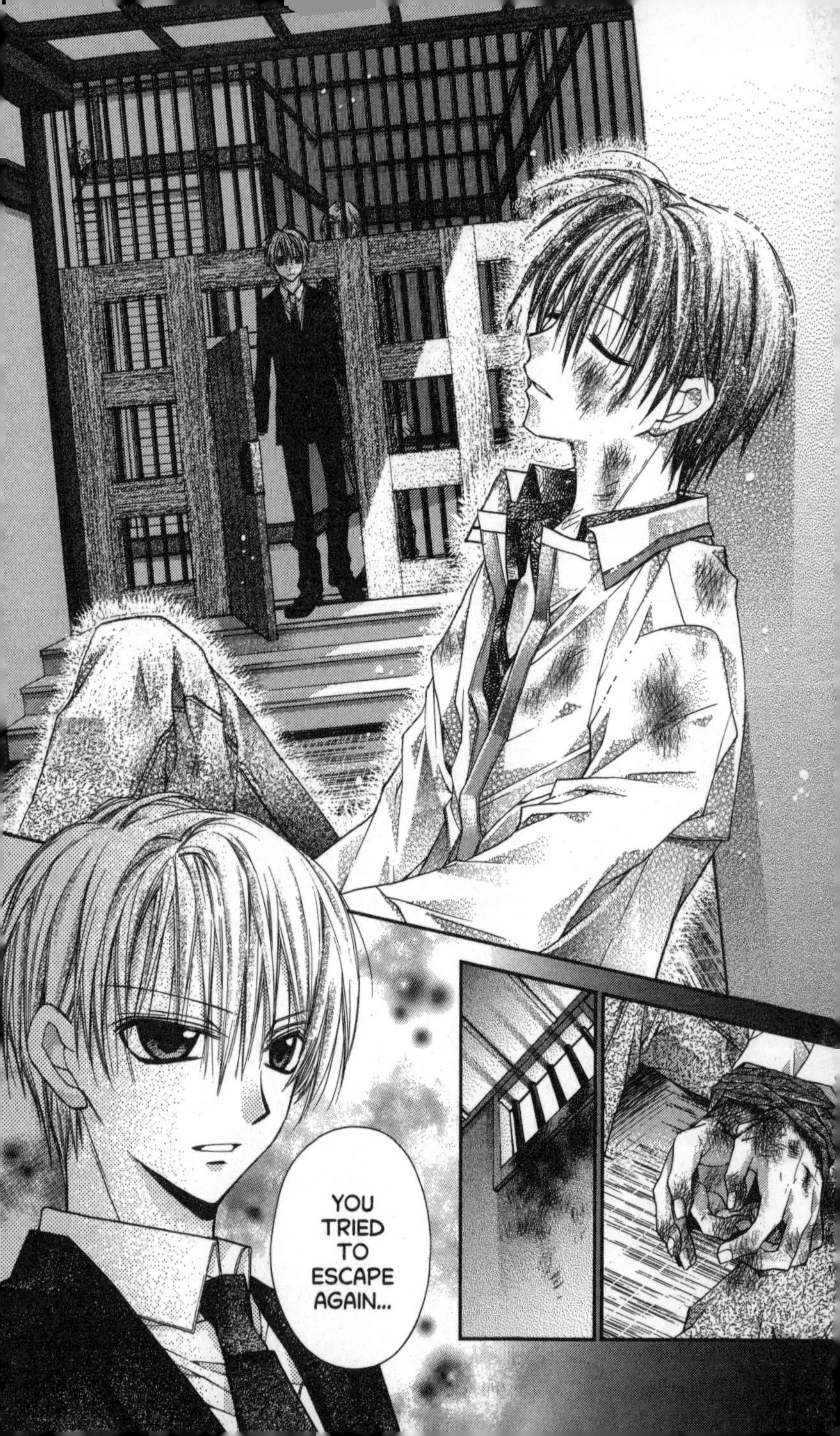
YOU TRIED TO ESCAPE AGAIN...

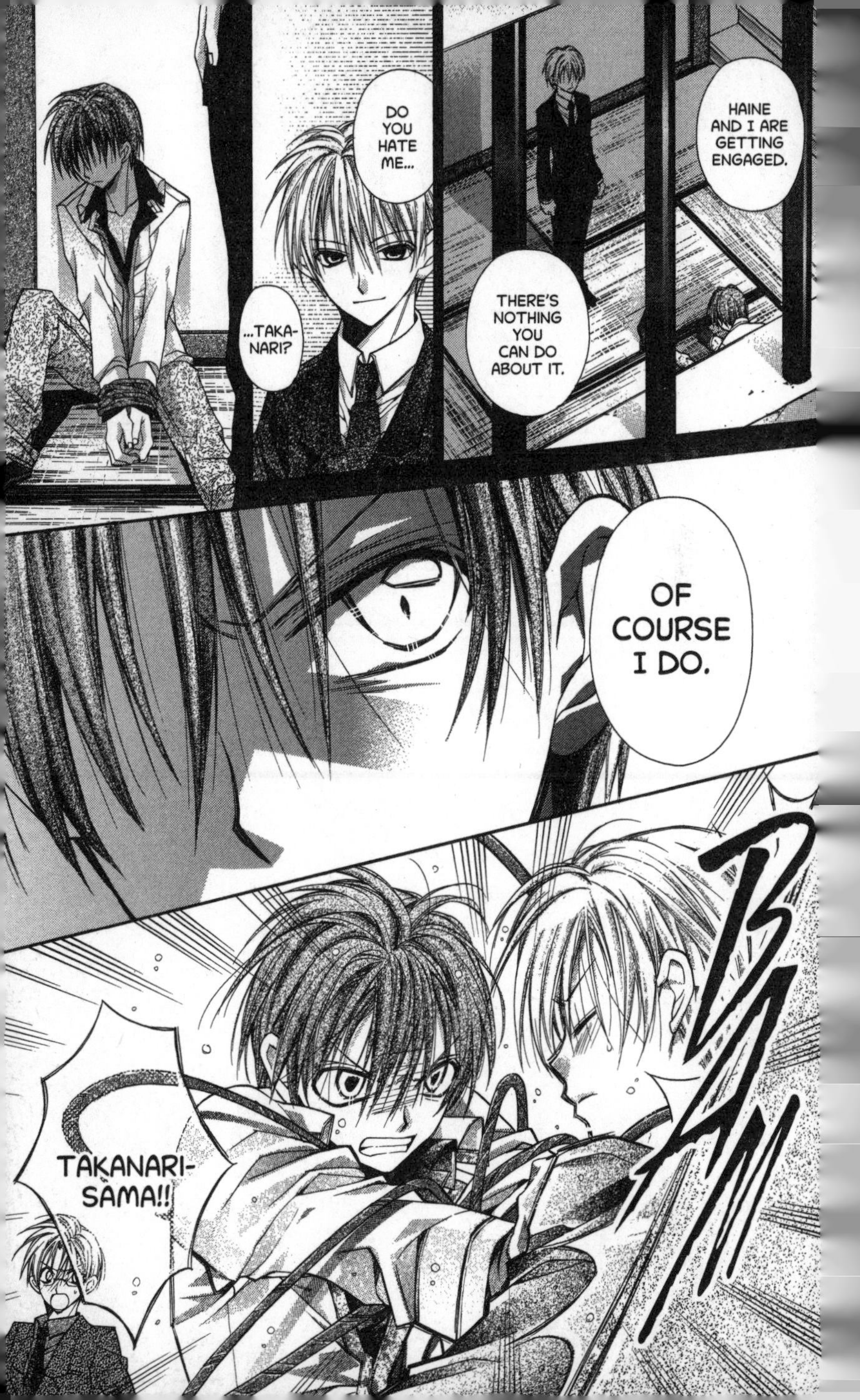
HAINE AND I ARE GETTING ENGAGED.
THERE'S NOTHING YOU CAN DO ABOUT IT.
DO YOU HATE ME...
...TAKANARI?
OF COURSE I DO.
TAKANARI-SAMA!!

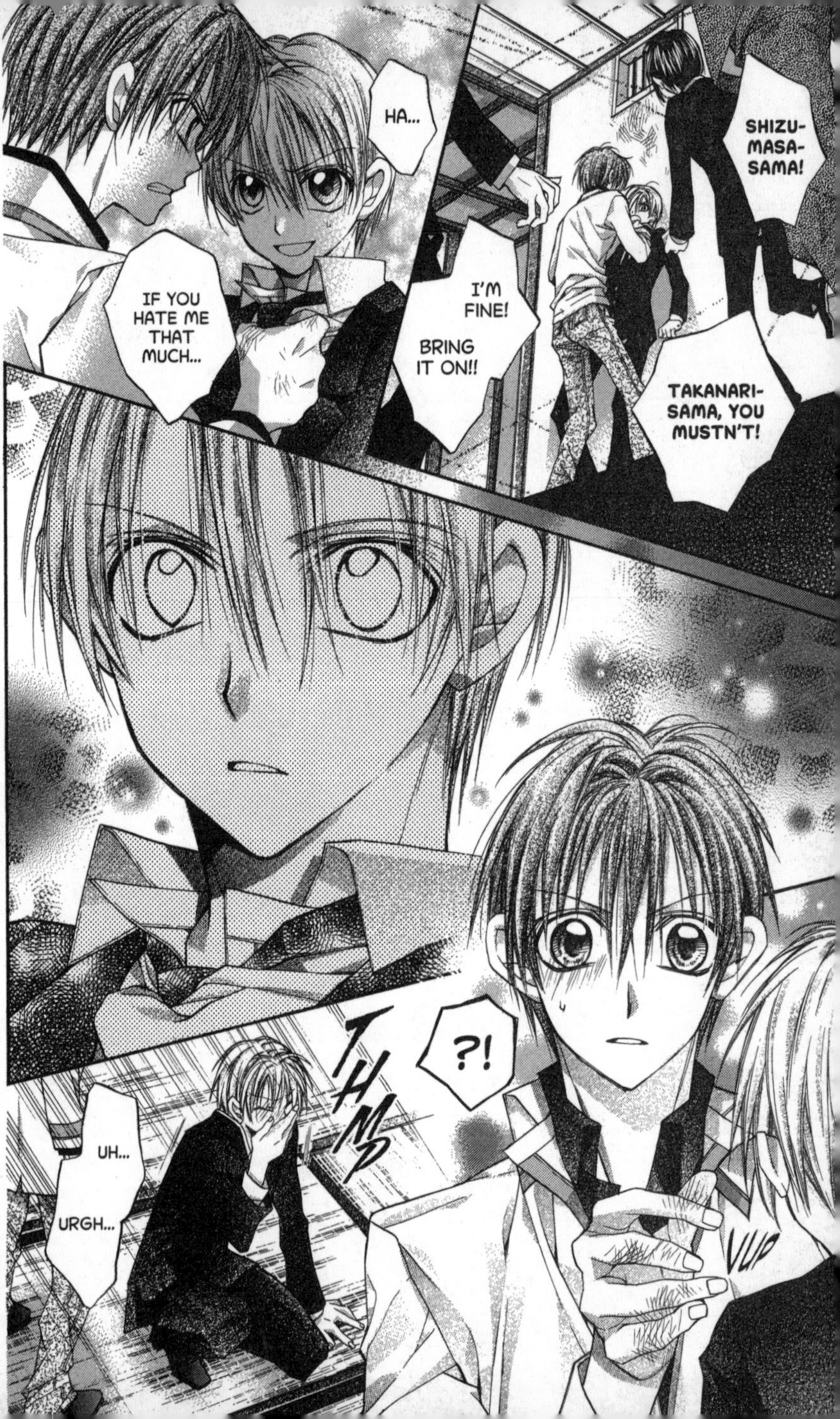
SHIZU-MASA-SAMA!
TAKANARI-SAMA, YOU MUSTN'T!
HA...
IF YOU HATE ME THAT MUCH...
I'M FINE!
BRING IT ON!!
?!
THMP
VUP
UH...
URGH...

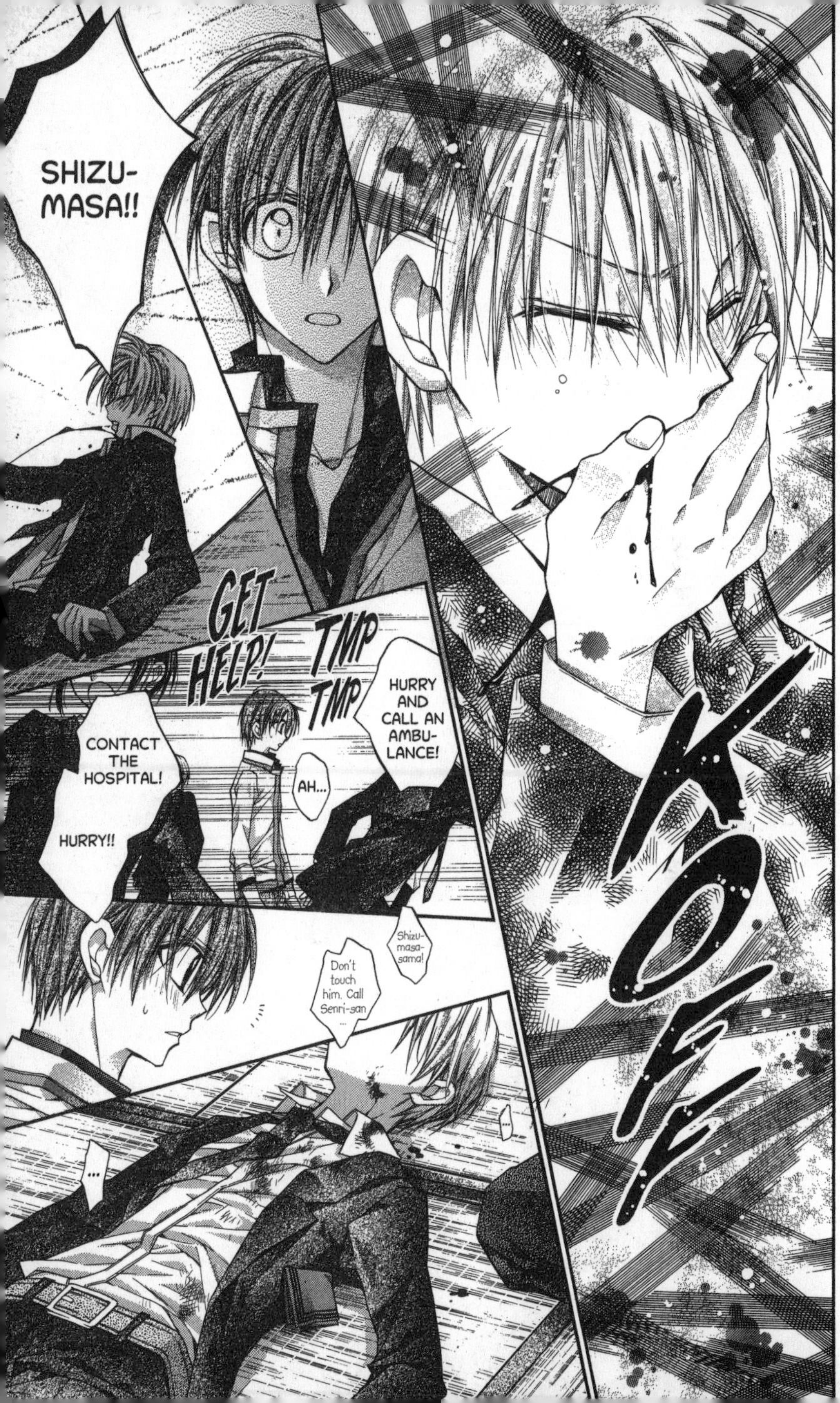
SHIZU-MASA!!
GET HELP!
TMP TMP
HURRY AND CALL AN AMBULANCE!
AH...
CONTACT THE HOSPITAL!
HURRY!!
Shizu-masa-sama!
Don't touch him. Call Senri-san ...
...
...

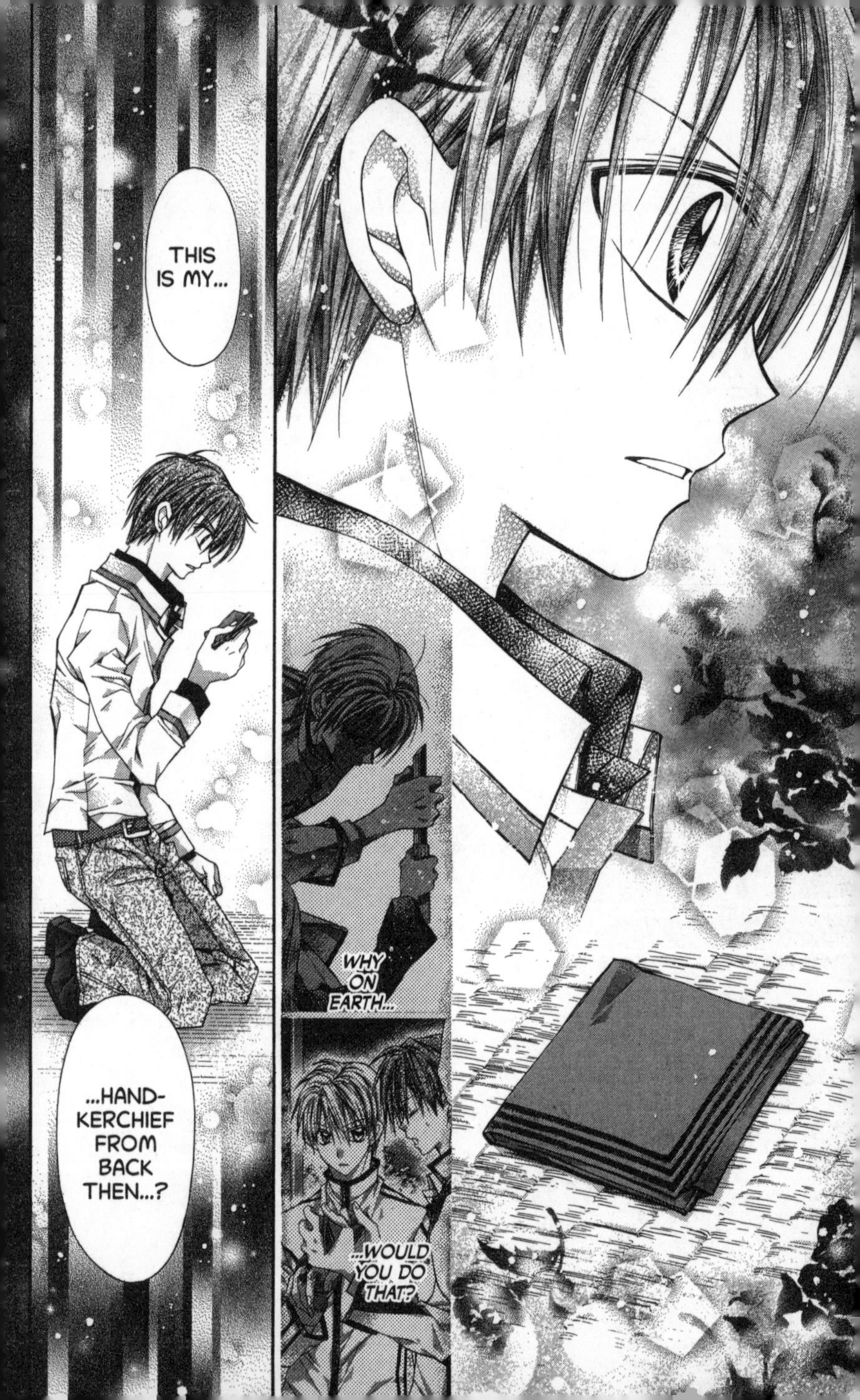
WHY ON EARTH...
...WOULD YOU DO THAT?
THIS IS MY...
...HAND-KERCHIEF FROM BACK THEN...?

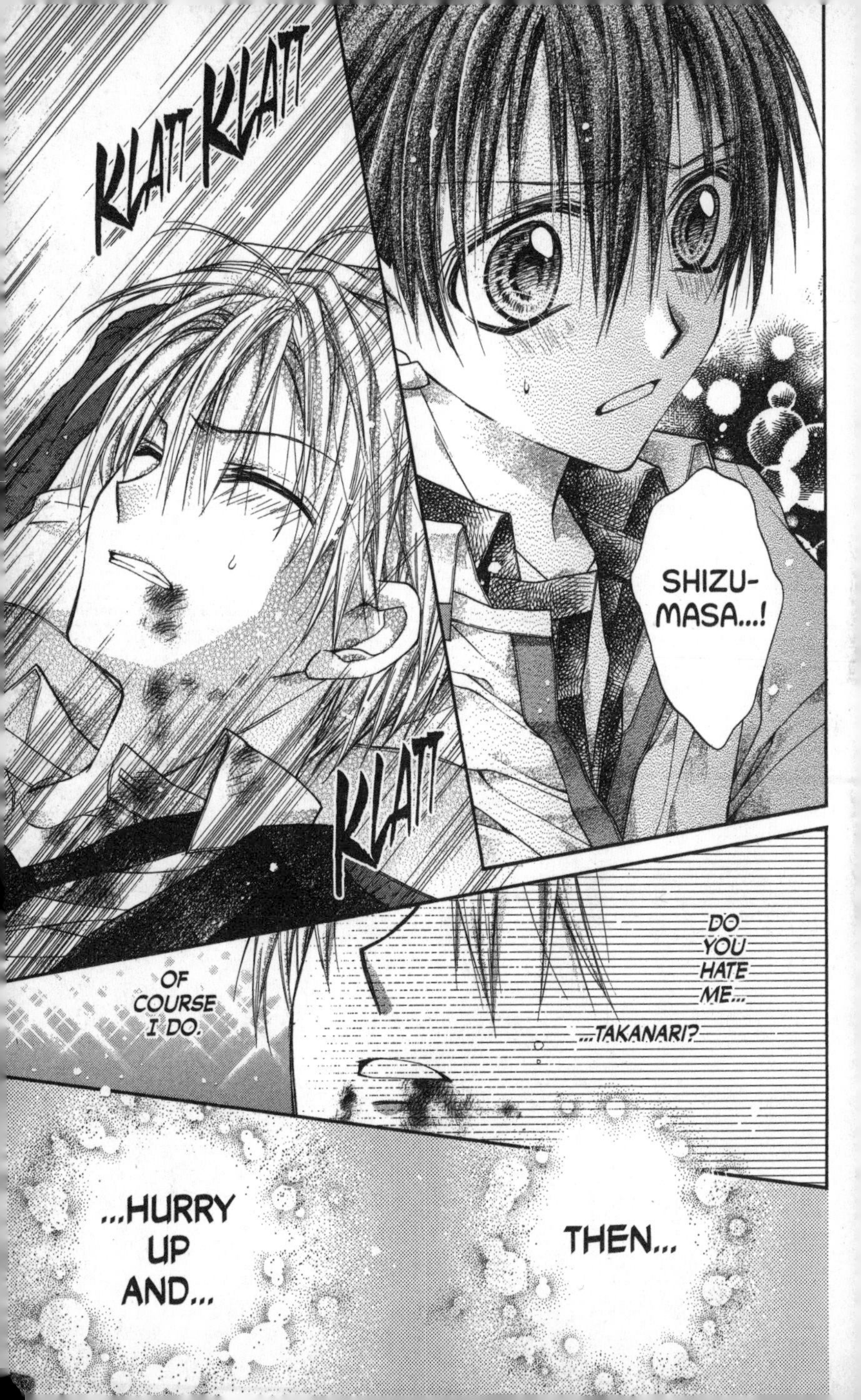
SHIZU-MASA...!
KLATT KLATT
KLATT
DO YOU HATE ME...
...TAKANARI?
OF COURSE I DO.
THEN...
...HURRY UP AND...

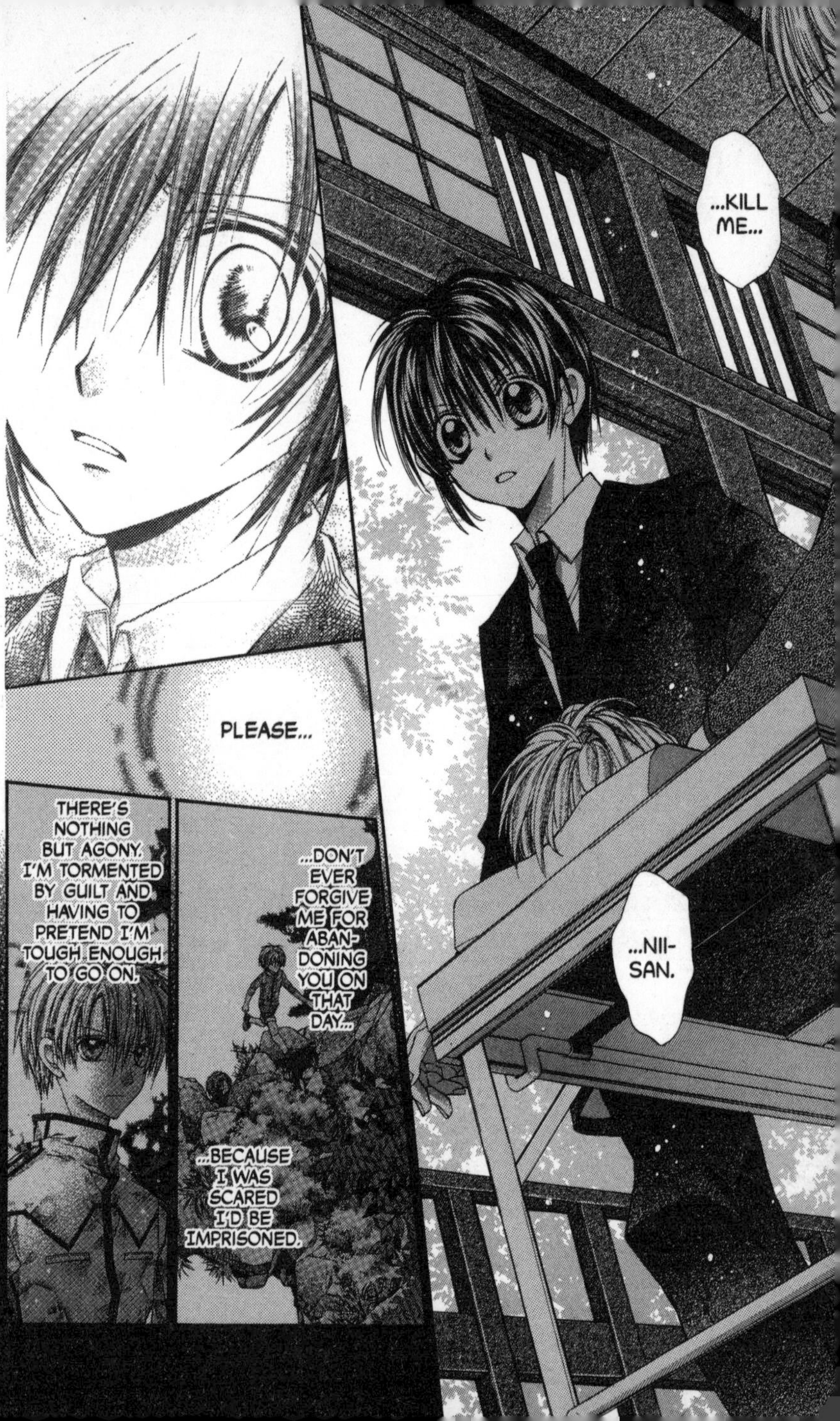
...KILL ME...
...NII-SAN.
PLEASE...
...DON'T EVER FORGIVE ME FOR ABANDONING YOU ON THAT DAY...
...BECAUSE I WAS SCARED I'D BE IMPRISONED.
THERE'S NOTHING BUT AGONY. I'M TORMENTED BY GUILT AND HAVING TO PRETEND I'M TOUGH ENOUGH TO GO ON.

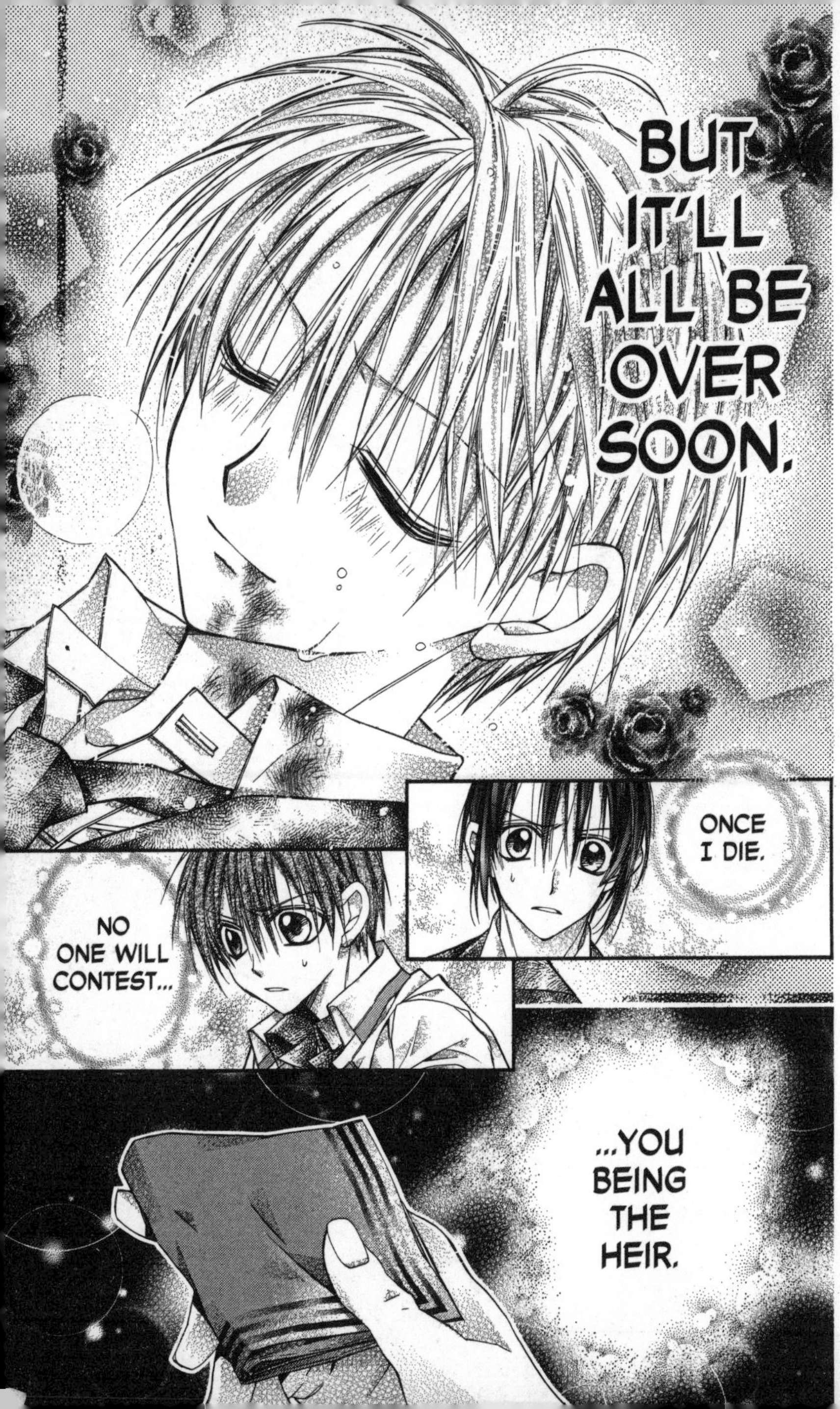
BUT IT'LL ALL BE OVER SOON.
ONCE I DIE.
NO ONE WILL CONTEST...
...YOU BEING THE HEIR.

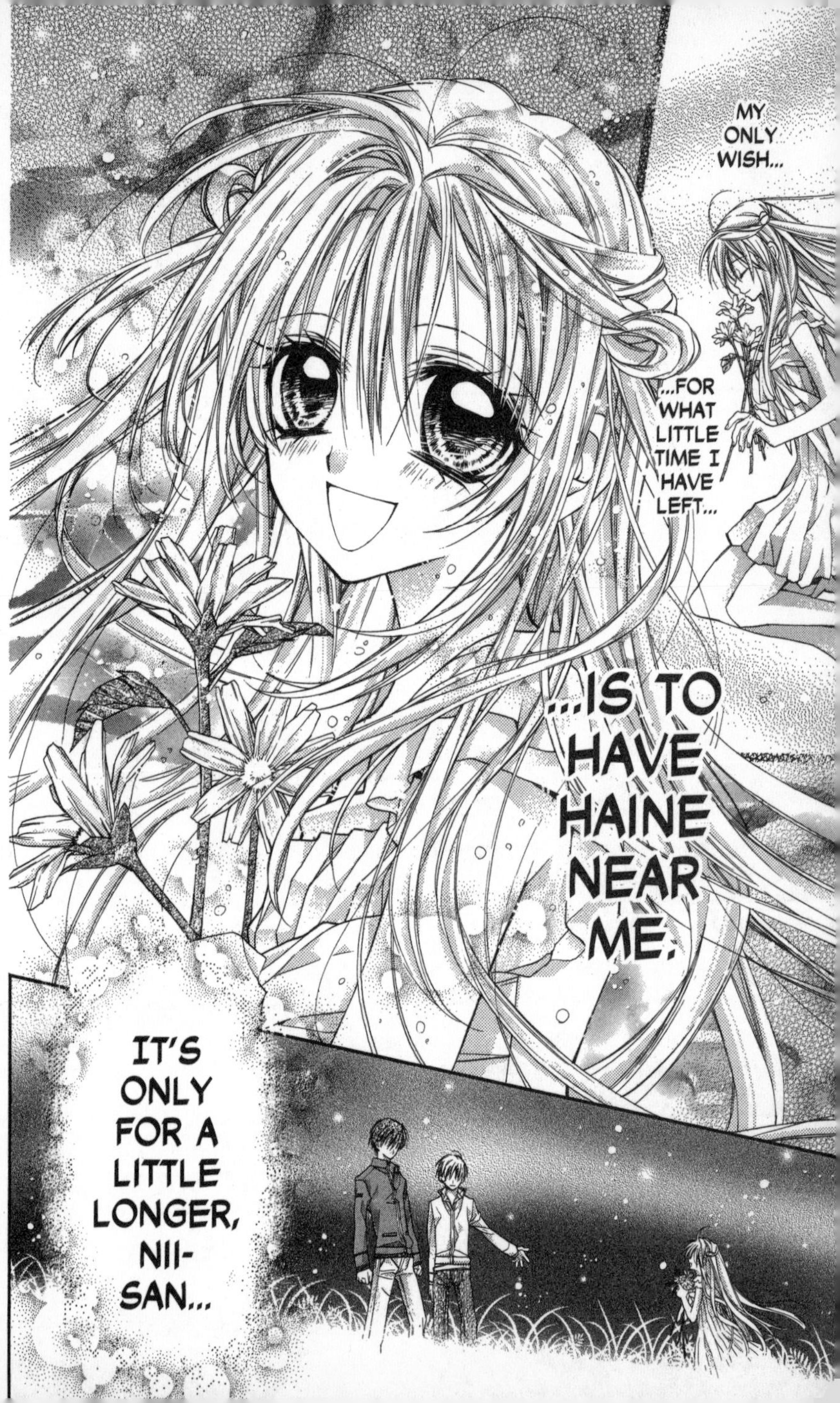
MY ONLY WISH...
...FOR WHAT LITTLE TIME I HAVE LEFT...
...IS TO HAVE HAINE NEAR ME.
IT'S ONLY FOR A LITTLE LONGER, NII-SAN...

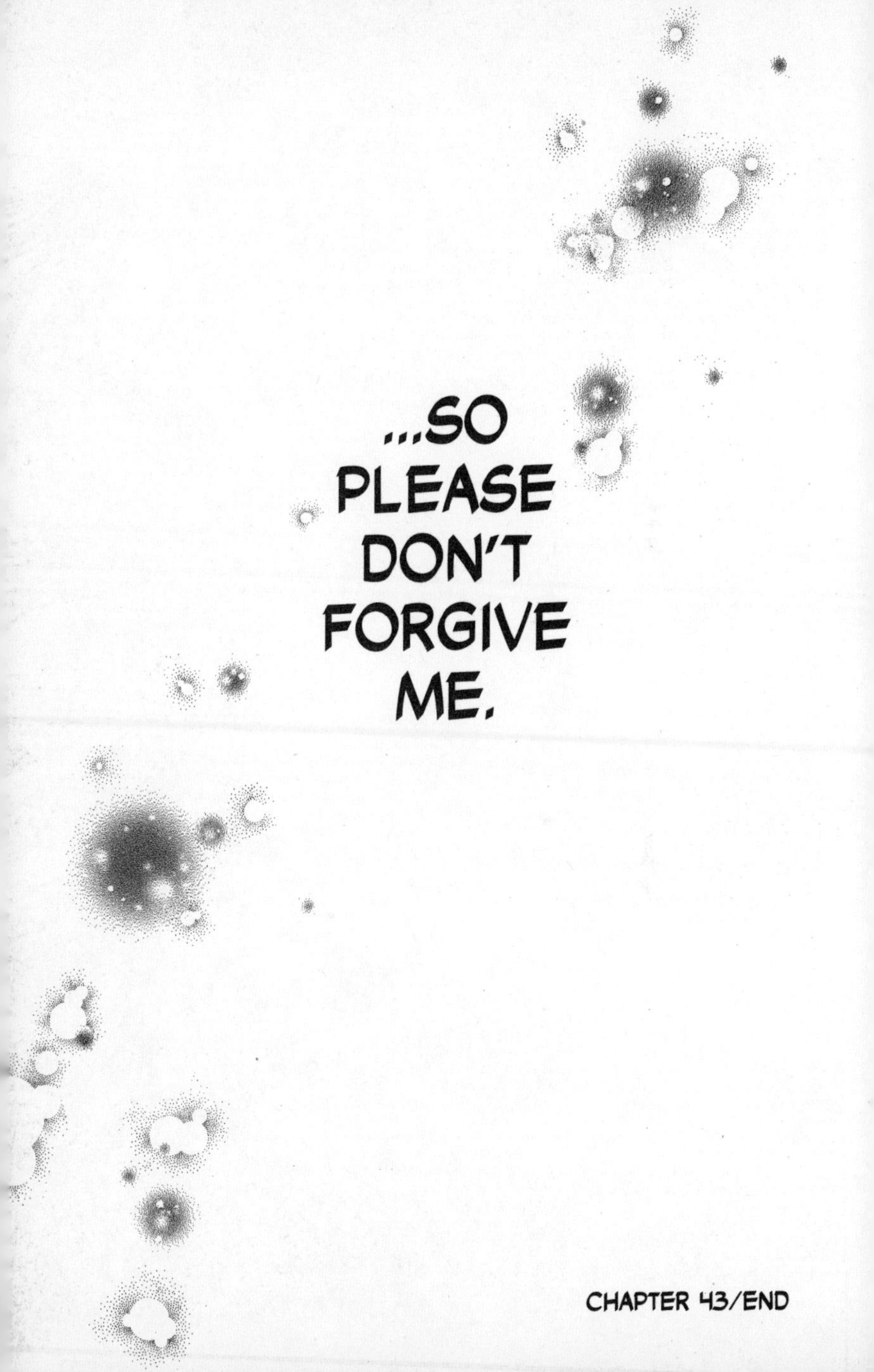
...SO PLEASE DON'T FORGIVE ME.
CHAPTER 43/END

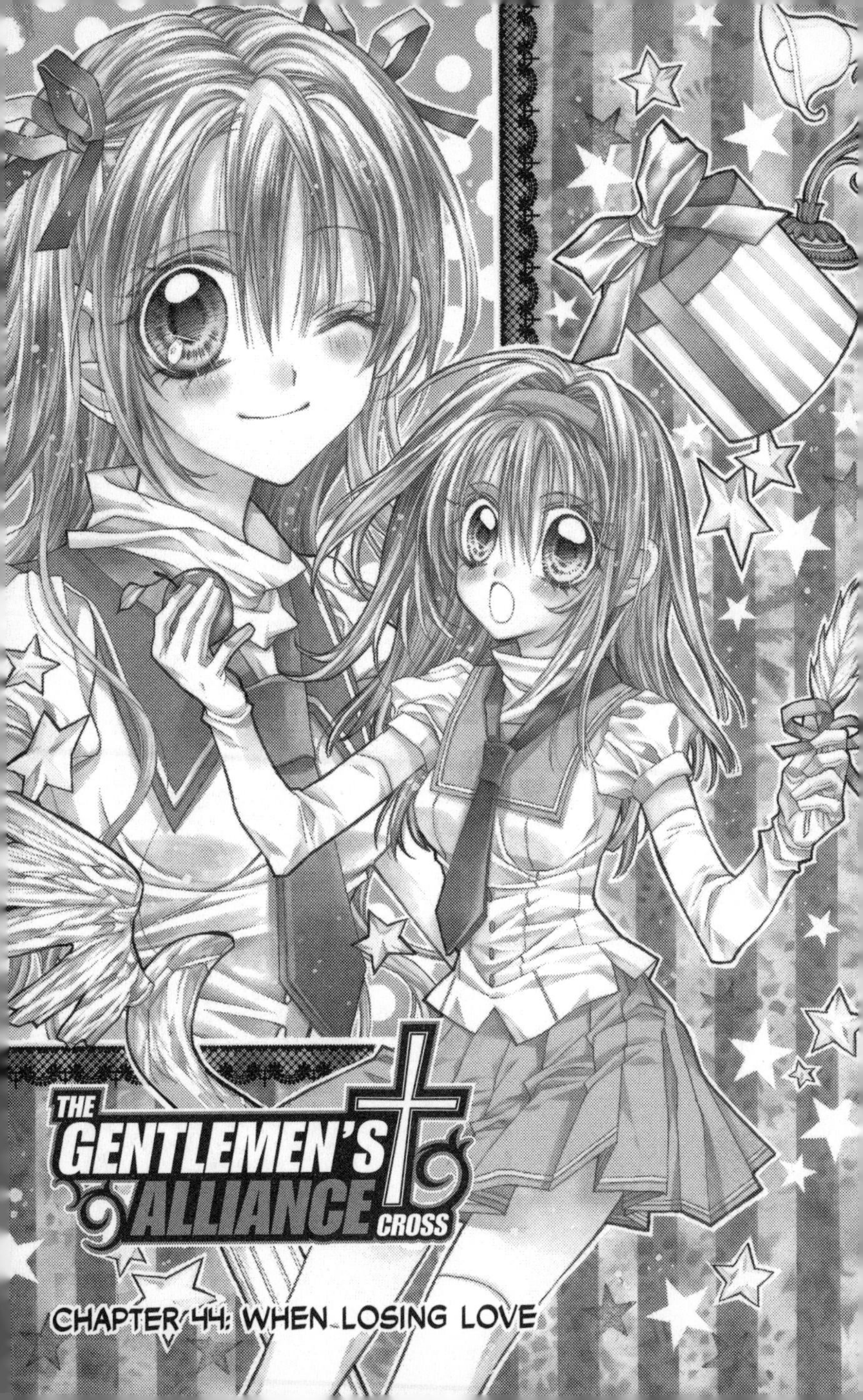
THE GENTLEMEN'S ALLIANCE CROSS
CHAPTER 44: WHEN LOSING LOVE

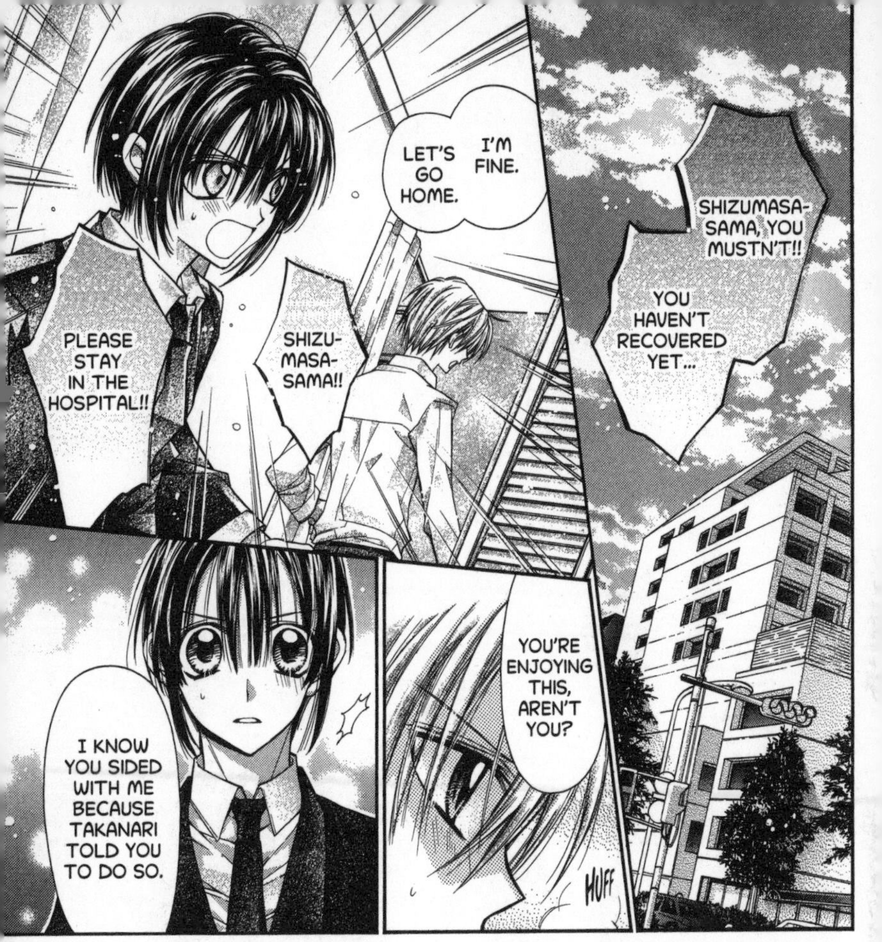
SHIZUMASA-SAMA, YOU MUSTN'T!!
YOU HAVEN'T RECOVERED YET...
I'M FINE.
LET'S GO HOME.
SHIZU-MASA-SAMA!!
PLEASE STAY IN THE HOSPITAL!!
YOU'RE ENJOYING THIS, AREN'T YOU?
HUFF
I KNOW YOU SIDED WITH ME BECAUSE TAKANARI TOLD YOU TO DO SO.

Chapter 44: When Losing Love

※ I'm giving away the story.

Lead-in Love is the last remaining magic spell in this world. The words are, of course, "I love you."

Kyoka, Takanari and Shizumasa's stepmother, appears for the first time. Did you know that all the mothers of the major characters in this series have "ka" in their names?! (Maika, Ryokka, Shoka, Kyoka) She's very much like Arina Tanemura. That's what I'm like.

The funniest thing about drawing this chapter was when Takanari says to Senri, "Why do you always take Shizumasa's side?!" What, were you sad that Senri wasn't on your side?? Taka-Taka...(laugh)

And this is just an inside? story but the "just hurry up and get into this" dress Kyoka-sama brought over is more expensive than the dress Haine was wearing. Hee! ♥

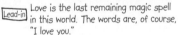

Kyoka-san was very popular—especially the part in which she's slamming the sliding door shut. By the way, I don't do things like that. (laugh)

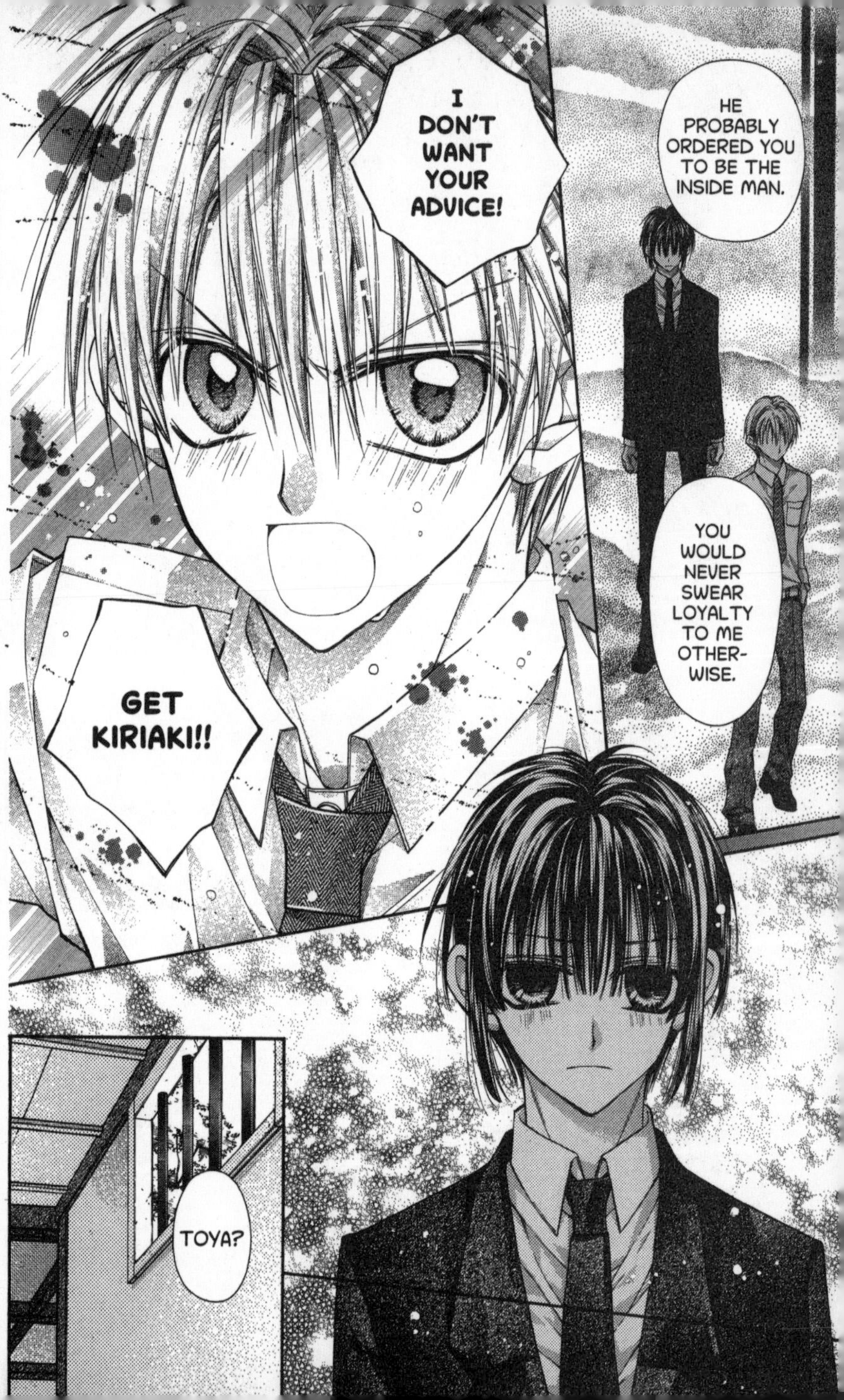
HE PROBABLY ORDERED YOU TO BE THE INSIDE MAN.
YOU WOULD NEVER SWEAR LOYALTY TO ME OTHER-WISE.
I DON'T WANT YOUR ADVICE!
GET KIRIAKI!!
TOYA?

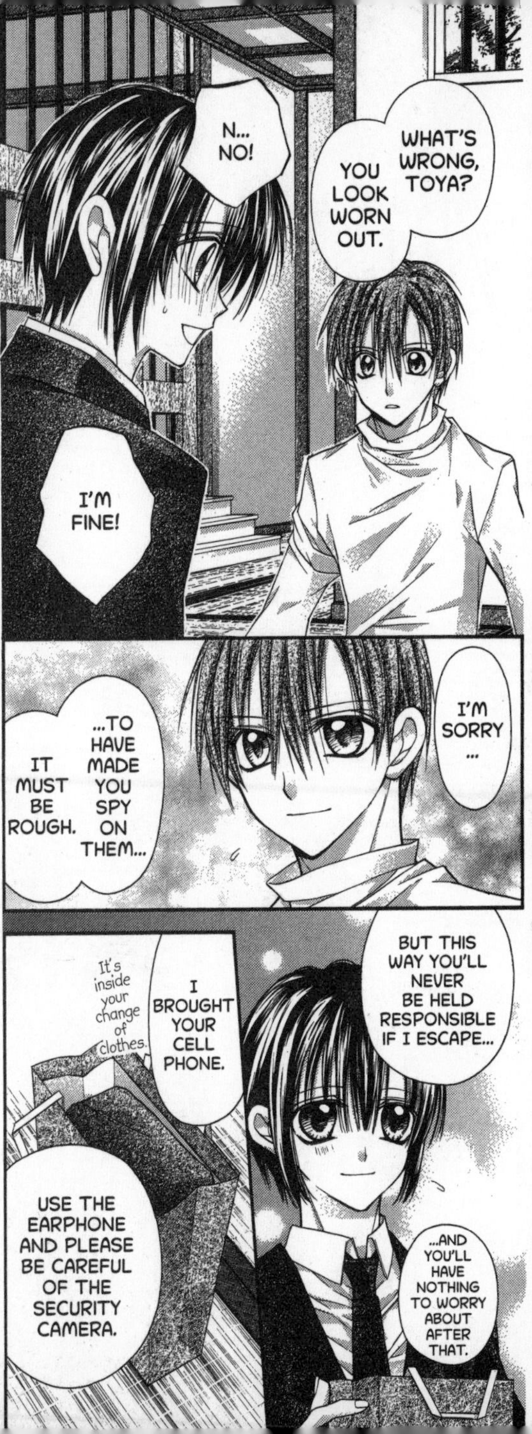
WHAT'S WRONG, TOYA?
YOU LOOK WORN OUT.
N... NO!
I'M FINE!
I'M SORRY...
...TO HAVE MADE YOU SPY ON THEM...
IT MUST BE ROUGH.
BUT THIS WAY YOU'LL NEVER BE HELD RESPONSIBLE IF I ESCAPE...
...AND YOU'LL HAVE NOTHING TO WORRY ABOUT AFTER THAT.
I BROUGHT YOUR CELL PHONE.
It's inside your change of clothes.
USE THE EARPHONE AND PLEASE BE CAREFUL OF THE SECURITY CAMERA.

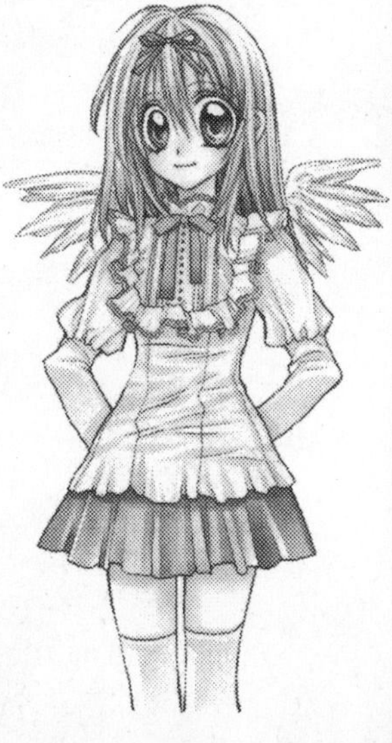

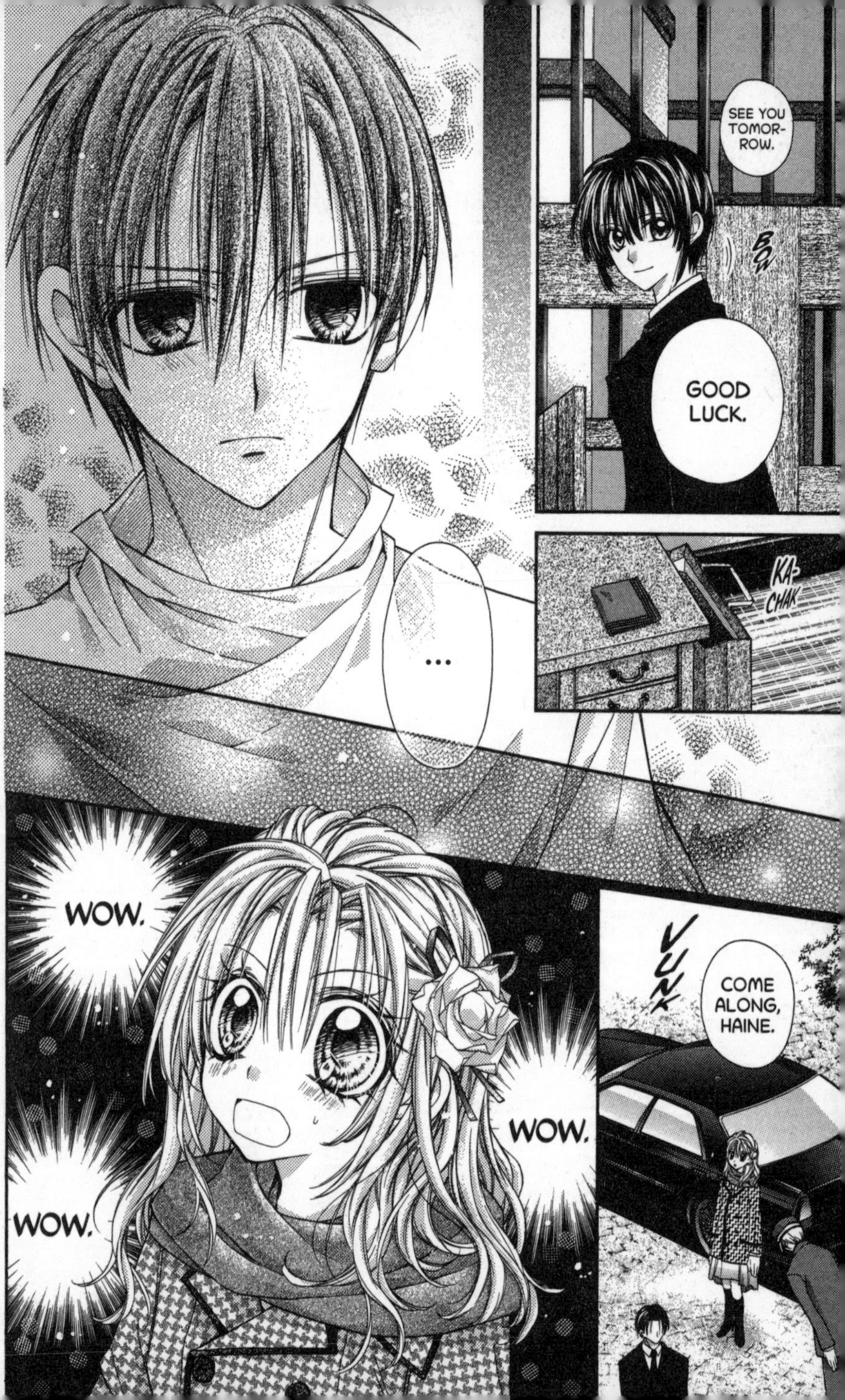
SEE YOU TOMOR-ROW.
BOW
GOOD LUCK.
KA-CHAK
...
VUNK
COME ALONG, HAINE.
WOW.
WOW.
WOW.

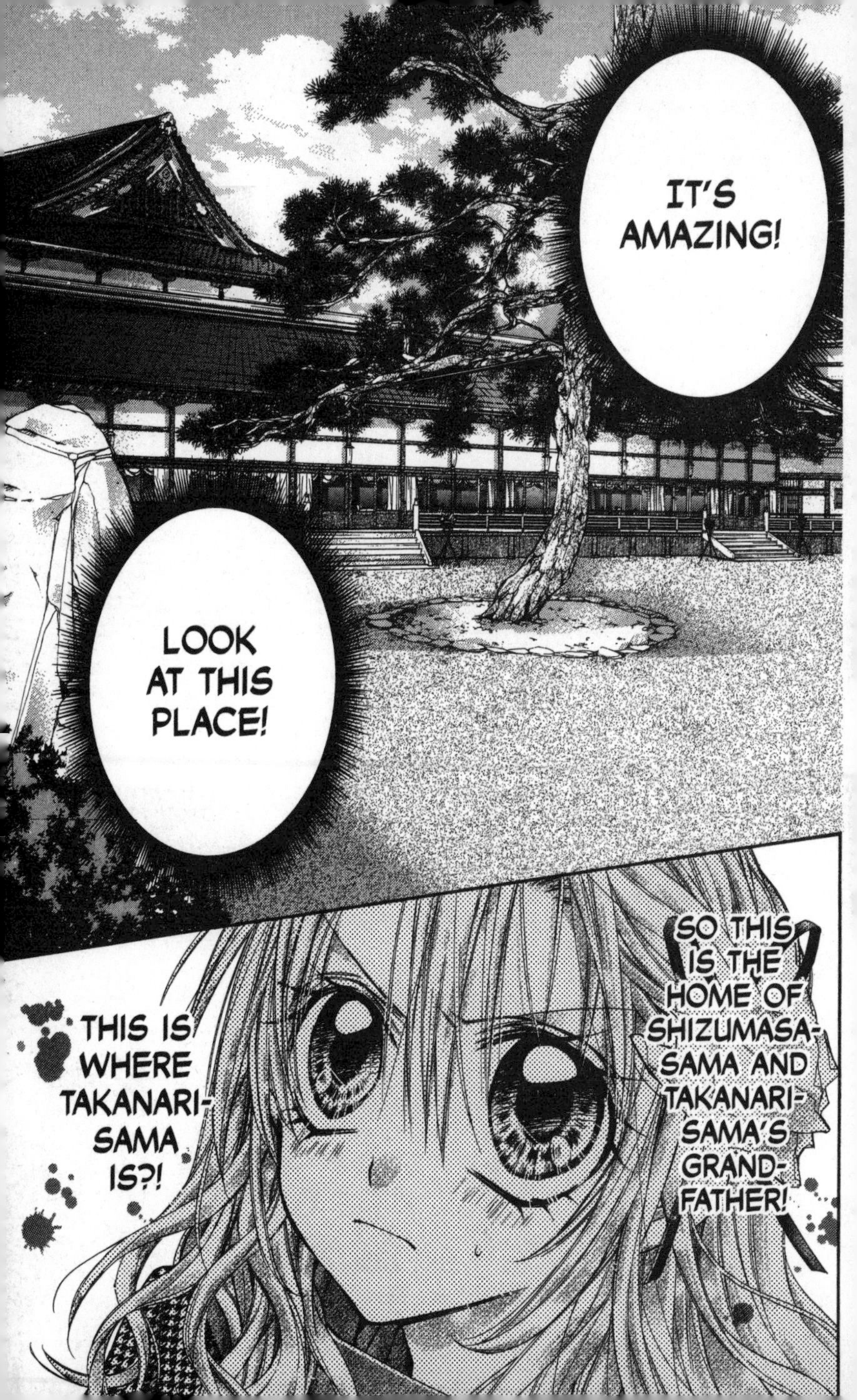
IT'S AMAZING!
LOOK AT THIS PLACE!
SO THIS IS THE HOME OF SHIZUMASA-SAMA AND TAKANARI-SAMA'S GRANDFATHER!
THIS IS WHERE TAKANARI-SAMA IS?!

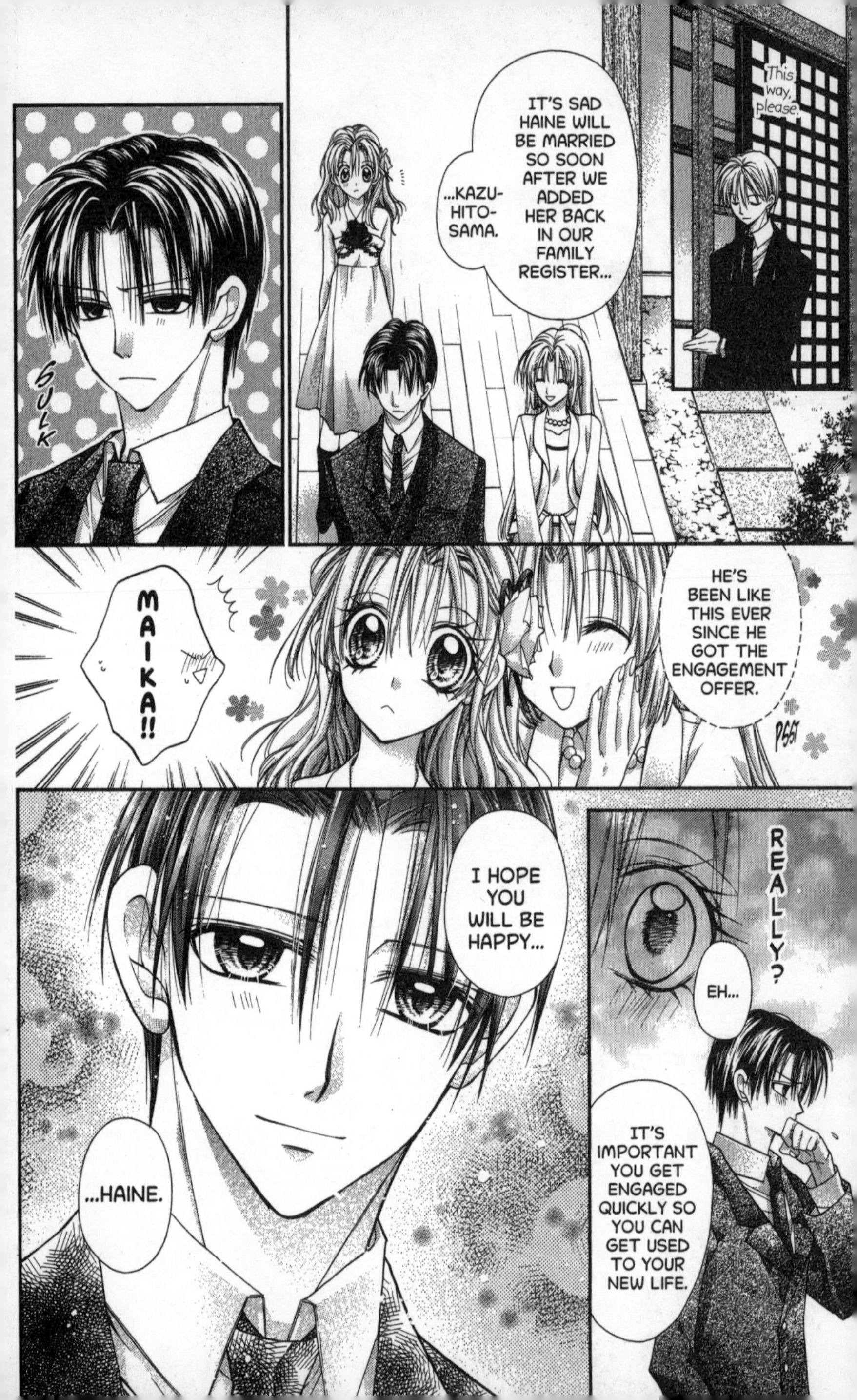
This way, please.
IT'S SAD HAINE WILL BE MARRIED SO SOON AFTER WE ADDED HER BACK IN OUR FAMILY REGISTER...
...KAZUHITO-SAMA.
GULK
HE'S BEEN LIKE THIS EVER SINCE HE GOT THE ENGAGEMENT OFFER.
PSST
MAIKA!!
REALLY?
EH...
IT'S IMPORTANT YOU GET ENGAGED QUICKLY SO YOU CAN GET USED TO YOUR NEW LIFE.
I HOPE YOU WILL BE HAPPY...
...HAINE.

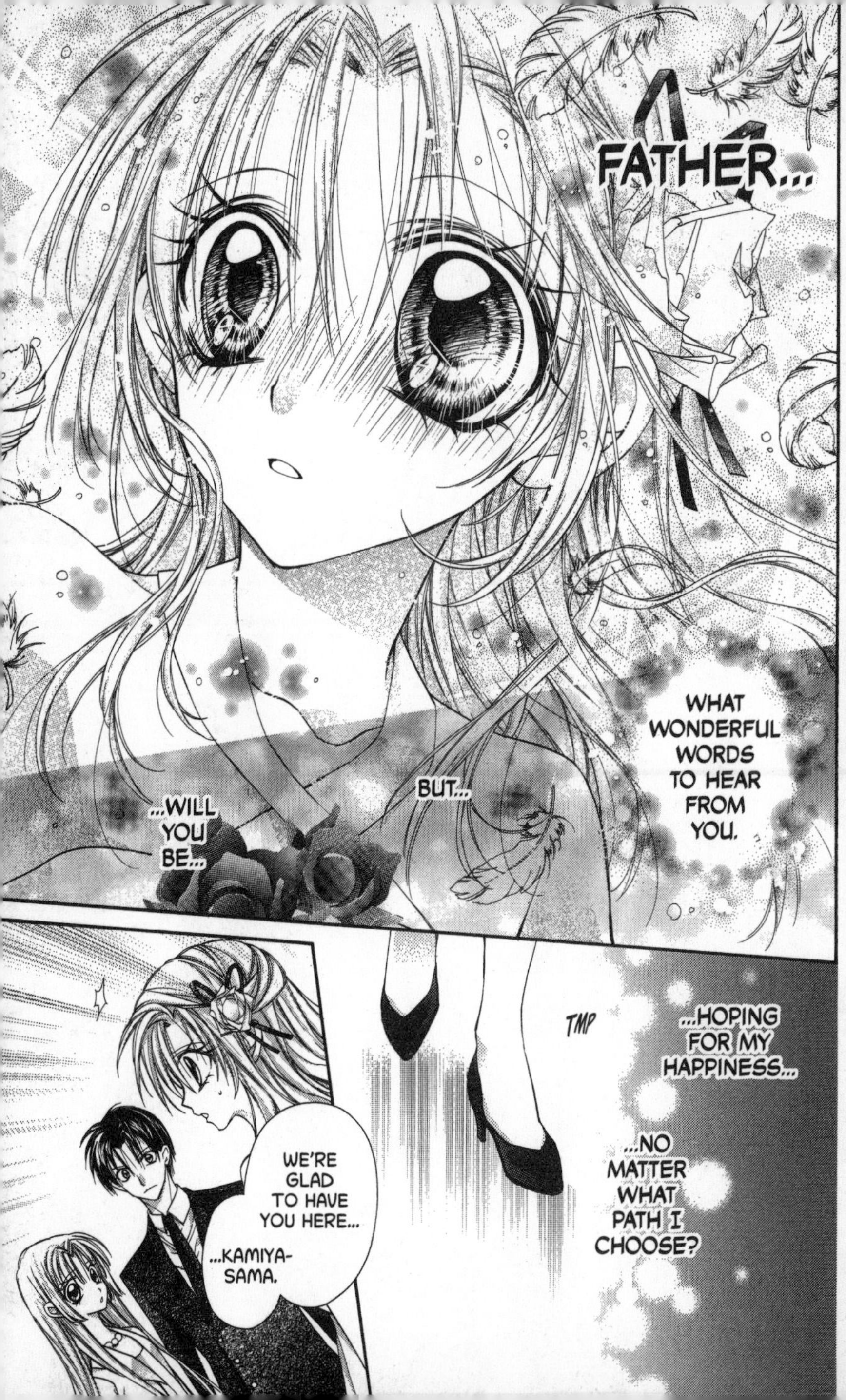
FATHER...
WHAT WONDERFUL WORDS TO HEAR FROM YOU.
BUT...
...WILL YOU BE...
TMP
...HOPING FOR MY HAPPINESS...
...NO MATTER WHAT PATH I CHOOSE?
WE'RE GLAD TO HAVE YOU HERE...
...KAMIYA-SAMA.

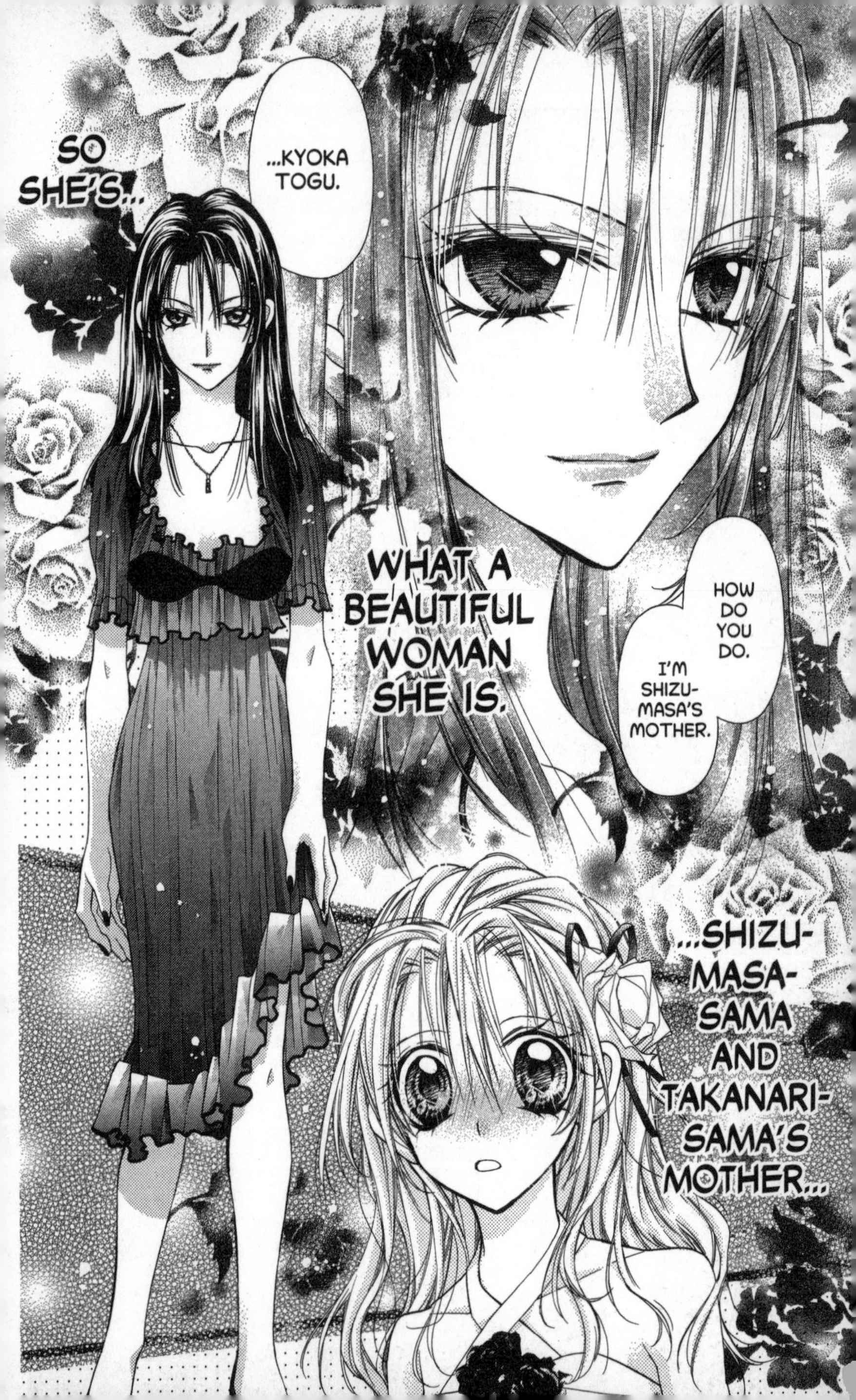
...KYOKA TOGU.
SO SHE'S...
HOW DO YOU DO.
I'M SHIZU-MASA'S MOTHER.
WHAT A BEAUTIFUL WOMAN SHE IS.
...SHIZU-MASA-SAMA AND TAKANARI-SAMA'S MOTHER...

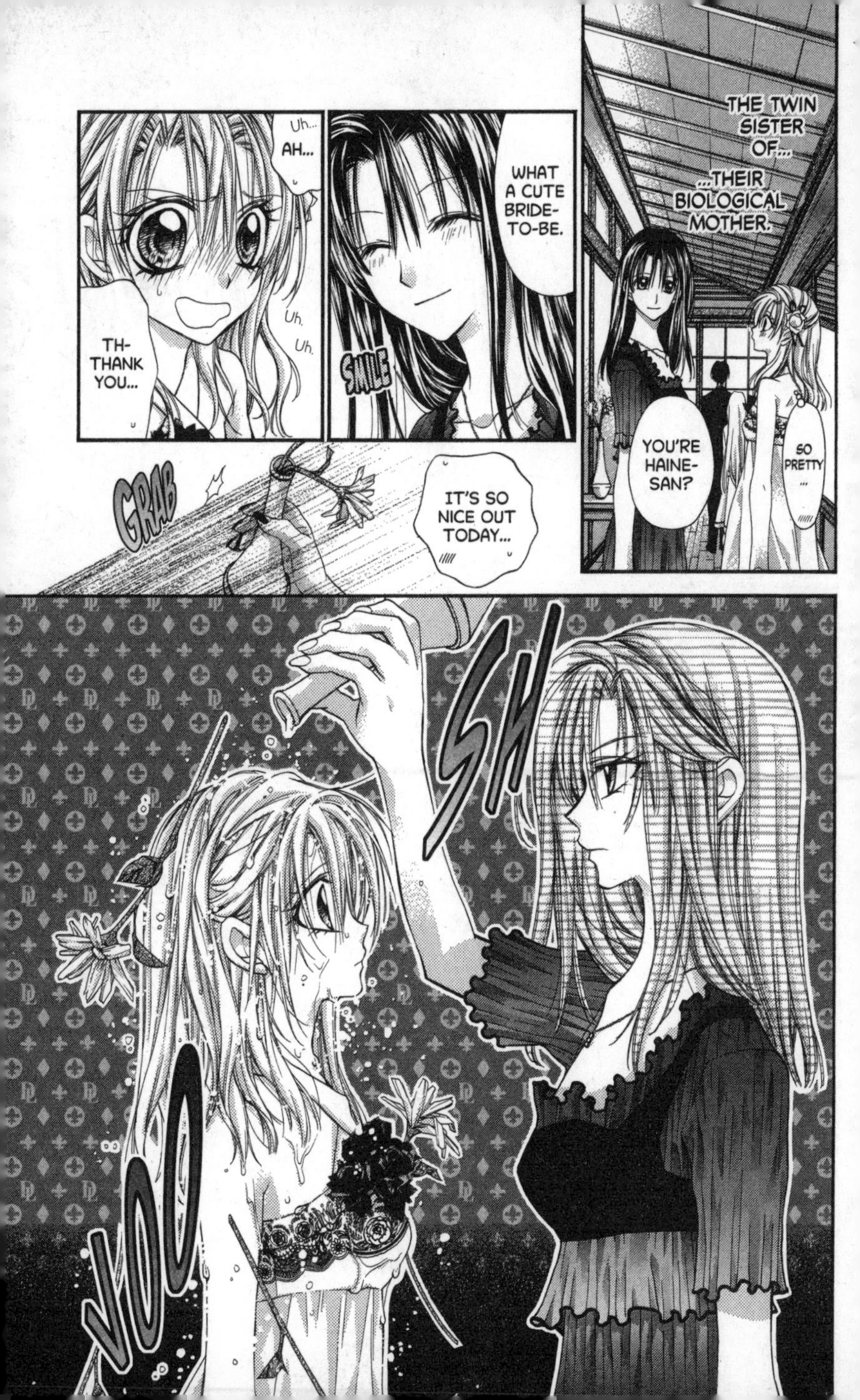
THE TWIN SISTER OF...
...THEIR BIOLOGICAL MOTHER.
SO PRETTY...
YOU'RE HAINE-SAN?
WHAT A CUTE BRIDE-TO-BE.
SMILE
Uh... AH...
Uh. Uh.
TH-THANK YOU...
IT'S SO NICE OUT TODAY...
GRAB
SH
VOO

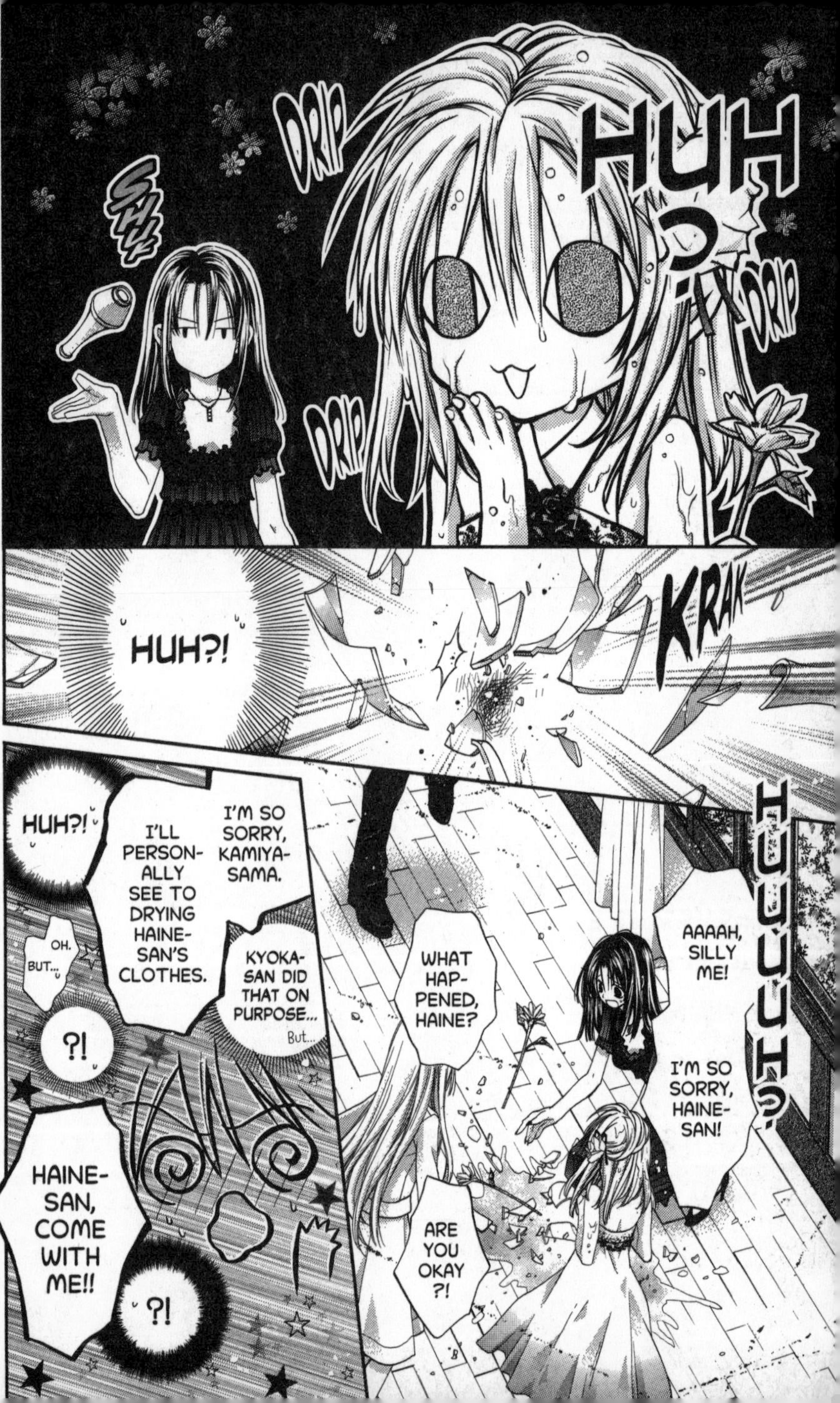
HUH?
DRIP
DRIP
DRIP
KRAK
HUH?!
HUUUUH?
AAAAH, SILLY ME!
I'M SO SORRY, HAINE-SAN!
WHAT HAP-PENED, HAINE?
ARE YOU OKAY?!
I'M SO SORRY, KAMIYA-SAMA.
I'LL PERSON-ALLY SEE TO DRYING HAINE-SAN'S CLOTHES.
HUH?!
KYOKA-SAN DID THAT ON PURPOSE...
But...
OH. BUT...
?!
HAINE-SAN, COME WITH ME!!
?!

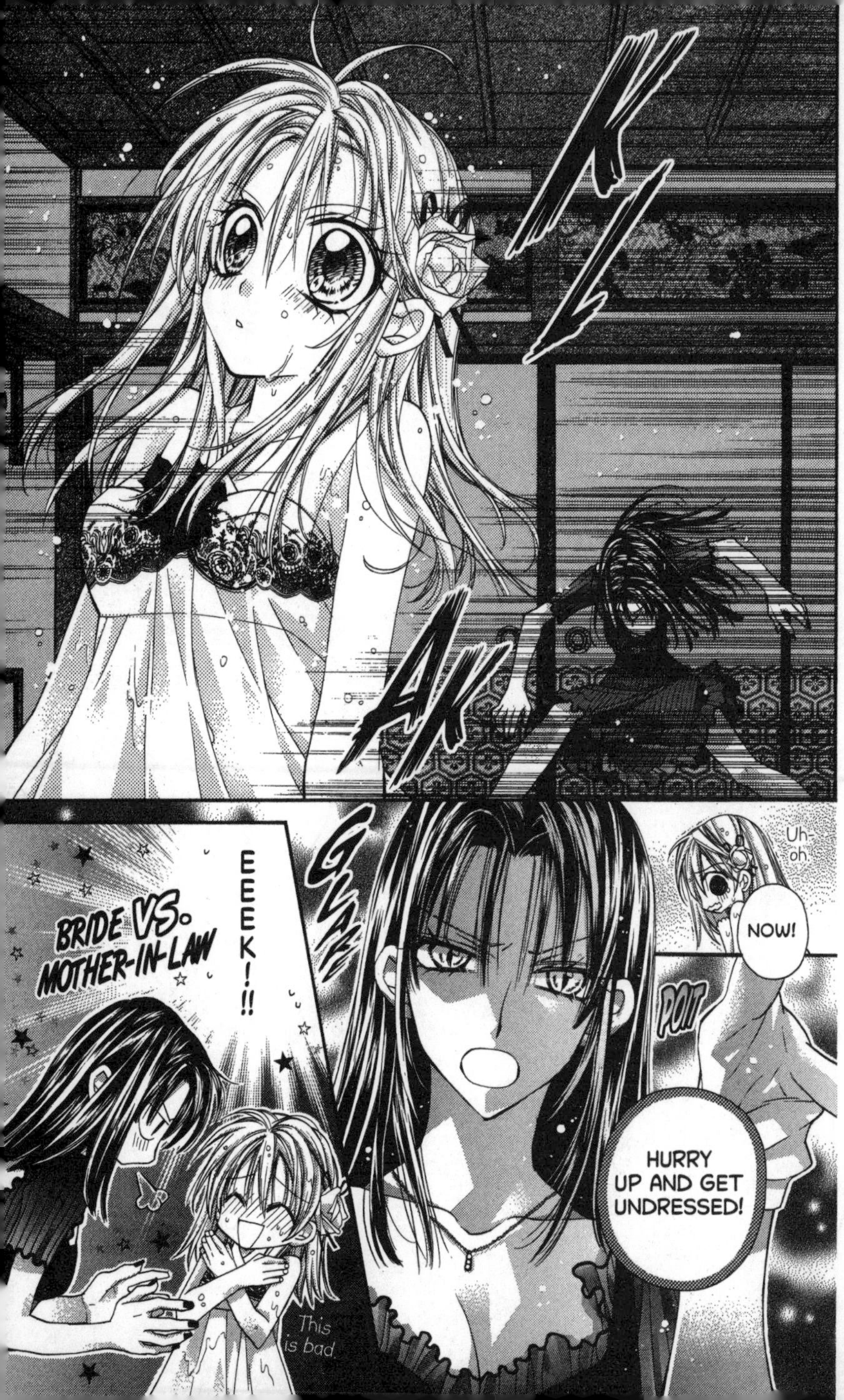

KA
GASHA
EEEEK!!!
BRIDE VS. MOTHER-IN-LAW
Uh-oh.
NOW!
POIT
HURRY UP AND GET UNDRESSED!
This is bad.

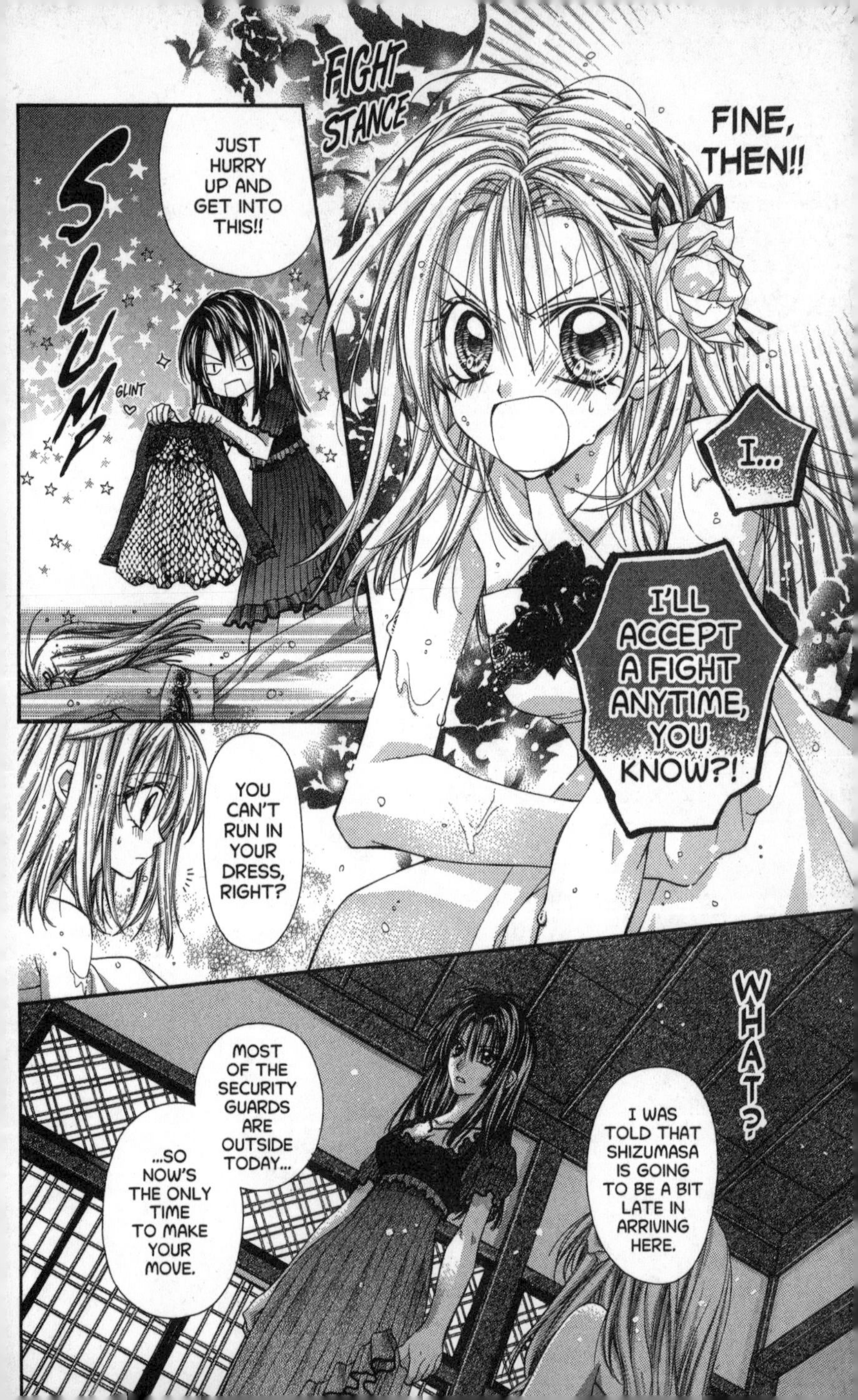
FIGHT STANCE
FINE, THEN!!
I...
I'LL ACCEPT A FIGHT ANYTIME, YOU KNOW?!
JUST HURRY UP AND GET INTO THIS!!
SLUMP
GLINT
YOU CAN'T RUN IN YOUR DRESS, RIGHT?
WHAT?
I WAS TOLD THAT SHIZUMASA IS GOING TO BE A BIT LATE IN ARRIVING HERE.
MOST OF THE SECURITY GUARDS ARE OUTSIDE TODAY...
...SO NOW'S THE ONLY TIME TO MAKE YOUR MOVE.

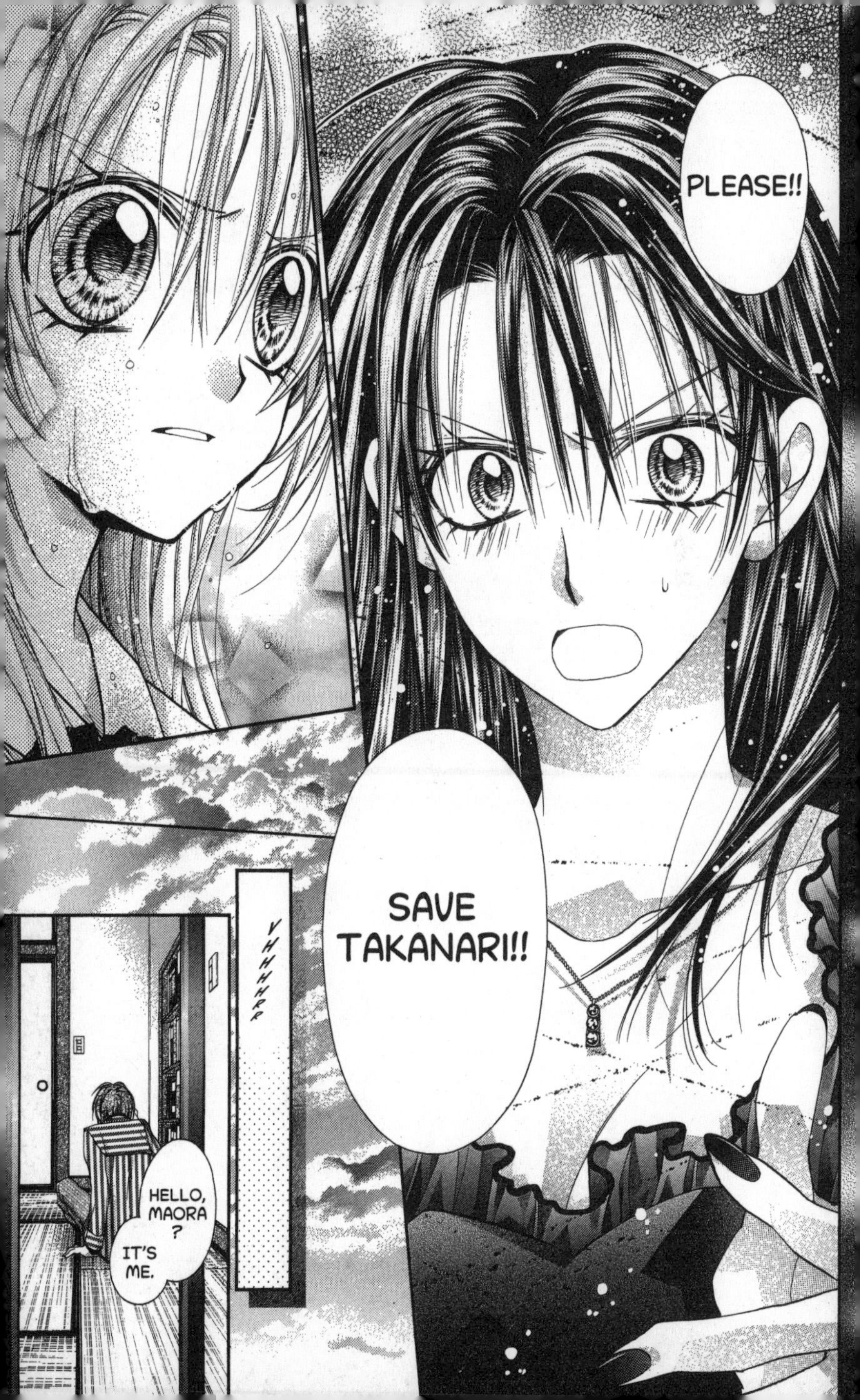
PLEASE!!
SAVE TAKANARI!!
VHHHHRR
HELLO, MAORA?
IT'S ME.

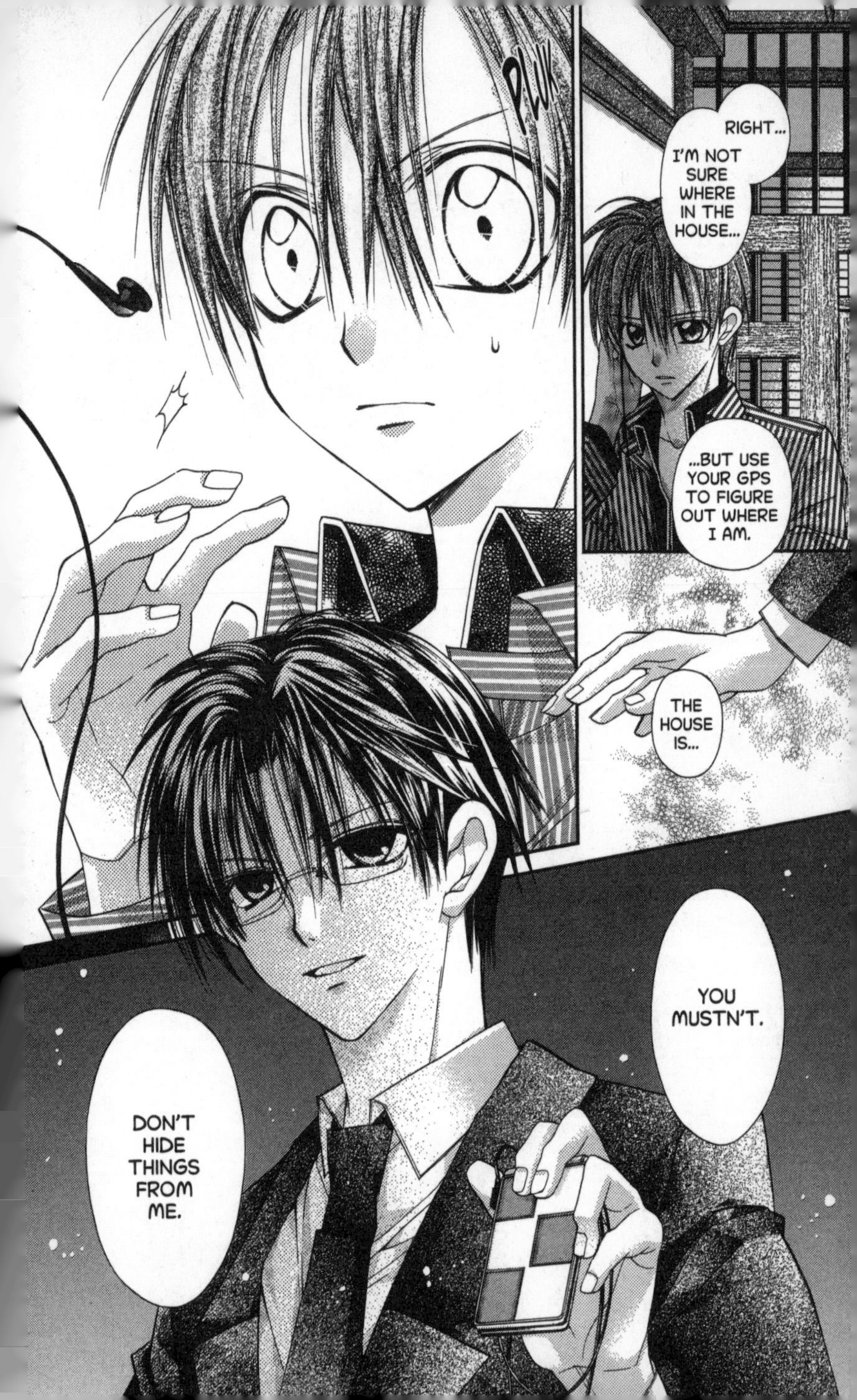
RIGHT...
I'M NOT SURE WHERE IN THE HOUSE...
...BUT USE YOUR GPS TO FIGURE OUT WHERE I AM.
PLUK
THE HOUSE IS...
YOU MUSTN'T.
DON'T HIDE THINGS FROM ME.

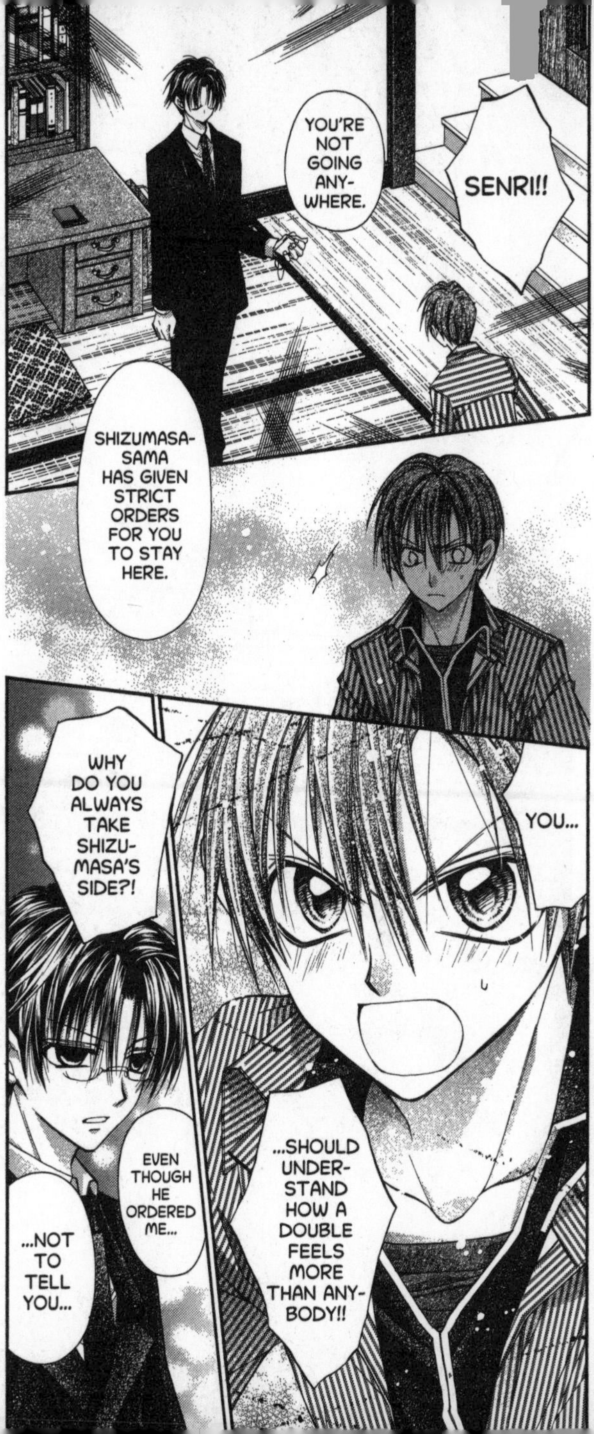
SENRI!!
YOU'RE NOT GOING ANYWHERE.
SHIZUMASA-SAMA HAS GIVEN STRICT ORDERS FOR YOU TO STAY HERE.
WHY DO YOU ALWAYS TAKE SHIZUMASA'S SIDE?!
YOU...
...SHOULD UNDERSTAND HOW A DOUBLE FEELS MORE THAN ANYBODY!!
EVEN THOUGH HE ORDERED ME...
...NOT TO TELL YOU...
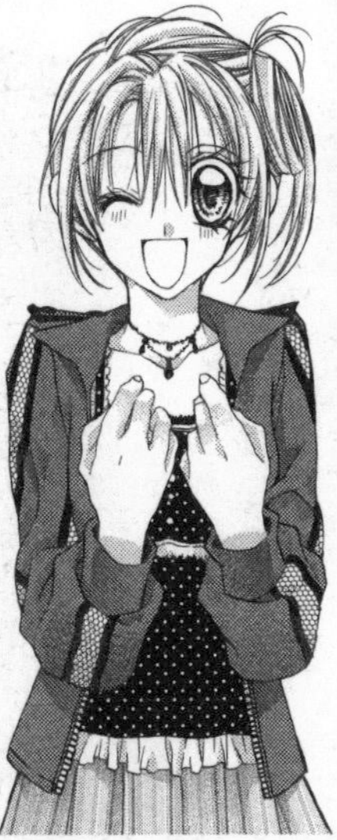

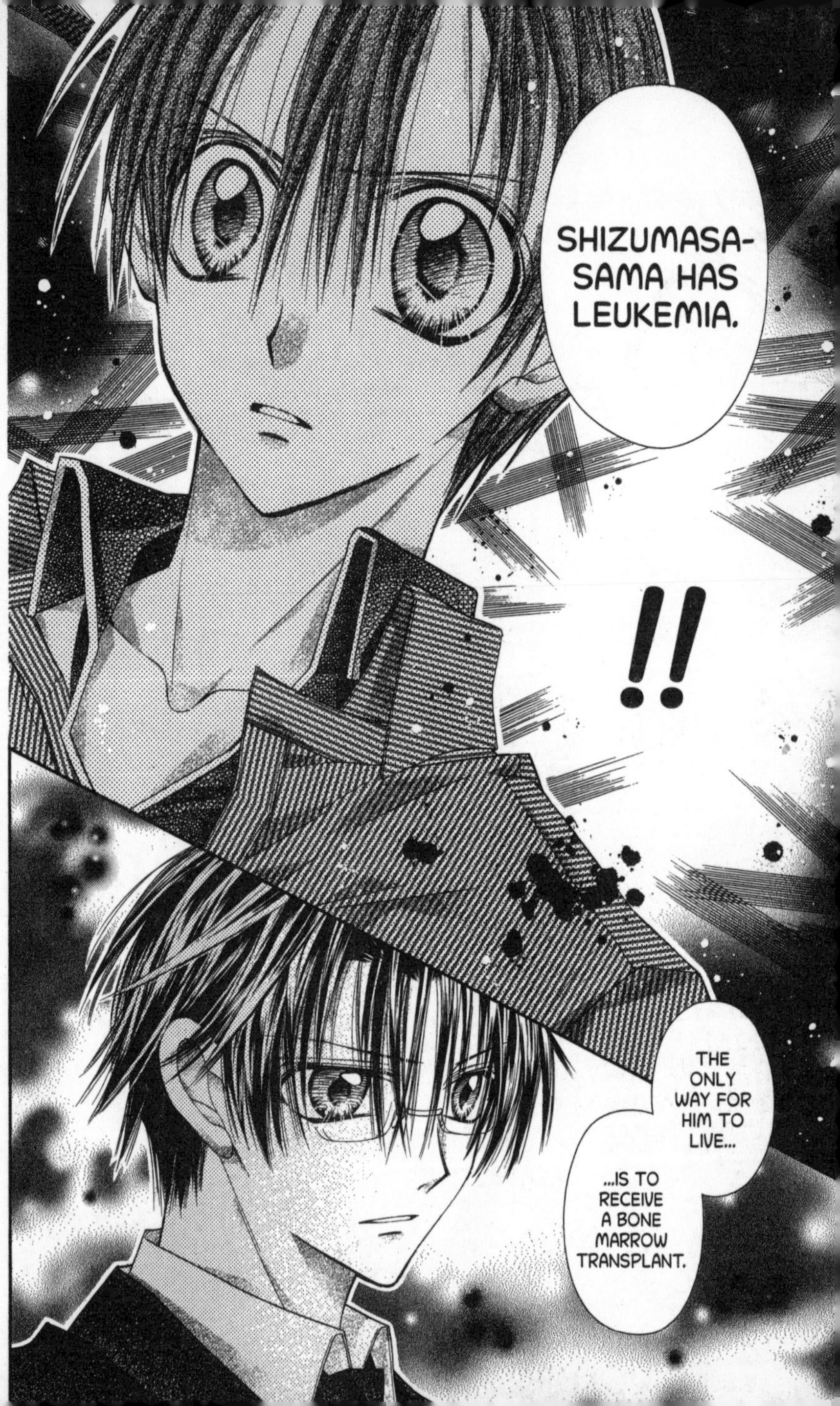
SHIZUMASA-SAMA HAS LEUKEMIA.
!!
THE ONLY WAY FOR HIM TO LIVE...
...IS TO RECEIVE A BONE MARROW TRANSPLANT.

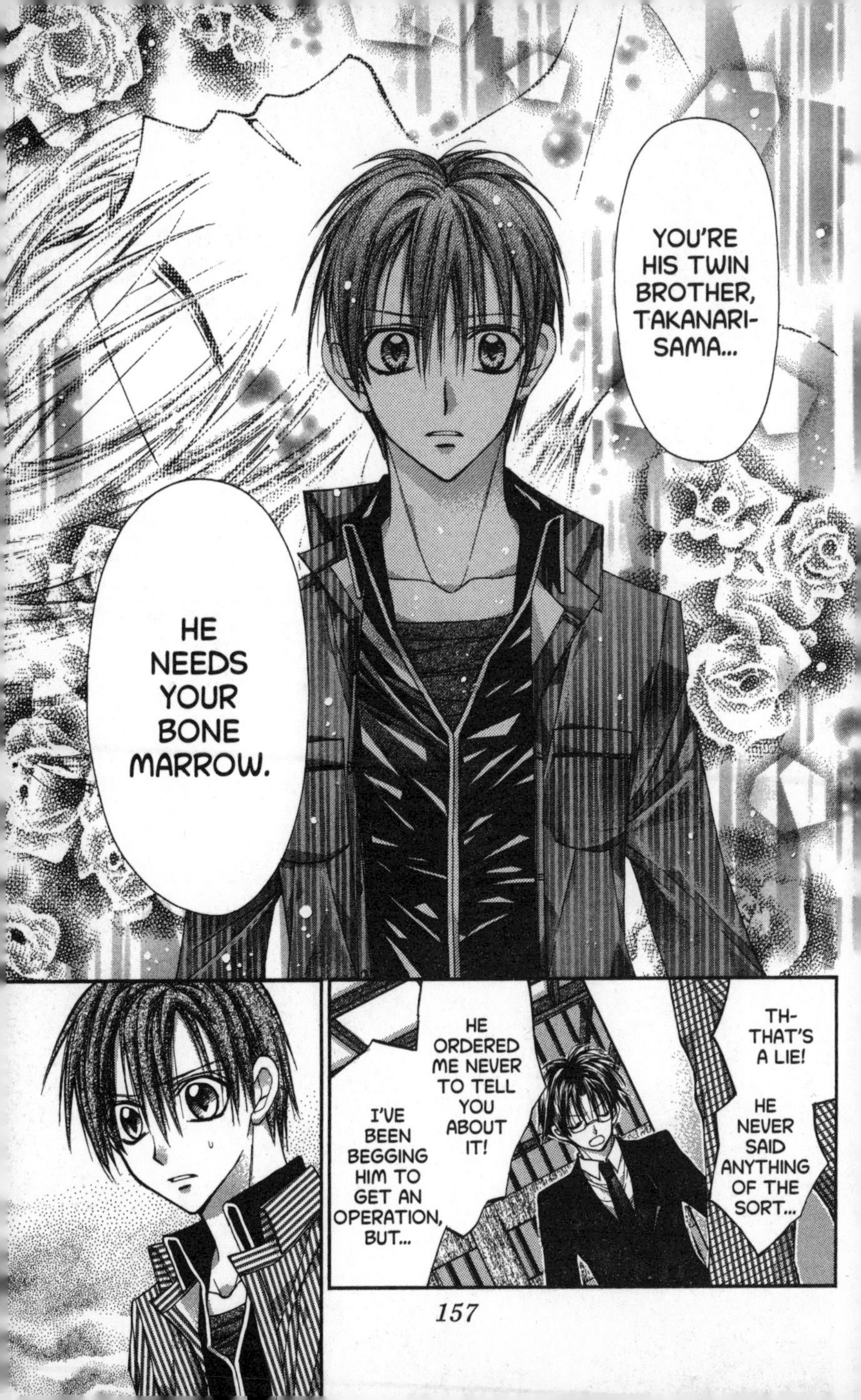
YOU'RE HIS TWIN BROTHER, TAKANARI-SAMA...
HE NEEDS YOUR BONE MARROW.
TH-THAT'S A LIE!
HE NEVER SAID ANYTHING OF THE SORT...
HE ORDERED ME NEVER TO TELL YOU ABOUT IT!
I'VE BEEN BEGGING HIM TO GET AN OPERATION, BUT...

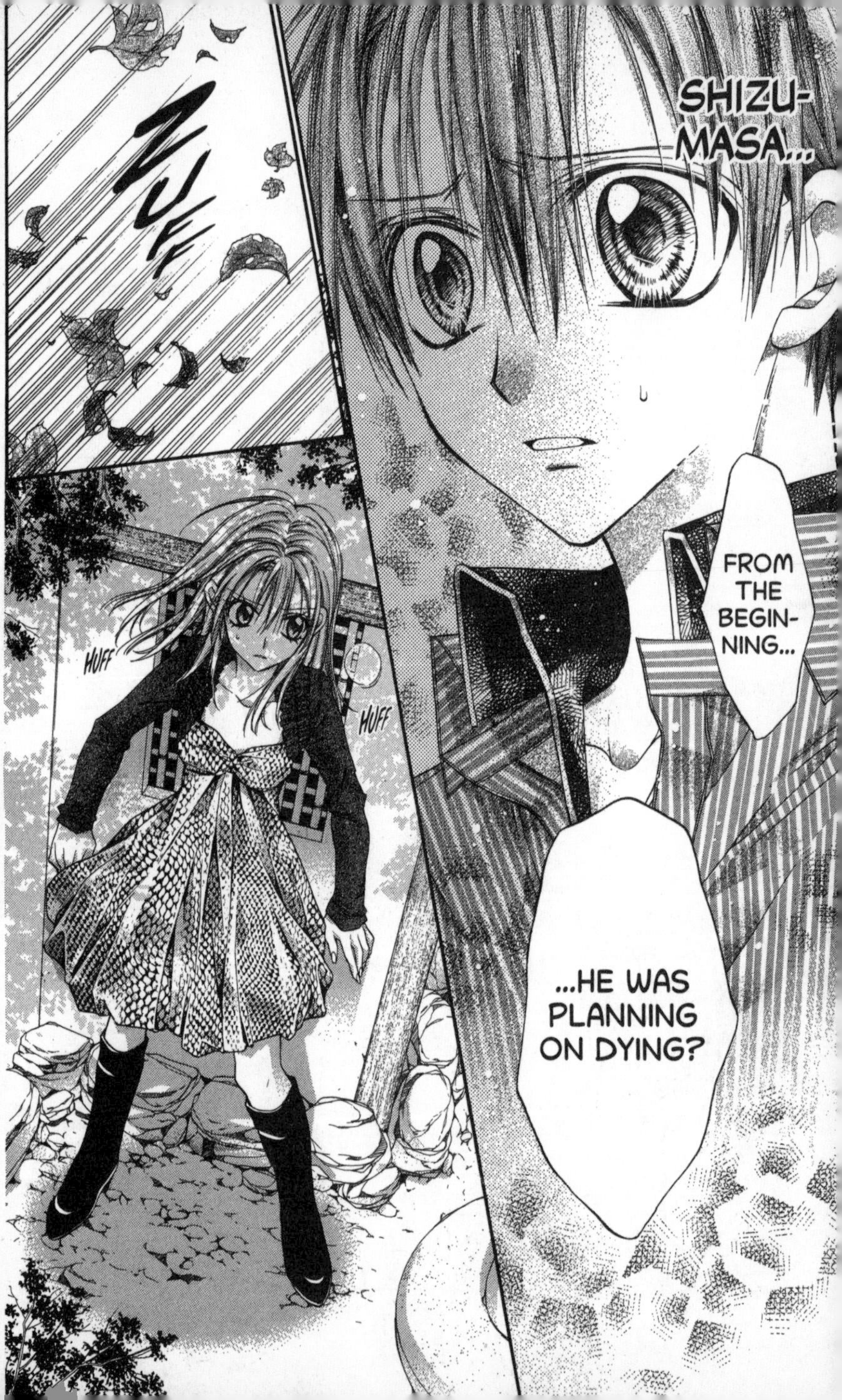
SHIZU-MASA...
FROM THE BEGINNING...
...HE WAS PLANNING ON DYING?
ZUFF
HUFF
HUFF

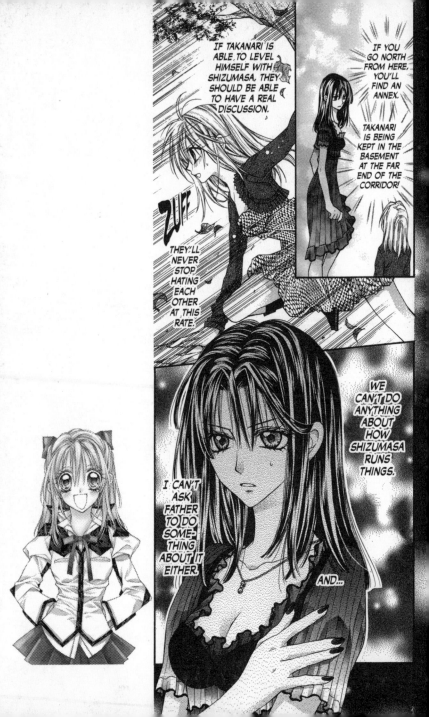

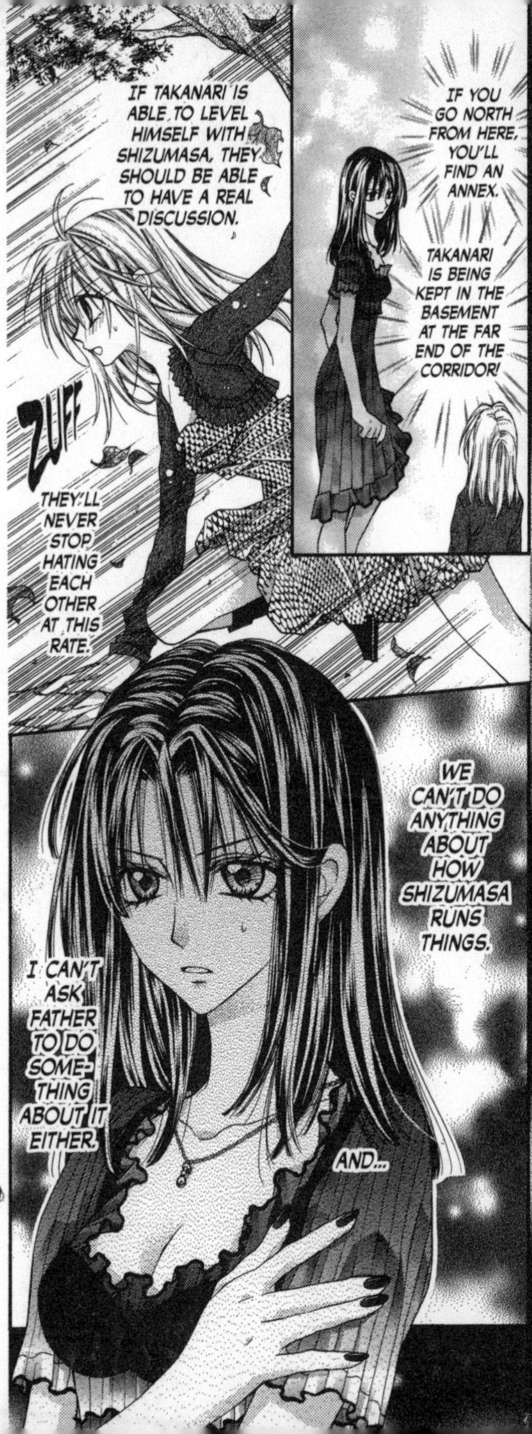
IF YOU GO NORTH FROM HERE, YOU'LL FIND AN ANNEX.
TAKANARI IS BEING KEPT IN THE BASEMENT AT THE FAR END OF THE CORRIDOR!
IF TAKANARI IS ABLE TO LEVEL HIMSELF WITH SHIZUMASA, THEY SHOULD BE ABLE TO HAVE A REAL DISCUSSION.
ZUFF
THEY'LL NEVER STOP HATING EACH OTHER AT THIS RATE.
WE CAN'T DO ANYTHING ABOUT HOW SHIZUMASA RUNS THINGS.
I CAN'T ASK FATHER TO DO SOME-THING ABOUT IT EITHER.
AND...

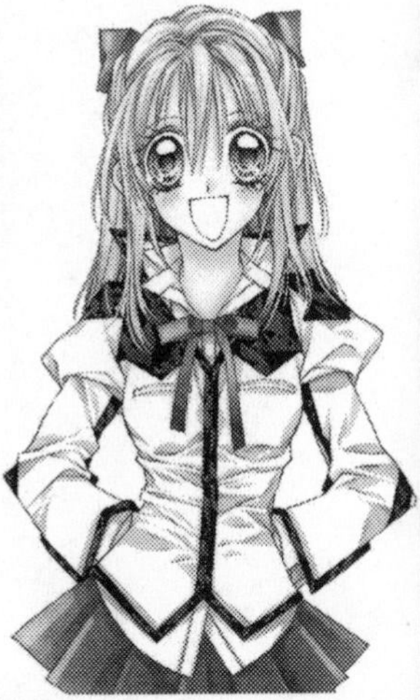

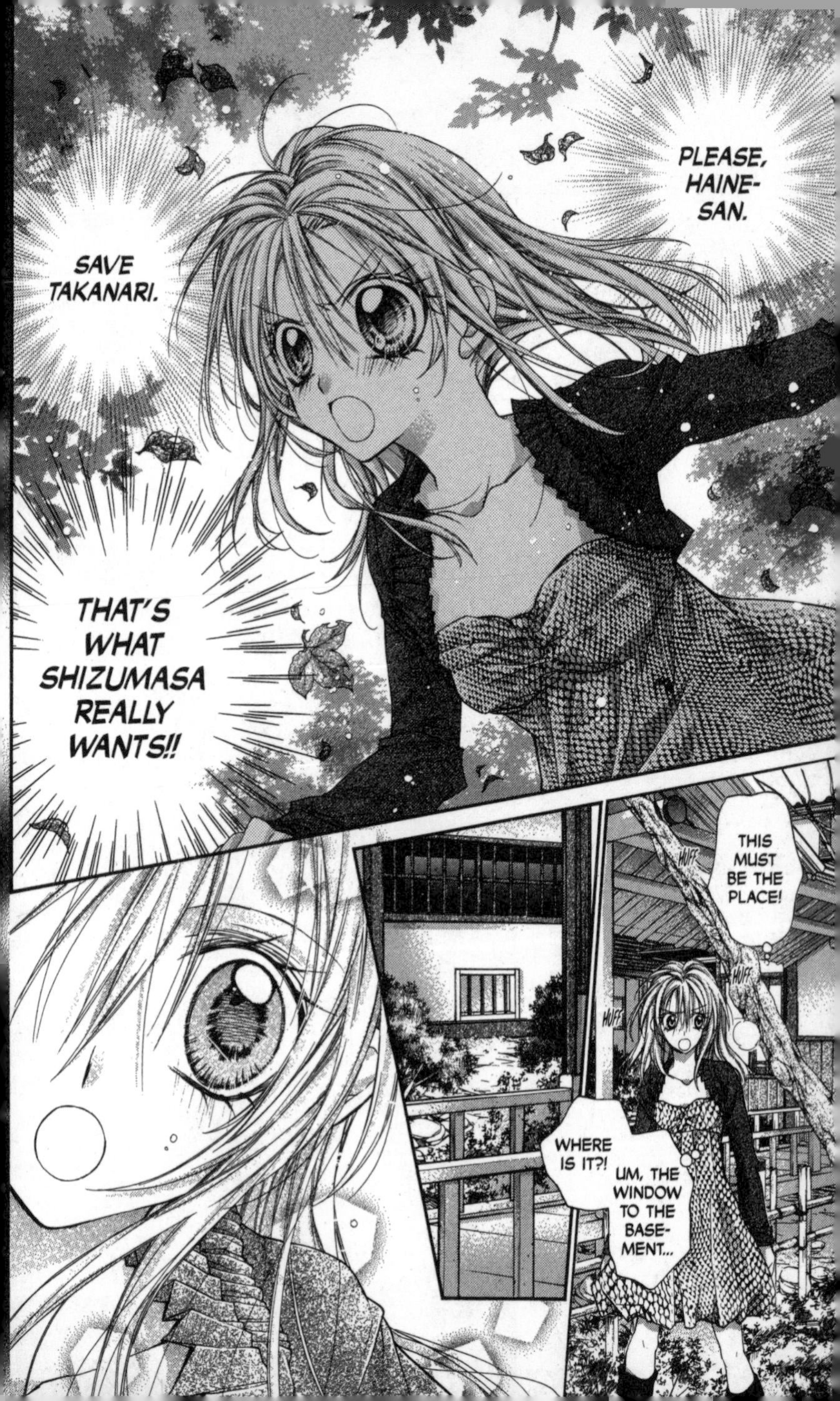
PLEASE, HAINE-SAN.
SAVE TAKANARI.
THAT'S WHAT SHIZUMASA REALLY WANTS!!
THIS MUST BE THE PLACE!
HUFF
HUFF
HUFF
WHERE IS IT?!
UM, THE WINDOW TO THE BASEMENT...

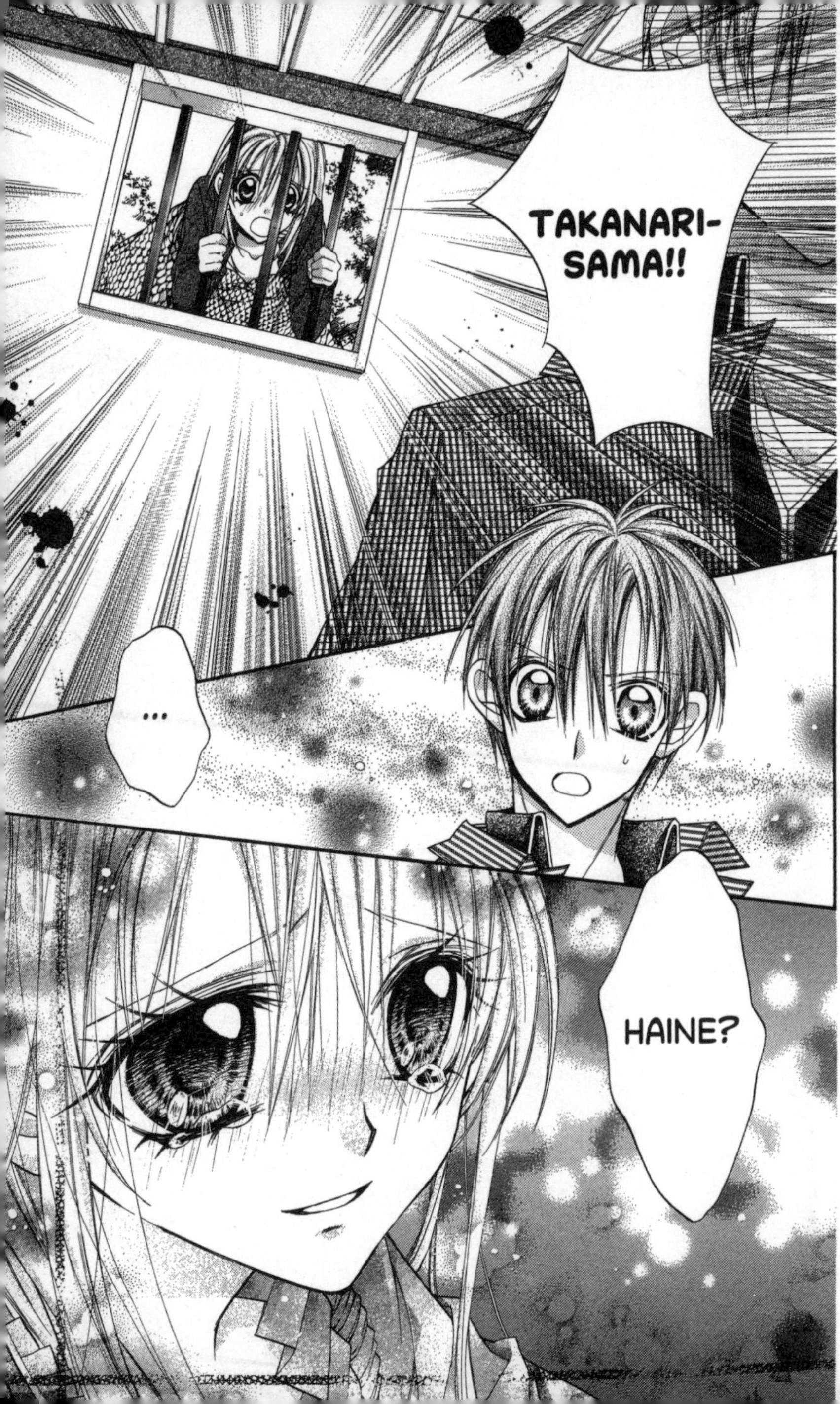
TAKANARI-SAMA!!
...
HAINE?

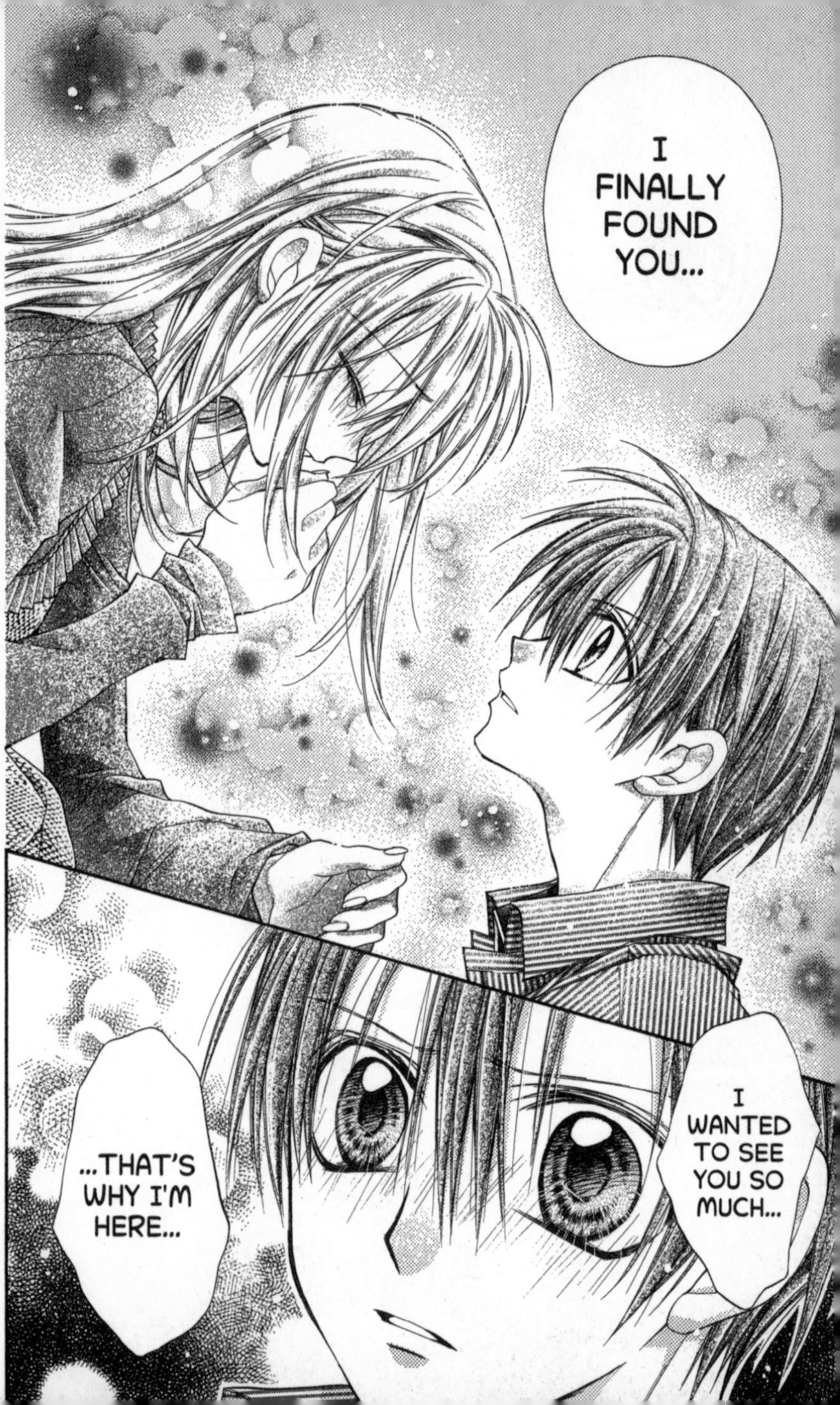
I FINALLY FOUND YOU...
I WANTED TO SEE YOU SO MUCH...
...THAT'S WHY I'M HERE...

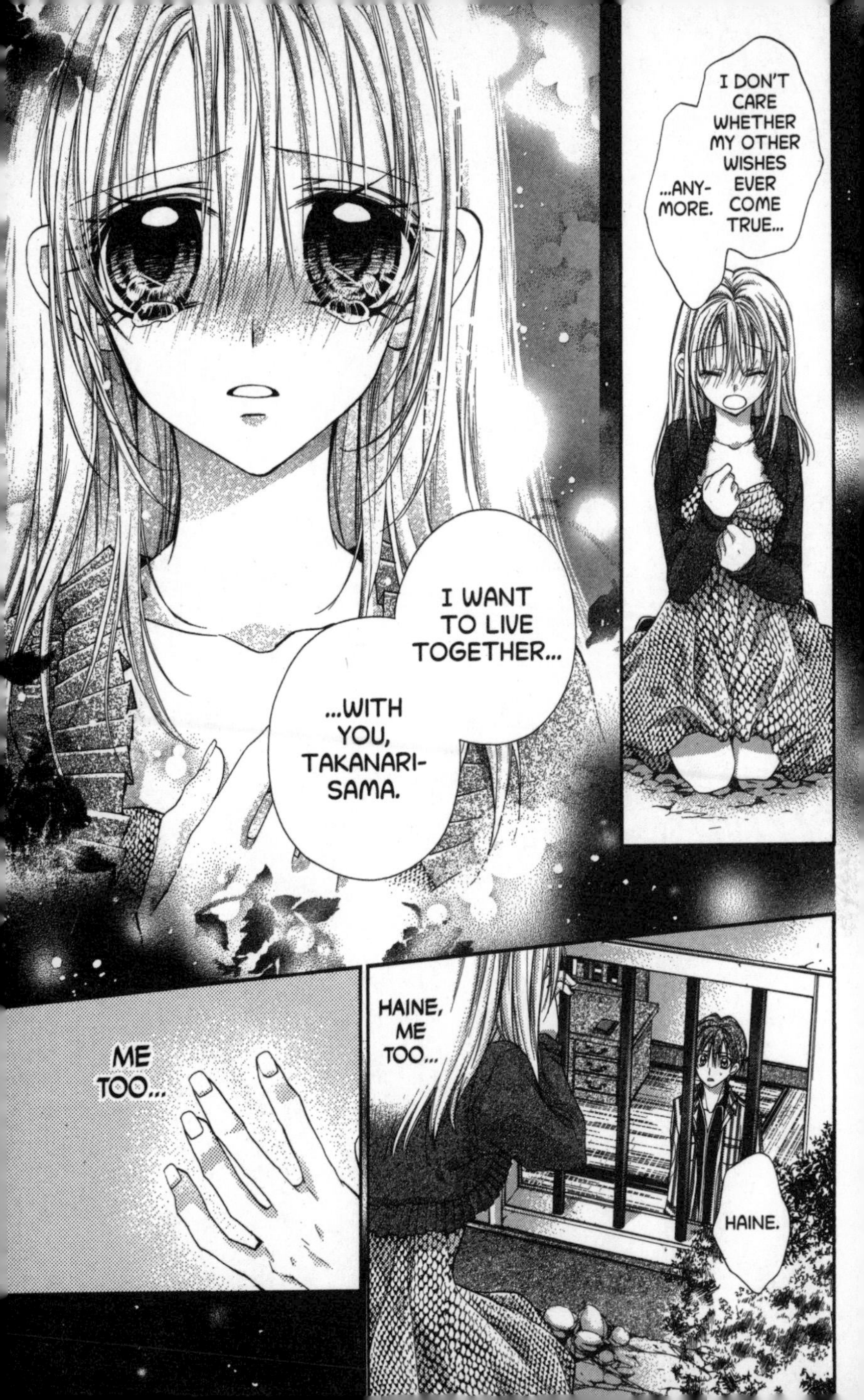
I DON'T CARE WHETHER MY OTHER WISHES EVER COME TRUE...
...ANY-MORE.
I WANT TO LIVE TOGETHER...
...WITH YOU, TAKANARI-SAMA.
HAINE, ME TOO...
HAINE.
ME TOO...

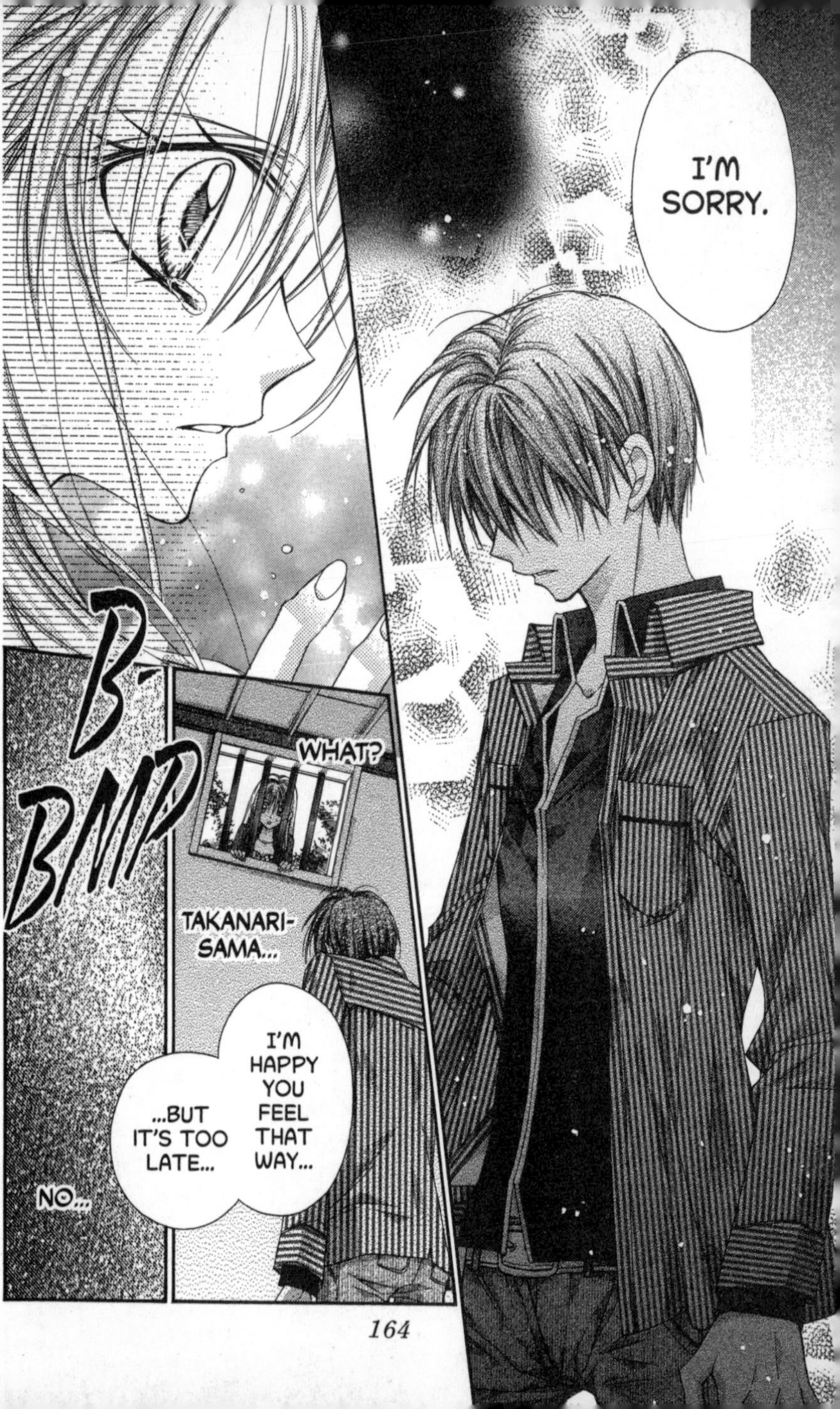
I'M SORRY.
B-BMP
WHAT?
TAKANARI-SAMA...
I'M HAPPY YOU FEEL THAT WAY...
...BUT IT'S TOO LATE...
NO...

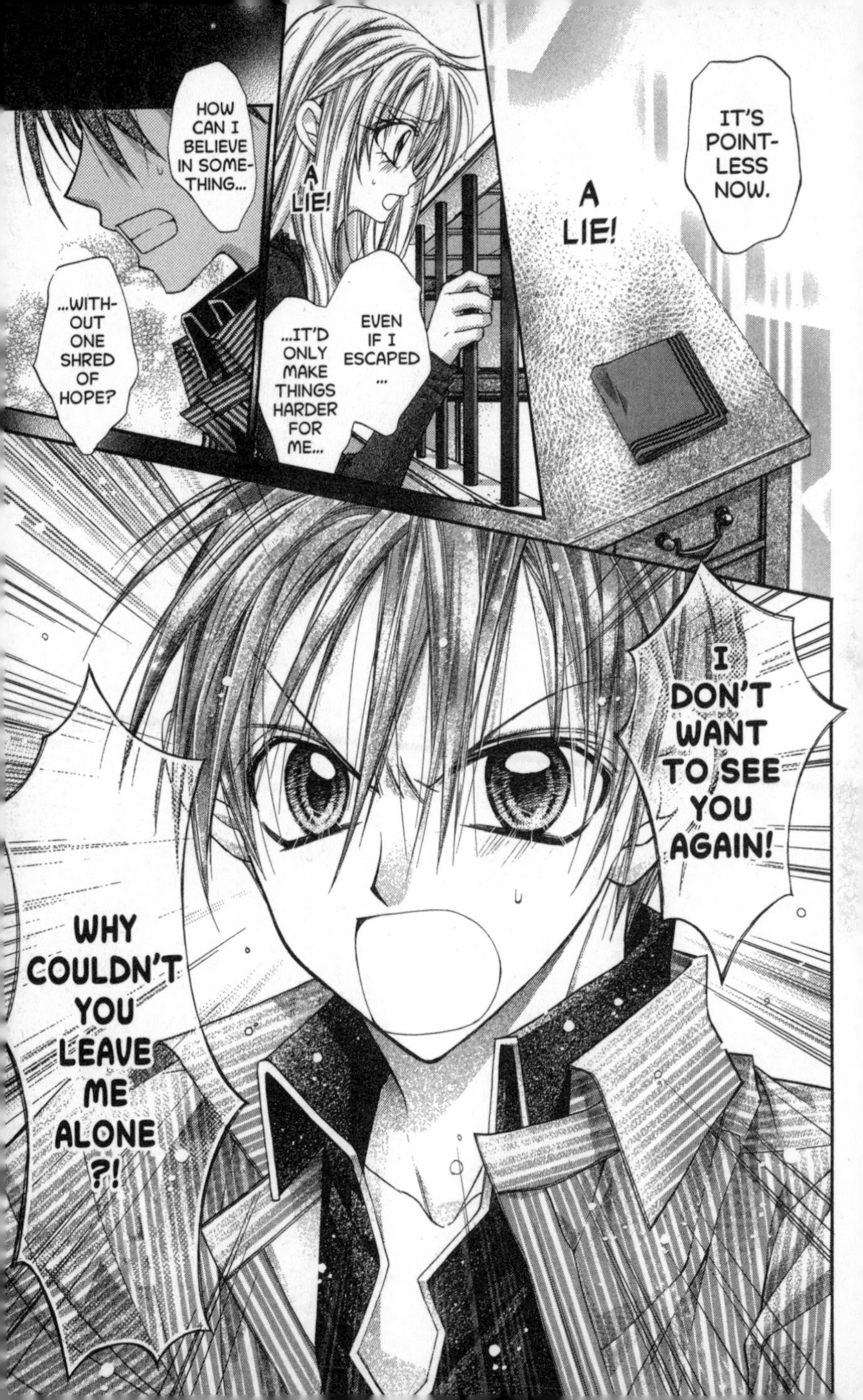
IT'S POINTLESS NOW.
A LIE!
A LIE!
EVEN IF I ESCAPED...
...IT'D ONLY MAKE THINGS HARDER FOR ME...
HOW CAN I BELIEVE IN SOMETHING...
...WITHOUT ONE SHRED OF HOPE?
I DON'T WANT TO SEE YOU AGAIN!
WHY COULDN'T YOU LEAVE ME ALONE?!

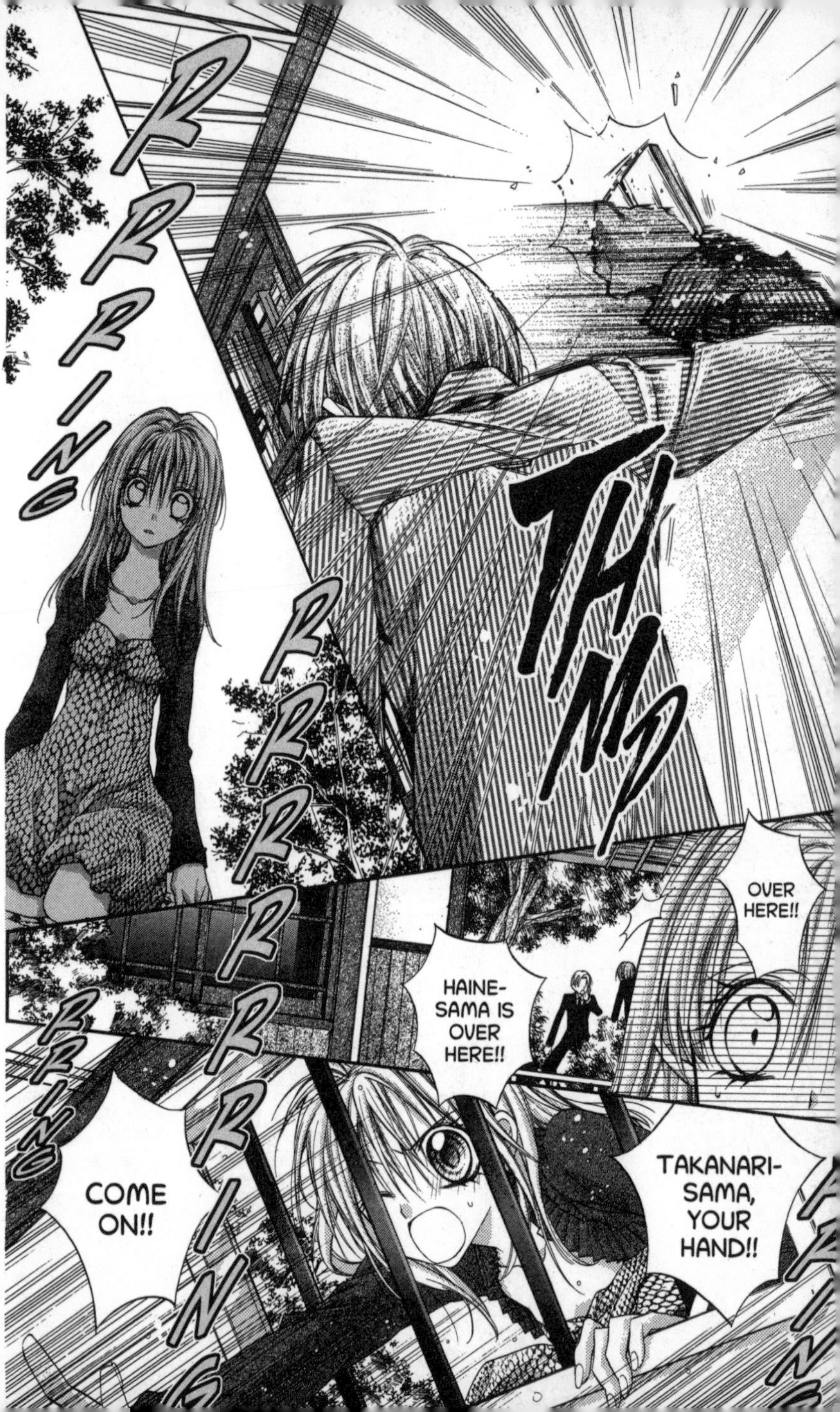
THMP
PRRRRING
OVER HERE!!
HAINE-SAMA IS OVER HERE!!
PRRRRRRRRING
TAKANARI-SAMA, YOUR HAND!!
COME ON!!
PRRING

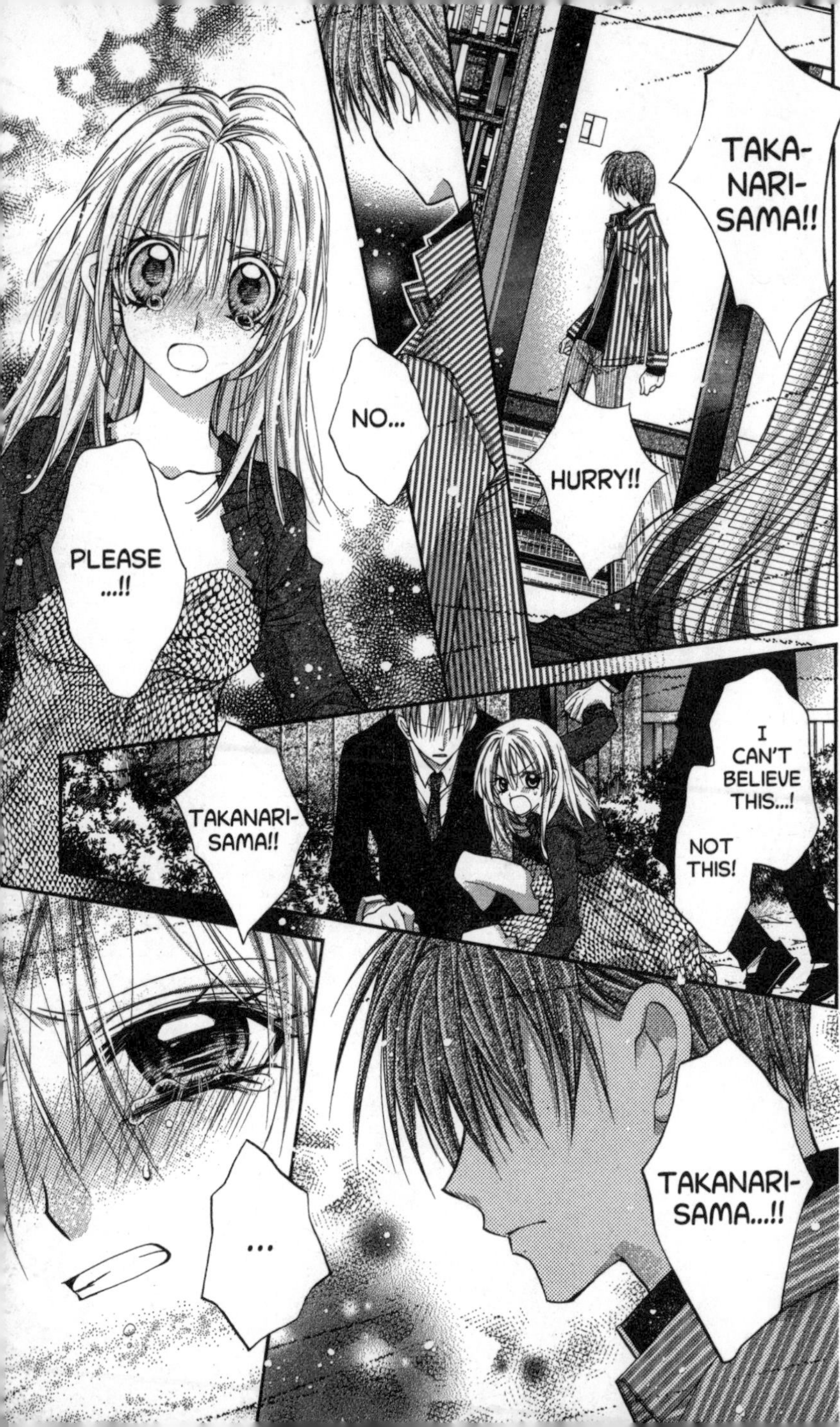
TAKA-NARI-SAMA!!
HURRY!!
NO...
PLEASE ...!!
I CAN'T BELIEVE THIS...!
NOT THIS!
TAKANARI-SAMA!!
TAKANARI-SAMA...!!
...

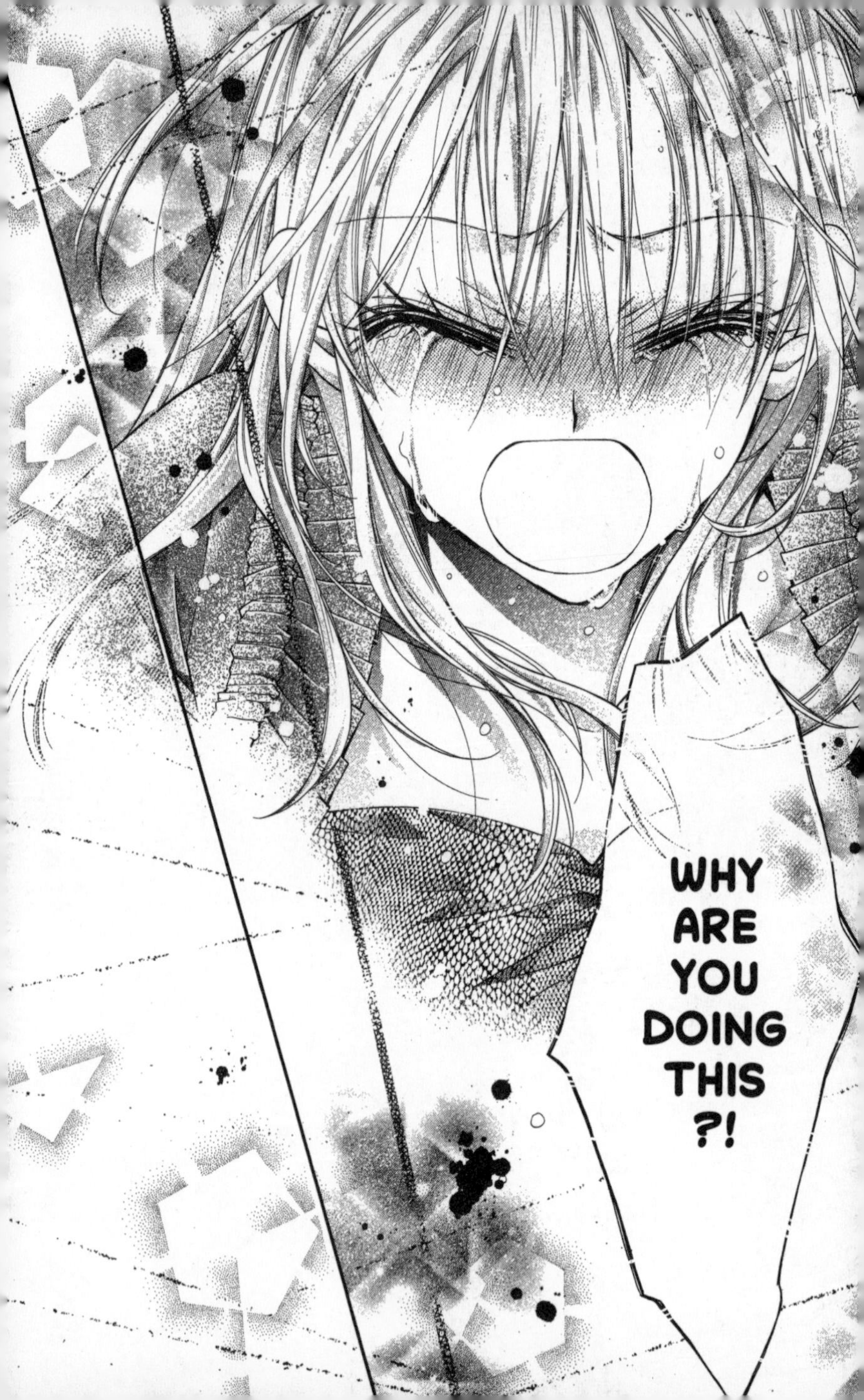
WHY ARE YOU DOING THIS?!

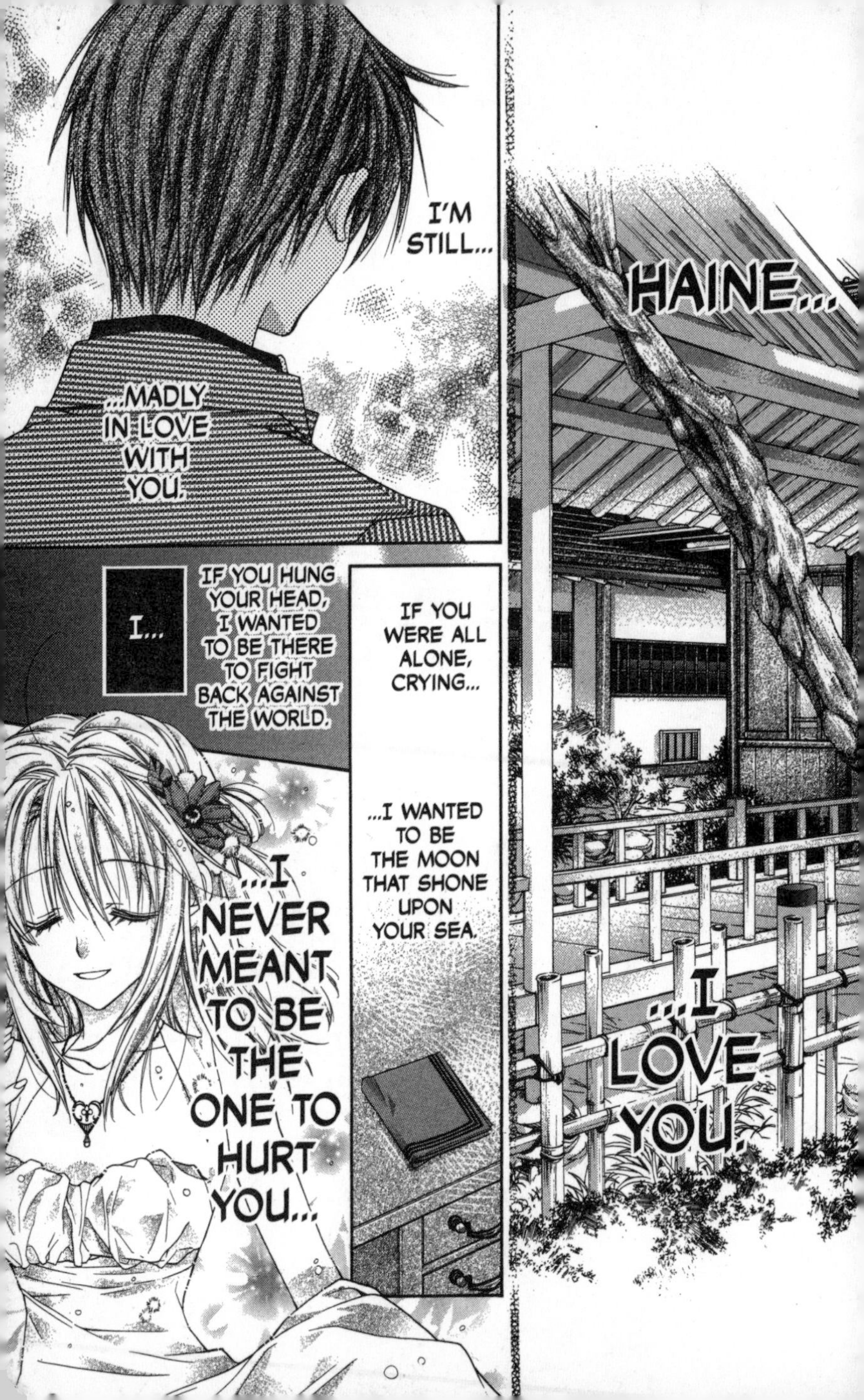
HAINE...
...I LOVE YOU.
I'M STILL...
...MADLY IN LOVE WITH YOU.
IF YOU WERE ALL ALONE, CRYING...
...I WANTED TO BE THE MOON THAT SHONE UPON YOUR SEA.
I...
IF YOU HUNG YOUR HEAD, I WANTED TO BE THERE TO FIGHT BACK AGAINST THE WORLD.
...I NEVER MEANT TO BE THE ONE TO HURT YOU...

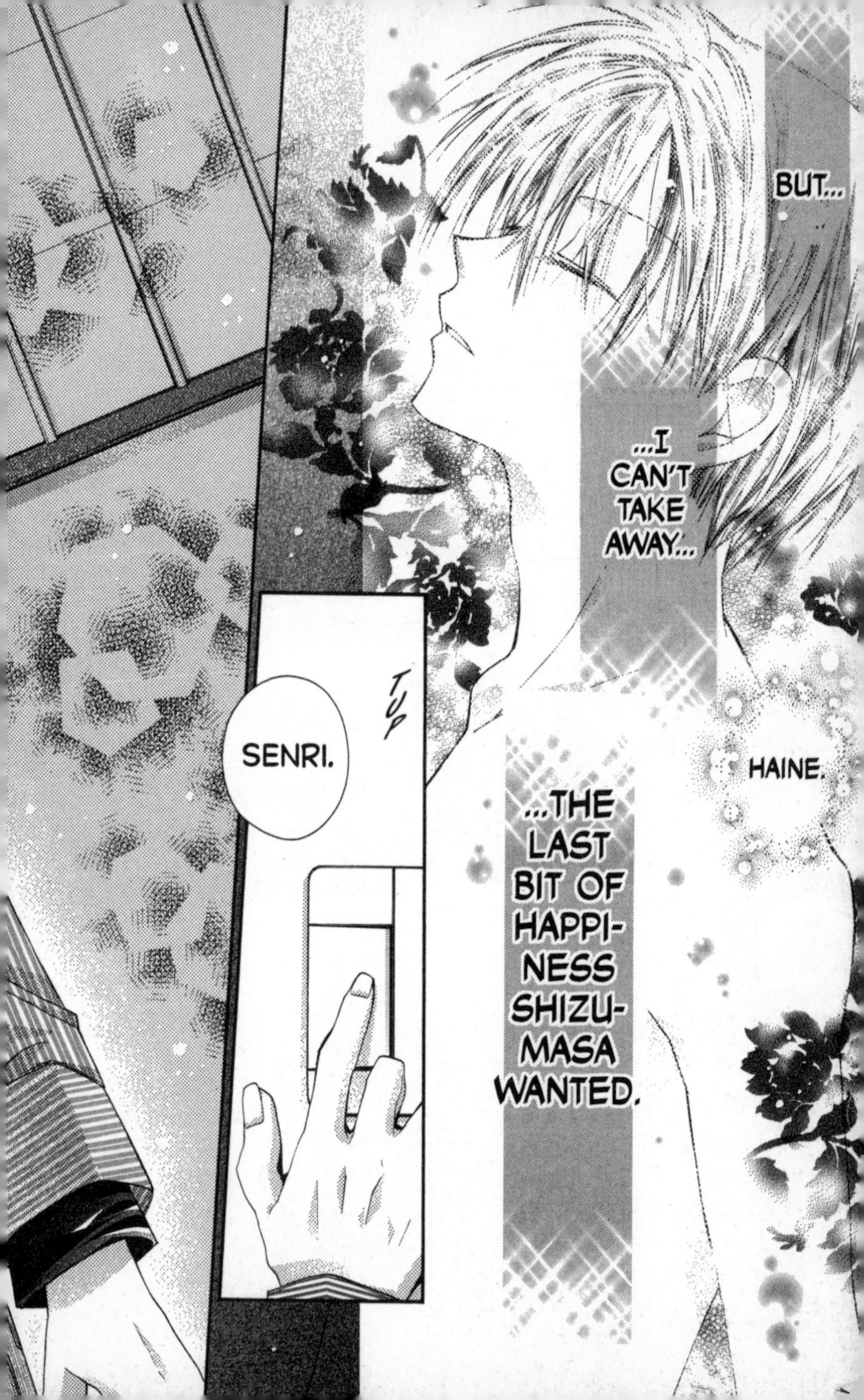
BUT...
...I CAN'T TAKE AWAY...
HAINE.
...THE LAST BIT OF HAPPINESS SHIZUMASA WANTED.
TUP
SENRI.

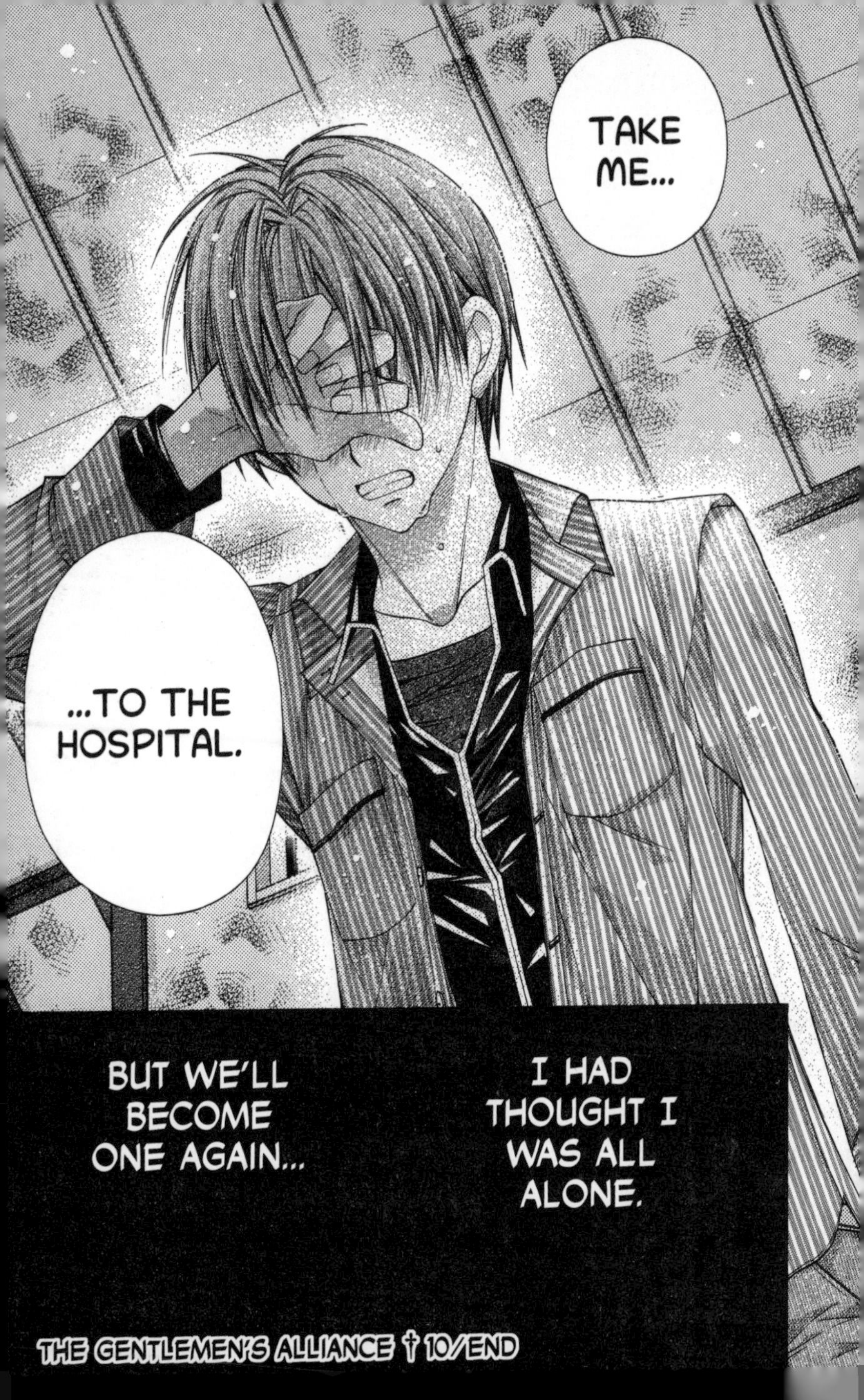
TAKE ME...
...TO THE HOSPITAL.
I HAD THOUGHT I WAS ALL ALONE.
BUT WE'LL BECOME ONE AGAIN...
THE GENTLEMEN'S ALLIANCE † 10/END

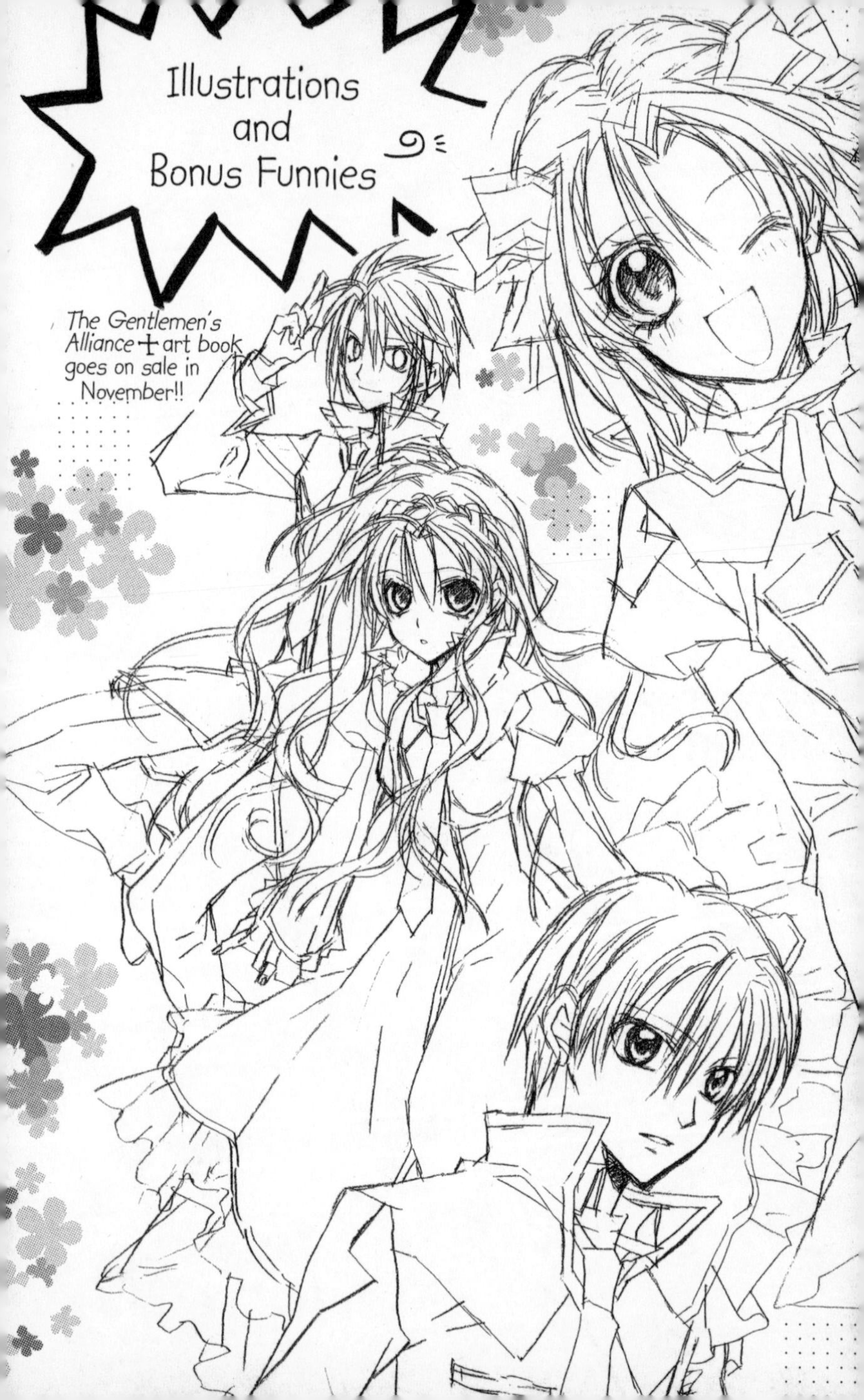
Illustrations and Bonus Funnies
The Gentlemen's Alliance † art book goes on sale in November!!

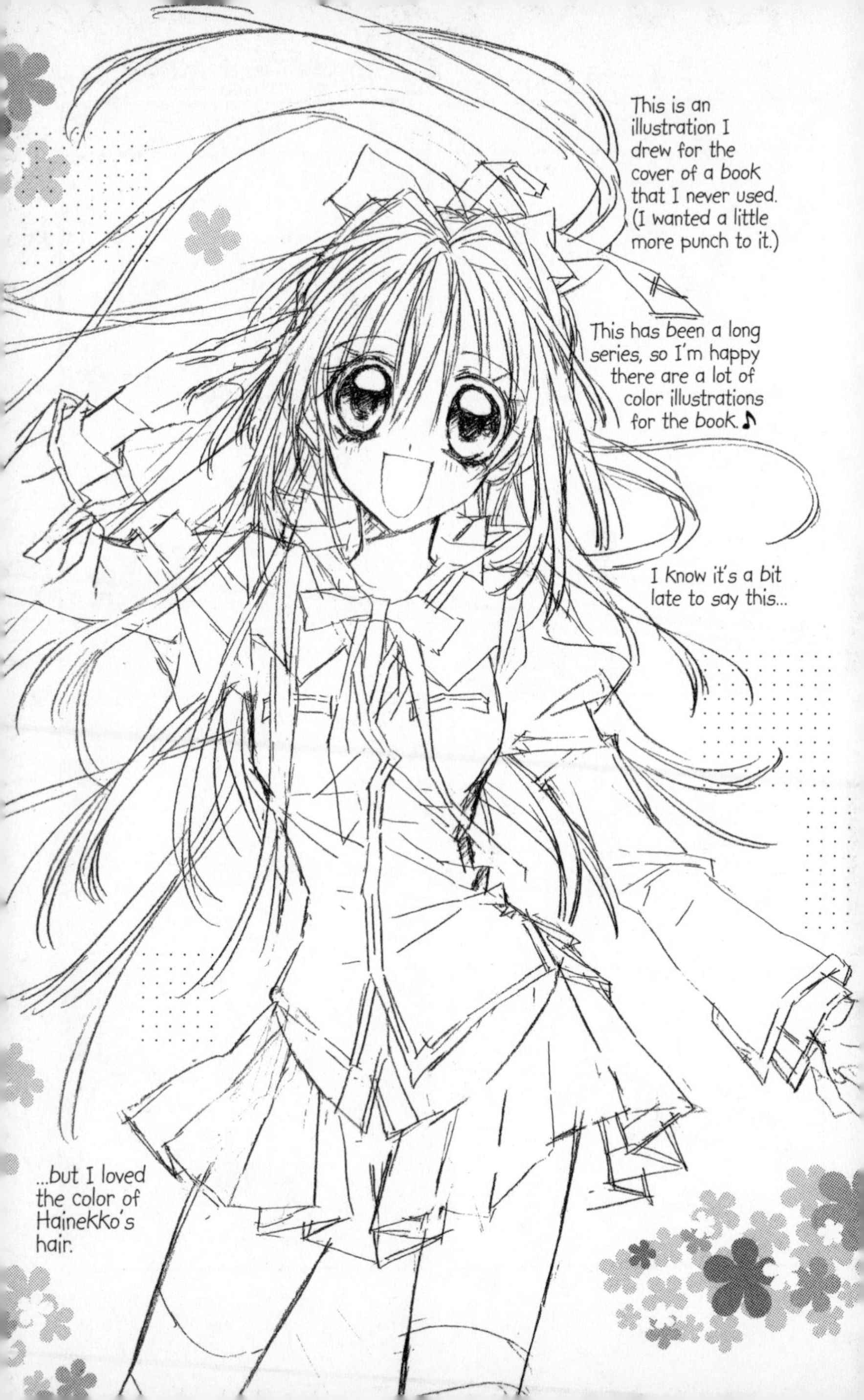
This is an illustration I drew for the cover of a book that I never used. (I wanted a little more punch to it.)
This has been a long series, so I'm happy there are a lot of color illustrations for the book.♪
I know it's a bit late to say this...
...but I loved the color of HaineKKo's hair.

Penchi de Shakin☆

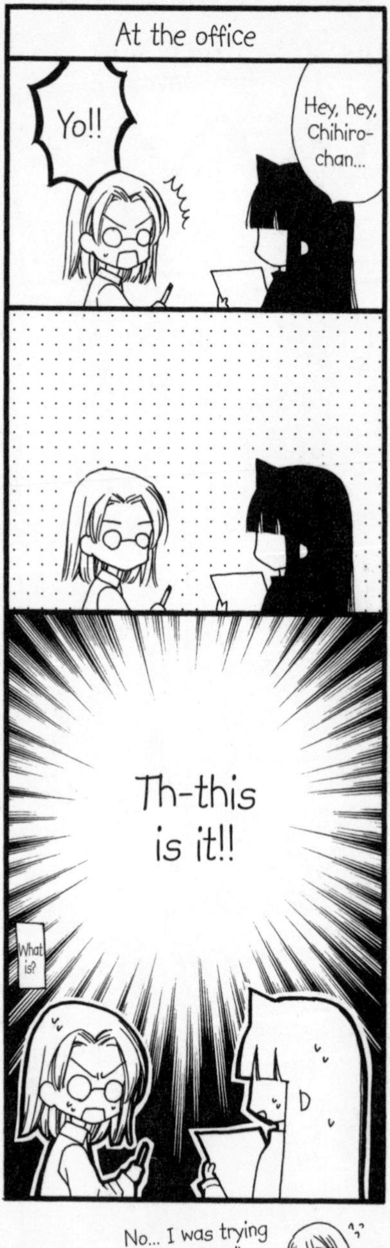
At the office
Hey, hey, Chihiro-chan...
Yo!!
Th-this is it!!
What is?

No... I was trying to say "Yes"...

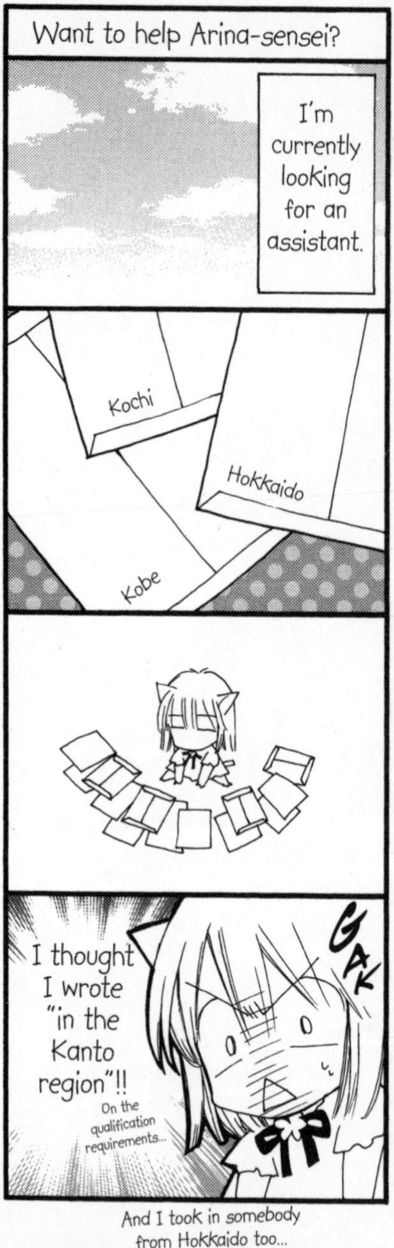
Want to help Arina-sensei?
I'm currently looking for an assistant.
Hokkaido
Kochi
Kobe
GAK
I thought I wrote "in the Kanto region"!!
On the qualification requirements...

And I took in somebody from Hokkaido too...
(I'm supposed to pay for travel expenses...)

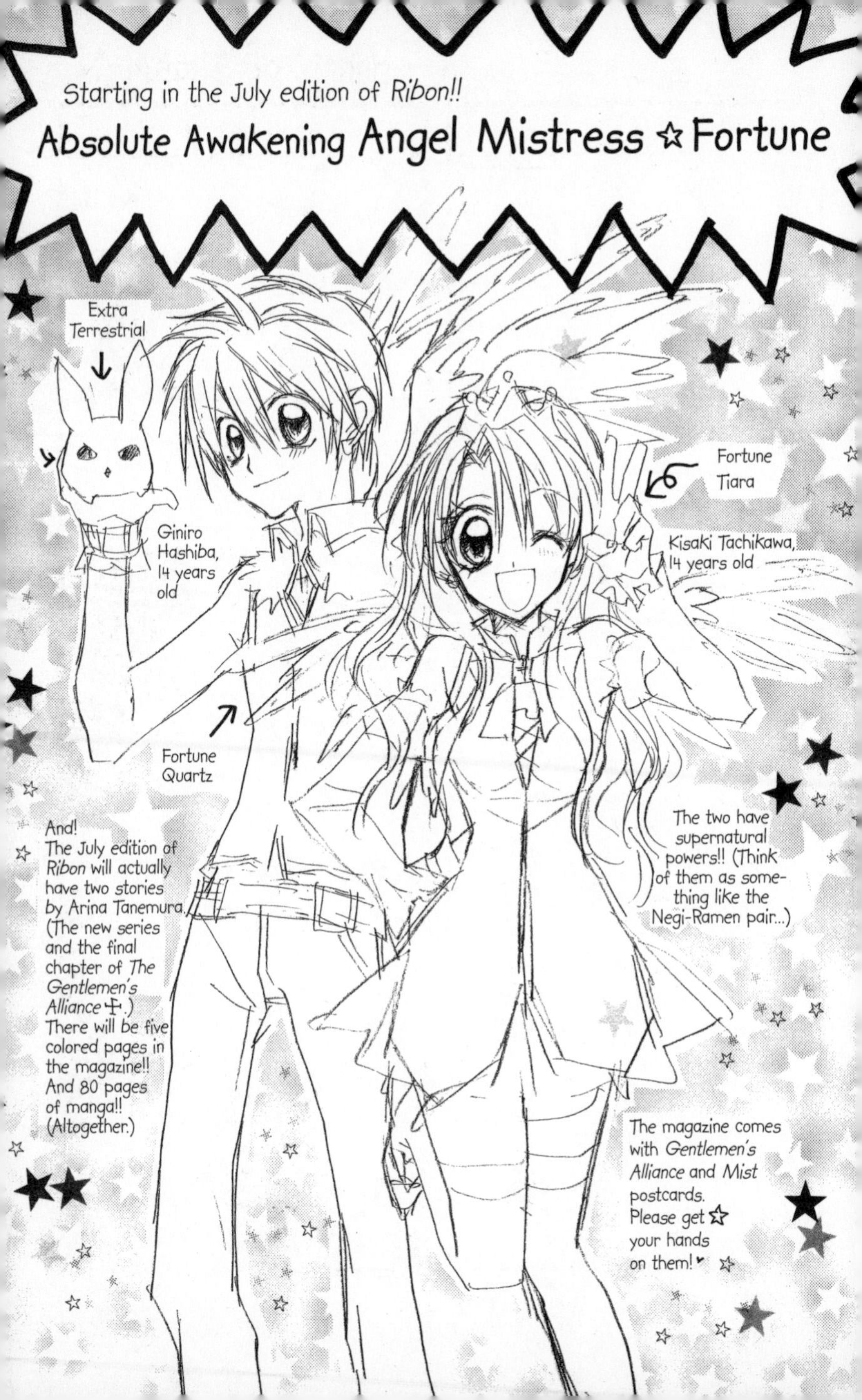
Starting in the July edition of *Ribon*!!
Absolute Awakening Angel Mistress ☆ Fortune
Extra Terrestrial
Giniro Hashiba, 14 years old
Fortune Quartz
Fortune Tiara
Kisaki Tachikawa, 14 years old
And! The July edition of *Ribon* will actually have two stories by Arina Tanemura. (The new series and the final chapter of *The Gentlemen's Alliance †*.) There will be five colored pages in the magazine!! And 80 pages of manga!! (Altogether.)
The two have supernatural powers!! (Think of them as something like the Negi-Ramen pair...)
The magazine comes with *Gentlemen's Alliance* and *Mist* postcards. Please get ☆ your hands on them! ♥

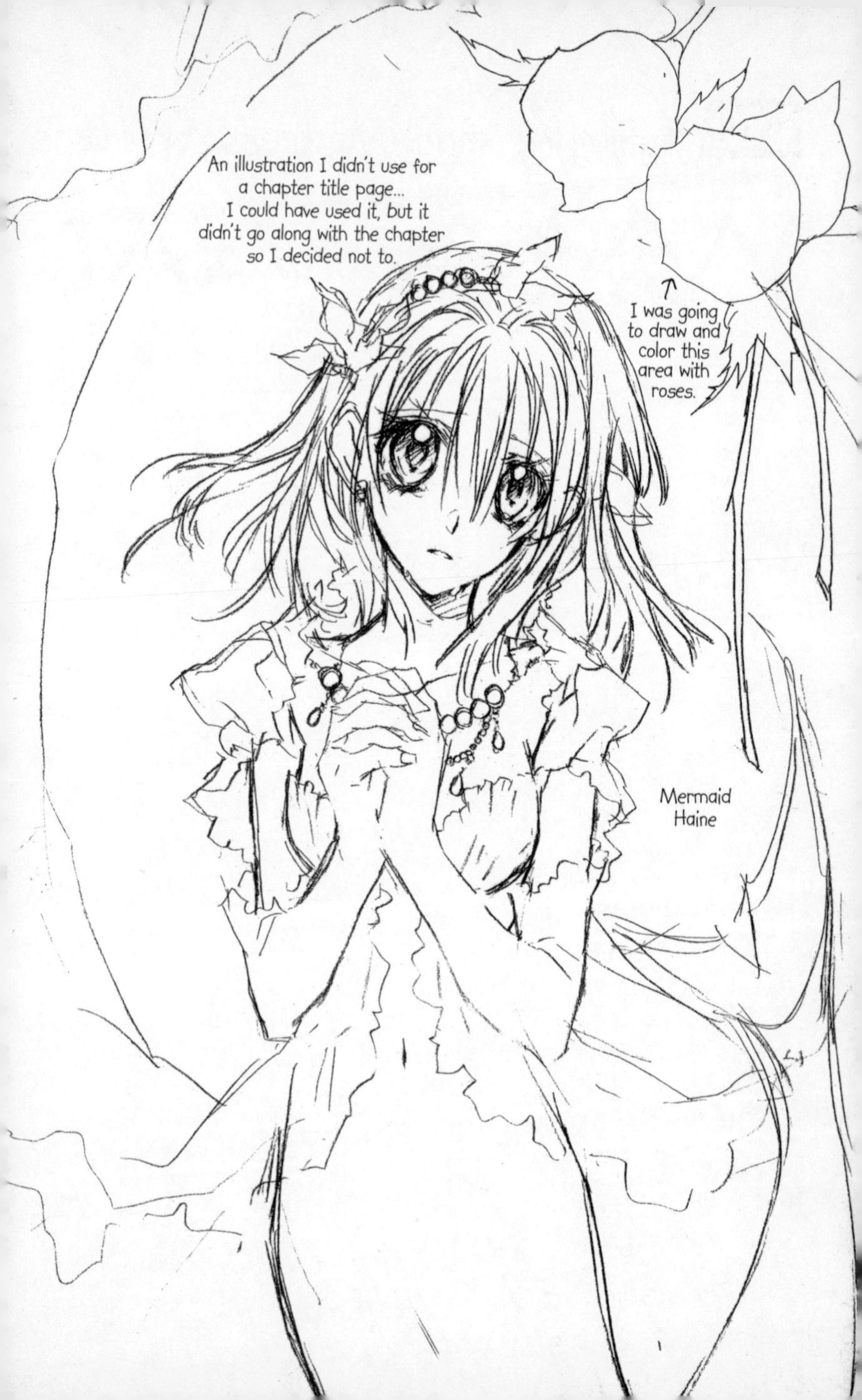
An illustration I didn't use for
a chapter title page...
I could have used it, but it
didn't go along with the chapter
so I decided not to.
I was going
to draw and
color this
area with
roses.
Mermaid
Haine

See you.

For everybody who bought both editions in Japan, thank you very much!

Please check out S-Raji if you have the chance to.

I'll be doing autograph sessions twice a month from May to August! You can read more about it in the magazine. I'll be having my first art book autograph session too!

I'll give it everything I've got!!

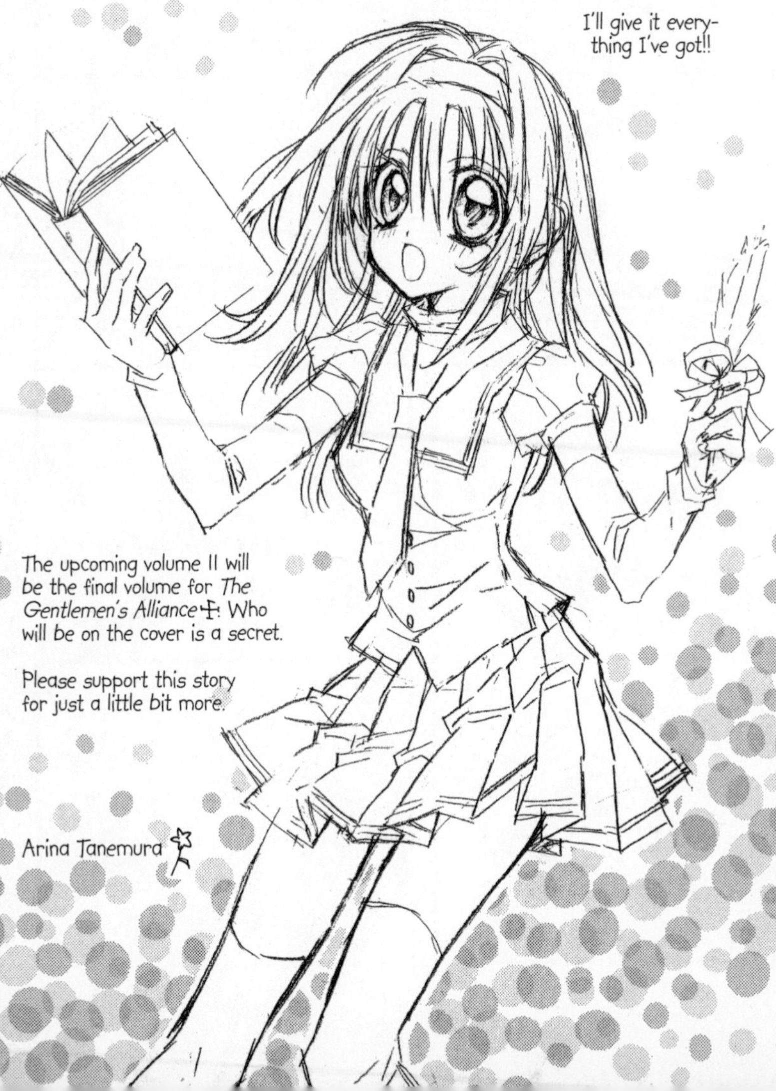

The upcoming volume 11 will be the final volume for *The Gentlemen's Alliance †*! Who will be on the cover is a secret.

Please support this story for just a little bit more.

Arina Tanemura

Penchi de Shakin☆

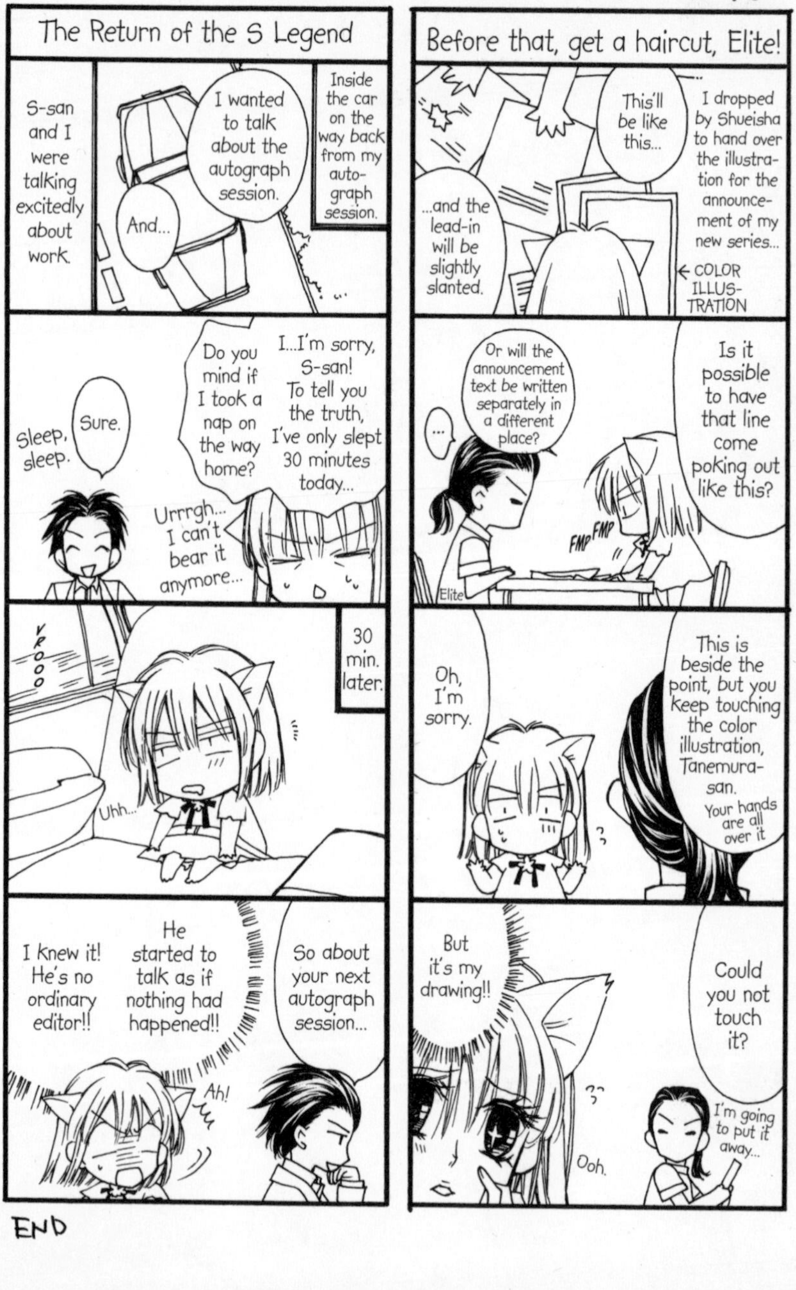
Before that, get a haircut, Elite!
I dropped by Shueisha to hand over the illustration for the announcement of my new series...
This'll be like this...
...and the lead-in will be slightly slanted.
← COLOR ILLUSTRATION
Is it possible to have that line come poking out like this?
Or will the announcement text be written separately in a different place?
...
FMP FMP
Elite
This is beside the point, but you keep touching the color illustration, Tanemura-san.
Your hands are all over it
Oh, I'm sorry.
Could you not touch it?
I'm going to put it away...
But it's my drawing!!
Ooh.
The Return of the S Legend
Inside the car on the way back from my autograph session.
I wanted to talk about the autograph session.
And...
S-san and I were talking excitedly about work.
I...I'm sorry, S-san! To tell you the truth, I've only slept 30 minutes today...
Do you mind if I took a nap on the way home?
Sure.
Sleep, sleep.
Urrrgh... I can't bear it anymore...
30 min. later.
VROOOO
Uhh...
So about your next autograph session...
He started to talk as if nothing had happened!!
I knew it! He's no ordinary editor!!
Ah!

END

● Special Edition ●

By the way, volume 10 went on sale with a special edition in Japan.

It came in a box with a special illustration and a copy of *The Unforgettable Song of the Witch* picture book! It's even got a different cover too!!

I drew the picture book using watercolor pencils, and it was a lot of fun!! (And to top it off, it's a hard cover. ♥)

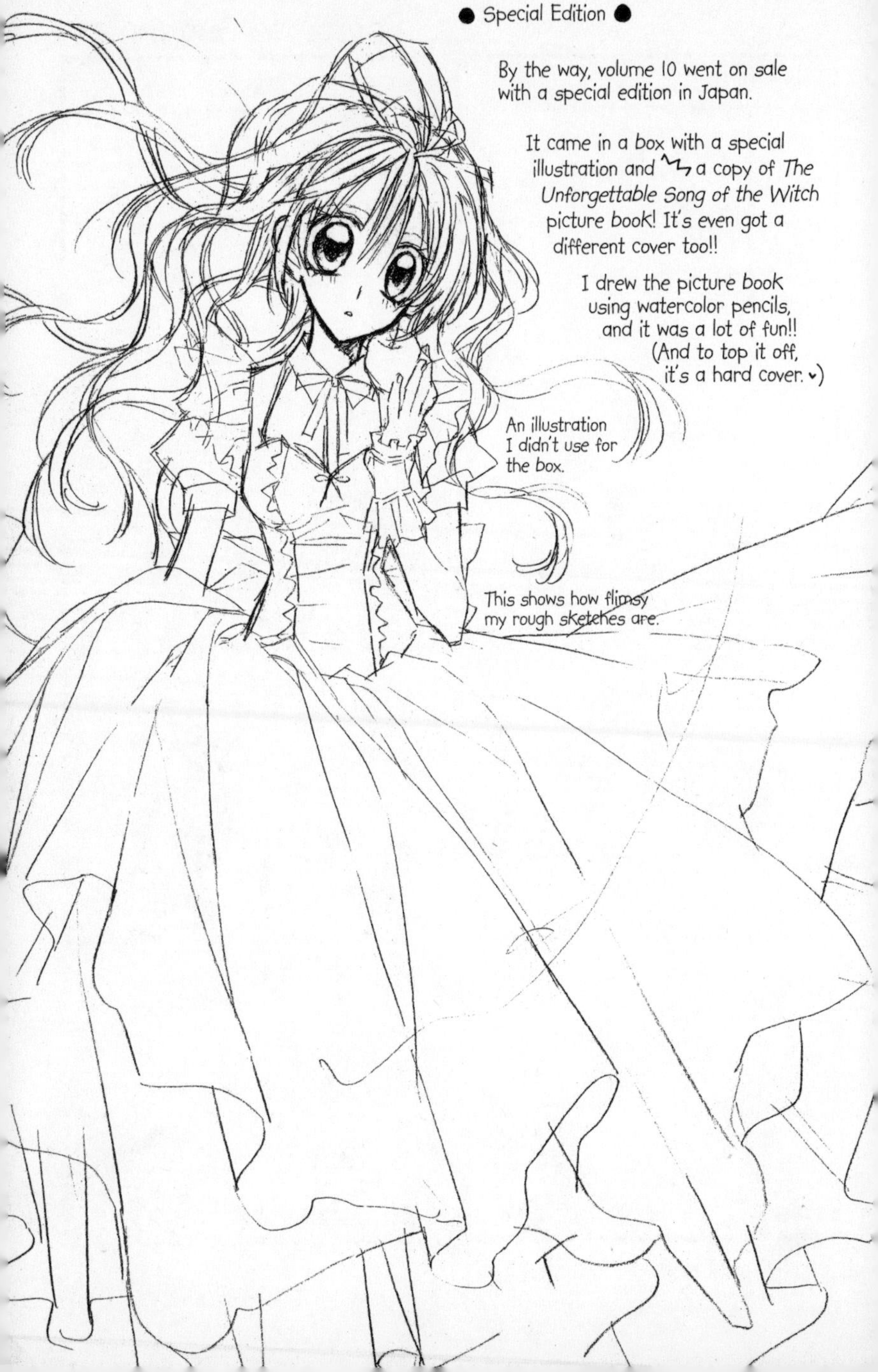

An illustration I didn't use for the box.

This shows how flimsy my rough sketches are.

Special Thanks

Nakame
Saori

Chihiro-chan Miwa-chan

Yuko-chan Yuki-chan
Asa-chan

Supervisor S-sama

Shueisha & Ribon
Editorial
Department

Riku & Kai

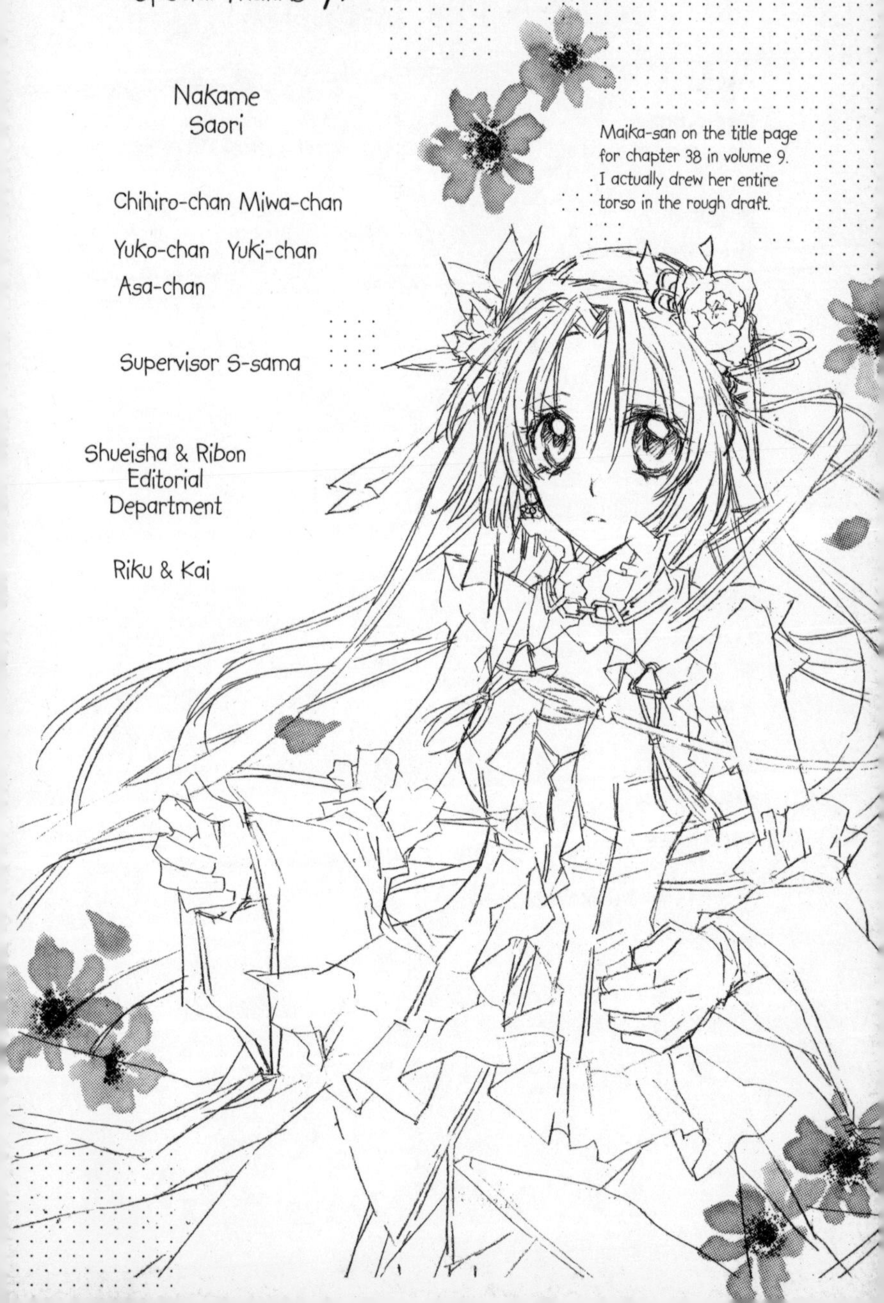

Maika-san on the title page for chapter 38 in volume 9. I actually drew her entire torso in the rough draft.

NOTES ON THE TEXT

PAGE 5:
Nee-sama
Nee-sama is a respectful way of saying "older sister."

PAGE 9:
Tankobon
Tankobon is what the actual volume of manga is called. In Japan, Tanemura's manga is first published in a magazine, and then chapters are collected into tankobon form.

PAGE 16:
Sensei
Sensei is a term used to refer to professionals, like doctors, teachers, and mangaka. It can also be used to show respect to nonprofessionals. Sensei can be used as a suffix or by itself.

PAGE 50:
Straps
The sign is referring to cell phone straps. Cell phone straps, or little charms that are hung on the phone, are extremely popular in Japan.

PAGE 96:
Taka-Taka
Taka-Taka seems to be Maguri's (and Tanemura-sensei's) nickname for Takanari.

PAGE 107:

Nii-san
Nii-san means "big brother." Takanari is the elder twin, so Shizumasa calls him "Nii-san."

PAGE 116:

"I shouldn't have looked back..."
Many myths warn against "looking back." In Japan, the most famous is the story about Izangi and Izanami, the god and goddess who created the islands of Japan.

PAGE 177:

"Please check out S-Raji if you have the chance to."
S-Raji is an abbreviation for "S Radio." (The "S" stands for "Shueisha.") S-Raji is an Internet radio site. Arina has her own radio program there called *Radio de shakin*. You can find the Japanese radio program here http://www.s-cast.net/radio/shakin/.

The final chapters begin. The long *Gentlemen's Alliance †* series has only three more chapters left after this volume. There is one promise I'll make for the last volume: "I won't leave anything left for you to imagine!" I intend to tie up everything.

Please look forward to the final volume of *The Gentlemen's Alliance †*, volume 11!

—*Arina Tanemura*

Arina Tanemura was born in Aichi, Japan. She got her start in 1996, publishing *Nibanme no Koi no Katachi* (The Style of the Second Love) in *Ribon Original* magazine. Her early work includes a collection of short stories called *Kanshaku Dama no Yuutsu* (Short-Tempered Melancholic). Two of her titles, *Kamikaze Kaito Jeanne* and *Full Moon*, were made into popular TV series. Tanemura enjoys karaoke and is a huge *Lord of the Rings* fan.

THE GENTLEMEN'S ALLIANCE † vol.10
The Shojo Beat Manga Edition

STORY & ART BY
ARINA TANEMURA

English Translation & Adaptation/Tetsuichiro Miyaki
Touch-up Art & Lettering/Gia Cam Luc
Design/Amy Martin
Editor/Nancy Thistlethwaite

VP, Production/Alvin Lu
VP, Publishing Licensing/Rika Inouye
VP, Sales & Product Marketing/Gonzalo Ferreyra
VP, Creative/Linda Espinosa
Publisher/Hyoe Narita

Printed in Canada

Published by VIZ Media, LLC
P.O. Box 77010
San Francisco, CA 94107

Shojo Beat Manga Edition
10 9 8 7 6 5 4 3 2 1
First printing, October 2009

Arina Tanemura Series

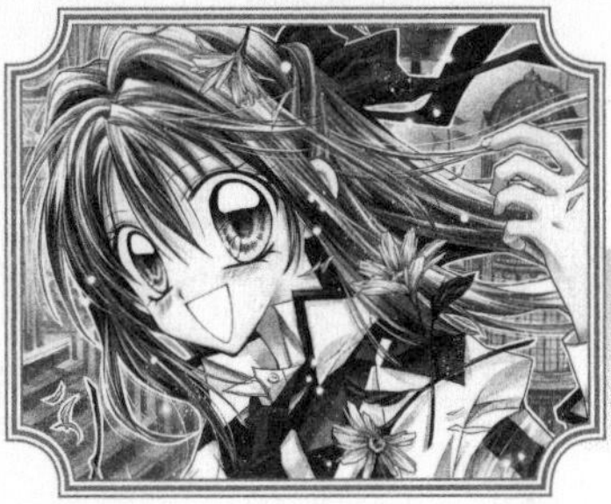

The Gentlemen's Alliance †

Haine Otomiya joins Imperial Academy in pursuit of the boy she's loved since she was a child, unaware that he has many secrets of his own.

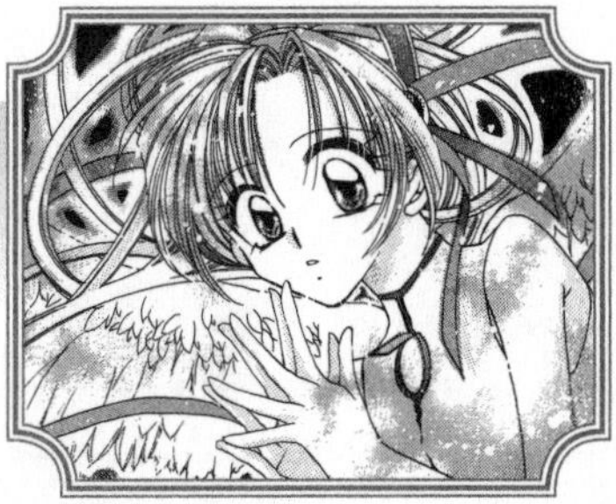

I•O•N

Chanting the letters of her first name has always brought Ion Tsuburagi good luck—but her good-luck charm is really the result of psychic powers!

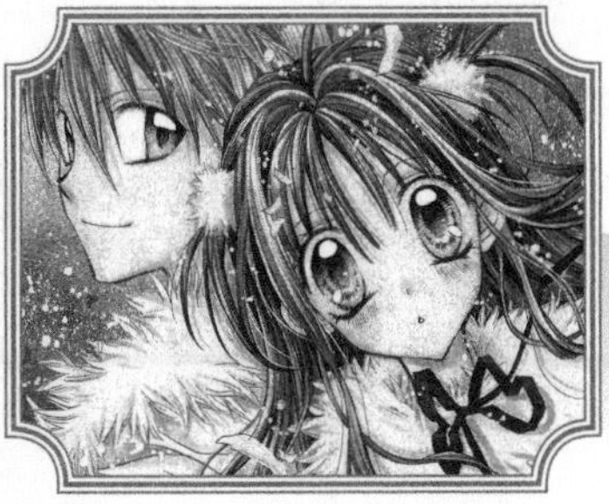

Full Moon

Mitsuki Koyama dreams of becoming a pop star, but she is dying of throat cancer. Can she live out a lifetime of dreams in just one year?

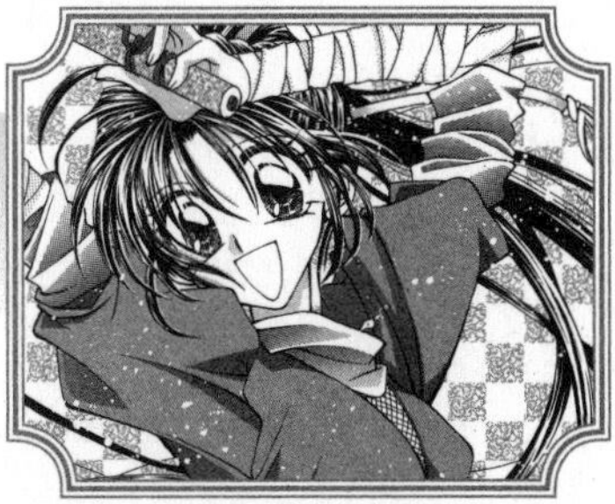

Short-Tempered Melancholic

A collection of short stories including Arina Tanemura's debut manga, "In the Style of the Second Love"!

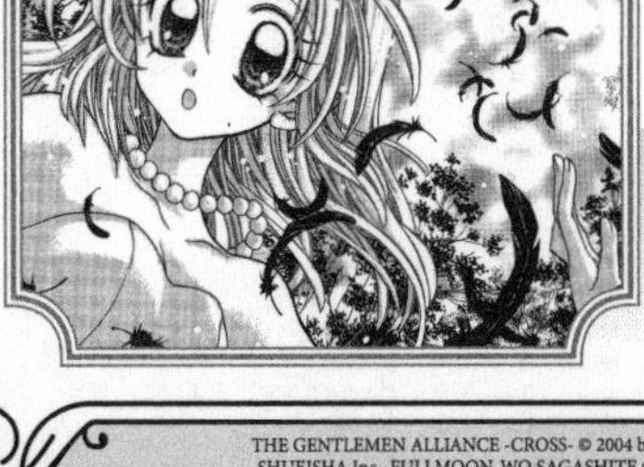

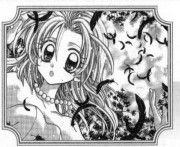

Time Stranger Kyoko

Kyoko Suomi must find 12 holy stones and 12 telepaths to awaken her sister who has been trapped in time since birth.

Kamikaze Girls

The last thing you want is sometimes the very thing you need

From Novala Takemoto
Creator of *Missin'* and *Missin' 2*

"...a hyperstylized, supercute female-bonding odyssey..."
-Scott Brown,
Entertainment Weekly

The critically acclaimed and award-winning film on DVD

The best-selling novel now available in English

Manga edition with bonus stories

Find out more at
www.kamikazegirls.net

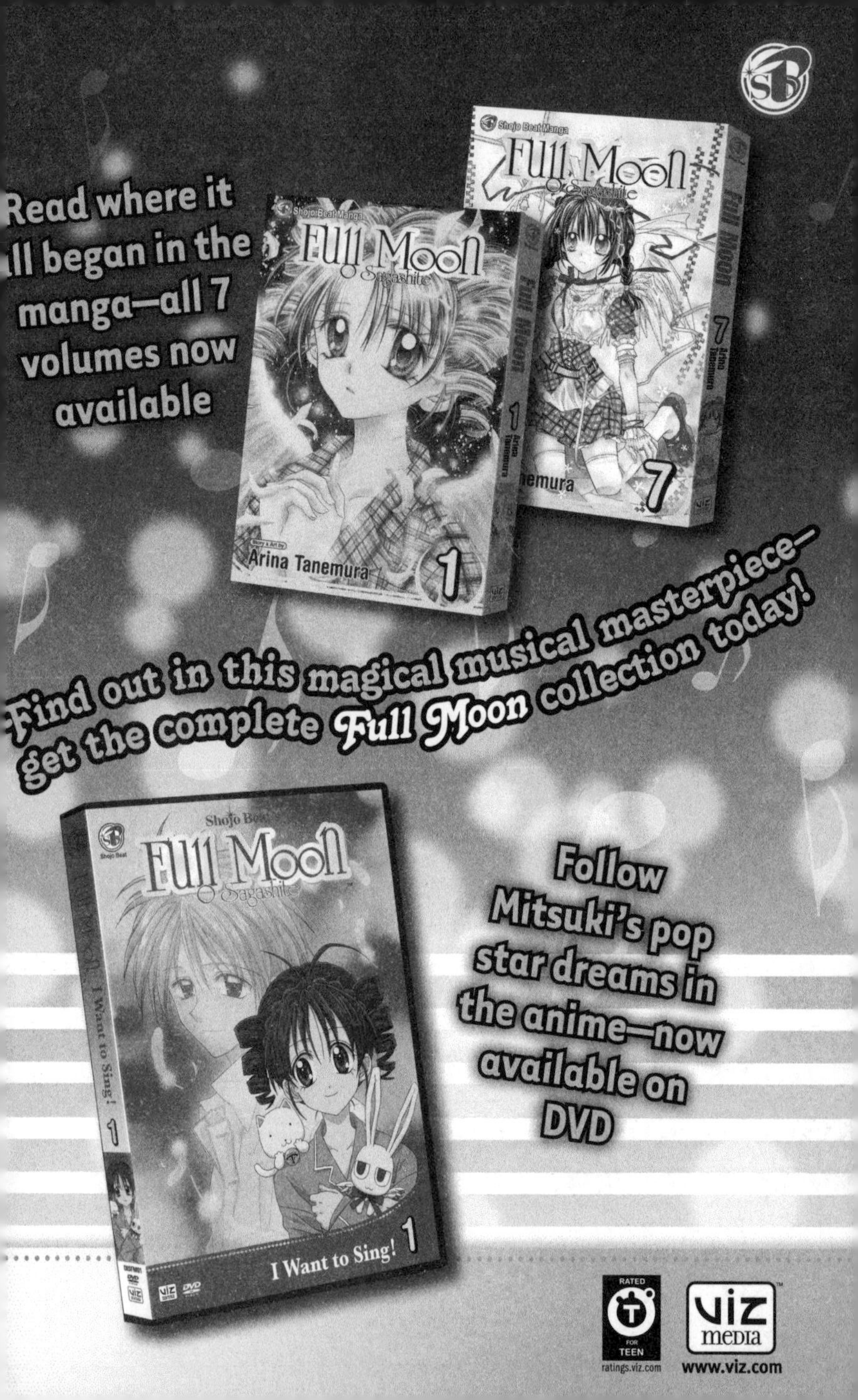

Read where it
ll began in the
manga—all 7
volumes now
available
Shojo Beat Manga
FULL MOON O Sagashite
Arina Tanemura
7
Shojo Beat Manga
FULL MOON O Sagashite
Story & Art by
Arina Tanemura
1
Find out in this magical musical masterpiece—
get the complete Full Moon collection today!
Shojo Beat
FULL MOON O Sagashite
I Want to Sing! 1
Follow
Mitsuki's pop
star dreams in
the anime—now
available on
DVD
RATED T FOR TEEN
ratings.viz.com
VIZ media
www.viz.com

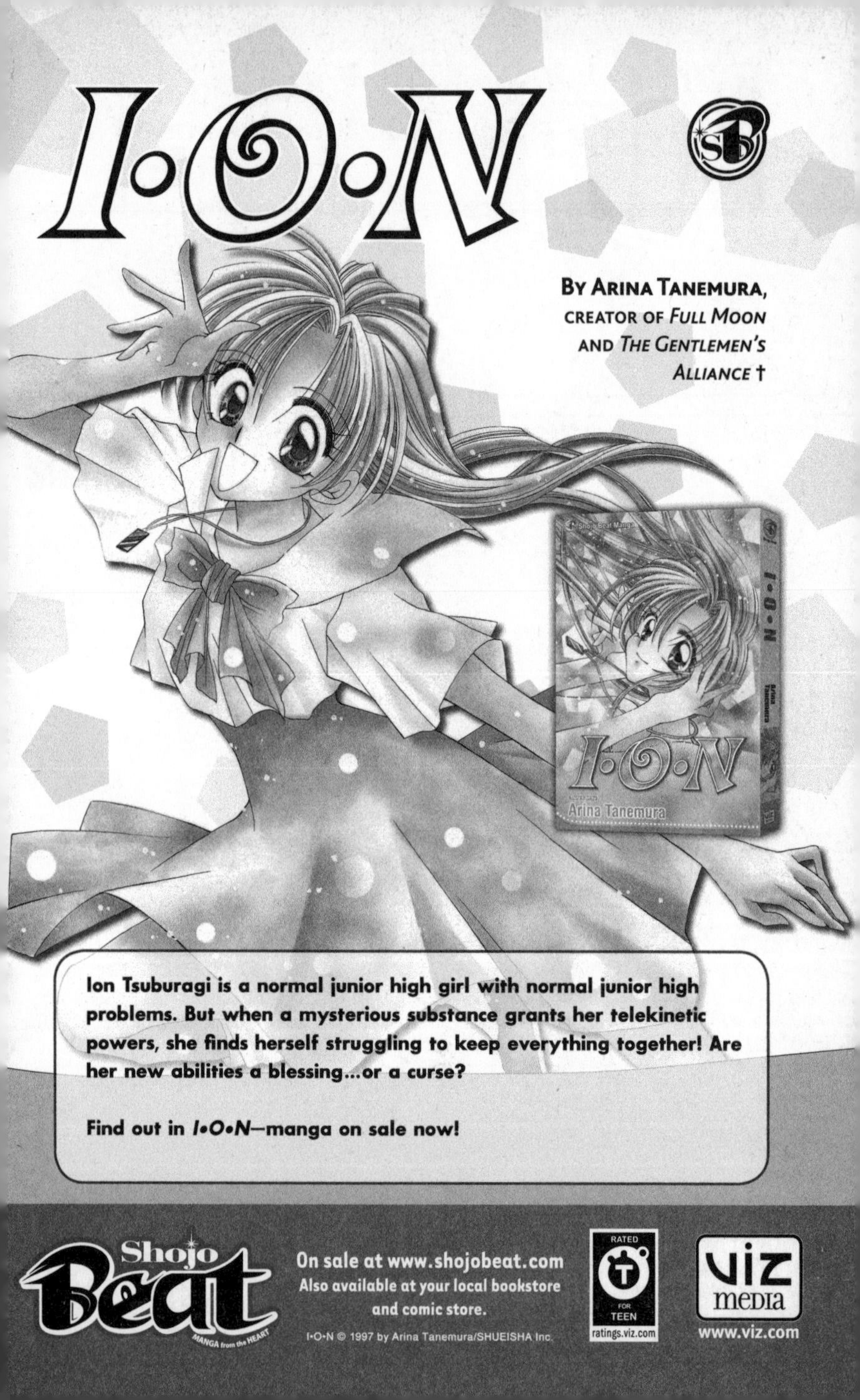
I•O•N
By Arina Tanemura, creator of Full Moon and The Gentlemen's Alliance †
Shojo Beat Manga
I•O•N
Arina Tanemura
Ion Tsuburagi is a normal junior high girl with normal junior high problems. But when a mysterious substance grants her telekinetic powers, she finds herself struggling to keep everything together! Are her new abilities a blessing...or a curse?
Find out in I•O•N—manga on sale now!
Shojo Beat
MANGA from the HEART
On sale at www.shojobeat.com
Also available at your local bookstore and comic store.
I•O•N © 1997 by Arina Tanemura/SHUEISHA Inc.
RATED
T
FOR
TEEN
ratings.viz.com
VIZ media
www.viz.com

Tell us what you think about Shojo Beat Manga!

Our survey is now available online. Go to:

shojobeat.com/mangasurvey

 Help us make our product offerings better!